San Diego Christian College
2100 Greenfield Drive
El Cajon, CA 92019

29.48
Am

Codependent No More
&
Beyond Codependency

Melody Beattie

HAZELDEN

MJF BOOKS
NEW YORK

Editor's note:
Hazelden Educational Materials offers a variety of information on chemical
dependency and related areas. Our publications do not necessarily represent
Hazelden or its programs, nor do they officially speak for any Twelve Step
organization. The Twelve Steps of Alcoholics Anonymous and The Twelve Steps of
A1-Anon are reprinted with permission of Alcoholics Anonymous World Services,
Inc. Permission to reprint the Twelve Steps of AA and A1-Anon does not mean that
AA has reviewed or approved the contents of this publication, nor that AA agrees
with the views expressed herein. The views expressed herein are solely those of the
author. AA is a program of recovery from alcoholism. Use of the Twelve Steps in
connection with programs which are patterned after AA, but which addresses other
problems, does not imply otherwise.

Published by MJF Books
Fine Communications
322 Eighth Avenue
New York, NY 10001

Codependent No More Copyright © 1987, 1992 by Hazelden Foundation.
Beyond Codependency Copyright © 1989 by Hazelden Foundation.
LC Control Number 97-70822
ISBN 1-56731-218-7

Copyright © 1990 by Hazelden Foundation

This edition published by arrangement with Hazelden Foundation.

Manufactured in the United States of America on acid-free paper

MJF Books and the MJF colophon are trademarks of Fine Creative Media,
Inc.

BG   17   16   15   14   13   12   11   10   9

Codependent No More

HOW TO STOP CONTROLLING OTHERS AND START CARING FOR YOURSELF

> "It is not easy to find happiness in ourselves, and it is not possible to find it elsewhere."
>
> —Agnes Repplier,
> *The Treasure Chest*

For helping make this book possible, I thank:

God, my mother, David, my children, Scott Egleston, Sharon George, Joanne Marcuson, and all the codependent people who have learned from me and allowed me to learn from them.

This book is dedicated to me.

Contents

Hazelden Publishing and Education is a division of the Hazelden Foundation, a not-for-profit organization. Since 1949, Hazelden has been a leader in promoting the dignity and treatment of people afflicted with the disease of chemical dependency.

The mission of the foundation is to improve the quality of life for individuals, families, and communities by providing a national continuum of information, education, and recovery services that are widely accessible; to advance the field through research and training; and to improve our quality and effectiveness through continuous improvement and innovation.

Stemming from that, the mission of the publishing division is to provide quality information and support to people wherever they may be in their personal journey—from education and early intervention, through treatment and recovery, to personal and spiritual growth.

Although our treatment programs do not necessarily use everything Hazelden publishes, our bibliotherapeutic materials support our mission and the Twelve Step philosophy upon which it is based. We encourage your comments and feedback.

The headquarters of the Hazelden Foundation is in Center City, Minnesota. Additional treatment facilities are located in Chicago, Illinois; New York, New York; Plymouth, Minnesota; St. Paul, Minnesota; and West Palm Beach, Florida. At these sites, we provide a continuum of care for men and women of all ages. Our Plymouth facility is designed specifically for youth and families.

For more information on Hazelden, please call 1-800-257-7800. Or you may access our World Wide Web site on the Internet at http://www.Hazelden.org.

PREFACE TO THE 1992 EDITION

Back in the early eighties, when I first envisioned writing a book about codependency—when I was desperately struggling to sort through my own pain—I vowed that if I ever figured out what happened to me and what I needed to do to get better, I'd write a book about it. That book, I decided, would be warm, gentle, nonjudgmental, nontechnical.

It would be kind. Because that's what I needed—information and kindness. I needed help with my healing process from my codependency issues.

About five years later, I sat down to write that book. Just separated from my husband of ten years, I went on welfare for four months, to help me support myself and my two children, Nichole and Shane, while I wrote *Codependent No More*.

When I wondered how I, a nonexpert, could write a book like that, I took comfort by telling myself that it was okay to say what I thought because only a few people would read it anyway. I also spent a great deal of time on the introduction, striving not only to introduce the book, but to introduce the concept of *codependency*—the word—to a world that, for the most part, had not heard about it.

Now, another five years later, I've been asked to write an anniversary preface to a book that has sold over two million copies.

"What do I put in it?" I asked my editor and friend, Rebecca Post, from Hazelden.

"Tell about the changes that have happened—to women, to people in our country, to *you*, since you wrote that book," she suggested.

"Hmmm," I pondered. "What changes have happened besides the Persian Gulf War, the breakdown of communism in the Soviet Union, and the Hill-Thomas hearings?"

I turn on the television. The movie of the week, I can't remember the name, is a story about a teenager struggling to deal with her alcoholism and the impact of being raped. Her mother, a nurse, has worked valiantly to break free from a dysfunctional and abusive relationship with her husband, the girl's father. Throughout the movie, mother and daughter talk directly about not rescuing each other because of the diminishing effects of such behavior. The movie ends with the daughter playing a guitar and singing a song she's written about not being a victim anymore.

I walk into a church, one I haven't attended for a long time. The sermon is somewhat unusual this cold, Sunday winter morning. The minister is speaking from his heart, telling the congregation that he is done leading a church that's based on shame, fear, guilt, and dishonesty. He wants instead, he says, to be part of a church that's based on equality, honesty, intimacy, acceptance, and the healing power of God's love. He wants to be part of a church where he can have his own issues and problems, and where people are functioning in healthy, honest relationships with each other and God.

My daughter comes home from her first week at a new school. "Guess what, Mom?" she says. "We're reading a meditation each day in homeroom class from your book, *The Language of Letting Go*. And at my friend's school, they're talking about codependency issues in health class."

Codependent No More, with a picture of handcuffs broken apart on the front cover, makes the best-seller list in France.

Catdependent No More, parodying the title of my book, makes the 1991 Christmas book list here in Minnesota.

Some things have changed. I've written four more books, traveled the world, divorced (but not remarried), and paid back the welfare department for the financial help they gave me.

I feel more passionately about the importance of healing from our abuse issues. I feel more passionately. I've become more spontaneous, embraced my femininity, and learned new lessons along the way—about boundaries, flexibility, and owning my power. And about love. I'm learning to respect men. My relationships have deepened. Some have changed.

The most significant change in my life has been the loss of my son, Shane. As you may have heard or read, in February of 1991, three days after his twelfth birthday, my beloved Shane—so much a part of my life and work—was killed suddenly in a ski accident on the slopes at Afton Alps.

I'm learning about death and life.

I've grown and changed. I've watched my friends grow and change Many of you have written to me about your growth and change.

I still struggle with feeling feelings and trusting my process, my path, and my Higher Power. I still feel afraid at times. Sometimes I forget and try to control everything. I may become obsessive, unless I catch myself.

And, despite its years on the best-seller list, the most common question I'm still asked by people and the media is, "Just exactly what is codependency?"

Some things haven't changed, at least not a lot. I still refuse to be an expert and permanently decline the title of "guru." But I'm still willing to tell you what I see, and believe.

Although some things appear not to have changed, things are constantly changing, Our consciousness, as individuals and as a society, has been raised. We've realized that women have souls, and men have feelings.

And I've gone deeper into my healing process than I ever intended.

*   *   *

I don't know how much my writing has contributed to this consciousness-raising, and how much the consciousness-raising has contributed to my writing. But I'm grateful to be part of what's happened.

I'm honored to be part of a movement influenced by people such as Anne Wilson Schaef, John Bradshaw, Patrick Carnes, Earnie Larsen, and led by people such as you, my readers—the real heroes—quietly and profoundly doing your own healing work and carrying the message to others, most significantly by example.

I've met many of you in my travels across the country. Some of you have written to me. Thank you for the love, support, and compassion you've shown me not only over the years, but throughout the rough, raw months of 1991 after Shane's death.

Many of you have written to me, saying how much I've helped you. Well, you've helped and touched me, too.

One woman wrote to me recently, saying she had read all my books and had been recovering from codependency for years. "I want to learn more, though," she wrote. "I want to go deeper into my codependency. Please write more about that."

Maybe we don't need to go deeper into our codependency. We can, instead, march forward into our destinies. We can remember and practice all we've learned about addictions, codependency, and abuse. With compassion and boundaries, we need to commit fully to loving God, ourselves, and others. We need to commit fully to trusting God, ourselves, and our process.

Then we can be open to the next step. We are on time, and we are where we need to be. We can be trusted. So can God. And letting go and gratitude still work. Keep your head up and your heart open. And let's see what's next. Happy five-year anniversary, *Codependent No More*.

Melody Beattie

INTRODUCTION

My first encounter with codependents occurred in the early sixties. This was before people, tormented by other people's behavior, were called *codependents,* and before people addicted to alcohol and other drugs were labeled *chemically dependent.* Although I didn't know *what* codependents were, I usually knew *who* they were. As an alcoholic and addict, I stormed through life, helping create other codependents.

Codependents were a necessary nuisance. They were hostile, controlling, manipulative, indirect, guilt producing, difficult to communicate with, generally disagreeable, sometimes downright hateful, and a hindrance to my compulsion to get high. They hollered at me, hid my pills, made nasty faces at me, poured my alcohol down the sink, tried to keep me from getting more drugs, wanted to know why I was doing this to them, and asked what was wrong with me. But they were always there, ready to rescue me from self-created disasters. The codependents in my life didn't understand me, and the misunderstanding was mutual. I didn't understand me, and I didn't understand them.

My first professional encounter with codependents occurred years later, in 1976. At that time in Minnesota, addicts and alcoholics had become *chemically dependent,* their families and friends had become *significant others,* and I had become a *recovering addict and alcoholic.* By then, I also worked as a counselor in the chemical dependency field, that vast network of institutions, programs, and agencies that helps chemically dependent people get well. Because I'm a woman and most of the significant others at that time were women, and because I had the least seniority and none of my co-workers wanted to do it, my employer at the Minneapolis treatment center told me to organize support groups for wives of addicts in the program.

I wasn't prepared for this task. I still found codependents hostile, controlling, manipulative, indirect, guilt producing, difficult to communicate with, and more.

In my group, I saw people who felt responsible for the entire world, but they refused to take responsibility for leading and living their own lives.

I saw people who constantly gave to others but didn't know how to receive. I saw people give until they were angry, exhausted, and emptied of everything. I saw some give until they gave up. I even saw one woman give and suffer so much that she died of "old age" and natural causes at age 33. She was the mother of five children and the wife of an alcoholic who had been sent to prison for the third time.

I worked with women who were experts at taking care of everyone around them, yet these women doubted their ability to take care of themselves.

I saw mere shells of people, racing mindlessly from one activity to another. I saw people-pleasers, martyrs, stoics, tyrants, withering vines, clinging vines, and, borrowing from H. Sackler's line in his play, *The Great White Hope*, "pinched up faces giving off the miseries."

Most codependents were obsessed with other people. With great precision and detail, they could recite long lists of the addict's deeds and misdeeds: what he or she thought, felt, did, and said; and what he or she didn't think, feel, do, and say. The codependents knew what the alcoholic or addict should and shouldn't do. And they wondered extensively why he or she did or didn't do it.

Yet these codependents who had such great insight into others couldn't see themselves. They didn't know what they were feeling. They weren't sure what they thought. And they didn't know what, if anything, they could do to solve their problems—if, indeed, they had any problems other than the alcoholics.

It was a formidable group, these codependents. They were aching, complaining, and trying to control everyone and everything but themselves. And, except for a few quiet pioneers in family therapy, many counselors (including me) didn't know how to help them. The chemical dependency field was flourishing, but help focused on the addict. Literature and training on family therapy were scarce. What did codependents need? What did they want? Weren't they just an extension of the alcoholic, a visitor to the treatment center? Why couldn't they cooperate, instead of always making problems? The alcoholic had an excuse for being so crazy—he was drunk. These significant others had no excuse. They were this way sober.

Soon, I subscribed to two popular beliefs. These crazy codependents (significant others) are sicker than the alcoholics. And, no wonder the alcoholic drinks; who wouldn't with a crazy spouse like that?

By then, I had been sober for a while. I was beginning to understand myself, but I didn't understand codependency. I tried, but couldn't—until years later, when I became so caught up in the chaos of a few alcoholics that I stopped living my own life. I stopped thinking. I stopped feeling positive emotions, and I was left with rage, bitterness, hatred, fear, depression, helplessness, despair, and guilt. At times, I wanted to stop living. I had no energy. I spent most of my time worrying about people and trying to figure out how to control them. I couldn't say no (to anything but fun activities) if my life depended on it, which it did. My relationships with friends and family members were in shambles. I felt terribly victimized. I lost myself and didn't know how it had happened. I didn't know *what* had happened. I thought I was going crazy. And, I thought, shaking a finger at the people around me, it's *their* fault.

Sadly, aside from myself, nobody knew how badly I felt. My problems were my secret. Unlike the alcoholics and other troubled people in my life, I wasn't going around making big messes and expecting someone to clean up after me. In fact, next to the alcoholics, I looked good. I was *so* responsible, *so* dependable. Sometimes *I* wasn't sure I had a problem. I knew I felt miserable, but I didn't understand why my life wasn't working.

After floundering in despair for a while, I began to understand. Like many people who judge others harshly, I realized I had just taken a very long and painful walk in the shoes of those I had judged. I now understood those crazy codependents. I had become one.

Gradually, I began to climb out of my black abyss. Along the way, I developed a passionate interest in the subject of codependency. As a counselor (although I no longer worked full-time in the field, I still considered myself one) and as a writer, my curiosity was provoked. As a "flaming, careening codependent" (a phrase borrowed from an Al-Anon member) who needed help, I also had a personal stake in the subject. What happens to people like me? How does it happen? Why? Most important, what do codependents need to do to feel better? And stay that way?

I talked to counselors, therapists, and codependents. I read the few available books on the subject and related topics. I reread the basics— the therapy books that have stood the test of time—looking for ideas that applied. I went to meetings of Al-Anon, a self-help group based on the Twelve Steps of Alcoholics Anonymous but geared toward the person who has been affected by another person's drinking.

Eventually, I found what I was seeking. I began to see, understand, and change. My life started working again. Soon, I was conducting another group for codependents at another Minneapolis treatment center. But this time, I had a vague notion of what I was doing.

I still found codependents hostile, controlling, manipulative, indirect, and all the things I had found them before. I still saw all the peculiar twists of personality I previously saw. But, I saw deeper.

I saw people who were hostile; they had felt so much hurt that hostility was their only defense against being crushed again. They were that angry because anyone who had tolerated what they had would be that angry.

They were controlling because everything around and inside them was out of control. Always, the dam of their lives and the lives of those around them threatened to burst and spew harmful consequences on everyone. And nobody but them seemed to notice or care.

I saw people who manipulated because manipulation appeared to be the only way to get anything done. I worked with people who were indirect because the systems they lived in seemed incapable of tolerating honesty.

I worked with people who thought they were going crazy because they had believed so many lies they didn't know what reality was.

I saw people who had gotten so absorbed in other people's problems they didn't have time to identify or solve their own. These were people who had cared so deeply, and often destructively, about other people that they had forgotten how to care about themselves. The codependents felt responsible for so much because the people around them felt responsible for so little; they were just taking up the slack.

I saw hurting, confused people who needed comfort, understanding, and information. I saw victims of alcoholism who didn't drink but were nonetheless victimized by alcohol. I saw victims struggling desperately to gain some kind of power over their perpetrators. They learned from me, and I learned from them.

Soon, I began to subscribe to some new beliefs about codependency. Codependents aren't crazier or sicker than alcoholics. But, they hurt as much or more. They haven't cornered the market on agony, but they have gone through their pain without the anesthetizing effects of alcohol or other drugs, or the other high states achieved by people with compulsive disorders. And the pain that comes from loving someone who's in trouble can be profound.

"The chemically dependent partner numbs the feelings and the non-abuser is doubled over in pain—relieved only by anger and occasional fantasies," wrote Janet Geringer Woititz in an article from the book *Co-Dependency, An Emerging Issue.*[1]

Codependents are that way sober because they went through what they did sober.

No wonder codependents are so crazy. Who wouldn't be, after living with the people they've lived with?

It's been difficult for codependents to get the information and practical help they need and deserve. It's tough enough to convince alcoholics (or other disturbed people) to seek help. It's more difficult to convince codependents—those who by comparison look, but don't feel, normal—that they have problems.

Codependents suffered in the backdrop of the sick person. If they recovered, they did that in the background too. Until recently, many counselors (like me) didn't know what to do to help them. Sometimes codependents were blamed; sometimes they were ignored; sometimes they were expected to magically shape up (an archaic attitude that has not worked with alcoholics and doesn't help codependents either). Rarely were codependents treated as individuals who needed help to get better. Rarely were they given a personalized recovery program for their problems and their pain. Yet, by its nature, alcoholism and other compulsive disorders turn everyone affected by the illness into victims—people who need help even if they are not drinking, using other drugs, gambling, overeating, or overdoing a compulsion.

That's why I wrote this book. It grew out of my research, my personal and professional experiences, and my passion for the subject. It is a personal and, in some places, prejudiced opinion.

I'm not an expert, and this isn't a technical book for experts. Whether the person you've let yourself be affected by is an alcoholic, gambler, foodaholic, workaholic, sexaholic, criminal, rebellious teenager, neurotic parent, another codependent, or any combination of the above, this book is for you, the codependent.

This book is not about how you can help your alcoholic or troubled person, although if you get better, his or her chance of recovery improves too.[2] There are plenty of good books on how to help the alcoholic. This book is about your most important and probably most neglected responsibility: taking care of yourself. It's about what you can do to start feeling better.

I've tried to round up some of the best, most helpful thoughts on codependency. I've included quotes from people I consider experts, to demonstrate their beliefs. I've also included case histories to show how people dealt with particular problems. Although I've changed names and certain details to protect privacy, all case histories are true and are not composites. I've inserted endnotes to document information, to suggest additional reading, and to attribute material to appropriate sources. But, much of what I've learned has been from many people and their similar thoughts on this subject. Many ideas have been handed down and passed around, and their sources have become indistinguishable. I've tried to attribute accurately, but in this field that is not always possible.

Although this is a self-help, how-to book, please remember it's not a cookbook for mental health. Each person is unique; each situation is unique. Try to tap into your own healing process. That may include seeking professional help, attending self-help groups such as Al-Anon, and calling on the assistance of a Power greater than yourself.

A friend, Scott Egleston, who is a professional in the mental health field, told me a therapy fable. He heard it from someone, who heard it from someone else. It goes:

Once upon a time, a woman moved to a cave in the mountains to study with a guru. She wanted, she said, to learn everything there was to know. The guru supplied her with stacks of books and left her alone so she could study. Every morning, the guru returned to the cave to monitor the woman's progress. In his hand, he carried a heavy wooden cane. Each morning, he asked her the same question: "Have you learned everything there is to know yet?" Each morning, her answer was the same. "No," she said, "I haven't." The guru would then strike her over the head with his cane.

This scenario repeated itself for months. One day the guru entered the cave, asked the same question, heard the same answer, and raised his cane to hit her in the same way, but the woman grabbed the cane from the guru, stopping his assault in midair.

Relieved to end the daily batterings but fearing reprisal, the woman looked up at the guru. To her surprise, the guru smiled. "Congratulations," he said, "you have graduated. You now know everything you *need* to know."

"How's that?" the woman asked.

"You have learned that you will never learn everything there is to know," he replied. "And you have learned how to stop the pain."

That's what this book is about: stopping the pain and gaining control of your life.

Many people have learned to do it. You can, too.

Part 1:

WHAT'S CODEPENDENCY, AND WHO'S GOT IT?

1

JESSICA'S STORY

The sun was shining, and it was a beautiful day when I met him.
Then, everything went crazy.

—Georgianne, married to an alcoholic

This is Jessica's story. I'll let her tell it.

*   *   *

I sat in the kitchen, drinking coffee, thinking about my unfinished
housework. Dishes. Dusting. Laundry. The list was endless, yet I couldn't
get started. It was too much to think about. Doing it seemed impossible.
Just like my life, I thought.

Fatigue, a familiar feeling, overtook me. I headed for the bedroom.
Once a luxury, naps had become a necessity. Sleeping was about all I
could do. Where had my motivation gone? I used to have an excess of
energy. Now, it was an effort to comb my hair and apply makeup daily—
an effort I frequently didn't put forth.

I lay on my bed and fell into a deep sleep. When I awoke, my first
thoughts and feelings were painful. This, also, was not new. I wasn't sure
which hurt most: the raw ache I felt because I was certain my marriage
was over—the love was gone, extinguished by the lies and the drinking
and the disappointments and the financial problems; the bitter rage I felt
toward my husband—the man who had caused it all; the despair I felt
because God, whom I had trusted, had betrayed me by allowing this to

happen; or the mixture of fear, helplessness, and hopelessness that blended into all the other emotions.

Damn him, I thought. Why did he have to drink? Why couldn't he have sobered up earlier? Why did he have to lie? Why couldn't he have loved me as much as I had loved him? Why didn't he stop drinking and lying years ago, when I still cared?

I never intended to marry an alcoholic. My father had been one. I had tried so hard to carefully choose my husband. Great choice. Frank's problem with drinking had become apparent on our honeymoon when he left our hotel suite late one afternoon and didn't return until 6:30 the next morning. Why didn't I see then? Looking back, the signs were clear. What a fool I had been. "Oh, no. He's not an alcoholic. Not him," I had defended, time and again. I had believed his lies. I had believed my lies. Why didn't I just leave him, get a divorce? Guilt, fear, lack of initiative, and indecision. Besides, I had left him before. When we were apart, all I did was feel depressed, think about him, and worry about money. Damn me.

I looked at the clock. Quarter to three. The kids would soon be home from school. Then he would be home, expecting supper. No housework done today. Nothing ever got done. And it's his fault, I thought. HIS FAULT!

Suddenly, I shifted emotional gears. Was my husband really at work? Maybe he had taken another woman to lunch. Maybe he was having an affair. Maybe he had left early to drink. Maybe he was at work, creating problems there. How long would he have this job, anyway? Another week? Another month? Then he'd quit or be fired, as usual.

The phone rang, interrupting my anxiety. It was a neighbor, a friend. We talked, and I told her about my day.

"I'm going to Al-Anon tomorrow," she said. "Want to come along?"

I had heard about Al-Anon. It was a group for people married to drunks. Visions charged into my mind of "the little women" huddled at this meeting, making the most of their husbands' drinking, forgiving them, and thinking of little ways to help them.

"I'll see," I lied. "I've got a lot of work to do," I explained, not lying.

Outrage poured through me, and I barely heard the rest of our conversation. Of course I didn't want to go to Al-Anon. I had helped and helped. Hadn't I already done enough for him? I felt furious at the suggestion that I do more and continue giving to this bottomless pit of unmet needs we called a marriage. I was sick of shouldering the burden and feeling responsible for the success or failure of the relationship. It's his problem, I railed silently. Let him find his solution. Leave me out of this. Don't ask another thing of me. Just make him better, and I'll feel better.

After I hung up the phone, I dragged myself into the kitchen to fix supper. Anyway, I'm not the one that needs help, I thought. I haven't drank, used drugs, lost jobs, and lied to and deceived those I loved. I've held this family together, sometimes by the skin of my teeth. I've paid the bills, maintained a home on a scant budget, been there for every emergency (and, married to an alcoholic, there had been plenty of emergencies), gone through most bad times alone, and worried to the point of frequent illness. No, I decided, I'm not the irresponsible one. To the contrary, I've been responsible for everything and everyone. There was nothing wrong with me. I just needed to get going, start doing my daily chores. I didn't need meetings to do that. I'd just feel guilty if I went out when I had all this work to do at home. God knows, I didn't need more guilt. Tomorrow, I'd get up and get busy. Things will be better—tomorrow.

When the kids came home, I found myself hollering at them. That didn't surprise them or me. My husband was easygoing, the good guy. I was the bitch. I tried to be pleasant, but it was hard. Anger was always just beneath the surface. For so long, I had tolerated so much. I was no longer willing or able to tolerate anything. I was always on the defensive, and I felt like I was, somehow, fighting for my life. Later, I learned I was.

By the time my husband came home, I had put a disinterested effort into preparing supper. We ate, barely talking.

"I had a good day," Frank said.

What does that mean? I wondered. What did you really do? Were you even at work? Furthermore, who cares?

"That's nice," I said back.

"How was your day?" he asked.

How in the hell do you think it was? I railed silently. After all you've done to me, how do you expect me to have any day? I flashed him daggers, forced a smile, and said, "My day was okay. Thanks for asking."

Frank looked away. He heard what I wasn't saying, more than what I had said. He knew better than to say anything else; I did too. We were usually one step way from a raving argument, a recount of past offenses, and screamed threats of divorce. We used to thrive on arguments, but we grew sick of them. So we did it silently.

The children interrupted our hostile silence. Our son said he wanted to go to a playground several blocks away. I said no, I didn't want him to go without his father or me. He wailed he wanted to go, he would go, and I never let him do anything. I yelled he wasn't going, and that was that. He yelled please, I have to go, all the other kids get to go. As usual, I backed down. Okay, go ahead, but be careful, I warned. I felt like I had lost. I always felt like I lost—with my kids and with my husband. No one ever listened to me; no one took me seriously.

I didn't take me seriously.

After supper, I washed dishes while my husband watched television. As usual, I work, and you play. I worry, and you relax. I care, and you don't. You feel good; I hurt. Damn you. I walked through the living room several times, purposely blocking his view of the television and secretly flashing him hateful looks. He ignored me. After tiring of this, I promenaded into the living room, sighed, and said I was going outside to rake the yard. It's really the man's job, I explained, but I guess I'll have to do it. He said he'd do it later. I said later never came, I couldn't wait, I was embarrassed by the yard, just forget it, I was used to doing everything, and I would do that, too. He said okay, he would forget it. I stormed outside and stomped around the yard.

As tired as I was, bedtime came too early. Sleeping with my husband had become as strained as our waking moments. We would either not speak, each curling up on opposite sides of the bed as far away from each other as possible, or he would make attempts—as though everything were fine—to have sex with me. Either way, it was tense. If we turned our backs to each other, I would lie there with confused, desperate thoughts. If he tried to touch me, I froze. How could he expect me to make love to him? How could he touch me as though nothing had happened? Usually I pushed him away with a sharp, "No, I'm too tired." Sometimes I agreed. Occasionally, I did it because I wanted to. But, usually, if I had sex with him, it was because I felt obligated to take care of his sexual needs and guilty if I didn't. Either way, sex was psychologically and emotionally unsatisfying. But, I told myself I didn't care. It didn't matter. Not really. Long ago, I had shut off my sexual desires. Long ago, I had shut off my need to give and receive love. I had frozen that part of me that felt and cared. I had to, to survive.

I had expected so much of this marriage. I had so many dreams for us. None of them had come true. I had been tricked, betrayed. My home and family—the place and people who should have been warm, nurturing, a comfort, a haven of love—had become a trap. And I couldn't find the way out. Maybe, I kept telling myself, it will get better. After all, the problems are his fault. He's an alcoholic. When he gets better, our marriage will get better.

But, I was beginning to wonder. He had been sober and attending Alcoholics Anonymous for six months. He was getting better. I wasn't. Was his recovery really enough to make me happy? So far, his sobriety didn't appear to be changing the way I felt, which was, at age 32, dried up, used up, and brittle. What had happened to our love? What had happened to me?

One month later, I began to suspect what I would soon learn was the truth. By then, the only thing that had changed was I felt worse. My life had ground to a halt; I wanted it to end. I had no hope that things would get better; I didn't even know what was wrong. I had no purpose, except to care for other people, and I wasn't doing a good job of that. I was stuck in the past and terrified of the future. God seemed to have abandoned me. I felt guilty all the time and wondered if I was going crazy. Something dreadful, something that I couldn't explain, had happened to

Final

me. It had snuck up on me and ruined my life. Somehow, I had been affected by his drinking, and the ways I had been affected had become *my* problems. It no longer mattered whose fault it was.

I had lost control.

* * *

I met Jessica at this point in her life. She was about to learn three fundamental ideas.

1) She wasn't crazy; she was codependent. Alcoholism and other compulsive disorders are truly family illnesses. The way the illness affects other family members is called codependency.

2) Once they have been affected—once "it" sets in—codependency takes on a life of its own. It is similar to catching pneumonia or picking up a destructive habit. Once you've got it, you've got it.

3) If you want to get rid of it, *you* have to do something to make it go away. It doesn't matter whose fault it is. Your codependency becomes your problem; solving your problems is your responsibility.

If you're codependent, you need to find your own recovery or healing process. To begin that recovery, it helps to understand codependency and certain attitudes, feelings, and behaviors that often accompany it. It is also important to change some of these attitudes and behaviors and understand what to expect as these changes occur.

This book will search for those understandings and encourage those changes. I'm happy to say Jessica's story had a happy ending or a new beginning. She got better. She started living her own life. I hope you do too.

2

OTHER STORIES

When I say I'm codependent, I don't mean I'm a little bit codependent. I mean I'm really codependent. I don't marry men who stop for a few beers after work. I marry men who won't work.

—Ellen, an Al-Anon member

Maybe you identified with Jessica in the last chapter. Her story is an extreme example of codependency, but it is one I hear frequently. However, Jessica's experience is not the only type of codependency. There are as many variations of that story as there are codependents to tell them.

Here are a few.

*   *   *

Gerald, a handsome and personable man in his early forties, calls himself "a success in business but a failure in relationships with women." During high school and college, Gerald dated many women. He was popular and considered a good catch. However, after graduation, Gerald stunned his family and friends when he married Rita. Rita treated Gerald worse than any other woman he had dated. She acted cool and hostile toward Gerald and his friends, shared few interests with him, and didn't seem to care much for or about Gerald. Thirteen years later, the marriage ended in divorce when Gerald discovered some things he had suspected for years were true: Rita had been dating other men since they were married, and she was (and had been for some time) abusing alcohol and other drugs.

Gerald was devastated. But, after mourning for about two months, he fell wildly in love with another woman, who was a start-in-the-morning-and-drink-'til-she-passes-out alcoholic. After spending several months worrying about her, trying to help her, trying to figure out what he was doing that caused her to drink, trying to control her drinking, and ultimately getting angry with her because she wouldn't stop drinking, Gerald terminated that relationship. Soon he met another woman, fell in love with her, and moved into her apartment. Within months, Gerald suspected she too was chemically dependent.

Soon, Gerald began spending much of his time worrying about his girlfriend. He checked up on her, rummaged through her purse looking for pills or other evidence, and questioned her about her activities. Sometimes, he simply denied she had a problem. During those times, he kept busy, tried to enjoy his time with his girlfriend (although he said he felt uneasy), and told himself, "It's just me. Something's wrong with me."

During one of the many crises in his most recent relationship, when Gerald was temporarily jolted out of denial, he went to a chemical dependency counselor for advice.

"I know I should end the relationship," Gerald said, "but I'm just not ready to let it go. We can talk about anything and everything together. We're such good friends. And I love her. Why? Why does this always happen to me?

"Give me a room full of women, and I'll fall in love with the one with the most problems—the one that will treat me the worst. Frankly, they're more of a challenge," Gerald confided. "If a woman treats me too well, it turns me off."

Gerald considered himself a social drinker who had never had problems as a result of his drinking. Gerald told the counselor he had never used drugs. Gerald's brother, now in his late forties, had been an alcoholic since he was a teenager. Gerald denied that either of his deceased parents was an alcoholic, but reluctantly admitted his dad may have "drunk too much."

The counselor suggested the alcoholism and excessive drinking in Gerald's immediate family may still be affecting him and his relationships.

"How could their problems be affecting me?" he asked. "Dad has been dead for years, and I rarely see my brother."

After a few counseling sessions, Gerald began to label himself codependent, but he wasn't sure exactly what that meant or what to do about it. When Gerald became less angry about the immediate problem in his relationship, he discontinued counseling. Gerald decided his girlfriend's problems with drugs weren't that bad. He became convinced his problems with women were due to bad luck. He said he hoped his luck would change someday.

Is Gerald's problem bad luck? Or is it codependency?

*   *   *

Patty was in her mid-thirties and had been married for eleven years when she sought help from a private therapist. She had three children, the youngest of whom had cerebral palsy. Patty had devoted her life to being a good wife and mother. She told her therapist she loved her children, didn't regret her decision to stay home and raise them, but hated her daily routine. Before her marriage, she had many friends and hobbies, worked as a nurse, and was interested in the world around her. However, in the years following the birth of her children, particularly her handicapped child, she had lost her enthusiasm for life. She had few friends, had gained over 80 pounds, didn't know what she was feeling, and if she did, felt guilty for feeling that way. She explained she had tried to stay active by helping her friends and doing volunteer work for various organizations, but her efforts usually resulted in feelings of ineffectiveness and resentment. She thought about returning to work, but she didn't because, "All I know is nursing, and I'm sick of taking care of people."

"My family and friends think I'm a tower of strength. Good ol' dependable Patty. Always there. Always in control. Always ready to help them. The truth is," Patty said, "I'm falling apart, very quietly but very certainly. I've been depressed for years. I can't shake it. I cry at the drop of a hat. I don't have any energy. I scream at the kids all the time. I don't have any interest in sex, at least not with my husband. I feel guilty all the time about everything. I even feel guilty about coming to see you," she told the counselor. "I should be able to solve my own problems. I should be able to just snap out of this. It's ridiculous to waste your time and my husband's money for my problems, problems I'm probably imagining and blowing way out of proportion.

"But I had to do something," Patty confessed. "Lately, I've been thinking about suicide. Of course," she added, "I'd never actually kill myself. Too many people need me. Too many people depend on me. I'd be letting them down. But I'm worried. I'm scared."

The counselor learned Patty and her husband had children, the youngest with cerebral palsy. Patty also said before their marriage, her husband had problems with alcohol. During their marriage, he had drank less, had held the same job, and had been a good provider. But, upon questioning, Patty told the counselor her husband had not attended Alcoholics Anonymous meetings or any other support group. Instead, he went "on the wagon" for months between weekend drinking binges. When he drank, he acted crazy. When he wasn't drinking, he was angry and hostile.

"I don't know what's happened to him. He's not the man I married. What's even more frightening is I don't know what's happening to me or who I am," Patty said. "It's difficult to explain exactly what the problem is. I don't understand it myself. There's no major problem I can point to and say, 'That's what's wrong.' But it feels like I've lost myself. At times, I wonder if I'm going crazy. What's wrong with me?" Patty asked.

"Maybe your husband is an alcoholic, and your problems are caused by the family disease of alcoholism," the counselor suggested.

"How could that be?" Patty asked. "My husband doesn't drink that often."

The counselor dug into Patty's background. Patty talked with fondness about her parents and her two adult brothers. She came from a good family that was close and successful.

The counselor dug deeper. Patty mentioned her father had attended Alcoholics Anonymous since she was a teenager.

"Dad sobered up when I was in high school," she said. "I really love him, and I'm proud of him. But his drinking years were some pretty crazy years for our family."

Not only was Patty married to someone who was probably an alcoholic, she is what is now called an adult child of an alcoholic. The entire family had been affected by the family disease of alcoholism. Her dad stopped drinking; her mother went to Al-Anon; family life improved. But Patty, too, had been affected. Was she expected to magically overcome the ways she had been affected, just because the drinking stopped?

Instead of additional counseling sessions, Patty's counselor referred Patty to a self-esteem course and an assertiveness class. The counselor also recommended Patty attend Al-Anon meetings or Adult Children of Alcoholics meetings, which are self-help groups based on the Twelve Steps of Alcoholics Anonymous.

Patty followed the counselor's advice. She didn't find an overnight cure, but as the months passed she found herself making decisions with greater ease, feeling and expressing her feelings, saying what she thought, paying attention to her needs, and feeling less guilty. She became more tolerant of herself and her daily routine. Gradually, her depression lifted. She cried less and laughed more. Her energy and enthusiasm for life returned. Incidentally, with no prodding from Patty, her husband joined Alcoholics Anonymous. He became less hostile, and their marriage began to improve. The point here is Patty gained control of her life. Her life started working.

Now, if you ask Patty what her problem is or was, she will answer: "I'm codependent."

*   *   *

Clients who seek help from mental health and chemical dependency agencies are not the only people who suffer from codependency. Randell was a chemical dependency counselor and a recovering alcoholic with several years of sobriety when he found himself having troubles. Randell was also an adult child of an alcoholic; his father and three brothers were alcoholics. An intelligent, sensitive man who enjoyed his work, Randell's problem was his leisure time. He spent most of it worrying about—obsessed with—other people and their problems. Sometimes he tried to untangle messes alcoholics created; other times he felt angry with the alcoholics for creating the messes he felt obligated to clean up; sometimes he felt upset because people, not necessarily alcoholics, behaved in particular ways. He ranted, felt guilty, sorry, and used by people. Rarely, however, did he feel close to them. Rarely did he have fun.

For many years, Randell believed his duty was to worry about people and get involved in their problems. He called his behavior kindness, concern, love, and, sometimes, righteous indignation. Now, after getting help for his problem, he calls it codependency.

*   *   *

Sometimes, codependent behavior becomes inextricably entangled with being a good wife, mother, husband, brother, or Christian. Now in her forties, Marlyss is an attractive woman—when she takes care of herself. Most of the time, however, she's busy taking care of her five children and her husband, who is a recovering alcoholic. She devoted her life to making them happy, but she didn't succeed. Usually, she feels angry and unappreciated for her efforts, and her family feels angry at her. She has sex with her husband whenever he wants, regardless of how she feels. She spends too much of the family's budget on toys and clothing for the children—whatever they want. She chauffeurs, reads to, cooks for, cleans for, cuddles, and coddles those around her, but nobody gives to her. Most of the time, they don't even say, "Thank you." Marlyss resents her constant giving to people in her life. She resents how her family and their needs control her life. She chose nursing as her profession, and she often resents that.

"But I feel guilty when I don't do what's asked of me. I feel guilty when I don't live up to my standards for a wife and mother. I feel guilty when I don't live up to other people's standards for me. I just plain feel guilty," she said. "In fact," she added, "I schedule my day, my priorities, according to guilt."

Does endlessly taking care of other people, resenting it, and expecting nothing in return mean Marlyss is a good wife and mother? Or could it mean Marlyss is codependent?

*   *   *

Alcoholism (or chemical dependency) is not the only family problem that can create a codependent person. Alissa, the mother of two teenagers, worked part-time at a mental health organization when she went to a family counselor. (She had previously gone to many family counselors in her search for help.) She went to counseling because her oldest child, a fourteen-year-old boy, was constantly causing problems. He ran away, broke curfew, skipped school, disobeyed other family rules, and generally did whatever he wanted, whenever he wanted.

"This child," Alissa told the counselor, "is driving me crazy."

She meant it. She was worried sick. Some days she was so depressed and troubled she couldn't get out of bed. Alissa had tried everything she could think of to help this child. She'd placed him in treatment three times, put him in two different foster homes, and dragged the whole family from counselor to counselor. Alissa had tried other techniques, too: She had threatened, cried, hollered, and begged. She had gotten tough and called the police on him. She had tried gentleness and forgiveness. She even tried acting like he hadn't done the inappropriate things he had done. She had locked him out. And she had traveled halfway across the state to bring him home after he ran away. Although her efforts hadn't helped her child, Alissa was obsessed with finding and doing the one thing that would "make him see the errors of his ways" and help him change.

"Why," she asked the counselor, "is he doing this to me? He's running and ruining my life!"

The counselor agreed the problem with Alissa's son was painful, upsetting, and required action. But the counselor also said the problem didn't have to run and ruin Alissa's life.

"You haven't been able to control your son, but you can gain control of yourself," he said. "You can deal with your own codependency."

*　　*　　*

Sheryl also labels herself codependent. Shortly after marrying the man of her dreams, she found herself in a nightmare. Her husband, she learned, was a sex addict. In his case, that meant he couldn't control his urges to indulge in pornography, he was compulsively drawn into affairs with other women, and as Sheryl put it, "God only knows what and who else." She learned her husband was a sex addict one week after their wedding, when she discovered him in bed with another woman.

Sheryl's first response was panic. Then she got angry. Then she felt concern—for her husband and his problem. Her friends advised her to leave him, but she decided to stay in the marriage. He needed help. He needed her. Maybe he would change. Besides, she wasn't ready to lose her dream of that rosy future they would have together.

Her husband joined Sex Addicts Anonymous, a Twelve Step self-help group similar to Alcoholics Anonymous. Sheryl refused to join Co-SA (similar to Al-Anon) for family members of sex addicts. She didn't want to go public with her problem; she didn't even want to discuss it privately.

Over a period of months, Sheryl, a successful fashion model, found herself accepting fewer work assignments, turning down evenings out with friends, and sticking closer to home. She wanted to answer the telephone, in case women called for her husband. She wanted to be home to see her husband when he left the house and returned. She wanted to see what he looked like, how he acted, and how he talked. She wanted to know exactly what he was doing and with whom he was doing it. She often called his S.A. sponsor to complain, to report, and to inquire about her husband's progress. She refused, she said, to be tricked and deceived again.

Gradually, she alienated herself from her friends and activities. She was too worried to work; she was too ashamed to talk to her friends. Her husband had several more affairs; her friends were frustrated with her for staying with him and constantly whining about how terrible it was to be his wife.

"I couldn't stand the sight of my husband. I had nothing but contempt for him. Yet, I couldn't bring myself to leave him," Sheryl reported later. "I couldn't make myself do much of anything except worry and check up on him.

"My turning point was the night I chased him with a butcher knife," Sheryl said. "It was my lowest point. I was running through the house screaming and raving, when I suddenly became aware, for the first time, of *me*. I had gone mad. I was crazy—completely out of control—and he just stood there, calmly looking at me. I knew then I had to do something to get help for me."

Sheryl joined Co-SA shortly after that incident. It was at those meetings that she began to label herself and her loss of control as codependency. Sheryl is now separated from her husband and seeking a divorce. She is also feeling better about herself.

*   *   *

Although the preceding examples have been dramatic, codependency doesn't necessarily have to be so intense. And it doesn't always involve experiences with deeply troubled people. Kristen is married, has two young children, and knows of no alcoholism or compulsive disorders in her immediate or extended family. Yet, she calls herself codependent. Her problem, she says, is that other people's moods control her emotions; she, in turn, tries to control their feelings.

"If my husband is happy, and I feel responsible for that, then I'm happy. If he's upset, I feel responsible for that, too. I'm anxious, uncomfortable, and upset until he feels better. I try to *make* him feel better. I feel guilty if I can't. And he gets angry with me for trying.

"And it's not only with him that I behave codependently," she added. "It's with everyone: my parents, my children, guests in my home. Somehow, I just seem to lose myself in other people. I get enmeshed in them.

"I'd like to do something about it—this thing called codependency—before it gets any worse. I'm not terribly unhappy," she said, "but I'd like to learn how to relax and start enjoying myself and other people."

A minister summarized the condition this way: "Some people are *really* codependent, and some of us are just a *little bit* codependent."

* * *

I chose the preceding examples because they're interesting and represent a variety of experiences. They also illuminate a point that needs to be made: No single example illustrates the typical codependent or his or her experience. Codependency is complex. People are complex. Each person is unique, and each person's situation is different. Some people have extremely painful and debilitating experiences with codependency. Others don't and may be only mildly affected. Sometimes codependency is a person's response to another person's alcoholism; sometimes it isn't. Each codependent has a unique experience born from his or her circumstances, history, and personality.

Yet, a common thread runs through all stories of codependency. It involves our responses and reactions to people around us. It involves our relationships with other people, whether they are alcoholics, gamblers, sex addicts, overeaters, or normal people. Codependency involves the effects these people have on us and how we, in turn, try to affect them.

As Al-Anon members say, "Identify, don't compare."

ACTIVITY

1. Did you identify with any people in this chapter? What helped you think of yourself? Which relationships did it bring to mind? Why?

2. You might find it helpful to buy a large notebook and record your responses to these activities. You can also write down other thoughts and feelings you have as you read this book.

3

CODEPENDENCY

Relationships are like a dance, with visible energy
racing back and forth between the partners.
Some relationships are the slow, dark dance of death.[1]

—Colette Dowling

Up to this point, I have been using the words *codependent* and *codependency* as lucid terms. However, the definitions of these words remain vague.

The definition of chemical dependency means being dependent (psychologically and/or physically) on alcohol or other drugs. Overeating and gambling are also words that bring specific ideas to mind. But what is codependency?

The obvious definition would be: being a partner in dependency. This definition is close to the truth but still unclear. It brings no specific image to mind. Codependency is part of treatment center jargon, professional slang that's probably unintelligible to people outside that profession and gibberish to some inside the trade.

Jargon may or may not mean anything in particular. Jargon may mean different things to different people. Or, people may sense what a term means but not be able to clearly define it, because it's never been clearly defined.

Those are some of the problems I've encountered with researching and attempting to define codependency and codependent. Many people haven't heard the terms. Others, who are familiar with the words, can't define them. If they can, each definition is different. Or people define the words by using more jargon. To complicate matters, I can't find the words in any dictionaries. My computer keeps tagging the words as misspelled, trying to convince me they're not words.

Yet, codependency does mean something in particular, something particularly important to me and millions of people. Let's get rid of the jargon and look at that meaning.

What's Codependency?

I have heard and read many definitions of codependency.

In an article from the book *Co-Dependency, An Emerging Issue*, Robert Subby wrote codependency is: "An emotional, psychological, and behavioral condition that develops as a result of an individual's prolonged exposure to, and practice of, a set of oppressive rules—rules which prevent the open expression of feeling as well as the direct discussion of personal and interpersonal problems."[2]

Earnie Larsen, another codependency specialist and a pioneer in that field, defines codependency as: "Those self-defeating, learned behaviors or character defects that result in a diminished capacity to initiate or to participate in loving relationships."

Some less professional definitions follow.

"Codependency means," said one woman, "that I'm a caretaker."

"Being codependent means I'm married to an alcoholic," responded one woman. "It also means I need to go to Al-Anon."

"Codependency," replied another, "means I'm up to my elbows in alcoholics."

"It means I'm always looking for someone to glob onto."

"Codependency? It means I know any man I'm attracted to, fall in love with, or marry will be chemically dependent or have some other equally serious problem."

"Codependency," explained one person, "is knowing all your relationships will either go on and on the same way (painfully), or end the same way (disastrously). Or both."

There are almost as many definitions of codependency as there are experiences that represent it. In desperation (or perhaps enlightenment), some therapists have proclaimed: "Codependency is *anything*, and *everyone* is codependent." So, who's got the inside story? Which definition is accurate? A brief history of codependency will help answer this question.

A Brief History

The word codependency appeared on the treatment scene in the late seventies. I don't know who discovered it. Although several people may claim to have done so, the word emerged simultaneously in several different treatment centers in Minnesota, according to information from the office of Sondra Smalley, C.C.D.P., a licensed psychologist and a leader in the codependency field. Maybe Minnesota, the heartland of chemical dependency treatment and Twelve Step programs for compulsive disorders, discovered it.

Robert Subby and John Friel, in an article from the book *Co-Dependency, An Emerging Issue,* wrote: "Originally, it was used to describe the person or persons whose lives were affected as a result of their being involved with someone who was chemically dependent. The codependent spouse or child or lover of someone who was chemically dependent was seen as having developed a pattern of coping with life that was not healthy, as a reaction to someone else's drug or alcohol abuse."[3]

It was a new name for an old game. Professionals had long suspected something peculiar happened to people who were closely involved with chemically dependent people. Some research had been done on the subject, indicating a physical, mental, emotional, and spiritual condition similar to alcoholism seemed to appear in many nonalcoholic or non-chemically dependent people who were close to an alcoholic. Words (more jargon which would later become synonymous for codependent) surfaced to describe this phenomenon: co-alcoholic, nonalcoholic, para-alcoholic.

Codependents certainly felt the effects of codependency long before the word was coined. In the 1940s, after the birth of Alcoholics Anonymous, a group of people—primarily wives of alcoholics—formed self-help, support groups to deal with the ways their spouses' alcoholism affected them.[4] They didn't know they would later be called codependents. They did know they had been directly affected by their mates' alcoholism. And, they were envious that alcoholics had a Twelve Step program to recover through. The wives also wanted a program. So they used the A.A. Twelve Step program, revised the A.A. Twelve Traditions, changed its name to Al-Anon, and it worked! Millions of people have since benefited from Al-Anon.[5]

The basic thought then, and in 1979 when the word codependency emerged, was codependents (co-alcoholics or para-alcoholics) *were people whose lives had become unmanageable as a result of living in a committed relationship with an alcoholic.*

However, the definition for codependency has expanded since then. Professionals began to better understand the effects of the chemically dependent person on the family, and the effects of the family on the chemically dependent person. Professionals began to identify other problems such as overeating and undereating, gambling, and certain sexual behaviors. These compulsive disorders paralleled the compulsive disorder, or *illness,* of alcoholism. Professionals also began to notice many people in close relationships with these compulsive people developed patterns of reacting and coping that resembled the coping patterns of people in relationships with alcoholics. Something peculiar had happened to these families, too.

As professionals began to understand codependency better, more groups of people appeared to have it: adult children of alcoholics; people in relationships with emotionally or mentally disturbed persons; people in relationships with chronically ill people; parents of children with behavior problems; people in relationships with irresponsible people; professionals—nurses, social workers, and others in "helping" occupations. Even recovering alcoholics and addicts noticed they were codependent and perhaps had been long before becoming chemically dependent.[7] Codependents started cropping up everywhere.

When a codependent discontinued his or her relationship with a troubled person, the codependent frequently sought another troubled person and repeated the codependent behaviors with that new person. These behaviors, or coping mechanisms, seemed to prevail throughout the codependent's life—if that person didn't change these behaviors.

Was it safe to assume codependency was triggered through relationships with people who have serious illnesses, behavior problems, or destructive compulsive disorders? Alcoholism in the family helped create codependency, but many other circumstances seemed to produce it, also.

One fairly common denominator was having a relationship, personally or professionally, with troubled, needy, or dependent people. But a second, more common denominator seemed to be the unwritten, silent rules that usually develop in the immediate family and set the pace for relationships.[8] These rules prohibit discussion about problems; open expression of feelings; direct, honest communication; realistic expectations, such as being human, vulnerable, or imperfect; selfishness; trust in other people and one's self; playing and having fun; and rocking the delicately balanced family canoe through growth or change—however healthy and beneficial that movement might be. These rules are common to alcoholic family systems but can emerge in other families too.

Now, I return to an earlier question: Which definition of codependency is accurate? They all are. Some describe the cause, some the effects, some the overall condition, some the symptoms, some the patterns, and some the pain. Codependency either meant, or has come to mean, all the definitions listed earlier.

I'm not trying to confuse you. Codependency has a fuzzy definition because it is a gray, fuzzy condition. It is complex, theoretical, and difficult to completely define in one or two sentences.

Why all this fuss about a definition? Because I'm going to attempt the difficult—define codependent in one sentence. And, I want you to see the broader picture before I show you the narrower one. I hope this approach might help you identify codependency in yourself, if that identification is appropriate. Defining the problem is important because it helps determine the solution. Here, the solution is vital. It means feeling better. It means recovery.

So, here is my definition of a codependent:

A codependent person is one who has let another person's behavior affect him or her, and who is obsessed with controlling that person's behavior.

The *other person* might be a child, an adult, a lover, a spouse, a brother, a sister, a grandparent, a parent, a client, or a best friend. He or she could be an alcoholic, a drug addict, a mentally or physically ill person, a normal person who occasionally has sad feelings, or one of the people mentioned earlier.

But, the heart of the definition and recovery lies not in the *other person*—no matter how much we believe it does. It lies in ourselves, in the ways we have let other people's behavior affect us and in the ways we try to affect them: the obsessing, the controlling, the obsessive "helping," caretaking, low self-worth bordering on self-hatred, self-repression, abundance of anger and guilt, peculiar dependency on peculiar people, attraction to and tolerance for the bizarre, other-centeredness that results in abandonment of self, communication problems, intimacy problems, and an ongoing whirlwind trip through the five-stage grief process.

Is codependency an illness? Some professionals say codependency isn't a disease; they say it's a normal reaction to abnormal people.[9]

Other professionals say codependency is a disease; it's a chronic, progressive illness. They suggest codependents want and need sick people around them to be happy in an unhealthy way. They say, for instance, the wife of an alcoholic needed to marry an alcoholic and chose him because she unconsciously thought he was an alcoholic. Furthermore, she needed him drinking and socking it to her to feel fulfilled.

This latter judgment may be overly harsh. I'm convinced codependents need less harshness in their lives. Other people have been hard enough on us. We have been hard enough on ourselves. Friends, we have suffered enough. We have been victimized by diseases and people. Each of us must decide what part we played in our victimization.

I don't *know* if codependency is or isn't an illness. I'm not an expert. But, to tell you what I *believe*, let me complete the brief history of codependency which I started earlier in this chapter.

Although the first Al-Anon groups were formed in the 1940s, I am certain we could go back to the beginning of time and human relationships and find glimmers of codependent behavior. People have always had problems, and others have always cared for their troubled friends and relatives. People have likely been caught up with the problems of others since relationships began.

Codependency probably trailed man as he struggled through the remaining B.C. years, right up to "these generally wretched times of the twentieth century," as Morley Safer of *60 Minutes* says. Ever since people first existed, they have been doing all the things we label "codependent." They have worried themselves sick about other people. They have tried to help in ways that didn't help. They have said yes when they meant no. They have tried to make other people see things their way. They have bent over backward to avoid hurting people's feelings and, in so doing, have hurt themselves. They have been afraid to trust their feelings. They have believed lies and then felt betrayed. They have wanted to get even and punish others. They have felt so angry they wanted to kill. They have struggled for their rights while other people said they didn't have any. They have worn sackcloth because they didn't believe they deserved silk.

Codependents have undoubtedly done good deeds too. By their nature, codependents are benevolent—concerned about and responsive to the needs of the world. As Thomas Wright writes in an article from the book *Co-Dependency, An Emerging Issue,* "I suspect codependents have historically attacked social injustice and fought for the rights of the underdog. Codependents want to help. I suspect they have helped. But they probably died thinking they didn't do enough and were feeling guilty.

"It is natural to want to protect and help the people we care about. It is also natural to be affected by and react to the problems of people around us. As a problem becomes more serious and remains unresolved, we become more affected and react more intensely to it."

The word *react* is important here. However you approach codependency, however you define it, and from whatever frame of reference you choose to diagnose and treat it, codependency is primarily a reactionary process. Codependents are reactionaries. They overreact. They underreact. But rarely do they *act*. They react to the problems, pains, lives, and behaviors of others. They react to their own problems, pains, and behaviors. Many codependent reactions are reactions to stress and uncertainty of living or growing up with alcoholism and other problems. It is normal to react to stress. It is not necessarily abnormal, but it is heroic and life-saving to learn how to *not* react and to act in more healthy ways. Most of us, however, need help to learn to do that.

Perhaps one reason some professionals call codependency a disease is because many codependents are reacting to an illness such as alcoholism.

Another reason codependency is called a disease is because it is progressive. As the people around us become sicker, we may begin to react more intensely. What began as a little concern may trigger isolation, depression, emotional or physical illness, or suicidal fantasies. One thing leads to another, and things get worse. Codependency may not be an illness, but it can make you sick. And, it can help the people around you stay sick.

Another reason codependency is called a disease is because codependent behaviors—like many self-destructive behaviors—become habitual. We repeat habits without thinking. Habits take on a life of their own.[10]

Whatever problem the other person has, codependency involves a habitual system of thinking, feeling, and behaving toward ourselves and others that can cause us pain. Codependent behaviors or habits are self-destructive. We frequently react to people who are destroying themselves; we react by learning to destroy ourselves. These habits can lead us into, or keep us in, destructive relationships, relationships that don't work. These behaviors can sabotage relationships that may otherwise have worked. These behaviors can prevent us from finding peace and happiness with the most important person in our lives—ourselves. These behaviors belong to the only person each of us can control—the only person we can change—ourselves. These are our problems. In the next chapter, we will examine these behaviors.

ACTIVITY

1. How would you define codependency?

2. Do you know anybody who has significantly affected your life, somebody whom you worry about and wish you could change? Who? Write several paragraphs about that person and your relationship. Later, read what you wrote. What are your feelings?

4

CODEPENDENT CHARACTERISTICS

God, grant me the serenity
To accept the things I cannot change,
Courage to change the things I can,
And wisdom to know the difference.

—The Serenity Prayer

Although two codependents might disagree on the definition of codependency, if they discuss the issues with each other, each will probably sense what the other person means. They will share ideas about things they have in common—things they do, think, feel, and say—that are characteristic of codependency. It is on these points—symptoms, problems, coping mechanisms, or reactions—that most definitions and recovery programs overlap and agree. These points dictate recovery. They are the things we need to recognize, accept, live with, deal with, struggle through, and frequently change.

Before I list the things codependents tend to do, however, I will make an important point: Having these problems does not mean we're bad, defective, or inferior. Some of us learned these behaviors as children. Other people learned them later in life. We may have learned some of these things from our interpretation of religion. Some women were taught these behaviors were desirable feminine attributes. Wherever we learned to do these things, most of us learned our lessons well.

Most of us started doing these things out of necessity to protect ourselves and meet our needs. We performed, felt, and thought these things to survive—emotionally, mentally, and sometimes physically. We tried to understand and cope with our complex worlds in the best ways. It is not always easy to live with normal, healthy people. It is particularly difficult to live with sick, disturbed, or troubled people. It is horrible having to live with a raving alcoholic. Many of us have been trying to cope with outrageous circumstances, and these efforts have been both admirable and heroic. We have done the best we could.

However, these self-protective devices may have outgrown their usefulness. Sometimes, the things we do to protect ourselves turn on us and hurt us. They become self-destructive. Many codependents are barely surviving, and most aren't getting their needs met. As counselor Scott Egleston says, codependency is a way of getting needs met that doesn't get needs met. We've been doing the wrong things for the right reasons.

Can we change? Can we learn healthier behaviors? I don't know if mental, spiritual, and emotional health can be taught, but we can be inspired and encouraged. We can learn to do things differently. We can change. I think most people want to be healthy and live the best lives they can. But many of us don't know it's okay to do things differently. Many of us don't even understand what we've been doing that hasn't been working. Most of us have been so busy responding to other people's problems that we haven't had time to identify, much less take care of, our own problems.

Many professionals say the first step toward change is awareness. The second step is acceptance.[1] With that in mind, let's examine the characteristics of codependency. These characteristics have been compiled from my entire bibliography and from my personal and professional experience.

CARETAKING

Codependents may:

- think and feel responsible for other people—for other people's feelings, thoughts, actions, choices, wants, needs, well-being, lack of well-being, and ultimate destiny.
- feel anxiety, pity, and guilt when other people have a problem.

- feel compelled—almost forced—to help that person solve the problem, such as offering unwanted advice, giving a rapid-fire series of suggestions, or fixing feelings.
- feel angry when their help isn't effective.
- anticipate other people's needs.
- wonder why others don't do the same for them.
- find themselves saying yes when they mean no, doing things they don't really want to be doing, doing more than their fair share of the work, and doing things other people are capable of doing for themselves.
- not know what they want and need or, if they do, tell themselves what they want and need is not important.
- try to please others instead of themselves.
- find it easier to feel and express anger about injustices done to others, rather than injustices done to themselves.
- feel safest when giving.
- feel insecure and guilty when somebody gives to them.
- feel sad because they spend their whole lives giving to other people and nobody gives to them.
- find themselves attracted to needy people.
- find needy people attracted to them.
- feel bored, empty, and worthless if they don't have a crisis in their lives, a problem to solve, or someone to help.
- abandon their routine to respond to or do something for somebody else.
- overcommit themselves.
- feel harried and pressured.
- believe deep inside other people are somehow responsible for them.
- blame others for the spot the codependents are in.
- say other people make the codependents feel the way they do.
- believe other people are making them crazy.
- feel angry, victimized, unappreciated, and used.
- find other people become impatient or angry with them for all the preceding characteristics.

LOW SELF-WORTH

Codependents tend to:

- come from troubled, repressed, or dysfunctional families.
- deny their family was troubled, repressed, or dysfunctional.
- blame themselves for everything.
- pick on themselves for everything, including the way they think, feel, look, act, and behave.
- get angry, defensive, self-righteous, and indignant when others blame and criticize the codependents—something codependents regularly do to themselves.
- reject compliments or praise.
- get depressed from a lack of compliments and praise (stroke deprivation).
- feel different from the rest of the world.
- think they're not quite good enough.
- feel guilty about spending money on themselves or doing unnecessary or fun things for themselves.
- fear rejection.
- take things personally.
- have been victims of sexual, physical, or emotional abuse, neglect, abandonment, or alcoholism.
- feel like victims.
- tell themselves they can't do anything right.
- be afraid of making mistakes.
- wonder why they have a tough time making decisions.
- expect themselves to do everything perfectly.
- wonder why they can't get anything done to their satisfaction.
- have a lot of "shoulds."
- feel a lot of guilt.
- feel ashamed of who they are.
- think their lives aren't worth living.
- try to help other people live their lives instead.

- get artificial feelings of self-worth from helping others.
- get strong feelings of low self-worth—embarrassment, failure, etc.— from other people's failures and problems.
- wish good things would happen to them.
- believe good things never will happen.
- believe they don't deserve good things and happiness.
- wish other people would like and love them.
- believe other people couldn't possibly like and love them.
- try to prove they're good enough for other people.
- settle for being needed.

REPRESSION

Many codependents:

- push their thoughts and feelings out of their awareness because of fear and guilt.
- become afraid to let themselves be who they are.
- appear rigid and controlled.

OBSESSION

Codependents tend to:

- feel terribly anxious about problems and people.
- worry about the silliest things.
- think and talk a lot about other people.
- lose sleep over problems or other people's behavior.
- worry.
- never find answers.
- check on people.
- try to catch people in acts of misbehavior.
- feel unable to quit talking, thinking, and worrying about other people or problems.

- abandon their routine because they are so upset about somebody or something.
- focus all their energy on other people and problems.
- wonder why they never have any energy.
- wonder why they can't get things done.

CONTROLLING

Many codependents:

- have lived through events and with people that were out of control, causing the codependents sorrow and disappointment.
- become afraid to let other people be who they are and allow events to happen naturally.
- don't see or deal with their fear of loss of control.
- think they know best how things should turn out and how people should behave.
- try to control events and people through helplessness, guilt, coercion, threats, advice-giving, manipulation, or domination.
- eventually fail in their efforts or provoke people's anger.
- get frustrated and angry.
- feel controlled by events and people.

DENIAL

Codependents tend to:

- ignore problems or pretend they aren't happening.
- pretend circumstances aren't as bad as they are.
- tell themselves things will be better tomorrow.
- stay busy so they don't have to think about things.
- get confused.
- get depressed or sick.

- go to doctors and get tranquilizers.
- become workaholics.
- spend money compulsively.
- overeat.
- pretend those things aren't happening, either.
- watch problems get worse.
- believe lies.
- lie to themselves.
- wonder why they feel like they're going crazy.

DEPENDENCY

Many codependents:

- don't feel happy, content, or peaceful with themselves.
- look for happiness outside themselves.
- latch onto whoever or whatever they think can provide happiness.
- feel terribly threatened by the loss of any thing or person they think provides their happiness.
- didn't feel love and approval from their parents.
- don't love themselves.
- believe other people can't or don't love them.
- desperately seek love and approval.
- often seek love from people incapable of loving.
- believe other people are never there for them.
- equate love with pain.
- feel they need people more than they want them.
- try to prove they're good enough to be loved.
- don't take time to see if other people are good for them.
- worry whether other people love or like them.
- don't take time to figure out if they love or like other people.
- center their lives around other people.
- look to relationships to provide all their good feelings.

- lose interest in their own lives when they love.
- worry other people will leave them.
- don't believe they can take care of themselves.
- stay in relationships that don't work.
- tolerate abuse to keep people loving them.
- feel trapped in relationships.
- leave bad relationships and form new ones that don't work either.
- wonder if they will ever find love.

POOR COMMUNICATION

Codependents frequently:

- blame.
- threaten.
- coerce.
- beg.
- bribe.
- advise.
- don't say what they mean.
- don't mean what they say.
- don't know what they mean.
- don't take themselves seriously.
- think other people don't take the codependents seriously.
- take themselves too seriously.
- ask for what they want and need indirectly—sighing, for example.
- find it difficult to get to the point.
- aren't sure what the point is.
- gauge their words carefully to achieve a desired effect.
- try to say what they think will please people.
- try to say what they think will provoke people.
- try to say what they hope will make people do what they want them to do.

- eliminate the word *no* from their vocabulary.
- talk too much.
- talk about other people.
- avoid talking about themselves, their problems, feelings, and thoughts.
- say everything is their fault.
- say nothing is their fault.
- believe their opinions don't matter.
- wait to express their opinions until they know other people's opinions.
- lie to protect and cover up for people they love.
- lie to protect themselves.
- have a difficult time asserting their rights.
- have a difficult time expressing their emotions honestly, openly, and appropriately.
- think most of what they have to say is unimportant.
- begin to talk in cynical, self-degrading, or hostile ways.
- apologize for bothering people.

WEAK BOUNDARIES

Codependents frequently:

- say they won't tolerate certain behaviors from other people.
- gradually increase their tolerance until they can tolerate and do things they said they never would.
- let others hurt them.
- keep letting people hurt them.
- wonder why they hurt so badly.
- complain, blame, and try to control while they continue to stand there.
- finally get angry.
- become totally intolerant.

LACK OF TRUST

Codependents:

- don't trust themselves.
- don't trust their feelings.
- don't trust their decisions.
- don't trust other people.
- try to trust untrustworthy people.
- think God has abandoned them.
- lose faith and trust in God.

ANGER

Many codependents:

- feel very scared, hurt, and angry.
- live with people who are very scared, hurt, and angry.
- are afraid of their own anger.
- are frightened of other people's anger.
- think people will go away if anger enters the picture.
- think other people make them feel angry.
- are afraid to make other people feel anger.
- feel controlled by other people's anger.
- repress their angry feelings.
- cry a lot, get depressed, overeat, get sick, do mean and nasty things to get even, act hostile, or have violent temper outbursts.
- punish other people for making the codependents angry.
- have been shamed for feeling angry.
- place guilt and shame on themselves for feeling angry.
- feel increasing amounts of anger, resentment, and bitterness.
- feel safer with their anger than with hurt feelings.
- wonder if they'll ever *not* be angry.

SEX PROBLEMS

Some codependents:

- are caretakers in the bedroom.
- have sex when they don't want to.
- have sex when they'd rather be held, nurtured, and loved.
- try to have sex when they're angry or hurt.
- refuse to enjoy sex because they're so angry at their partner.
- are afraid of losing control.
- have a difficult time asking for what they need in bed.
- withdraw emotionally from their partner.
- feel sexual revulsion toward their partner.
- don't talk about it.
- force themselves to have sex, anyway.
- reduce sex to a technical act.
- wonder why they don't enjoy sex.
- lose interest in sex.
- make up reasons to abstain.
- wish their sex partner would die, go away, or sense the codependent's feelings.
- have strong sexual fantasies about other people.
- consider or have an extramarital affair.

MISCELLANEOUS

Codependents tend to:

- be extremely responsible.
- be extremely irresponsible.
- become martyrs, sacrificing their happiness and that of others for causes that don't require sacrifice.
- find it difficult to feel close to people.
- find it difficult to have fun and be spontaneous.

- have an overall passive response to codependency—crying, hurt, helplessness.
- have an overall aggressive response to codependency—violence, anger, dominance.
- combine passive and aggressive responses.
- vacillate in decisions and emotions.
- laugh when they feel like crying.
- stay loyal to their compulsions and people even when it hurts.
- be ashamed about family, personal, or relationship problems.
- be confused about the nature of the problem.
- cover up, lie, and protect the problem.
- not seek help because they tell themselves the problem isn't bad enough, or they aren't important enough.
- wonder why the problem doesn't go away.

PROGRESSIVE

In the later stages of codependency, codependents may:

- feel lethargic.
- feel depressed.
- become withdrawn and isolated.
- experience a complete loss of daily routine and structure.
- abuse or neglect their children and other responsibilities.
- feel hopeless.
- begin to plan their escape from a relationship they feel trapped in.
- think about suicide.
- become violent.
- become seriously emotionally, mentally, or physically ill.
- experience an eating disorder (over- or undereating).
- become addicted to alcohol and other drugs.

*   *   *

The preceding checklist is long but not all-inclusive. Like other people, codependents do, feel, and think many things. There are not a certain number of traits that guarantees whether a person is or isn't codependent. Each person is different; each person has his or her way of doing things. I'm just trying to paint a picture. The interpretation, or decision, is up to you. What's most important is that you first identify behaviors or areas that cause you problems, and then decide what you want to do.

At the end of Chapter Three, I asked you to define codependency. As Earnie Larsen says, if you defined your problem as, "living with an alcoholic," you may think *not* living with an alcoholic is the solution to your problem. That may be partially correct. But our real problems as codependents are our own characteristics—our codependent behaviors.

Who's codependent? I am.

An estimated 80 million people are chemically dependent or in a relationship with someone who is.[2] They are probably codependent.

People who love, care about, or work with troubled people may be codependent.

People who care about people with eating disorders are probably codependent. In her book, *Fat Is a Family Affair,* Judi Hollis wrote that one eating disorder person can keep fifteen to twenty codependents busy.[3] Many people with eating disorders are codependents, too. "In an informal survey, I discovered at least 40 percent of the wives of alcoholics were obese," Hollis wrote.[4]

You may be reading this book for yourself; you may be codependent. Or, you may be reading this book to help someone else; if so, you probably are codependent. If concern has turned into obsession; if compassion has turned into caretaking; if you are taking care of other people and not taking care of yourself—you may be in trouble with codependency. Each person must decide for him- or herself if codependency is a problem. Each person must decide for him- or herself what needs to be changed and when that should happen.

Codependency is many things. It is a dependency on people—on their moods, behaviors, sickness or well-being, and their love. It is a paradoxical dependency.[5] Codependents appear to be depended upon, but they are dependent. They look strong but feel helpless. They appear controlling but in reality are controlled themselves, sometimes by an illness such as alcoholism.

These are the issues that dictate recovery. It is solving these problems that makes recovery fun. Many recoveries from problems that involve a person's mind, emotions, and spirit are long and grueling. Not so, here. Except for normal human emotions we would be feeling anyway, and twinges of discomfort as we begin to behave differently, recovery from codependency is exciting. It is liberating. It lets us be who we are. It lets other people be who they are. It helps us own our God-given power to think, feel, and act. It feels good. It brings peace. It enables us to love ourselves and others. It allows us to receive love—some of the good stuff we've all been looking for. It provides an optimum environment for the people around us to get and stay healthy. And recovery helps stop the unbearable pain many of us have been living with.

Recovery is not only fun, it is simple. It is not always easy, but it is simple. It is based on a premise many of us have forgotten or never learned: Each person is responsible for him- or herself. It involves learning one new behavior that we will devote ourselves to: taking care of ourselves. In the second half of this book, we'll discuss specific ideas for doing that.

ACTIVITY

1. Go through the checklist in this chapter. Mark each characteristic with a 0 if it is never a problem for you. Mark the characteristic with a 1 if it is occasionally a problem. And mark it with a 2 if it is frequently a problem. Later, in another chapter, you will use this to establish goals. You may wish to use it now as a guide to the chapters you want to read.

2. How do you feel about changing yourself? What do you think would happen if you began to change? Do you think you can change? Why or why not? Write several paragraphs answering these questions.

Part II:

THE BASICS OF SELF-CARE

5

DETACHMENT

It (detachment) is not detaching from the person
whom we care about, but from the agony of involvement.[1]

—Al-Anon member

When I was trying to choose the topic for the first chapter in this section of the book, many subjects competed for first place. I chose detachment not because it is significantly more important than the other concepts. I selected it because it is an underlying concept. It is something we need to do frequently, as we strive to live happy lives. It is the goal of most recovery programs for codependents. And, it is also something we must do first—before we can do the other things we need to do. We cannot begin to work on ourselves, to live our own lives, feel our own feelings, and solve our own problems until we have detached from the object of our obsession. From my experiences (and those of others), it appears that even our Higher Power can't do much with us until we have detached.

Attachment

When a codependent says, "I think I'm getting attached to you," look out! He or she probably means it.

Most codependents are attached to the people and problems in their environments. By "attachment," I don't mean normal feelings of liking people, being concerned about problems, or feeling connected to the world. Attachment is becoming overly-involved, sometimes hopelessly entangled.

Attachment can take several forms:

- We may become excessively worried about, and preoccupied with, a problem or person (our mental energy is attached).
- Or, we may graduate to becoming obsessed with and controlling of the people and problems in our environment (our mental, physical, and emotional energy is directed at the object of our obsession).
- We may become reactionaries, instead of acting authentically of our own volition (our mental, emotional, and physical energy is attached).
- We may become emotionally dependent on the people around us (now we're really attached).
- We may become caretakers (rescuers, enablers) to the people around us (firmly attaching ourselves to their need for us).

The problems with attachment are many. (In this chapter I will focus on worry and obsession. In following chapters I will cover the other forms of attachment.) Overinvolvement of any sort can keep us in a state of chaos; it can keep the people around us in a state of chaos. If we're focusing all our energies on people and problems, we have little left for the business of living our own lives. And, there is just so much worry and responsibility in the air. If we take it all on ourselves, there is none left for the people around us. It overworks us and underworks them. Furthermore, worrying about people and problems doesn't help. It doesn't solve problems, it doesn't help other people, and it doesn't help us. It is wasted energy.

"If you believe that feeling bad or worrying long enough will change a fact, then you are residing on another planet with a different reality system," wrote Dr. Wayne W. Dyer in *Your Erroneous Zones*.[2]

Worrying and obsessing keep us so tangled in our heads we can't solve our problems. Whenever we become attached in these ways to someone or something, we become detached from ourselves. We lose touch with ourselves. We forfeit our power and ability to think, feel, act, and take care of ourselves. We lose control.

Obsession with another human being, or a problem, is an awful thing to be caught up in. Have you ever seen someone who is obsessed with someone or something? That person can talk about nothing else, can think of nothing else. Even if he appears to be listening when you talk, you know that person doesn't hear you. His mind is tossing and turning, crashing and banging, around and around on an endless racetrack of compulsive thought. He is preoccupied. He relates whatever you say, no matter how unrelated it actually is, to the object of his obsession. He says the same things, over and over, sometimes changing the wording slightly, sometimes using the same words. Nothing you say makes any difference. Even telling him to stop doesn't help. He probably would if he could. The problem is he can't (at that moment). He is bursting with the jarring energy that obsession is made of. He has a problem or a concern that is not only bothering him—it is controlling him.

Many of the people I've worked with in family groups have been *that* obsessed with people they care about. When I asked them what they were feeling, they told me what the other person was feeling. When I asked what they did, they told me what the other person had done. Their entire focus was on someone or something other than themselves. Some of them had spent years of their lives doing this—worrying about, reacting to, and trying to control other human beings. They were shells, sometimes almost invisible shells, of people. Their energy was depleted—directed at someone else. They couldn't tell me what they were feeling and thinking because they didn't know. Their focus was not on themselves.

Maybe you've been obsessed with someone or something. Someone does or says something. A thought occurs to you. Something reminds you of a past event. A problem enters your awareness. Something happens or doesn't happen. Or you sense something's happening, but you're not sure what. He doesn't call, and he usually calls by now. He doesn't answer the phone, and he should. It's payday. In the past he always got drunk on payday. He's only been sober three months. Will it happen again today? You may not know what, you may not know why, and you're not sure when, but you *know* something bad—something terrible—has happened, is happening, or is about to happen.

It hits you in the stomach. The feeling fills you up—that gut-twisting, handwringing anxiety that is *so* familiar to codependents. It is what causes us to do much of what we do that hurts ourselves; it is the substance worry and obsession feed upon. It is fear at its worst. Fear usually comes and goes, leaving us in flight, ready to fight, or just temporarily frightened. But anxiety hangs in there. It grips the mind, paralyzing it for all but its own purposes—an endless rehashing of the same useless thoughts. It is the fuel that propels us into controlling behaviors of all sorts. We can think of nothing but keeping a lid on things, controlling the problem, and making it go away; it is the stuff codependency is made of.

When you're obsessed, you can't get your mind off that person or that problem. You don't know what you are feeling. You didn't know what you were thinking. You're not even sure what you should do, but by God, you should do something! And fast!

Worrying, obsessing, and controlling are illusions. They are tricks we play on ourselves. We feel like we are doing something to solve our problems, but we're not. Many of us have reacted this way with justifiably good reason. We may have lived with serious, complicated problems that have disrupted our lives, and they would provoke any normal person to become anxious, upset, worried, and obsessed. We may love someone who is in trouble—someone who's out of control. His or her problem may be alcoholism, an eating disorder, gambling, a mental or emotional problem, or any combination of these.

Some of us may be living with less serious problems, but they concern us anyway. People we love or care about may have mood swings. They may do things we wish they wouldn't do. We may think he or she should do things differently, a better way, a way that we believe wouldn't cause so many problems.

Out of habit, some of us may have developed an attitude of attachment—of worrying, reacting, and obsessively trying to control. Maybe we have lived with people and through events that were out of control.

Maybe obsessing and controlling is the way we kept things in balance or temporarily kept things from getting worse. And then we just kept on doing it. Maybe we're afraid to let go, because when we let go in the past, terrible, hurtful things happened.

Maybe we've been attached to people—living their lives for and through them—for so long that we don't have any life of our own left to live. It's safer to stay attached. At least we know we're alive if we're reacting. At least we've got something to do if we're obsessing or controlling.

For various reasons codependents tend to attach themselves to problems and people. Never mind that worrying isn't solving anything. Never mind that those problems rarely have solutions. Never mind that they're so obsessed they can't read a book, watch television, or go for a walk. Never mind that their emotions are constantly in turmoil over what she said or didn't say, what she did or didn't do, or what she will do next. Never mind that the things we're doing aren't helping anyone! No matter what the cost, we will hang on. We will grit our teeth, clutch the rope, and grab more tightly than ever.

Some of us may not even be aware we've been holding on so tightly. Some of us may have convinced ourselves we have to hang on this tightly. We believe there is simply no other choice but to react to this particular problem or person in this obsessive manner. Frequently, when I suggest to people that they detach from a person or problem, they recoil in horror. "Oh, no!" they say. "I could never do that. I love him, or her, too much. I care too much to do *that*. This problem or person is too important to me. I *have* to stay attached!"

My answer to that is, "WHO SAYS YOU HAVE TO?"

I've got news—good news. We don't "have to." There's a better way. It's called "detachment."[3] It may be scary at first, but it will ultimately work better for everyone involved.

A Better Way

Exactly what is detachment? What am I asking of you? (The term, as you may have guessed, is more jargon.)

First, let's discuss what detachment isn't. Detachment is not a cold, hostile withdrawal; a resigned, despairing acceptance of anything life and people throw our way; a robotical walk through life oblivious to, and totally unaffected by people and problems; a Pollyanna-like ignorant bliss; a shirking of our *true* responsibilities to ourselves and others; a severing of our relationships. Nor is it a removal of our love and concern, although sometimes these ways of detaching might be the best we can do, for the moment.

Ideally, detachment is releasing, or detaching from, a person or problem *in love*. We mentally, emotionally, and sometimes physically disengage ourselves from unhealthy (and frequently painful) entanglements with another person's life and responsibilities, and from problems we cannot solve, according to a handout, entitled "Detachment," that has been passed around Al-Anon groups for years.

Detachment is based on the premises that each person is responsible for himself, that we can't solve problems that aren't ours to solve, and that worrying doesn't help. We adopt a policy of keeping our hands off other people's responsibilities and tend to our own instead. If people have created some disasters for themselves, we allow them to face their own proverbial music. We allow people to be who they are. We give them the freedom to be responsible and to grow. And we give ourselves that same freedom. We live our own lives to the best of our ability. We strive to ascertain what it is we can change and what we cannot change. Then we stop trying to change things we can't. We do what we can to solve a problem, and then we stop fretting and stewing. If we cannot solve a problem and we have done what we could, we learn to live with, or in spite of, that problem. And we try to live happily—focusing heroically on what is good in our lives today, and feeling grateful for that. We learn the magical lesson that making the most of what we have turns it into more.

Detachment involves "present moment living"—living in the here and now. We allow life to happen instead of forcing and trying to control it. We relinquish regrets over the past and fears about the future. We make the most of each day.

Detachment also involves accepting reality—the facts. It requires faith—in ourselves, in God, in other people, and in the natural order and destiny of things in this world. We believe in the rightness and appropriateness of each moment. We release our burdens and cares, and give ourselves the freedom to enjoy life in spite of our unsolved problems. We trust that all is well in spite of the conflicts. We trust that Someone greater than ourselves knows, has ordained, and cares about what is happening. We understand that this Someone can do much more to solve the problem than we can. So we try to stay out of His way and let Him do it. In time, we *know* that all is well because we see how the strangest (and sometimes most painful) things work out for the best and for the benefit of everyone.

Judi Hollis wrote of detachment in a section on codependency in her book, *Fat Is a Family Affair.* There she described detachment as "a healthy neutrality."[4]

Detaching does not mean we don't care. It means we learn to love, care, and be involved without going crazy. We stop creating all this chaos in our minds and environments. When we are not anxiously and compulsively thrashing about, we become able to make good decisions about how to love people, and how to solve our problems. We become free to care and to love in ways that help others and don't hurt ourselves.[5]

The rewards from detachment are great: serenity; a deep sense of peace; the ability to give and receive love in self-enhancing, energizing ways; and the freedom to find real solutions to our problems. We find the freedom to live our own lives without excessive feelings of guilt about, or responsibility toward others.[6] Sometimes detachment even motivates and frees people around us to begin to solve their problems. We stop worrying about them, and they pick up the slack and finally start worrying about themselves. What a grand plan! We each mind our own business.

Earlier, I described a person caught in the entanglement of obsessions and worry. I have known many people who have had to (or have chosen to) live with serious problems such as an alcoholic spouse who never sobered up, a severely handicapped child, and a teenager hell-bent on destroying himself through drugs and criminal behavior. These people learned to live with, and in spite of, their problems. They grieved for their losses, then found a way to live their lives not in resignation, martyrdom, and despair, but with enthusiasm, peace, and a true sense of gratitude for that which was good. They took care of their actual responsibilities. They gave to people, they helped people, and they loved people. But they also gave to and loved themselves. They held themselves in high esteem. They didn't do these things perfectly, or without effort, or instantly. But they strived to do these things, and they learned to do them well.

I owe a debt of gratitude to these people. They taught me that detachment was possible. They *showed me* it could work. I would like to pass that same hope on to you. It is my wish that you will find other people to pass that hope on to, for detachment is real and thrives with reinforcement and nurturing.

Detachment is both an act and an art. It is a way of life. I believe it is also a gift. And it will be given to those who seek it.

How do we detach? How do we extricate our emotions, mind, body, and spirit from the agony of entanglement? As best we can. And, probably, a bit clumsily at first. An old A.A. and Al-Anon saying suggests a three-part formula called "HOW": Honesty, Openness, and Willingness to try.[7]

In the chapters ahead, I will discuss some specific concepts for detaching from certain forms of attachment. Many of the other concepts I will discuss later will lead to detachment. You will have to decide how these ideas apply to you and your particular situation and then find your own path. With a little humility, surrender, and effort on your part, I believe you can do it. I believe detachment can become a habitual response, in the same manner that obsessing, worrying, and controlling became habitual responses—by practice. You may not do it perfectly, but no one has. However, and at whatever pace, you practice detachment in your life, I believe it will be right for you. I hope you will be able to detach with love for the person or persons you are detaching from. I think it is better to do everything in an attitude of love. However, for a variety of reasons, we can't always do that. If you can't detach in love, it is my opinion that it is better to detach in anger rather than to stay attached. If we are detached, we are in a better position to work on (or through) our resentful emotions. If we're attached, we probably won't do anything other than stay upset.

When should we detach? When we can't stop thinking, talking about, or worrying about someone or something; when our emotions are churning and boiling; when we feel like we *have* to do something about someone because we can't stand it another minute; when we're hanging on by a thread, and it feels like that single thread is frayed; and when we believe we can no longer live with the problem we've been trying to live with. It is time to detach! You will learn to recognize when detachment is advisable. A good rule of thumb is: You need to detach most when it seems the least likely or possible thing to do.

I'll close this chapter with a true story. One night about midnight my telephone rang. I was in bed and wondered, as I picked up the receiver, who was calling me at that hour. I thought it had to be an emergency.

In a way it was an emergency. It was a stranger. She had been calling various friends all evening, trying to find some kind of consolation. Apparently, she hadn't been able to find it. Someone had given her someone else's phone number, that person had given her someone else's phone number, and the last person had suggested she call me.

Immediately upon introducing herself, the woman exploded in a tirade. Her husband used to go to Alcoholics Anonymous. He had separated from her, and now he was seeing another woman because he wanted to "find himself." Furthermore, before he left her, he had been acting really crazy and didn't go to meetings. And she wondered, isn't he acting crazy now by dating a woman who is *that much younger than him*?

I was speechless at first, then found it hard to find a chance to talk. She went on and on. Finally she asked, "Don't you think he's sick? Don't you think he's acting crazy? Don't you think something should be done about him?"

"That could be," I replied. "But obviously I can't do it, and neither can you. I'm more concerned about you. What are *you* feeling? What do *you* think? What do *you* need to do to take care of *yourself*?"

I shall say the same thing to you, dear reader. I know you have problems. I understand that many of you are deeply grieved over, and concerned about, certain people in your lives. Many of them may be destroying themselves, you, and your family, right before your eyes. But I can't do anything to control those people; and you probably can't either. If you could, you probably would have done it by now.

Detach. Detach in love, or detach in anger, but strive for detachment. I know it's difficult, but it will become easier with practice. If you can't let go completely, try to "hang on loose."[8] Relax. Sit back. Now, take a deep breath. The focus is on you.

ACTIVITY

1. Is there a problem or person in your life that you are excessively worried about? Write about that person or problem. Write as much as you need to write to get it out of your system. When you have written all you need to write about that person or problem, focus on yourself. What are you thinking? What are you feeling?

2. How do you feel about detaching from that person or problem? What might happen if you detach? Will that probably happen anyway? How has staying "attached"—worrying, obsessing, trying to control—helped so far?

3. If you did not have that person or problem in your life, what would you be doing with your life that is different from what you are doing now? How would you be feeling and behaving? Spend a few minutes visualizing yourself living your life, feeling and behaving that way—in spite of your unsolved problem. Visualize your hands placing in God's hands the person or problem you are concerned about.[9] Visualize His hands gently and lovingly holding that person or willingly accepting that problem. Now, visualize His hands holding you. All is well for the moment. All is as it should and as it needs to be. All will be well—better than you think.

6

Don't Be Blown About by Every Wind

Easy Does It.

—Twelve Step program slogan

I am a reactionary.

That thought burned deeply into my consciousness one day while I was sitting in my office. I had heard people discuss reacting, but until that moment I didn't understand how much I reacted.

I reacted to other people's feelings, behaviors, problems, and thoughts. I reacted to what they *might* be feeling, thinking, or doing. I reacted to my own feelings, my own thoughts, my own problems. My strong point seemed to be reacting to crises—I thought almost everything was a crisis. I overreacted. Hidden panic (which bordered on hysteria) brewed in me much of the time. I sometimes underreacted. If the problem I faced was significant, I often used the tool of denial. I reacted to almost everything that came into my awareness and environment. My entire life had been a reaction to other people's lives, desires, problems, faults, successes, and personalities. Even my low self-worth, which I dragged around like a bag of stinking garbage, had been a reaction. I was like a puppet with strings hanging out, inviting and allowing anyone or anything to yank them.

Most codependents are reactionaries. We react with anger, guilt, shame, self-hate, worry, hurt, controlling gestures, caretaking acts, depression, desperation, and fury. *We react with fear and anxiety.* Some of us react so much it is painful to be around people, and torturous to be in large groups of people. It is normal to react and respond to our environment. Reacting is part of life. It's part of interacting, and it's part of being alive and human. But we allow ourselves to get *so* upset, and *so* distracted. Little things, big things—anything—have the power to throw us off the track. And the way we respond after we react is frequently not in our best interests.

We may have started reacting and responding urgently and compulsively in patterns that hurt us. Just *feeling* urgent and compulsive is enough to hurt us. We keep ourselves in a crisis state—adrenaline flowing and muscles tensed, ready to react to emergencies that usually aren't emergencies. Someone does something, so we must do something back. Someone says something, so we must say something back. Someone feels a certain way, so we must feel a certain way. WE JUMP INTO THE FIRST FEELING THAT COMES OUR WAY AND THEN WALLOW IN IT. We think the first thought that comes into our heads and then elaborate on it. We say the first words on our tongues and sometimes regret them. We do the first thing that comes to mind, usually without thinking about it. That is the problem: we are reacting without thinking—without honest thought about what we need to do, and how we want to handle the situation. Our emotions and behaviors are being controlled—triggered— by everyone and everything in our environment. We are indirectly allowing others to tell us what to do. That means we have lost control. We are being controlled.

When we react we forfeit our personal, God-given power to think, feel, and behave *in our best interests.* We allow others to determine when we will be happy; when we will be peaceful; when we will be upset; and what we will say, do, think, and feel. We forfeit our right to feel peaceful at the whim of our environments. We are like a wisp of paper in a thunderstorm, blown about by every wind.

Here is an example of a way I tend to react (one of many): My office is in my home, and I have two young children. Sometimes when I'm working they start going wild in the other rooms—fighting, running, messing up the house, and eating and drinking everything in the kitchen. My first, instinctive reaction is to screech at them to, "Stop that!" My second reaction is to holler some more. It comes naturally. Reacting that way appears to be easier than leaving my office, working my way through the laundry room, and walking upstairs. It also appears easier than taking the time to think about how I want to handle the situation. The problem is: bellowing and screaming do not work. It is not really easier. It makes my throat sore and teaches the children how to make me sit in my office and screech.

Reacting usually does not work. We react too quickly, with too much intensity and urgency. Rarely can we do our best at anything in this state of mind. I believe the irony is that we are not called upon or required to do things in this state of mind. There is little in our lives we need to do that we cannot do better if we are peaceful. Few situations—no matter how greatly they appear to demand it—can be bettered by us going berserk.

Why do we do it, then?

We react because we're anxious and afraid of what has happened, what might happen, and what is happening.

Many of us react as though everything is a crisis because we have lived with so many crises for so long that crisis reaction has become a habit.

We react because we think things *shouldn't* be happening the way they are.

We react because we don't feel good about ourselves.

We react because most people react.

We react because we think we have to react.

We don't have to.

We don't have to be so afraid of people. They are just people like us.

We don't have to forfeit our peace. It doesn't help. We have the same facts and resources available to us when we're peaceful that are available to us when we're frantic and chaotic. Actually we have more resources available because our minds and emotions are free to perform at peak level.

We don't have to forfeit our power to think and feel for anyone or anything. That is also not required of us.

We don't have to take things so seriously (ourselves, events, and other people). We blow things out of proportion—our feelings, thoughts, actions, and mistakes. We do the same thing with other people's feelings, thoughts, and actions. We tell ourselves things are awful, terrible, a tragedy, and the end of the world. Many things might be sad, too bad, and unpleasant—but the only thing that's the end of the world is the end of the world. Feelings are important, but they're only feelings. Thoughts are important, but they're only thoughts—and we all think a lot of different things, and our thoughts are subject to change. What we say and do is important, what others say and do is important, but the world doesn't hinge on any particular speech or action. And if it is particularly important that something gets done or said, don't worry: It'll happen. Lighten up. Give yourself and others room to move, to talk, to be who they are—to be human. Give life a chance to happen. Give yourself an opportunity to enjoy it.

We don't have to take other people's behaviors as reflections of our self-worth. We don't have to be embarrassed if someone we love chooses to behave inappropriately. It's normal to react that way, but we don't have to continue to feel embarrassed and *less than* if someone else continues to behave inappropriately. Each person is responsible for his or her behavior. If another person behaves inappropriately, let him or her feel embarrassed for him- or herself. If you have done nothing to feel embarrassed about, don't feel embarrassed. I know this is a tough concept, but it can be mastered.

We don't have to take rejection as a reflection of our self-worth. If somebody who is important (or even someone unimportant) to you rejects you or your choices, you are still real, and you are still worth every bit as much as you would be if you had not been rejected. Feel any feelings that go with rejection; talk about your thoughts; but don't forfeit your self-esteem to another's disapproval or rejection of who you are or what you have done. Even if the most important person in your world rejects you, you are still real, and you are still okay. If you have done something inappropriate or you need to solve a problem or change a behavior, then take appropriate steps to take care of yourself. But don't reject yourself, and don't give so much power to other people's rejection of you. It isn't necessary.

We don't have to take things so personally. We take things to heart that we have no business taking to heart. For instance, saying "If you loved me you wouldn't drink" to an alcoholic makes as much sense as saying "If you loved me, you wouldn't cough" to someone who has pneumonia. Pneumonia victims will cough until they get appropriate treatment for their illness. Alcoholics will drink until they get the same. When people with a compulsive disorder do whatever it is they are compelled to do, they are not saying they don't love you—they are saying they don't love themselves.

We don't have to take little things personally either. If someone has a bad day or gets angry, don't assume it has something to do with you. It may or may not have something to do with you. If it does you'll find out. Usually things have far less to do with us than we think.

An interruption, someone else's bad mood, sharp tongue, bad day, negative thoughts, problems, or active alcoholism does not have to run or ruin our lives, our day, or even an hour of our day. If people don't want to be with us or act healthy, it is not a reflection on *our* self-worth. It reflects on *their* present circumstances. By practicing detachment we can lessen our destructive reactions to the world around us. Separate yourself from things. Leave things alone, and let people be who they are. Who are you to say that the interruption, mood, word, bad day, thought, or problem is not an important and necessary part of life? Who are you to say that this problem won't ultimately be beneficial to you or someone else?

We don't have to react. We have options. That is the joy of recovery from codependency. And each time we exercise our right to choose how we want to act, think, feel, and behave, we feel better and stronger.

"But," you might protest, "why shouldn't I react? Why shouldn't I say something back? Why shouldn't I be upset? He or she deserves to bear the brunt of my turmoil." That may be, but *you* don't. We're talking here about your lack of peace, your lack of serenity, your wasted moments. As Ralph Edwards used to say, "This is your life." How do you want to spend it? You're not detaching for him or her. You're detaching for you. Chances are everyone will benefit by it.

We are like singers in a large chorus. If the guy next to us gets off key, must we? Wouldn't it help him, and us, more to strive to stay on key? We can learn to hold our part.

We don't need to eliminate all our reactions to people and problems. Reactions can be useful. They help us identify what we like and what feels good. They help us identify problems in and around us. But most of us react too much. And much of what we react to is nonsense. It isn't all that important, and it doesn't merit the time and attention we're giving it. Some of what we react to is other people's reactions to us. (I'm mad because he got mad; he got mad because I was angry; I was angry because I thought he was angry with me; he wasn't angry, he was hurt because . . .)

Our reactions can be such a chain reaction that frequently everyone's upset and nobody knows why. They're just upset. Then, everyone's out of control and being controlled. Sometimes people behave in certain ways to provoke us to react in certain ways. If we stop reacting in these certain ways, we take all the fun out of it for them. We remove ourselves from their control and take away their power over us.

Sometimes our reactions provoke other people to react in certain ways. We help them justify certain behaviors. (We don't need any more of that, do we?) Sometimes reacting narrows our vision so much that we get stuck reacting to symptoms of problems. We may stay so busy reacting we never have the time or energy to identify the real problem, much less figure out how to solve it. We can spend years reacting to each drinking incident and resulting crisis, completely failing to recognize that the true problem is alcoholism! Learn to stop reacting in ways that aren't necessary and don't work. Eliminate the reactions that hurt *you*.

Some suggestions follow to help you detach from people and your destructive reactions to them. These are only suggestions. There is no precise formula for detachment. You need to find your own way, a way that works for you.

1. Learn to recognize when you're reacting, when you are allowing someone or something to yank your strings. Usually when you start to feel anxious, afraid, indignant, outraged, rejected, sorry for yourself, ashamed, worried, or confused, something in your environment has snagged you. (I'm not saying it's wrong to feel these feelings. Probably anybody would feel that way. The difference is, we're learning to decide how long we want to feel that way, and what we want to do about it.) Using the words "he or it or she *made me feel*" often indicates we are reacting. Losing our sense of peace and serenity is probably the strongest indication that we are caught up in some sort of reaction.

2. Make yourself comfortable. When you recognize that you're in the midst of a chaotic reaction, say or do as little as possible until you can restore your level of serenity and peace. Do whatever you need to do (that is not self- or other-destructive) to help yourself relax. Take a few deep breaths. Go for a walk. Clean the kitchen. Go sit in the bathroom. Go to a friend's house. Go to an Al-Anon meeting. Read a meditation book. Take a trip to Florida. Watch a television program. Find a way to emotionally, mentally, and (if necessary) physically separate yourself from whatever you are reacting to. Find a way to ease your anxiety. Don't take a drink or drive the car down a side street at 85 miles per hour. Do something safe that will help restore your balance.

3. Examine what happened. If it's a minor incident, you may be able to sort through it yourself. If the problem is serious, or is seriously upsetting you, you may want to discuss it with a friend to help clear your thoughts and emotions. Troubles and feelings go wild when we try to keep them caged inside. Talk about your feelings. Take responsibility for them. Feel whatever feeling you have. Nobody made you feel. Someone might have helped you feel a particular way, but you did your feeling all by yourself. Deal with it. Then, tell yourself the truth about what happened.[1] Was someone trying to sock it to you? (If in doubt about whether to interpret something as an insult or rejection, I prefer to believe it had nothing to do with me. It saves my time and helps me feel good about myself.) Were you trying to control someone or some event? How serious

is the problem or issue? Are you taking responsibility for someone else? Are you angry because someone didn't guess what you really wanted or what you were really trying to say? Are you taking someone's behavior too personally? Did someone push your insecurity or guilt buttons? Is it truly the end of the world, or is it merely sad and disappointing?

4. Figure out what you need to do to take care of yourself. Make your decisions based on reality, and make them from a peaceful state. Do you need to apologize? Do you want to let it go? Do you need to have a heart-to-heart talk with someone? Do you need to make some other decision to take care of yourself? When you make your decision keep in mind what your responsibilities are. You are not responsible for making other people "see the light," and you do not need to "set them straight." You are responsible for helping yourself see the light and for setting yourself straight. If you can't get peaceful about a decision, let it go. It's not time to make it yet. Wait until your mind is consistent and your emotions are calm.

Slow down. You don't have to feel so frightened. You don't have to feel so frantic. Keep things in perspective. Make life easier for *you*.

ACTIVITY

1. Are you spending too much time reacting to someone or something in your environment? Who or what? How are you reacting? Is that how you would choose to behave or feel if you had a choice?

2. Go through the previous steps on detachment for whatever or whoever is bothering you the most. If you need to talk to someone select a trusted friend. If necessary seek professional help.

3. What activities help you feel peaceful and comfortable? (A Twelve Step meeting, a steaming hot shower, a good movie, and dancing are my favorite ones.)

7

SET YOURSELF FREE

Let Go and Let God.

—Twelve Step program slogan

People say codependents are controllers.

We nag; lecture; scream; holler; cry; beg; bribe; coerce; hover over; protect; accuse; chase after; run away from; try to talk into; try to talk out of; attempt to induce guilt in; seduce; entrap; check on; demonstrate how much we've been hurt; hurt people in return so they'll know how it feels; threaten to hurt ourselves; whip power plays on; deliver ultimatums to; do things for; refuse to do things for; stomp out on; get even with; whine; vent fury on; act helpless; suffer in loud silence; try to please; lie; do sneaky little things; do sneaky big things; clutch at our hearts and threaten to die; grab our heads and threaten to go crazy; beat on our chests and threaten to kill; enlist the aid of supporters; gauge our words carefully; sleep with; refuse to sleep with; have children with; bargain with; drag to counseling; drag out of counseling; talk mean about; talk mean to; insult; condemn; pray for miracles; pay for miracles; go to places we don't want to go; stay nearby; supervise; dictate; command; complain; write letters about; write letters to; stay home and wait for; go out and look for; call all over looking for; drive down dark alleys at night hoping to see; chase down dark alleys at night hoping to catch; run down alleys at night to get away from; bring home; keep home; lock out; move away from; move with; scold; impress upon; advise; teach lessons to; set straight; insist; give in to; placate; provoke; try to make jealous; try to make afraid; remind; inquire; hint; look through pockets; peek in wallets; search dresser drawers; dig through glove boxes; look in the toilet tank; try to look into the future; search through the past; call relatives about; reason with; settle issues once and for all; settle them again; punish; reward; almost give up on; then try even harder; and a list of other handy maneuvers I've either forgotten or haven't tried yet.

We aren't the people who "make things happen." Codependents are the people who consistently, and with a great deal of effort and energy, try to force things to happen.

We control in the name of love.

We do it because we're "only trying to help."

We do it because we know best how things should go and how people should behave.

We do it because we're right and they're wrong.

We control because we're afraid not to do it.

We do it because we don't know what else to do.

We do it to stop the pain.

We control because we think we have to.

We control because we don't think.

We control because controlling is all we can think about.

Ultimately we may control because that's the way we've always done things.

Tyrannical and dominating, some rule with an iron hand from a self-appointed throne. They are powerful. They know best. And by God, it will be done this way. They will see to it.

Others do their dirty work undercover. They hide behind a costume of sweetness and niceties, and secretly go about their business—OTHER PEOPLE'S BUSINESS.

Others, sighing and crying, claim inability, proclaim their dependence, announce their overall victimization, and successfully control through weakness. They are *so* helpless. They need your cooperation so badly. They can't live without it. Sometimes the weak are the most powerful manipulators and controllers.[1] They have learned to tug at the guilt and pity strings of the world.

Many codependents combine tactics, using a variety of methods. Whatever works! (Or, more accurately, whatever doesn't work although we continue to hope it will.)

Despite tactics, the goals remain the same. Make other people do what you want them to. Make them behave as you think they should. Don't let them behave in ways you think they shouldn't, but probably would, without your "assistance." Force life's events to unravel and unfold in the manner and at such times as you have designated. Do not let what's happening, or what might happen, occur. Hold on tightly and don't let go. We have written the play, and we will see to it that the actors behave and the scenes unfold exactly as we have decided they should. Never mind that we continue to buck reality. If we charge ahead insistently enough, we can (we believe) stop the flow of life, transform people, and change things to our liking.

We are fooling ourselves.

Let me tell you about Maria. She married a man who turned out to be an alcoholic. He was a binge drinker. He didn't drink every day, every weekend, or every month, but when he did—look out. He stayed drunk for days, sometimes weeks. He started drinking at eight in the morning and drank until he passed out. He vomited all over, devastated the family's finances, got fired from jobs, and created unbearable chaos each time he drank. Between binges life was not perfect either. A sense of impending doom and unresolved feelings filled the air. Other unresolved problems, residues from the drinking, cluttered their lives. They could never get ahead of the disasters. They were always starting over with a dirty slate. But, it was better—for Maria and her three children—when her husband wasn't drinking. There was hope, too, that this time it would be different.

It never was different. For years, each time Maria turned around or turned her back, her husband went on a binge. When she went away for a weekend, when she went to the hospital to deliver her babies, when her husband left town on a trip, or when he was out of her sight for any reason—he drank.

Whenever Maria returned or retrieved him from wherever he was drinking, he would abruptly quit drinking. Maria decided that the key to her husband's sobriety was her presence. She could control the drinking (and all the pain it caused) by sticking close to home and standing guard over her husband. Because she learned this method of control, and because of increasing feelings of shame, embarrassment, anxiety, and the overall trauma that accompanies codependency, Maria became a recluse. She turned down opportunities to travel, and she refused to attend church conferences she was interested in. Even leaving the house for more than a trip to the grocery store began to threaten the balance she had created—or thought she had created. In spite of her determined and desperate efforts, her husband still found opportunities to drink. He found ways to drink at home without her knowing about it, and he drank when she had no choice but to spend the night away from home.

After one particularly disruptive drinking bout, Maria's husband informed her that the impossible financial predicament they were in caused him to drink. (He neglected to mention that his drinking had caused the impossible financial predicament.) He said if she would take a job and help out financially, he would not feel like he had to drink any more. The pressure would be off. Maria thought about his request, then reluctantly agreed. She was afraid to leave home and felt concerned about setting up appropriate baby-sitting arrangements for the children. She did not feel emotionally or mentally able to work. She especially resented taking a job to earn extra money when her husband was so irresponsible with money. But it was worth a try. Anything to keep this man sober!

Before long Maria located a job as a legal secretary. She did well— better than she thought she would. Codependents make great employees. They don't complain; they do more than their share; they do whatever is asked of them; they please people; and they try to do their work perfectly—at least for a while, until they become angry and resentful.

Maria started feeling a little better about herself. She enjoyed her contact with people—something that had been missing in her life. She liked the feeling of earning her own money (although she still resented her husband's irresponsibility with it). And her employers appreciated her. They gave her increasing amounts of responsibility and were on the verge of promoting her to a paralegal position. But about that time Maria began to feel that old familiar anxious feeling—her cue that her husband was about to drink again.

The feeling came and went for days. Then one day, it hit hard. That handwringing, gut-twisting anxiety came back in full force. Maria started calling her husband on the phone. He was not at work where he was supposed to be. His employer didn't know where he was. She made more phone calls. Nobody knew where he was. She spent the day biting her nails, making frantic phone calls, and hoping her fellow employees wouldn't see through her "everything's fine—no problem" veneer. When she arrived home that evening she discovered that her husband was not at home and had not picked up the children from day care as he was supposed to. Things were out of control again. He was drinking again. The next morning she quit her job—walked out with no appropriate notice. By 10:00 A.M., she was back in her house—guarding her husband.

Years later she said, "I felt like I had to do this. I had to get things under control—MY CONTROL."

My question is this: Who's controlling whom?

Maria learned she was not controlling her husband or his drinking at all. He and his alcoholism were controlling her.

This point was further clarified for me one evening during a family group facilitation I had at a treatment center. (Many of my clients are wise—wiser than I am. I have learned much by listening to them.) During the group, the wife of an alcoholic talked openly to her husband—a man who had spent many years of their marriage drinking, unemployed, and in prison.

"You accuse me of trying to control you, and I guess I have," she said. "I've gone to bars with you so you wouldn't drink so much. I've let you come home when you were abusive and drunk so you wouldn't drink anymore or hurt yourself. I've measured your drinks, drank with you (and I hate drinking), hid your bottles, and taken you to Alcoholics Anonymous meetings.

"But the truth is," she said, "you've been controlling me. All those letters from prison telling me what I've wanted to hear. All those promises, all those words. And every time I'm ready to leave you—to walk out for good—you do or say just the right thing to keep me from leaving. You know just what I want to hear, and that's what you tell me. But you never change. You've never intended to change. You just want to control me."

He smiled a half-smile and nodded when she said that. "Yes," he said, "I have been trying to control you. And I've been doing a pretty good job of it at that."

When we attempt to control people and things that we have no business controlling, we are controlled. We forfeit our power to think, feel, and act in accordance with our best interests. We frequently lose control of ourselves. Often, we are being controlled not just by people but by diseases such as alcoholism, eating disorders, and compulsive gambling. Alcoholism and other destructive disorders are powerful forces. Never forget that alcoholics and other troubled persons are expert controllers. We have met our match when we attempt to control them or their disease. We lose the battles. We lose the wars. We lose our selves—our lives. Borrowing a tidbit from Al-Anon: You didn't cause it; you can't control it; and you can't cure it.

So stop trying! We become utterly frustrated when we try to do the impossible. And we usually prevent the possible from happening. I believe that clutching tightly to a person or thing, or forcing my will on any given situation eliminates the possibility of my Higher Power doing anything constructive about that situation, the person, or me. My controlling blocks God's power. It blocks other people's ability to grow. It stops events from happening naturally. It prevents me from enjoying people or events.

Control is an illusion. It doesn't work. We cannot control alcoholism. We cannot control anyone's compulsive behaviors—overeating, sexual, gambling—or any of their behaviors. We cannot (and have no business trying to) control anyone's emotions, mind, or choices. We cannot control the outcome of events. We cannot control life. Some of us can barely control ourselves.

People ultimately do what they want to do. They feel how they want to feel (or how they are feeling); they think what they want to think; they do the things they believe they need to do; and they will change only when they are ready to change. It doesn't matter if they're wrong and we're right. It doesn't matter if they're hurting themselves. It doesn't matter that we could help them if they'd only listen to, and cooperate with, us. IT DOESN'T MATTER, DOESN'T MATTER, DOESN'T MATTER, DOESN'T MATTER.

We cannot change people. Any attempts to control them are a delusion as well as an illusion. People will either resist our efforts or redouble their efforts to prove we can't control them. They may temporarily adapt to our demands, but the moment we turn our backs they will return to their natural state. Furthermore, people will punish us for making them do something they don't want to do, or be something they don't want to be. No amount of control will effect a permanent or desirable change in another person. We can sometimes do things that increase the probability that people will want to change, but we can't even guarantee or control that.

And that's the truth. It's too bad. It's sometimes hard to accept, especially if someone you love is hurting him- or herself and you. But that's the way it is. The only person you can now or ever change is yourself. The only person that it is your business to control is yourself.

Detach. Surrender. Sometimes when we do that the result we have been waiting and hoping for happens quickly, almost miraculously. Sometimes it doesn't. Sometimes it never happens. But you will benefit. You don't have to stop caring or loving. You don't have to tolerate abuse. You don't have to abandon constructive, problem-solving methods such as professional intervention. You only need to put your emotional, mental, spiritual, and physical hands back in your own pockets and leave things and people alone. Let them be. Make any decisions you need to make to take care of yourself, but don't make them to control other people. Start taking care of yourself!

"But this is so important to me," many people protest. "I can't detach."

If it's that important to you, I suggest that is all the more reason to detach.

I heard some wisdom on detachment out of the mouths of babes—my babies. Sometimes, my youngest son, Shane, hangs on too tightly and too long after a hug. He starts tipping me over. I lose my balance, and become impatient for him to stop hugging me. I begin to resist him. Perhaps he does it to keep me close to him a little longer. Maybe it's a form of control over me. I don't know. One night when he did this my daughter watched until even she became frustrated and impatient.

"Shane," she said, "there comes a time to let go."

For each of us, there comes a time to let go. You will know when that time has come. When you have done all that you can do, it is time to detach. Deal with your feelings. Face your fears about losing control. Gain control of yourself and your responsibilities. Free others to be who they are. In so doing, you will set yourself free.

ACTIVITY

1. Is there an event or person in your life that you are trying to control? Why? Write a few paragraphs about it.

2. In what ways (mentally, physically, emotionally, etc.) are you being controlled by whatever or whomever you are attempting to control?

3. What would happen (to you and the other person) if you detached from this situation or person? Will that probably happen anyway, in spite of your controlling gestures? How are you benefitting by attempting to control the situation? How is the other person benefitting by your attempts to control? How effective are your attempts at controlling the outcomes of events?

8

REMOVE THE VICTIM

We're so careful to see that no one gets hurt.
No one, that is, but ourselves.

—Al-Anon member

About a year into my recovery from codependency, I realized I was still doing something over and over that caused me pain. I sensed this pattern had something to do with why many of my relationships went sour. But I didn't know what "it" was that I was doing, so I couldn't stop doing it.

One sunny day, as I was walking down the sidewalk with my friend Scott, I stopped, turned to him, and asked, "What is the one thing codependents do over and over? What is it that keeps us feeling so bad?"

He thought about my question for a moment before answering. "Co-dependents are caretakers—rescuers. They rescue, then they persecute, then they end up victimized. Study the Karpman Drama Triangle," he said. The Karpman Drama Triangle and the accompanying roles of rescuer, persecutor, and victim, are the work and observation of Stephen B. Karpman.[1]

What he said didn't make sense, but I went home, dragged out some therapy books that were collecting dust on my shelves, and studied.[2] After a while, a light went on inside my head. I saw. I understood. And I felt like I had discovered fire.

This was it. This was my pattern. This is *our* pattern. This is what we repeatedly do with friends, family, acquaintances, clients, or anybody around us. As codependents, we may do many things, but this pattern is what we do best and most often. This is our favorite reaction.

We are the rescuers, the enablers. We are the great godmothers or godfathers to the entire world, as Earnie Larsen says. We not only meet people's needs, we anticipate them. We fix, nurture, and fuss over others. We make better, solve, and attend to. And we do it all so well. "Your wish is my command," is our theme. "Your problem is my problem," is our motto. We are the caretakers.

What's a Rescue?

Rescuing and *caretaking* mean almost what they sound like. We rescue people from their responsibilities. We take care of people's responsibilities for them. Later we get mad at *them* for what *we've* done. Then we feel used and sorry for ourselves. That is the pattern, the triangle.

Rescuing and caretaking are synonymous. Their definitions are closely connected to enabling. *Enabling* is therapeutic jargon that means a destructive form of helping. Any acts that help an alcoholic continue drinking, prevent the alcoholic from suffering consequences, or in any way make it easier for an alcoholic to continue drinking are considered enabling behaviors.

As counselor Scott Egleston says, we rescue anytime we take responsibility for another human being—for that person's thoughts, feelings, decisions, behaviors, growth, well-being, problems, or destiny. The following acts constitute a rescuing or caretaking move:

- Doing something we really don't want to do.
- Saying yes when we mean no.
- Doing something for someone although that person is capable of and should be doing it for him- or herself.
- Meeting people's needs without being asked and before we've agreed to do so.
- Doing more than a fair share of work after our help is requested.
- Consistently giving more than we receive in a particular situation.
- Fixing people's feelings.

- Doing people's thinking for them.
- Speaking for another person.
- Suffering people's consequences for them.
- Solving people's problems for them.
- Putting more interest and activity into a joint effort than the other person does.
- Not asking for what we want, need, and desire.

We rescue whenever we take care of other people.

At the time we rescue or caretake we may feel one or more of the following feelings: discomfort and awkwardness about the other person's dilemma; urgency to do something; pity; guilt; saintliness; anxiety; extreme responsibility *for* that person or problem; fear; a sense of being forced or compelled to do something; mild or severe reluctance to do anything; more competency than the person we are "helping"; or occasional resentment at being put in this position. We also think the person we are taking care of is helpless and unable to do what we are doing for him or her. We feel needed temporarily.

I am not referring to acts of love, kindness, compassion, and true helping—situations where our assistance is legitimately wanted and needed and we want to give that assistance. These acts are the good stuff of life. Rescuing or caretaking isn't.

Caretaking looks like a much friendlier act than it is. It requires incompetency on the part of the person being taken care of. We rescue "victims"—people who we believe are not capable of being responsible for themselves. The victims actually are capable of taking care of themselves, even though we and they don't admit it. Usually, our victims are just hanging around that corner of the triangle, waiting for us to make our move and jump on the triangle with them.

After we rescue, we will inevitably move to the next corner of the triangle: persecution. We become resentful and angry at the person we have so generously "helped." We've done something we didn't want to do, we've done something that was not our responsibility to do, we've ignored our own needs and wants, and we get angry about it. To complicate matters, this victim, this poor person we've rescued, is not grateful for our help. He or she is not appreciative enough of the sacrifice we have made. The victim isn't behaving the way he or she should. This person is not even taking our advice, which we offered so readily. This person is not letting us fix that feeling. Something doesn't work right or feel right, so we rip off our halos and pull out our pitchforks.

Sometimes, people don't notice or choose not to notice our peeved mood. Sometimes we do our best to hide it. Sometimes we let loose with the full force of our fury; we particularly do this with family members. Something about family tends to bring out the *real* us. Whether we show, hide, or partially hide our agitation and resentment, WE KNOW what's going on.

Most of the time, the people we rescue immediately sense our shift in mood. They saw it coming. It's just the excuse they needed to turn on us. It's *their* turn in the persecution corner. This may precede, happen at the same time as, or follow our feelings of anger. Sometimes, the victims respond to our anger. Usually it is a response to our taking responsibility for that person, which directly or indirectly tells him or her how incapable we believe he or she is. People resent being told or shown they are incompetent, no matter how loudly they plead incompetency. And they resent us for adding insult to injury by becoming angry with them after we point out their incompetency.

Then it's time for our final move. We head right for our favorite spot: the victim corner on the *bottom*. This is the predictable and unavoidable result of a rescue. Feelings of helplessness, hurt, sorrow, shame, and self-pity abound. We have been used—again. We have gone unappreciated—again. We try so hard to help people, to be good to them. We moan, "Why? Why does this ALWAYS happen to me?" Another person has trampled on us, socked it to us. We wonder, shall we forever be victims? Probably, if we don't stop rescuing and caretaking.

Many codependents, at some time in their lives, *were* true victims—of someone's abuse, neglect, abandonment, alcoholism, or any number of situations that can victimize people. We were, at some time, truly helpless to protect ourselves or solve our problems. Something came our way, something we didn't ask for, and it hurt us terribly. That is sad, truly sad. But an even sadder fact is that many of us codependents began to see ourselves as victims. Our painful history repeats itself. As caretakers, we allow people to victimize us, and we participate in our victimization by perpetually rescuing people. Rescuing or caretaking is not an act of love. The Drama Triangle is a hate triangle. It fosters and maintains self-hate, and it hinders our feelings for other people.

The triangle and the shifting roles of rescuer, persecutor, and victim are a visible process we go through. The role changes and the emotional changes come over us as certainly and as intensely as if we were reading a script. We can complete the process in seconds, experiencing only mild emotions as we shift roles. Or, we can take years to complete the triangle and really work up to a major explosion. We can, and many of us do, rescue twenty times in one day.

Let me illustrate a rescue. A friend of mine was married to an alcoholic. Whenever he got drunk, she would drive all over town, enlist the aid of friends, and relentlessly pursue her husband until she found him. She usually felt benevolent, concerned, and sorry for him—a warning that a rescue was about to take place—until she got him home and tucked into bed—taking responsibility for him and his sobriety. When his head hit the pillow, things changed. She charged into the persecutor position. She didn't want this man in her home. She expected him to whine for days about how sick he was. He was unable to assume his responsibilities in the family, and he generally acted pitiful. He had done this so many times! So, she would start in on him, beginning with little snipes and working up to a full-blown blast. He would briefly tolerate her persecution before switching from a helpless victim to vengeful persecutor. She then took a downward dip into the victim role. Self-pity, feelings of helplessness, shame, and despair set in. This was the story of her life, she would moan. After all she had done for him, how could he treat her this way? Why did this always happen to her? She felt like a victim of circumstance, a victim of her husband's outrageous behavior, a victim of life. It never occurred to her that she was also a victim of herself and her own behavior.

Here's another illustration of a rescue. One summer, a friend wanted me to take her to an apple farm. Originally, I wanted to go, and we set a date. By the time that date came, however, I was extremely busy. I called her, and instead of telling her I didn't want to go, I asked to postpone it. I felt guilty and responsible for her feelings—another rescue on the way. I couldn't disappoint her because I thought she couldn't handle or be responsible for her feelings. I couldn't tell the truth, because I thought she might be angry with me—more emotional responsibility—as if someone else's anger is my business. The next weekend rolled around, and I squeezed the trip into my even busier schedule. But I did not want to go. I didn't even need any apples; I had two drawers in my refrigerator crammed with apples. Before I stopped my car in front of her house, I had already switched into the persecuting role. I seethed with resentful, tense thoughts as we drove to the apple orchard. When we arrived at the orchard and began tasting and looking at apples, it became apparent neither of us was enjoying herself. After a few minutes, my friend turned to me. "I really don't want any apples," she said. "I bought some last week. I only came because I thought you wanted to, and I didn't want to hurt your feelings."

This example is only one of the thousands of rescues I have devoted my life to performing. When I began to understand this process, I realized that I spent most of my waking moments flipping around the jagged edges of this triangle taking responsibility for anybody and everybody besides myself. Sometimes I managed big rescues; sometimes I managed little rescues. My friendships were initiated, maintained, and ultimately discontinued according to the rescue progression. Rescuing infiltrated my relationships with family members and clients. It kept me in a tizzy most of the time.

Two codependents in a relationship can really play havoc with each other. Consider two people-pleasers in a relationship with each other. Now consider two people-pleasers in a relationship with each other when they both want out of the relationship. They will, as Earnie Larsen says, do horrible things. They'll nearly destroy each other and themselves before one will stop rescuing and say, "I want out."

As codependents, we spend much of our time rescuing. We try to be living proof that people can outgive God. I can usually spot a codependent within the first five minutes of meeting and talking. He or she will either offer me unrequested help, or the person will keep talking to me although he or she is obviously uncomfortable and wants to discontinue the conversation. The person begins the relationship by taking responsibility for me and not taking responsibility for him- or herself.

Some of us become so tired from the enormous burden—total responsibility for all human beings—that we may skip the feelings of pity and concern that accompany the rescue act and move ahead to anger. We're angry all the time; we feel anger and resentment toward potential victims. A person with a need or problem provokes us to feel we have to do something or feel guilty. After a rescue, we make no bones about our hostility toward this uncomfortable predicament. I have frequently seen this happen to people in helping professions. After so many years of rescuing—giving so much and receiving far less in return—many professional helpers adopt a hostile attitude toward their clients. They may continue to hang in there and keep "helping" them, anyway, but they will usually leave their profession feeling terribly victimized, according to some counselors.

Caretaking doesn't help; it causes problems. When we take care of people and do things we don't want to do, we ignore personal needs, wants, and feelings. We put *ourselves* aside. Sometimes, we get so busy taking care of people that we put our entire lives on hold. Many caretakers are harried and overcommitted; they enjoy none of their activities. Caretakers look so responsible, but we aren't. We don't assume responsibility for our highest responsibility—ourselves.

We consistently give more than we receive, then feel abused and neglected because of it. We wonder why, when we anticipate the needs of others, no one notices *our* needs. We may become seriously depressed as a result of not getting our needs met. Yet, a good caretaker feels safest when giving; we feel guilty and uncomfortable when someone gives to us or when we do something to meet our needs. Sometimes, codependents may become so locked into a caretaker role that we feel dismayed and rejected when we can't caretake or rescue someone—when someone re fuses to be "helped."

The worst aspect of caretaking is we become and stay victims. I believe many serious self-destructive behaviors—chemical abuse, eating disorders, sexual disorders—are developed through this victim role. As victims, we attract perpetrators. We believe we need someone to take care of us, because we feel helpless. Some caretakers will ultimately present ourselves to somebody or some institution, needing to be taken care of mentally, physically, financially, or emotionally.

Why, you might ask, would apparently rational people do this rescuing? Many reasons. Most of us aren't even aware of what we're doing. Most of us truly believe we're helping. Some of us believe we *have to* rescue. We have confused ideas about what constitutes help and what doesn't. Many of us are convinced that rescuing is a charitable deed. We may even think it cruel and heartless to do something as cold-blooded as allowing a person to work through or face a legitimate feeling, suffer a consequence, be disappointed by hearing "no," be asked to respond to our needs and wants, and generally be held responsible and accountable for him- or herself in this world. Never mind that they will certainly pay a price for our "helping"—a price that will be as harsh as or more severe than any feeling they may be facing.

Many of us do not understand what we are responsible for and what we are not responsible for. We may believe we have to get into a tizzy when someone has a problem because it is our responsibility to do that. Sometimes, we become sick of feeling responsible for so much that we reject all responsibility and become totally irresponsible.

However, at the heart of most rescues is a demon: low self-worth. We rescue because we don't feel good about ourselves. Although the feelings are transient and artificial, caretaking provides us with a temporary hit of good feelings, self-worth, and power. Just as a drink helps an alcoholic momentarily feel better, a rescue move momentarily distracts us from the pain of being who we are. We don't feel lovable, so we settle for being needed. We don't feel good about ourselves, so we feel compelled to do a particular thing to *prove* how good we are.

We rescue because we don't feel good about other people either. Sometimes with justification, sometimes without, we decide other people simply cannot be held responsible for themselves. Although this may appear to be true, it simply is not a fact. Unless a person has brain damage, a serious physical impairment, or is an infant, that person can be responsible for him- or herself.

Sometimes we rescue because it's easier than dealing with the discomfort and awkwardness of facing other people's unsolved problems. We haven't learned to say, "It's too bad you're having that problem. What do you need from me?" We've learned to say, "Here. Let me do that *for* you."

Some of us learned to be caretakers when we were children. Perhaps we were almost forced to as a result of living with an alcoholic parent or some other family problem. Some of us may have started caretaking later in life, as a result of being in a committed relationship with an alcoholic or other person who refused and appeared unable to take care of him- or herself. We decided to cope—to survive—the best way we could, by picking up the slack and assuming other people's responsibilities.

Many codependents have been taught other ways to be caretakers. Maybe someone taught us these lies, and we believed them: don't be selfish, always be kind and help people, never hurt other people's feelings because we "make them feel," never say no, and don't mention personal wants and needs because it's not polite.

We may have been taught to be responsible for other people but not responsible for ourselves. Some women were taught that good, desirable wives and mothers were caretakers. Caretaking was expected and required of them. It was their duty. Some men believe good husbands and fathers are caretakers—superheroes responsible for meeting every need of each family member.

Sometimes a state resembling codependency sets in when a person is taking care of infants or young children. Taking care of infants requires a person to forfeit his or her needs, to do things he or she doesn't want to do, to squelch his or her feelings and desires (4 A.M. feedings usually only meet the needs of the person being fed), and to assume total responsibility for another human being. Taking care of children is not rescuing. That is an actual responsibility and is not the kind of caretaking I'm talking about. But if that person doesn't take care of him- or herself, he or she may begin to feel the codependent blues.

Others may have interpreted religious beliefs as a mandate to caretake. Be cheerful givers, we are told. Go the extra mile. Love our neighbors, and we try. We try so hard. We try too hard. And then we wonder what's wrong with us because our Christian beliefs aren't working. Our lives aren't working either.

Christian beliefs work just fine. Your life can work just fine. It's rescuing that doesn't work. "It's like trying to catch butterflies with a broomstick," observed a friend. Rescuing leaves us bewildered and befuddled every time. It's a self-destructive reaction, another way codependents attach themselves to people and become detached from themselves. It's another way we attempt to control, but instead become controlled by people. Caretaking is an unhealthy parent-child relationship—sometimes between two consenting adults, sometimes between an adult and a child.

Caretaking breeds anger. Caretakers become angry parents, angry friends, angry lovers. We may become unsatisfied, frustrated, and confused Christians. The people we help either are or they become helpless, angry victims. Caretakers become victims.

Most of us have heard the Biblical parable about Mary and Martha. While Mary sat and talked with Jesus and His friends, Martha cleaned and cooked. Before long, the story goes, Martha started banging pans, accusing Mary of being lazy. Martha complained that she had to do everything while Mary relaxed and enjoyed herself. Does this sound familiar? Jesus didn't let this one go by. He told Martha to hush. Mary knows what's important, He said. Mary made the right decision.

His message might be that Mary made the right choice because it's more important to enjoy people than it is to cook and clean. But I also believe there's a message here about taking responsibility for our choices, doing what we *want* to be doing, and realizing how we become angry when we don't. Maybe Mary's choice was right because she acted as she wanted to. Jesus helped many people, but He was honest and straightforward about it. He didn't persecute people after He helped them. And He *asked* them what they wanted from Him. Sometimes He asked why, too. He held people responsible for their behavior.

I think caretaking perverts Biblical messages about giving, loving, and helping. Nowhere in the Bible are we instructed to do something for someone, then scratch his or her eyes out. Nowhere are we told to walk the extra mile with someone, and then grab the person's cane and beat him or her with it. Caring about people and giving are good, desirable qualities—something we need to do—but many codependents have misinterpreted the suggestions to "give until it hurts." We continue giving long after it hurts, usually until we are doubled over in pain. It's good to give some away, but we don't have to give it all away. It's okay to keep some for ourselves.

I believe God wants us to help people and share our time, talents, and money. But I also believe He wants us to give from a position of high self-esteem. I believe acts of kindness are not kind unless we feel good about ourselves, what we are doing, and the person we are doing it for. I think God is in each of us and speaks to each of us. If we absolutely can't feel good about something we're doing, then we shouldn't do it—no matter how charitable it seems. We also shouldn't do things for others that they ought to and are capable of doing for themselves. Other people aren't helpless. Neither are we.

"God told us to lose our lives. He told us to give to people," says the Reverend Daniel Johns, Senior Pastor at Trinity Lutheran Church in Stillwater, Minnesota. "But I don't think He ever intended people to use the Scriptures to behave in unhealthy ways."

Giving to and doing things for and with people are essential parts of healthy living and healthy relationships. But learning when not to give, when not to give in, and when not to do things for and with people are also essential parts of healthy living and healthy relationships. It is not good to take care of people who take advantage of us to avoid responsibility. It hurts them, and it hurts us. There is a thin line between helping and hurting people, between beneficial giving and destructive giving. We can learn to make that distinction.

Caretaking is an act and an attitude. For some of us, it becomes a role, an approach to our entire lives and to all the people around us. Caretaking is, I believe, closely associated with martyrdom (a state codependents are frequently accused of being in), and people-pleasing (another accusation hurled at us). Martyrs, according to Earnie Larsen, "screw things up." We need to keep sacrificing our happiness as well as others' for the good of some unknown cause that doesn't demand sacrifice. People-pleasers, according to Earnie Larsen, can't be trusted. We lie. And as caretakers, we don't take care of ourselves.

The most exciting thing about caretaking is learning to understand what it is and when we are doing it, so we can stop doing it.

We can learn to recognize a rescue. *Refuse to rescue. Refuse to let people rescue us.* Take responsibility for ourselves, and let others do the same. Whether we change our attitudes, our circumstances, our behaviors, or our minds, the kindest thing we can do is remove the victims—ourselves.

ACTIVITY

1. This assignment may take some time, but if caretaking is causing your problems, it may be a breakthrough experience for you. On a sheet of paper, detail all the things you consider your responsibilities. Do this for your participation at work, with children, with friends, and with your spouse or lover. Now, list detail by detail what responsibilities belong to the other people in your life. If any responsibilities are shared, list what percentage you think is appropriate for each person. For instance, if your spouse is working and you have chosen to be a homemaker and work part-time, list what percentage of the financial responsibilities you assume, and what percentage of the household chores he or she assumes. You may be surprised at how much inappropriate responsibility you have taken on and how little you have allowed others to assume. You may

also find you have been so busy with other people's business that you have been neglecting some of your true responsibilities.

2. Become familiar with the Karpman Drama Triangle and how you go through the process in your life. When you find yourself rescuing, watch for the role and mood shifts. When you catch yourself feeling resentful or used, figure out how you rescued. Practice non-rescuing behaviors: Say no when you want to say no. Do things you want to do. Refuse to guess what people want and need; instead insist that others ask you directly for what they want and need from you. Begin asking directly for what you want and need. Refuse to assume other people's responsibilities. When you initially stop taking care of people who are used to having you take care of them, they may become angry or frustrated. You've changed the system, rocked the boat. It means more work for them, and they can't use you anymore. Explain to them what you are doing, and allow them to be responsible for their feelings. They may thank you for it later. They may even surprise you—sometimes the people we thought least able to take care of themselves can, when we stop taking care of them.

9

UNDEPENDENCE

"What is it about me?" she asked.
"Do I need a dead body laying in my bed
in order to feel good about myself?"

—Alice B., a codependent who has been married to two alcoholics

"I'm real independent—as long as I'm in a relationship," announced a policewoman who has been involved with several emotionally troubled men.

"My husband has been lying on the couch drunk and hasn't brought home a paycheck in ten years," said another woman, the director of a large human services organization. "Who needs this?" she asked. "I must," she said, answering her own question. "But why? And for what?"

A woman who had recently joined Al-Anon called me one afternoon. This married woman worked part-time as a registered nurse, had assumed all the responsibility for raising her two children, and did all the household chores, including repairs and finances. "I want to separate from my husband," she sobbed. "I can't stand him or his abuse any longer. But tell me, please tell me," she asked, "do you think I can take care of myself?"

The words vary, but the thought is the same. "I'm not happy living with this person, but I don't think I can live *without* him (or her). I cannot, for some reason, find it within myself to face the aloneness that every human being must face or continue to run from: that of being ultimately and solely responsible for taking care of myself. I don't believe I *can* take care of myself. I'm not sure I *want* to. I need a person, any person, to buffer the shock of my solitary condition. No matter what the cost."

Colette Dowling wrote about this thought pattern in *The Cinderella Complex.* Penelope Russianoff discussed it in *Why Do I Think I'm Nothing Without a Man?* I've said it many times.

Whether codependents appear fragile and helpless, or sturdy and powerful, most of us are frightened, needy, vulnerable children who are aching and desperate to be loved and cared for.

This child in us believes we are unlovable and will never find the comfort we are seeking; sometimes this vulnerable child becomes too desperate. People have abandoned us, emotionally and physically. People have rejected us. People have abused us, let us down. People have never been there for us; they have not seen, heard, or responded to our needs. We may come to believe that people will never be there for us. For many of us, even God seems to have gone away.

We have been there for so many people. Most of us desperately want someone to finally be there for us. We need someone, anyone, to rescue us from the stark loneliness, alienation, and pain. We want some of the good stuff, and the good stuff is not in us. Pain is in us. We feel so helpless and uncertain. Others look so powerful and assured. We conclude the magic must be in them.

So we become dependent on them. We can become dependent on lovers, spouses, friends, parents, or our children. We become dependent on their approval. We become dependent on their presence. We become dependent on their need for us. We become dependent on their love, even though we believe we will never receive their love; we believe we are unlovable and nobody has ever loved us in a way that met our needs.

I am not saying codependents are peculiar ducks because they want and need love and approval. Most people want to be in a love relationship. They want a special person in their lives. Most people want and need friends. Most people want the people in their lives to love and approve of them. These are natural, healthy desires. A certain amount of emotional dependency is present in most relationships, including the healthiest ones.[1] But many men and women don't just want and need people—we *need* people. We may become driven, controlled by this need.

Needing people too much can cause problems. Other people become the key to our happiness. I believe much of the other-centeredness, orbiting our lives around other people, goes hand in hand with codependency and springs out of our emotional insecurity. I believe much of this incessant approval seeking we indulge in also comes from insecurity. The magic is in others, not us, we believe. The good feelings are in them, not us. The less good stuff we find in ourselves, the more we seek it in others. *They* have it all; we have nothing. *Our* existence is not important. We have been abandoned and neglected so often that we also abandon ourselves.

Needing people so much, yet believing we are unlovable and people will never be there for us, can become a deeply ingrained belief. Sometimes, we think people aren't there for us when they really are. Our need may block our vision, preventing us from seeing the love that is there for us.

Sometimes, no human being could be there for us the way we need them to be—to absorb us, care for us, and make us feel good, complete, and safe.

Many of us expect and need other people so much that we settle for too little. We may become dependent on troubled people—alcoholics and other people with problems. We can become dependent on people we don't particularly like or love. Sometimes, we need people so badly we settle for nearly anyone. We may need people who don't meet our needs. Again, we may find ourselves in situations where we need someone to be there for us, but the person we have chosen cannot or will not do that.

We may even convince ourselves that we can't live without someone and will wither and die if that person is not in our lives. If that person is an alcoholic or deeply troubled, we may tolerate abuse and insanity to keep him or her in our lives, to protect our source of emotional security. Our need becomes so great that we settle for too little. Our expectations drop below normal, below what we ought to expect from our relationships. Then, we become trapped, stuck.

". . . It is no longer Camelot. It is no longer even person to person," wrote Janet Geringer Woititz in an article from the book *Co-Dependency, An Emerging Issue.* "The distortion is bizarre. I will stay because . . . 'He doesn't beat me.' 'She doesn't run around.' 'He hasn't lost his job.' Imagine getting credit for the behaviors we ordinary mortals do as a matter of course. Even if the worst is true. Even if he does beat you. Even if she does run around. Even if he is no longer working. Even with all this, you will then say, 'But I love him/her!' When I respond, 'Tell me, what is so lovable?' there is no response. The answer doesn't come, but the power of being emotionally stuck is far greater than the power of reason."[2]

I am not suggesting all our intimate relationships are based on insecurities and dependencies. Certainly the power of love overrides common sense, and perhaps that is how it should be at times. By all means, if we love an alcoholic and want to stick with him or her, we should keep loving that person. But the driving force of emotional insecurity can also become far greater than the power of reason or love. Not being centered in ourselves and not feeling emotionally secure with ourselves may trap us.[3] We may become afraid to terminate relationships that are dead and destructive. We may allow people to hurt and abuse us, and that is never in our best interest.

People who feel trapped look for escapes. Codependents who feel stuck in a relationship may begin planning an escape. Sometimes our escape route is a positive, healthy one; we begin taking steps to become undependent, financially and emotionally. "Undependence" is a term Penelope Russianoff uses in her book to describe that desirable balance wherein we acknowledge and meet our healthy, natural needs for people and love, yet we don't become overly or harmfully dependent on them.

We may go back to school, get a job, or set other goals that will bring freedom. And we usually begin setting those goals when we are sick enough of being trapped. Some codependents, however, plan destructive escapes. We may try to escape our prison by using alcohol or drugs. We may become workaholics. We may seek escape by becoming emotionally dependent on another person who is like the person we were attempting to escape—another alcoholic, for example. Many codependents begin to contemplate suicide. For some, ending our lives appears to be the only way out of this terribly painful situation.

Emotional dependency and feeling stuck can also cause problems in salvageable relationships. If we are in a relationship that is still good, we may be too insecure to detach and start taking care of ourselves. We may stifle ourselves and smother or drive away the other person. That much need becomes obvious to other people. It can be sensed, felt.

Ultimately, too much dependency on a person can kill love. Relationships based on emotional insecurity and need, rather than on love, can become self-destructive. They don't work. Too much need drives people away and smothers love. It scares people away. It attracts the wrong kind of people. And our real needs don't get met. Our real needs become greater and so does our despair. We center our lives around this person, trying to protect our source of security and happiness. We forfeit our lives to do this. And we become angry at this person. We are being controlled by him or her. We are dependent on that person. We ultimately become angry and resentful at what we are dependent on and controlled by, because we have given our personal power and rights to that person.[4]

Feeling desperate or dependent can expose us to other risks too. If we let the desperate part of us make our choices, we may unwittingly put ourselves in situations where we expose ourselves to sexually transmitted diseases such as herpes or AIDS (Acquired Immune Deficiency Syndrome). It is not safe to be that needy in intimate relationships.

Sometimes, we may play tricks on ourselves to disguise our dependency. Some of these tricks, according to Colette Dowling, are making someone more than he or she is ("He's such a genius; that's why I stick with him."), making someone less than he or she is ("Men are such babies; they can't take care of themselves."), and—the favorite trick of codependents—caretaking. Dowling demonstrated these characteristics in *The Cinderella Complex,* where she cited the case history of Madeleine, a woman who was extricating herself from a destructive relationship with Manny, her alcoholic husband.

That is the last trick of the dependent personality—believing that you're responsible for "taking care of" the other one. Madeleine had always felt more responsible for Manny's survival than for her own. As long as she was concentrating on Manny— *his* passivity, *his* indecisiveness, *his* problems with alcohol—she focused all her energy on devising solutions for him, or for "them," and never had to look inside herself. It was why it had taken twenty-two years for Madeleine to catch on to the fact that if things continued as they had always been, she would end up shortchanged. She would end up *never having lived a life.*

    . . . From the time she was eighteen until she was forty—years when people are supposed to reap, and grow, and experience the world—Madeleine Boroff had been hanging on, pretending to herself that life was not what it was, that her husband would get his bearings before long, and that she would one day spring free to live her own inner life—peacefully, creatively.

    For twenty-two years she had not been able to cope with what it would mean to face down the lie, and so, without intending any harm, but too frightened to live authentically, she turned her back on truth.

    It may seem dramatic in its surface details, but in its fundamental dynamic Madeleine's story is not so unusual. The go-along quality she exhibited, the seeming inability to extricate herself, or even *think* of extricating herself, from an utterly draining relationship—these signs of helplessness are characteristic of women who are psychologically dependent.[5]

    Why do we do this to ourselves? Why do we feel so uncertain and vulnerable that we can't go about the business of living our lives? Why, when we have proved we are so strong and capable by the sheer fact that many of us have endured and survived what we have, can't we believe in ourselves? Why, when we are experts at taking care of everybody around us, do we doubt our ability to take care of ourselves? What is it about us?

Many of us learned these things because when we were children, someone very important to us was unable to give us the love, approval, and emotional security we needed. So we've gone about our lives the best way we could, still looking vaguely or desperately for something we never got. Some of us are still beating our heads against the cement trying to get this love from people who, like Mother or Father, are unable to give what we need. The cycle repeats itself until it is interrupted and stopped. It's called unfinished business.

Maybe we've been taught to not trust ourselves. This happens when we have a feeling and we're told it's wrong or inappropriate. Or when we confront a lie or an inconsistency and we're told we're crazy. We lose faith in that deep, important part of ourselves that feels appropriate feelings, senses truth, and has confidence in its ability to handle life's situations. Pretty soon, we may believe what we are told about ourselves—that we're off, a tad crazy, not to be trusted. We look at the people around us— sometimes sick, troubled, out of control people—and we think, "They're okay. They must be. They told me so. So it must be me. There must be something fundamentally wrong with me." We abandon ourselves and lose faith in our ability to take care of ourselves.

Some women were taught to be dependent. They learned to center their lives around other people and to be taken care of. Even since the women's liberation movement, many women, deep inside, fear being alone.[6] Many people, not just women, fear being alone and taking care of themselves. It is part of being human.

Some of us may have entered an adult relationship with our emotional security intact, only to discover we were in a relationship with an alcoholic. Nothing will destroy emotional security more quickly than loving someone who is alcoholic or has any other compulsive disorder. These diseases demand us to center our lives around them. Confusion, chaos, and despair reign. Even the healthiest of us may begin to doubt ourselves after living with an alcoholic. Needs go unmet. Love disappears. The needs become greater and so does the self-doubt. Alcoholism creates emotionally insecure people. Alcoholism creates victims of us—

drinkers and nondrinkers, alike—and we doubt our ability to take care of ourselves.

If we have decided, for whatever reason, that we can't take care of ourselves, I have good news. The theme of this book is encouragement to begin taking care of ourselves. The purpose of this chapter is to say we *can* take care of ourselves. We are not helpless. Being ourselves and being responsible for ourselves do not have to be so painful and scary. We can handle things, whatever life brings our way. We don't have to be so dependent on the people around us. Unlike Siamese twins, we can live without any particular human being. As one woman put it: "For years, I kept telling myself I couldn't live without a particular man. I was wrong. I've had four husbands. They're all dead, and I'm still living." Knowing we can live without someone does not mean we *have* to live without that person, but it may free us to love and live in ways that work.

Now, let me give what I shall call the "rest" of the news. There is no magic, easy, overnight way to become undependent.

Emotional security and our present level of insecurity are penetrating issues that we must keep in mind as we make our decisions. Sometimes we become financially as well as emotionally dependent on a person, and we are then faced with two real concerns—two concerns that may or may not be connected.[7] Neither issue is to be taken lightly; each demands consideration. My words or our hopes will not diminish the reality of these facts. If we are financially or emotionally dependent, that is a fact, and facts need to be accepted and taken into account. But I believe we can strive to become less dependent. And I know we can become undependent, if we want to.

Here are some ideas that may help:

1. *Finish up business from our childhoods, as best as we can. Grieve. Get some perspective. Figure out how events from our childhoods are affecting what we're doing now.*

A client who has been in committed love relationships with two alcoholics told me the following story. Her father left home when she was five years old. He had been drunk for most of those five years. Although they lived in the same city, she rarely saw her father after he moved out. He visited her a few times after her mother divorced him, but there was no substance to the relationship. As she grew up, she called her father from time to time to tell him about important events in her life: high school graduation, her marriage, the birth of her first child, her divorce, her remarriage, her second pregnancy. Each time she called, her father talked to her for five minutes, mentioned seeing her sometime, then hung up. She said she didn't feel particularly hurt or angry; she expected this from him. He had never been there for her. He never would be there for her. He didn't participate in the relationship. There was nothing, including love, coming back from him. But it was a fact of life, and it did not particularly upset her. She truly thought she had resigned herself to and dealt with her father's alcoholism. This relationship went on this way for years. Her relationships with alcoholics went on for years.

When she was in the midst of her most recent divorce, the phone rang one evening. It was her father. It was the first time he had ever called her. Her heart nearly jumped out of her chest, she reported later. Her father asked how she and her family were—a question he usually avoided. Just as she was wondering if she could tell him about her divorce (something she wanted to do; she had always wanted to cry and be comforted by her father) he began whining about how he had been locked up in a psychiatric ward, he had no rights, it wasn't fair, and couldn't she do something to help him? She quickly wrapped up the conversation, hung up the phone, sat down on the floor, and bawled.

"I remember sitting on the floor screaming: 'You've never been there for me. Never. And now I need you. I let myself need you just once, and you weren't there for me. Instead, you wanted *me* to take care of *you*.'

"When I quit crying, I felt strangely peaceful," she said. "I think it was the first time I ever let myself grieve or get angry at my father. Over the next few weeks, I began to understand—really understand. Of course he had never been there for me. He was an alcoholic. He had never been there for anyone, including himself. I also began to realize that underneath my sophisticated veneer, I felt unlovable. Very unlovable. Somewhere, hidden inside me, I had maintained a fantasy that I had a loving father who was staying away from me—who was rejecting me—because I wasn't good enough. There was something wrong with me. Now I knew the truth. It wasn't me that was unlovable. It wasn't me that was screwed up, although I know I've got problems. It was *he.*

"Something happened to me after that," she said. "I no longer *need* an alcoholic to love me. The truth has indeed set me free."

I am not suggesting that all of this woman's problems were solved when she finished her grieving or by one moment of awareness. She may have more grieving to do; she still needs to deal with her codependent characteristics. But I think what happened helped her.

2. *Nurture and cherish that frightened, vulnerable, needy child inside us. The child may never completely disappear, no matter how self-sufficient we become. Stress may cause the child to cry out. Unprovoked, the child may come out and demand attention when we least expect it.*

I had a dream about this that I think illustrates the point. In my dream, a girl about nine years old had been left alone, abandoned by her mother for several days and nights. Without supervision, the child ran around the neighborhood late at night. She didn't cause any serious problems. She seemed to be looking for something, trying to fill her empty hours. *The child did not want to stay in her house alone when it got dark.* The loneliness was too frightening. When the mother finally returned, the neighbors approached her and complained about this child running all over, unsupervised. The mother became angry, and started yelling at the child for her misbehavior. "I told you to stay in the house while I was gone. I told you to not cause problems, didn't I?" the mother screamed. The child offered no retort, didn't even cry. She just stood there with downcast eyes and quietly said, "I think I have a stomachache."

Don't pound on that vulnerable child when he or she doesn't want to stay in the dark all alone, when he or she becomes frightened. We don't have to let the child make our choices for us, but don't ignore the child either. Listen to the child. Let the child cry if he or she needs to. Comfort the child. Figure out what he or she needs.

3. *Stop looking for happiness in other people. Our source of happiness and well-being is not inside others; it's inside us. Learn to center ourselves in ourselves.*

Stop centering and focusing on other people. Settle down with and in ourselves. Stop seeking so much approval and validation from others. We don't need the approval of everyone and anyone. We only need *our* approval. We have all the same sources for happiness and making choices inside us that others do. Find and develop our own internal supply of peace, well-being, and self-esteem. Relationships help, but they cannot be our source. Develop personal cores of emotional security with ourselves.

4. *We can learn to depend on ourselves. Maybe other people haven't been there for us, but we can start being there for us.*

Stop abandoning ourselves, our needs, our wants, our feelings, our lives, and everything that comprises us. Make a commitment to always be there for ourselves. We can trust ourselves. We can handle and cope with the events, problems, and feelings life throws our way. We can trust our feelings and our judgments. We can solve our problems. We can learn to live with our unsolved problems, too. We must trust the people we are learning to depend upon—ourselves.

5. *We can depend on God, too. He's there, and He cares. Our spiritual beliefs can provide us with a strong sense of emotional security.*

Let me illustrate this idea. One night, when I lived in a rough neighborhood, I had to walk down the alley behind my house to get to my car. I asked my husband to watch from a window on the second floor to make sure nothing happened to me. He agreed. As I walked across the backyard, away from the security of my home and into the blackness of the night, I began to feel afraid. I turned around and saw my husband in the window. He was watching; he was there. Immediately, the fear left, and I felt comforted and safe. It occurred to me that I believe in God, and I can find the same feelings of comfort and security in knowing that He is always watching over my life. I strive to look to this security.

Some codependents begin to believe God has abandoned us. We have had so much pain. So many needs have gone unmet, sometimes for so long that we may cry out, "Where has God gone? Why has He gone away? Why has He let this happen? Why won't He help? Why has He abandoned me?"

God hasn't abandoned us. We abandoned ourselves. He's there, and He cares. But He expects us to cooperate by caring for ourselves.

6. *Strive for undependence. Begin examining the ways we are dependent, emotionally and financially, on the people around us.*

Start taking care of ourselves whether we are in relationships that we intend to continue, or whether we are in relationships we are trying to get out of. In *The Cinderella Complex*, Colette Dowling suggested doing this with an attitude of "courageous vulnerability."[8] That means: You feel scared, but you do it anyway.

We can feel our feelings, talk about our fears, accept ourselves and our present conditions, and then get started on the journey toward undependence. We *can* do it. We don't have to feel strong all the time to be undependent and taking care of ourselves. We can and probably will have feelings of fear, weakness, and even hopelessness. That is normal and even healthy. Real power comes from feeling our feelings, not from ignoring them. Real strength comes, not from pretending to be strong all the time, but from acknowledging our weaknesses and vulnerabilities when we feel this way.

Many of us have dark nights. Many of us have uncertainty, loneliness, and the pang of needs and wants that beg to be met and yet go seemingly unnoticed. Sometimes the way is foggy and slippery, and we have no hope. All we can feel is fear. All we can see is the dark. I was driving one night in weather like this. I don't like driving, and I particularly don't like driving in bad weather. I was stiff and frightened at the wheel. I could barely see; the headlights were only illuminating a few feet of the road. I was almost blind. I started to panic. Anything could happen! Then, a calming thought entered my mind. The path was only lit for a few feet, but each time I progressed those few feet, a new section was lit. It didn't matter that I couldn't see far ahead. If I relaxed, I could see as far as I needed for the moment. The situation wasn't ideal, but I could get through it if I stayed calm and worked with what was available.

You can get through dark situations, too. You can take care of yourself and trust yourself. Trust God. Go as far as you can see, and by the time you get there, you'll be able to see farther.

It's called *One Day at a Time.*

ACTIVITY

1. Examine the following characteristics, and decide if you are in a dependent (addicted) or healthy (love) relationship:

Characteristics

Love (Open System)	Addiction (Closed System)
Room to grow, expand; desire for other to grow.	Dependent, based on security and comfort; use intensity of need and infatuation as proof of love (may really be fear, insecurity, loneliness).
Separate interests; other friends; maintain other meaningful relationships.	Total involvement; limited social life; neglect old friends, interests.
Encouragement of each other's expanding; secure in own worth.	Preoccupation with other's behavior; dependent on other's approval for own identity and self-worth.
Trust; openness.	Jealousy, possessiveness, fears competition, "protects supply."
Mutual integrity preserved.	One partner's needs suspended for the other's; self-deprivation.
Willingness to risk and be real.	Search for perfect invulnerability—eliminates possible risks.
Room for exploration of feelings in and of relationship.	Reassurance through repeated, ritualized activity.
Ability to enjoy being alone.	Intolerance—unable to endure separations (even in conflict); hang on even tighter. Undergo withdrawal—loss of appetite, restless, lethargic, disoriented agony.

BREAKUPS

Accept breakup without feeling a loss of own adequacy and self-worth.

Feel inadequate, worthless; often one-sided decision.

Wants best for partner, though apart; can become friends.

Violent ending—often hate other; try to inflict pain; manipulation to get other back.

ONE-SIDED ADDICTION

Denial, fantasy; overestimation of other's commitment.

Seeks solutions outside self—drugs, alcohol, new lover, change of situation.

10

LIVE YOUR OWN LIFE

Live and let live.

—Twelve Step program slogan

If I make one point in this book, I hope it is that *the surest way to make ourselves crazy is to get involved in other people's business, and the quickest way to become sane and happy is to tend to our own affairs.*

I have discussed concepts and ideas pertaining to that thought. We've examined reactions typical of codependency. We've discussed ways of learning how to react differently using detachment. But, after we've detached and taken our grip off the people around us, what's left? Each of us is left with ourselves.

I remember the day I faced that truth. For a long time I had blamed my unfortunate circumstances on other people. "You are the reason I am the way I am!" I had screeched. "Look what you made me do—with my minutes, my hours, my life." After I detached and took responsibility for myself, I wondered, maybe other people weren't the reason I hadn't been living my own life; maybe they were just the excuse I needed. My destiny—my todays and tomorrows—looked pretty glum.

Living our lives may not be an exciting prospect to some of us either. Maybe we've been so wrapped up in other people that we've forgotten how to live and enjoy our lives.

We may be in so much emotional distress we think we have no life; all we are is our pain. That's not true. We are more than our problems. We can be more than our problems. We will be more than our problems.¹ Just because life has been this painful so far doesn't mean it has to keep hurting. Life doesn't have to hurt so much, and it won't—if we begin to change. It may not be all roses from here on out, but it doesn't have to be all thorns either. We need to and can develop our own lives. As one friend says, "Get a life."

Some codependents think a life with no future, no purpose, no great shakes, and no great breaks isn't worth living. That's not true, either. I believe God has exciting, interesting things in store for each of us. I believe there is an enjoyable, worthwhile purpose—besides taking care of people and being an appendage to someone—for each of us. I believe we tap into this attitude by taking care of ourselves. We begin to cooperate. We open ourselves up to the goodness and richness available in us and to us.²

Throughout this book I have used the phrase *taking care of ourselves*. I have heard that phrase used and abused. I have heard people use it to control, impose upon, or force their wills on people. (I dropped in, uninvited, with my five kids and cat. We're going to spend the week. I'm just taking care of myself!) I have heard the phrase used manipulatively to justify persecuting and punishing people, instead of dealing appropriately with angry feelings. (I'm going to holler and scream at you all day because you didn't do what I wanted you to do. Don't get mad at me though. I'm just taking care of myself.) I have heard people use these words to avoid responsibility. (I know my son is up in his bedroom shooting heroin, but that's his problem. I'm not going to worry. I'm going to the store and charge $500, and I'm not going to worry about how I'll pay that either. I'm just taking care of myself.)

Those behaviors are not what I mean by taking care of ourselves. Self-care is an attitude toward ourselves and our lives that says, I am responsible for myself. I am responsible for leading or not living my life. I am responsible for tending to my spiritual, emotional, physical, and financial well-being. I am responsible for identifying and meeting my needs. I am responsible for solving my problems or learning to live with those I cannot solve. I am responsible for my choices. I am responsible for what I give and receive. I am also responsible for setting and achieving my goals. I am responsible for how much I enjoy life, for how much pleasure I find in daily activities. I am responsible for whom I love and how I choose to express this love. I am responsible for what I do to others and for what I allow others to do to me. I am responsible for my wants and desires. All of me, every aspect of my being, is important. I count for something. I matter. My feelings can be trusted. My thinking is appropriate. I value my wants and needs. I do not deserve and will not tolerate abuse or constant mistreatment. I have rights, and it is my responsibility to assert these rights. The decisions I make and the way I conduct myself will reflect my high self-esteem. My decisions will take into account my responsibilities to myself.

My decisions will also take into account my responsibilities to other people—my spouse, my children, my relatives, my friends. I will examine and decide exactly what these responsibilities are as I make my decisions. I will also consider the rights of those around me—the right to live their lives as they see fit. I do not have the right to impose on others' rights to take care of themselves, and they have no right to impose on my rights.

Self-care is an attitude of mutual respect. It means learning to live our lives responsibly. It means allowing others to live their lives as they choose, as long as they don't interfere with our decisions to live as we choose. Taking care of ourselves is not as selfish as some people assume it is, but neither is it as selfless as many codependents believe.

In the chapters that follow, we will discuss some specific ways of taking care of ourselves: goal setting, dealing with feelings, working a Twelve Step program, and more. I believe taking care of ourselves is an art, and this art involves one fundamental idea that is foreign to many: giving ourselves what we need.

This may be a shock to us and our family systems at first. Most codependents don't ask for what we need. Many codependents don't know or haven't given much thought to what we want and need. (Throughout this book, I have used and will use the terms *needs* and *wants* interchangeably. I consider wants and needs important, and I will treat these terms with equal respect.)

Many of us have falsely believed our needs aren't important and we shouldn't mention them. Some of us even began to believe our needs are bad or wrong, so we've learned to repress them and push them out of our awareness. We haven't learned to identify what we need, or listen to what we need because it didn't matter anyway—our needs weren't going to get met. Some of us haven't learned how to get our needs met appropriately.

Giving ourselves what we need is not difficult. I believe we can learn quickly. The formula is simple: In any given situation, detach and ask, "What do I need to do to take care of myself?"

Then we need to listen to ourselves and to our Higher Power. Respect what we hear. This insane business of punishing ourselves for what we think, feel, and want—this nonsense of not listening to who we are and what our selves are struggling to tell us—must stop. How do you think God works with us? As I've said before, no wonder we think God has abandoned us; we've abandoned ourselves. We can be gentle with ourselves and accept ourselves. We're not only or merely human, we were created and intended to be human. And we can be compassionate with ourselves. Then, perhaps, we may develop true compassion for others.[3] Listen to what our precious self is telling us about what we need.

Maybe we need to hurry and get to an appointment. Maybe we need to slow down and take the day off work. Maybe we need exercise or a nap. We might need to be alone. We may want to be around people. Maybe we need a job. Maybe we need to work less. Maybe we need a hug, a kiss, or a back rub.

Sometimes giving ourselves what we need means giving ourselves something fun: a treat, a new hairdo, a new dress, a new pair of shoes, a new toy, an evening at the theater, or a trip to the Bahamas. Sometimes, giving ourselves what we need is work. We need to eliminate or develop a certain characteristic; we need to work on a relationship; or we need to tend to our responsibilities to other people or to our responsibilities to ourselves. Giving ourselves what we need does not only mean giving presents to ourselves; it means doing what's necessary to live responsibly— not an excessively responsible or an irresponsible existence.

Our needs are different and vary from moment to moment and day to day. Are we feeling the crazy anxiety that goes with codependency? Maybe we need to go to an Al-Anon meeting. Are our thoughts negative and despairing? Maybe we need to read a meditation or inspirational book. Are we worried about a physical problem? Maybe we need to go to a doctor. Are the kids going wild? Maybe we need to figure out a family plan for discipline. Are people stomping on our rights? Set some boundaries. Are our stomachs churning with emotions? Deal with our feelings. Maybe we need to detach, slow down, make an amend, do an intervention, initiate a relationship, or file for divorce. It's up to us. What do we think we need to do?

Besides giving ourselves what we need, we begin to ask people for what we need and want from them because this is part of taking care of ourselves and being a responsible human being.

Giving ourselves what we need means we become, as the Reverend Phil L. Hansen suggests, our personal counselor, confidante, spiritual advisor, partner, best friend, and caretaker in this exciting, new venture we have undertaken—living our own lives. The Reverend Hansen is nationally active in the addiction field. We base all our decisions on reality, and we make them in our best interests. We take into account our responsibilities to other people, because that is what responsible people do. But we also know we count. We try to eliminate "shoulds" from our decisions and learn to trust ourselves. If we listen to ourselves and our Higher Power, we will not be misled. Giving ourselves what we need and learning to live self-directed lives requires faith. We need enough faith to get on with our lives, and we need to do at least a little something each day to begin moving forward.

As we learn how to care for and meet our own needs, we forgive ourselves when we make mistakes and we congratulate ourselves when we do well. We also get comfortable doing some things poorly and some things with mediocrity, for that is part of life too. We learn to laugh at ourselves and our humanity, but we don't laugh when we need to cry. We take ourselves seriously but not too seriously.

Ultimately, we may even discover this astounding truth: Few situations in life are ever improved by not taking care of ourselves and not giving ourselves what we need. In fact, we may learn most situations are improved when we take care of ourselves and tend to our needs.

I am learning to identify how to take care of myself. I know many people who have either learned or are learning to do this too. I believe all codependents can.

ACTIVITY

1. As you go through the days ahead, stop and ask yourself what you need to do to take care of yourself. Do it as often as you need to, but do it at least once daily. If you are going through a crisis, you may need to do it every hour. Then give yourself what you need.

2. What do you need from the people around you? At an appropriate time, sit down with them and discuss what you need from them.

11

HAVE A LOVE AFFAIR WITH YOURSELF

This above all:
to thine own self be true,
and it must follow, as the night the day,
thou canst not then be false to any man.

—William Shakespeare

"Love thy neighbor as thyself." The problem with many codependents is we do just that. What's worse, many of us wouldn't dream of loving or treating other people the way we treat ourselves. We wouldn't dare, and others probably wouldn't let us.

Most codependents suffer from that vague but penetrating affliction, low self-worth. We don't feel good about ourselves, we don't like ourselves, and we wouldn't consider loving ourselves. For some of us, low self-worth is an understatement. We don't merely dislike ourselves, we hate ourselves.[1]

We don't like the way we look. We can't stand our bodies. We think we're stupid, incompetent, untalented, and, in many cases, unlovable.[2] We think our thoughts are wrong and inappropriate. We think our feelings are wrong and inappropriate. We believe we're not important, and even if our feelings aren't wrong, we think they don't *matter*. We're convinced our needs aren't important. And we shame someone else's desires or plans. We think we're inferior to and different from the rest of the world—not unique, but oddly and inappropriately different.

We have never come to grips with ourselves, and we look at ourselves not through rose-colored glasses but through a dirty, brownish-gray film. We may have learned to disguise our true feelings about ourselves by dressing right, fixing our hair right, living in the right home, and working at the right job. We may boast of our accomplishments, but underneath the trappings lies a dungeon where we secretly and incessantly punish and torture ourselves. At times, we may punish ourselves openly before the whole world, by saying demeaning things about ourselves. Sometimes, we even invite others to help us hate ourselves, such as when we allow certain people or religious customs to help us feel guilty, or when we allow people to hurt us. But our worst beatings go on privately, inside our minds.

We pick on ourselves endlessly, heaping piles of shoulds on our conscience and creating mounds of worthless, stinking guilt. Don't confuse this with true, authentic guilt, which motivates change, teaches valuable lessons, and brings us into a close relationship with ourselves, others, and our Higher Power. We constantly put ourselves in impossible situations where we have no choice but to feel badly about ourselves. We think a thought, then tell ourselves we shouldn't think that way. We feel a feeling, then tell ourselves we shouldn't feel that way. We make a decision, act on it, then tell ourselves we shouldn't have acted that way. There is nothing to correct in these situations, no amends to make; we have done nothing wrong. We are engaged in a form of punishment designed to keep us feeling anxious, upset, and stifled. We trap ourselves.

One of my favorite forms of self-torture involves a dilemma between two things to do. I make a decision to do one of them first. The minute I act on this decision, I say: "I should be doing the other thing." So I switch gears, begin doing the other thing, and I start in on myself again: "I really shouldn't be doing this. I should be doing what I was doing before." Another one of my favorites is this: I fix my hair, put on makeup, look in the mirror, and say, "Gee, I look weird. I shouldn't look this way."

Some of us believe we have made such bad mistakes that we can't reasonably expect forgiveness. Some of us believe our lives are a mistake. Many of us believe everything we've done is a mistake. A few of us believe we can't do anything right, but at the same time, we demand perfection of ourselves. We put ourselves in impossible situations, then wonder why we can't get out.

Then we finish the job by shaming ourselves. We don't like what we do, and we don't like who we are. Fundamentally, we are not good enough. For some reason, God created in us a person totally inappropriate for life.

In codependency, as in many other areas of life, everything is connected to everything, and one thing leads to another. In this case, our low self-worth is frequently connected to much of what we do or don't do, and it leads to many of our problems.

As codependents, we frequently dislike ourselves so much that we believe it's wrong to take ourselves into account, in other words, appear selfish. Putting ourselves first is out of the question. Often, we think we're only worth something if we do things for others or caretake, so we never say no. Anyone as insignificant as us must go an extra mile to be liked. No one in their right minds could like and enjoy being with us. We think we have to do something for people to get and keep their friendships. Much of the defensiveness I've seen in codependents comes not because we think we're above criticism, but because we have so little self-worth that any perceived attack threatens to annihilate us. We feel so bad about ourselves and have such a need to be perfect and avoid shame that we cannot allow anyone to tell us about something we've done wrong. One reason some of us nag and criticize other people is because that's what we do to ourselves.

I believe, as Earnie Larsen and other authorities do, that our low self-worth or self-hatred is tied into all aspects of our codependency: martyrdom, refusal to enjoy life; workaholism, staying so busy we can't enjoy life; perfectionism, not allowing ourselves to enjoy or feel good about the things we do; procrastination, heaping piles of guilt and uncertainty on ourselves; and preventing intimacy with people such as running from relationships, avoiding commitment, staying in destructive relationships; initiating relationships with people who are not good for us, and avoiding people who are good for us.

We can find endless means of torturing ourselves: overeating, neglecting our needs, comparing ourselves to others, competing with people, obsessing, dwelling on painful memories, or imagining future painful scenes. We think, what if she drinks again? What if she has an affair? What if a tornado hits the house? This "what if" attitude is always good for a strong dose of fear. We scare ourselves, then wonder why we feel so frightened.

We don't like ourselves, and we're not going to let ourselves get any of the good stuff because we believe we don't deserve it.

As codependents, we tend to enter into totally antagonistic relationships with ourselves.[3] Some of us learned these self-hating behaviors in our families, possibly with the help of an alcoholic parent. Some of us reinforced our self-disdain by leaving an alcoholic parent and marrying an alcoholic. We may have entered into adult relationships with fragile self-worth, then discovered our remaining self-esteem disintegrated. A few of us may have had our self-worth completely intact until we met him or her or until *that problem* came along; we suddenly or gradually found ourselves hating ourselves. Alcoholism and other compulsive disorders destroy self-worth in alcoholics and codependents. Remember, alcoholism and other compulsive disorders are self-destructive. Some of us may not even be aware of our low self-esteem and self-hatred because we have been comparing ourselves to the alcoholics and other crazy people in our lives; by comparison, we come out on top. Low self-worth can sneak up on us any time we let it.

Actually, it doesn't matter when we began torturing ourselves. We must stop now. Right now, we can give ourselves a big emotional and mental hug. We are okay. It's wonderful to be who we are. Our thoughts are okay. Our feelings are appropriate. We're right where we're supposed to be today, this moment. There is nothing wrong with us. There is nothing fundamentally wrong with us. If we've done wrongs, that's okay; we were doing the best we could.

In all our codependency, with all our controlling, rescuing, and assorted character defects, we are okay. We are exactly as we are meant to be. I've talked a lot about problems, issues, and things to change—these are goals, things we will do to enhance our lives. Who we are right now is okay. In fact, codependents are some of the most loving, generous, good-hearted, and concerned people I know. We've just allowed ourselves to be tricked into doing things that hurt us, and we're going to learn how to stop doing those things. But those tricks are our problems; they are not us. If we have one character defect that is abhorrent, it is the way we hate and pick on ourselves. That is simply not tolerable nor acceptable any longer. We can stop picking on ourselves for picking on ourselves.[4] This habit is not our *fault* either, but it is our *responsibility* to learn to stop doing it.

We can cherish ourselves and our lives. We can nurture ourselves and love ourselves. We can accept our wonderful selves, with all our faults, foibles, strong points, weak points, feelings, thoughts, and everything else. It's the best thing we've got going for us. It's who we are, and who we were meant to be. And it's not a mistake. We are the greatest thing that will ever happen to us. Believe it. It makes life much easier.

The only difference between codependents and the rest of the world is that the other people don't pick on themselves for being who they are. All people think similar thoughts and have a range of feelings. All people make mistakes and do a few things right. So we can leave ourselves alone.

We aren't second-class citizens. We don't deserve to lead second-hand lives. And we don't deserve second-best relationships! We are lovable, and we are worth getting to know. People who love and like us aren't stupid or inferior for doing that. We have a right to be happy.[5] We deserve good things.

The people who look the most beautiful are the same as us. The only difference is they're telling themselves they look good, and they're letting themselves shine through. The people who say the most profound, intelligent, or witty things are the same as us. They're letting go, being who they are. The people who appear the most confident and relaxed are no different from us. They've pushed themselves through fearful situations and told themselves they could make it. The people who are successful are the same as us. They've gone ahead and developed their gifts and talents, and set goals for themselves. We're even the same as the people on television: our heroes, our idols. We're all working with approximately the same material—humanity. It's how we feel about ourselves that makes the difference. It's what we tell ourselves that makes the difference. We are good. We are good enough. We are appropriate to life. Much of our anxiety and fearfulness stems, I believe, from constantly telling ourselves that we're just not up to facing the world and all its situations. Nathaniel Branden calls this "a nameless sense of being unfit for reality."[6] I'm here to say we are fit for reality. Relax. Wherever we need to go and whatever we need to do, we are appropriate for that situation. We will do fine. Relax. It's okay to be who we are. Who or what else can we be? Just do our best at whatever we are called upon to do. What more can we do? Sometimes, we can't even do our best; that's okay, too. We may have feelings, thoughts, fears, and vulnerabilities as we go through life, but we all do. We need to stop telling ourselves we're different for doing and feeling what everyone else does.

We need to be good to ourselves. We need to be compassionate and kind to ourselves. How can we expect to take care of ourselves appropriately if we hate or dislike ourselves?

We need to refuse to enter into an antagonistic relationship with ourselves. Quit blaming ourselves and being victimized, and take responsible steps to remove the victim. Put the screws to guilt. Shame and guilt serve no long-term purpose. They are only useful to momentarily indicate when we may have violated our own moral codes. Guilt and shame are not useful as a way of life. Stop the "shoulds." Become aware of when we're punishing and torturing ourselves and make a concerted effort to tell ourselves positive messages. If we should be doing something, do it. If we're torturing ourselves, stop it. It gets easier. We can laugh at ourselves, tell ourselves we won't be tricked, give ourselves a hug, then go about the business of living as we choose. If we have real guilt, deal with it. God will forgive us. He knows we did our best, even if it was our worst. We don't have to punish ourselves by feeling guilty to prove to God or anyone else how much we care.[7] We need to forgive ourselves. Take the Fourth and Fifth Steps (see the chapter on working a Twelve Step program); talk to a clergy person; talk to God; make amends; and then be done with it.

We need to stop shaming ourselves. Shame, like guilt, serves absolutely no extended purpose. If people tell us, directly or indirectly, that we ought to be ashamed, we don't have to believe it. Hating or shaming ourselves doesn't help except for a moment. Name one situation that is improved by continuing to feel guilt or shame. Name one time when that has solved a problem. How did it help? Most of the time, guilt and shame keep us so anxious we can't do our best. Guilt makes *everything* harder.

We need to value ourselves and make decisions and choices that enhance our self-esteem.

"Each time you learn to act as if you are valuable, not desperate, you make it easier the next time," advises Toby Rice Drew in *Getting Them Sober*.[8]

We can be gentle, loving, listening, attentive, and kind to ourselves, our feelings, thoughts, needs, wants, desires, and everything we're made of. We can accept ourselves—all of us. Start where we're at, and we will become more. Develop our gifts and talents. Trust ourselves. Assert ourselves. We can be trusted. Respect ourselves. Be true to ourselves. Honor ourselves, for that is where our magic lies. That is our key to the world.

Following is an excerpt from *Honoring the Self,* an excellent book on self-esteem written by Nathaniel Branden. Read closely what he writes.

Of all the judgments that we pass in life, none is as important as the one we pass on ourselves, for that judgment touches the very center of our existence.

. . . No significant aspect of our thinking, motivation, feelings, or behavior is unaffected by our self-evaluation. . . .

The first act of honoring the self is the assertion of consciousness: the choice to think, to be aware, to send the searchlight of consciousness outward toward the world and inward toward our own being. To default on this effort is to default on the self at the most basic level.

To honor the self is to be willing to think independently, to live by our own mind, and to have the courage of our own perceptions and judgments.

To honor the self is to be willing to know not only what we think but also what we feel, what we want, need, desire, suffer over, are frightened or angered by—and to accept our right to experience such feelings. The opposite of this attitude is denial, disowning, repression—self-repudiation.

To honor the self is to preserve an attitude of self-acceptance—which means to accept what we are, without self-oppression or self-castigation, without any pretense about the truth of our own being, pretense aimed at deceiving either ourselves or anyone else.

To honor the self is to live authentically, to speak and act from our innermost convictions and feelings.

To honor the self is to refuse to accept unearned guilt, and to do our best to correct such guilt as we may have earned.

To honor the self is to be committed to our right to exist which proceeds from the knowledge that our life does not belong to others and that we are not here on earth to live up to someone else's expectations. To many people, this is a terrifying responsibility.

To honor the self is to be in love with our own life, in love with our possibilities for growth and for experiencing joy, in love with the process of discovery and exploring our distinctively human potentialities.

Thus we can begin to see that to honor the self is to practice *selfishness* in the highest, noblest, and least understood sense of that word. And this, I shall argue, requires enormous independence, courage, and integrity.[9]

We need to love ourselves and make a commitment to ourselves. We need to give ourselves some of the boundless loyalty that so many codependents are willing to give others. Out of high self-esteem will come true acts of kindness and charity, not selfishness.

The love we give and receive will be enhanced by the love we give ourselves.

ACTIVITY

1. How do you feel about yourself? Write about it. Include the things you like or don't like about yourself. Reread what you have written.

12

LEARN THE ART OF ACCEPTANCE

I'd like to make a motion that we face reality.

—Bob Newhart, from the *Bob Newhart Show*

Accepting reality is touted and encouraged by most sane people. It is the goal of many therapies, as well it should be. Facing and coming to terms with *what is* is a beneficial act. Acceptance brings peace. It is frequently the turning point for change. It is also much easier said than done.

People, not just codependents, are faced daily with the prospect of either accepting or rejecting the reality of that particular day and present circumstances. We have many things to accept in the course of normal living from the moment we open our eyes in the morning until we close them at night. Our present circumstances include who we are, where we live, who we live with or without, where we work, our method of transportation, how much money we have, what our responsibilities are, what we shall do for fun, and any problems that arise. Some days, accepting these circumstances is a breeze. It comes naturally. Our hair behaves, our kids behave, the boss is reasonable, the money's right, the house is clean, the car works, and we like our spouse or lover. We know what to expect, and what we expect is acceptable. It's okay. Other days might not go so well. The brakes go out on the car, the roof leaks, the kids sass, we break an arm, we lose our job, or our spouse or lover says he or she doesn't love us any more. Something has happened. We have a problem. Things are different. Things are changing. We're *losing* something. Our present circumstances are no longer as comfortable as they were. Circumstances have been altered, and we have a new situation to accept. We may initially respond by denying or resisting the change, problem, or loss. We want things to be the way they were. We want the problem to be quickly solved. We want to be comfortable again. We want to know what to expect. We are not peaceful with reality. It feels awkward. We have temporarily lost our balance.

Codependents never know what to expect, particularly if we are in a close relationship with an alcoholic, a drug addict, a criminal, a gambler, or any other person with a serious problem or compulsive disorder. We are bombarded by problems, losses, and change. We endure shattered windows, missed appointments, broken promises, and outright lies. We lose financial security, emotional security, faith in the people we love, faith in God, and faith in ourselves. We may lose our physical well-being, our material goods, our ability to enjoy sex, our reputation, our social life, our career, our self-control, our self-esteem, and ourselves.

Some of us lose respect for and trust in the people we love. Sometimes we even lose our love for and our commitment to a person we once loved. This is common. It is a natural, normal consequence of the *disease*. The booklet, *A Guide for the Family of the Alcoholic* discusses this:

"Love cannot exist without the dimension of justice. Love must also have compassion which means to bear with or to suffer with a person. Compassion does not mean to suffer because of the injustice of a person. Yet injustice is often suffered repeatedly by families of alcoholics."[1]

Even though this injustice is common, it makes it no less painful. Betrayal can be overwhelming when someone we love does things that deeply hurt us.

Perhaps the most painful loss many codependents face is the loss of our dreams, the hopeful and sometimes idealistic expectations for the future that most people have. This loss can be the most difficult to accept. As we looked at our child in the hospital nursery, we had certain hopes for him or her. Those hopes didn't include our child having a problem with alcohol or other drugs. Our dreams didn't include this. On our wedding day, we had dreams. The future with our beloved was full of wonder and promise. This was the start of something great, something loving, something we had long hoped for. The dreams and promises may have been spoken or unspoken but for most of us, they were there.

"For each couple the beginning is different," wrote Janet Woititz in an article from the book *Co-Dependency, An Emerging Issue*. "Even so, the process that occurs in the chemically dependent marital relationship is essentially the same. For the starting point, let's take a look at the marriage vows. Most wedding services include the following statements—for better or worse—for richer or poorer—in sickness and in health—until death do us part. Maybe that's where all the trouble began. Did you mean what you said when you said it? If you knew at that time that you were going to have not the better but the worse, not the health but the sickness, not the richer but the poorer, would the love that you felt have made it worth it? You may say yes, but I wonder. If you were more realistic than romantic you may have interpreted the vows to mean— through the bad as well as the good, assuming that the bad times would be transitory and the good ones permanent. The contract is entered into in good faith. There is no benefit of hindsight."[2]

The dreams were there. Many of us held on for so long, clutching those dreams through one loss and disappointment after another. We flew in the face of reality, shaking these dreams at the truth, refusing to believe or accept anything less. But one day the truth caught up to us and refused to be put off any longer. This wasn't what we wanted, planned on, asked for, or hoped for. It never would be. The dream was dead, and it would never breathe again.

Some of us may have had our dreams and hopes crushed. Some of us may be facing the failure of something extremely important such as marriage or another important relationship. I know there's a lot of pain at the prospect of losing love or losing the dreams we had. There's nothing we can say to make that less painful or to lessen our grief. It hurts deeply to have our dreams destroyed by alcoholism or any other problem. The disease is deadly. It kills everything in sight, including our noblest dreams. "Chemical dependency destroys slowly, but thoroughly," concluded Janet Woititz.[3] How true. How sadly true. And nothing dies slower or more painfully than a dream.

Even recovery brings losses, more changes we must struggle to accept.[4] When an alcoholic spouse gets sober, things change. Patterns of relating change. Our codependent characteristics, the ways we have been affected, are losses of self-image we must face. Although these are good changes, they are still losses—losses of things that may not have been desirable but may have become oddly comfortable. These patterns became a fact of our present circumstances. At least we knew what to expect, even if that meant not expecting anything.

The losses many codependents must daily face and accept are enormous and ongoing. They are not the usual problems and losses most people encounter as part of normal living. These are losses and problems which are caused by people we care about. Although the problems are a direct result of an illness, condition, or compulsive disorder, they may appear as deliberate and malicious acts. We are suffering at the hands of someone we loved and trusted.

We are continually off balance, struggling to accept changes and problems. We don't know what to expect, nor do we know when to expect it. Our present circumstances are always in a state of flux. We may experience loss or change in all areas. We feel crazy; our kids are upset; our spouse or lover is acting crazy; the car has been repossessed; nobody has worked for weeks; the house is a mess; and the money has dwindled. The losses may come barrelling down all at once, or they may occur gradually. Things then may stabilize briefly, until once more we lose the car, job, home, money, and relationships with the people we care about. We dared to have hope, only to have our dreams smashed again. It doesn't matter that our hopes were falsely based on wishful thinking that the problem would magically go away. Crushed hopes are crushed hopes. Disappointments are disappointments. Lost dreams are dead dreams, and they all bring pain.

Accept reality? Half the time we don't even know what reality is. We're lied to; we lie to ourselves; and our heads are spinning. The other half of the time, facing reality is simply more than we can bear, more than anyone can bear. Why should it be so mysterious that denial is an integral part of alcoholism or any serious problem that causes ongoing losses? We have too much to accept; our present circumstances are over-whelming. Frequently, we are so caught up in crises and chaos trying to solve other people's problems that we're too busy to worry about accepting anything. Yet, we must sometime come to terms with *what is*. If things are ever to be any different, we must accept reality. If we are ever to re-place our lost dreams with new dreams and feel sane and peaceful again, we must accept reality.

Please understand acceptance does not mean adaptation. It doesn't mean resignation to the sorry and miserable way things are. *It doesn't mean accepting or tolerating any sort of abuse.* It means, for the present moment, we acknowledge and accept our circumstances, including our-selves and the people in our lives, as we and they are. It is only from that state that we have the peace and the ability to evaluate these circum-stances, make appropriate changes, and solve our problems. A person who is being abused will not make the decisions necessary to stop that abuse until he or she acknowledges the abuse. The person must then stop pretending the abuse will somehow magically end, stop pretending it doesn't exist, or stop making excuses for its existence. In a state of accep-tance we are able to respond responsibly to our environment. In this state we receive the power to change the things we can. Alcoholics cannot quit drinking until they accept their powerlessness over alcohol and their al-coholism. People with eating disorders cannot solve their food problems until they accept their powerlessness over food. Codependents cannot change until we accept our codependent characteristics—our powerlessness over people, alcoholism, and other circumstances we have so desperately tried to control. Acceptance is the ultimate paradox: we cannot change who we are until we accept ourselves the way we are.

Here is an excerpt from *Honoring the Self* on self-acceptance:

> . . . If I can accept that I am who I am, that I feel what I feel, that I have done what I have done—if I can accept it whether I like all of it or not—then I can accept myself. I can accept my short-comings, my self-doubts, my poor self-esteem. And when I can ac-cept all that, I have put myself on the side of reality rather than

attempting to fight reality. I am no longer twisting my consciousness in knots to maintain delusions about my present condition. And so I clear the road for the first steps of strengthening my self-esteem. . . .

So long as we cannot accept the fact of what we are at any given moment of our existence, so long as we cannot permit ourselves fully to be aware of the nature of our choices and actions, cannot admit the truth into our consciousness, we cannot change.[5]

It has also been my experience that my Higher Power seems reluctant to intervene in my circumstances until I accept what He has already given me. Acceptance is not forever. It is for the present moment. But it must be sincere and at gut-level.

How do we achieve this peaceful state? How do we stare at stark reality without blinking or covering our eyes? How do we accept all the losses, changes, and problems that life and people hurl at us?

Not without a little kicking and screaming. We accept things through a five-step process. Elisabeth Kübler-Ross first identified the stages and this process as the way dying people accept their death, the ultimate loss.[6] She called it the grief process. Since then, mental health professionals have observed people go through these stages whenever they face any loss. The loss could be minor—a five-dollar bill, not receiving an expected letter—or it could be significant—the loss of a spouse through divorce or death, the loss of a job. Even positive change brings loss—when we buy a new house and leave the old one—and requires a progression through the following five stages.[7]

1. Denial

The first stage is denial. This is a state of shock, numbness, panic, and general refusal to accept or acknowledge reality. We do everything and anything to put things back in place or pretend the situation isn't happening. There is much anxiety and fear in this stage. Reactions typical of denial include: refusing to believe reality ("No, this can't be!"); denying or minimizing the importance of the loss ("It's no big deal."); denying any feelings about the loss ("I don't care."); or mental avoidance (sleeping, obsessing, compulsive behaviors, and keeping busy).[8] We may feel somewhat detached from ourselves, and our emotional responses may be flat, nonexistent, or inappropriate (laughing when we should be crying; crying when we should be happy).

I am convinced we do most of our codependent behaviors in this stage—obsessing, controlling, repressing feelings. I also believe many of our feelings of "craziness" are connected to this state. We feel crazy because we are lying to ourselves. We feel crazy because we are believing other people's lies. Nothing will help us feel crazy faster than being lied to. Believing lies disrupts the core of our being. The deep, instinctive part of us knows the truth, but we are pushing that part away and telling it, "You're wrong. Shut up." According to counselor Scott Egleston, we then decide there's something fundamentally wrong with us for being suspicious, and we label ourselves and our innermost, intuitive being as untrustworthy.

We are not denying whatever we are denying because we are stupid, stubborn, or deficient. We are not even consciously lying to ourselves. "Denial isn't lying," explained Noel Larsen, a licensed consulting psychologist. "It's not letting yourself know what reality is."

Denial is the bugaboo of life. It's like sleeping. We aren't aware of our actions until we've done them. We, on some level, really believe the lies *we* tell *ourselves*. There is a reason for that, too.

"In times of great stress, we shut down our awareness emotionally, sometimes intellectually, and occasionally physically," explained Claudia L. Jewett in *Helping Children Cope with Separation and Loss*. "A built-in mechanism operates to screen out devastating information and to prevent us from becoming overloaded. Psychologists tell us denial is a conscious or unconscious defense that all of us use to avoid, reduce, or prevent anxiety when we are threatened," Jewett continued. "We use it to shut out our awareness of things that would be too disturbing to know."[9]

Denial is the shock absorber for the soul. It is an instinctive and natural reaction to pain, loss, and change. It protects us. It wards off the blows of life until we can gather our other coping resources.

2. Anger

When we have quit denying our loss, we move into the next stage: anger. Our anger may be reasonable or unreasonable. We may be justified in venting our wrath, or we may irrationally vent our fury on anything and anyone. We may blame ourselves, God, and everyone around us for what we have lost. Depending on the nature of the loss, we may be a little peeved, somewhat angry, downright furious, or caught in the grips of a soul-shaking rage.

This is why setting someone straight, showing someone the light, or confronting a serious problem often does not turn out the way we expect. If we are denying a situation, we won't move directly into acceptance of reality—we'll move into anger. That is also why we need to be careful about major confrontations.

"The vocation of putting people straight, of tearing off their masks, of forcing them to face the repressed truth, is a highly dangerous and destructive calling," wrote John Powell in *Why Am I Afraid To Tell You Who I Am?* "He cannot live with some realization. In one way or another, he keeps his psychological pieces intact by some form of self-deception. . . . If the psychological pieces come unglued, who will pick them up and put poor Humpty Dumpty Human Being together again?"[10]

I have witnessed frightening and violent acts when people finally face a long-denied truth. If we are planning an intervention, we need to seek professional help.

3. Bargaining

After we have calmed down, we attempt to strike a bargain with life, ourselves, another person, or God. If we do such and such or if someone else does this or that, then we won't have to suffer the loss. We are not attempting to postpone the inevitable; we are attempting to prevent it.

Sometimes the deals we negotiate are reasonable and productive: "If my spouse and I get counseling, then we won't have to lose our relationship." Sometimes our bargains are absurd: "I used to think if I just kept the house cleaner or if I cleaned the refrigerator good enough this time, then my husband wouldn't drink any more," recalls the wife of an alcoholic.

4. Depression

When we see our bargain has not worked, when we finally become exhausted from our struggle to ward off reality, and when we decide to acknowledge what life has socked to us we become sad, sometimes terribly depressed. This is the essence of grief: mourning at its fullest. This is what we have been attempting at all costs to avoid. This is the time to cry, and it hurts. This stage of the process begins when we humbly surrender, says Esther Olson, a family counselor who works with the grief or, as she calls it, "forgiveness process." It will disappear, she says, only when the process has been worked out and through.

5. Acceptance

This is it. After we have closed our eyes, kicked, screamed, negotiated, and finally felt the pain, we arrive at a state of acceptance.

"It is not a resigned and hopeless 'giving up,' a sense of 'what's the use?' or 'I just cannot fight it any longer,' though we hear such statements too," wrote Elisabeth Kübler-Ross. "They also indicate the beginning of the end of the struggle, but the latter are not indications of acceptance. Acceptance should not be mistaken for a happy stage. It is almost void of feelings. It is as if the pain had gone, the struggle is over. . . ."[11]

We are at peace with what is. We are free to stay; free to go on; free to make whatever decisions we need to make. We are free! We have accepted our loss, however minor or significant. It has become an acceptable part of our present circumstances. We are comfortable with it and our lives. We have adjusted and reorganized. Once more, we are comfortable with our present circumstances and ourselves.

Not only are we comfortable with our circumstances and the changes we have endured, but we believe we have in some way benefitted from our loss or change even if we cannot fully understand how or why. We have faith that all is well, and we have grown from our experience. We deeply believe our present circumstances—every detail of them—are exactly as they ought to be for the moment. In spite of our fears, feelings, struggles, and confusion, we understand everything is okay even if we lack insight. We accept what is. We settle down. We stop running, ducking, controlling, and hiding. And we know it is only from this point that we can go forward.

This is how people accept things. Besides being called the grief process, counselor Esther Olson calls it the forgiveness process, the healing process, and the "way God works with us." It is not particularly comfortable. In fact, it is awkward and sometimes painful. We may feel like we're falling apart. When the process begins, we usually feel shock and panic. As we go through the stages, we often feel confused, vulnerable, lonely, and isolated. A sense of loss of control is usually present, as is hope, which is sometimes unrealistic.

We will probably go through this process for anything that is a fact in our lives that we have not accepted. A codependent person or a chemically dependent person may be in many stages of the grief process for several losses, all during the same time. Denial, depression, bargaining, and anger may all come rushing in. We may not know what we're trying to accept. We may not even know we're struggling to accept a situation. We may simply feel like we've gone crazy.

We haven't. Become familiar with this process. The entire process may take place in thirty seconds for a minor loss; it may last years or a lifetime when the loss is significant. Because this is a model, we may not go through the stages exactly as I have outlined them. We may travel back and forth: from anger to denial, from denial to bargaining, from bargaining back to denial. Regardless of the speed and route we travel through these stages, we must travel through them. Elisabeth Kübler-Ross says it is not only a normal process, it is a necessary process, and each stage is necessary. We must ward off the blows of life with denial until we are better prepared to deal with them. We must feel anger and blame until we have gotten them out of our system. We must try to negotiate, and we must cry. We don't necessarily have to let the stages dictate our behaviors, but each of us, for our well-being and ultimate acceptance, needs to spend individually appropriate time in each stage. Judi Hollis quoted Fritz Perls, the father of Gestalt therapy, in this manner: "The only way out is through."[12]

We are sturdy beings. But in many ways, we are fragile. We can accept change and loss, but this comes at our own pace and in our own way. And only we and God can determine that timing.

"Healthy are those who mourn," writes Donald L. Anderson, a minister and psychologist, in *Better Than Blessed*. "Only very recently have we begun to realize that to deny grief is to deny a natural human function and that such denial sometimes produces dire consequences," he continues. "Grief, like any genuine emotion, is accompanied by certain physical changes and the release of a form of psychic energy. If that energy is not expended in the normal process of grieving, it becomes destructive within the person. . . . Even physical illness can be a penalty for unresolved grief. . . . Any event, any awareness that contains a sense of loss for you can, and should, be mourned. This doesn't mean a life of incessant sadness. It means being willing to admit to an honest feeling rather than always having to laugh off the pain. It's not only permissible to admit the sadness that accompanies any loss—it's the healthy option."[13]

We can give ourselves permission to go through this process when we face loss and change, even minor losses and changes. Be gentle with ourselves. This is a draining, exhausting process. It can deplete our energy and throw us off balance. Watch how we pass through the stages and feel what we need to feel. Talk to people, people who are safe and will provide the comfort, support, and understanding we need. Talk it out; talk it through. One thing that helps me is thanking God for the loss—for my present circumstances—regardless of how I feel or what I think about them. Another thing that helps many people is the Serenity Prayer. We don't have to act or behave inappropriately, but we need to go through this. Other people do too. Understanding this process helps us be more supportive to other people, and it gives us the power to decide how we will behave and what to do to take care of ourselves when we go through it.

Learn the art of acceptance. It's a lot of grief.

ACTIVITY

1. Are you or is someone in your life going through this grief process for a major loss? Which stage do you think you or that person is in?

2. Review your life and consider the major losses and changes you have gone through. Recall your experiences with the grief process. Write about your feelings as you remember them.

13

FEEL YOUR OWN FEELINGS

When I repress my emotions,
my stomach keeps score . . .[1]

—John Powell

"I used to facilitate groups to help people deal with their feelings," says the wife of an alcoholic. "I used to openly express my emotions. Now, after eight years in this relationship, I couldn't tell you what I was feeling if my life depended on it."

As codependents, we frequently lose touch with the emotional part of ourselves. Sometimes we withdraw emotionally to avoid being crushed. Being emotionally vulnerable is dangerous. Hurt becomes piled upon hurt, and no one seems to care. It becomes safer to go away. We become overloaded with pain, so we short-circuit to protect ourselves.

We may withdraw emotionally from certain people—people we think may hurt us. We don't trust them, so we hide the emotional part of us when we are around them.

Sometimes we feel forced to withdraw our emotions. Family systems, suffering from the effects of alcoholism and other disorders, reject emotional honesty and at times appear to demand dishonesty. Consider our attempts to tell a drunk how we *felt* about him or her smashing up the car, ruining the birthday party, or throwing up in our bed. Our feelings may provoke unpleasant reactions in others, such as anger. Expressing our feelings may even be dangerous to our physical well-being, because they rock the family boat.

Even families that have no history of alcoholism reject feelings. "Don't feel that way. That feeling is inappropriate. In fact, don't even feel," may be the message we hear. We quickly learn the lie that our feelings don't count, that our feelings are somehow wrong. Our feelings are not listened to, so we quit listening to them too.

It may appear easier, at times, to not feel. We have so much responsibility because we have taken on so much responsibility for the people around us. We must do what is necessary anyway. Why take the time to feel? What would it change?

Sometimes we try to make our feelings disappear because we are afraid of them. To acknowledge how we really feel would demand a decision—action or change—on our part.[2] It would bring us face to face with reality. We would become aware of what we're thinking, what we want, and what we need to do. And we're not ready to do that yet.

Codependents are oppressed, depressed, and repressed. Many of us can quickly tell what someone else is feeling, why that person is feeling that way, how long they've felt that way, and what that person is probably going to do because of that feeling. Many of us spend our lives fussing about other people's feelings. We try to fix people's feelings. We try to control other people's feelings. We don't want to hurt people, we don't want to upset them, and we don't want to offend them. We feel so responsible for other people's feelings. Yet, we don't know what we are feeling. If we do, we don't know what to do to fix ourselves. Many of us have abandoned or never taken responsibility for our emotional selves.

Just how important are feelings, anyway? Before I answer that question, let me tell you about when I was in treatment for chemical dependency at Willmar State Hospital, Willmar, Minnesota, in 1973. I was faced with kicking a ten-year habit of alcohol, heroin, dilaudid, morphine, methadone, cocaine, barbiturate, amphetamine, marijuana, and any other substance that even remotely promised to change the way I felt. When I asked my counselor, Ruth Anderson, and other counselors how to do this, they replied: "Deal with your feelings." (They also suggested I attend Alcoholics Anonymous. More on that later.) I did start dealing with my feelings. It felt terrible at first. I had emotional explosions that I thought would rip the top of my head off. But it worked. I experienced my first days and months of sobriety. Then, it came time to leave treatment. I was faced with the unlikely prospect of trying to fit myself into society. I had no resume; it can be difficult for a heroin addict to find and maintain gainful employment. I had to discontinue my relationships with everyone I knew who used chemicals, which was everyone I knew. My family was skeptical about my recovery and still understandably peeved about some of the things I had done. Generally, I had left a trail of destruction and chaos behind me, and I didn't think there was any place in society for me. My life stretched ahead of me, and it held little promise. At the same time, my counselor was telling me to go ahead and start living. Again, I asked her exactly how I should do that. Again, she and others replied: "Keep dealing with your feelings. Go to A.A. And everything will be okay."

It sounded a bit simplistic to me, but I didn't have much choice. Amazingly, and thanks to the help of a Higher Power, it's worked so far. I got into deep water with my codependency when I thought myself too sophisticated to deal with feelings. The moral of this story is that dealing with feelings and going to A.A. can help us recover from chemical dependency. But it goes beyond that, and it answers the question I asked earlier, "How important are feelings?"

Feelings are not the end all and be all to living. Feelings must not dictate or control our behaviors, but we can't ignore our feelings either. They won't be ignored.

Our feelings are very important. They count. They matter. The emotional part of us is special. If we make feelings go away, if we push them away, we lose an important part of us and our lives. Feelings are our source of joy, as well as sadness, fear, and anger. The emotional part of us is the part that laughs as well as cries. The emotional part of us is the center for giving and receiving the warm glow of love. That part of us lets us feel close to people. That part of us lets us enjoy touch and other sensual feelings.

Our feelings are also indicators. When we feel happy, comfortable, warm, and content, we usually know all is well in our world, for the present moment. When we feel uncomfortable with anger, fear, or sadness, our feelings are telling us there's a problem. The problem may be inside us—something we're doing or thinking—or it may be external. But something is going wrong.

Feelings can be positive motivators too. Anger can motivate us to solve a bothersome problem. Fear encourages us to run from danger. Repeated hurt and emotional pain tell us to stay away.

Our feelings can also provide us with clues to ourselves: our desires, wants, and ambitions. They help us discover ourselves, what we are really thinking. Our emotions also tap into that deep part of us that seeks and knows truth, and desires self-preservation, self-enhancement, safety, and goodness. Our emotions are connected to our conscious, cognitive thought process and to that mysterious gift called instinct or intuition.

There is, however, a darker side to emotions. Emotional pain hurts. It can hurt so badly we think all we are or ever will be is our emotional part. Pain and sadness can linger. Fear can be a stopper; it can prevent us from doing the things we want and need to do to live our lives.

Sometimes we can get stuck in emotions—trapped in a well of a certain dark feeling—and think we'll never get out. Anger can fester into resentments and bitterness and threaten to linger indefinitely. Sadness can turn into depression, almost smothering us. Some of us live with fear for long periods of time.

Our feelings can trick us too. Our emotions can lead us into situations where our heads tell us not to go. Sometimes feelings are like cotton candy; they appear to be more than they actually are.

In spite of the darker side of emotions—the painful ones, the ones that linger, and the tricky ones—there is an even bleaker picture if we choose to become unemotional. Not feeling our feelings, withdrawing emotionally, and pushing that part of us away can be unpleasant, unhealthy, and self-destructive.

Repressing or denying feelings can lead to headaches, stomach disorders, backaches, and generally weakened physical conditions which can open the door to many illnesses. Repressing feelings—particularly if we are doing it during the denial stage of the grief process—can lead us into trouble with overeating, undereating, alcohol and other drug use, compulsive sexual behaviors, compulsive spending, not sleeping enough, sleeping too much, obsessing, controlling gestures, and other compulsive behaviors.[3]

Feelings are energy. Repressed feelings block our energy. We don't do our best when we're blocked.

Another problem with repressed feelings is they don't go away. They linger, sometimes growing stronger and causing us to do many peculiar things. We have to stay one step ahead of the feeling, we have to stay busy, we have to do *something*. We don't dare get quiet and peaceful because we might then feel these emotions. And the feeling might squeak out anyway, causing us to do something we never intended to do: scream at the kids, kick the cat, spill on our favorite dress, or cry at the party. We get stuck in feelings because we're trying to repress them, and like a persistent neighbor, they will not go away until we acknowledge their presence.

The big reason for not repressing feelings is that emotional withdrawal causes us to lose our positive feelings. We lose the ability to feel. Sometimes, this may be a welcome relief if the pain becomes too great or too constant, but this is not a good plan for living. We may shut down our deep needs—our need to love and be loved—when we shut down our emotions. We may lose our ability to enjoy sex, the human touch. We lose the ability to feel close to people, otherwise known as intimacy. We lose our capacity to enjoy the pleasant things in life.

We lose touch with ourselves and our environment. We are no longer in touch with our instincts. We become unaware of what our feelings are telling us and any problems in our environment. We lose the motivating power of feelings. If we aren't feeling, we're probably not examining the thinking that goes with it, and we don't know what our selves are telling us. And if we don't deal with our feelings we don't change and we don't grow. We stay stuck.

Feelings might not always be a barrel of gladness, but repressing them can be downright miserable. So what's the solution? What do we do with these pesky feelings that seem to be both a burden and a delight?

We feel them. We *can* feel. It's okay to feel our feelings. It's okay for us to have feelings—all of them. It's even okay for men to feel. Feelings are not wrong. They're not inappropriate. We don't need to feel guilty about feelings. Feelings are not acts; feeling homicidal rage is entirely different from committing homicide. Feelings shouldn't be judged as either good or bad. Feelings are emotional energy; they are not personality traits.

People say there are hundreds of different feelings, ranging from peeved to miffed to exuberant to delighted and so on. Some therapists have cut the list to four: mad, sad, glad, and scared. These are the four primary feeling groups, and all the rest are shades and variations. For instance, lonely and "down in the dumps" would fall in the sad category; anxiety and nervousness would be variations of the scared theme; tickled pink and happy would qualify as glad. You can call them whatever you want; the important idea is to feel them.

That doesn't mean we have to always be on guard for one feeling or the other. It doesn't mean we have to devote an extraordinary amount of our lives to wallowing in emotional muck. In fact, dealing with our feelings means we can move out of the muck. It means if a feeling—emotional energy—comes our way, we feel it. We take a few moments, acknowledge the sensation, and move on to the next step. We don't censor. We don't block. We don't run from. We don't tell ourselves, "Don't feel that. Something must be wrong with me." We don't pass judgment on ourselves for our feelings. We experience them. We allow the energy to pass through our bodies, and we accept it as being our emotional energy, our feeling. We say, "Okay."

Next, we do that mystical thing so many people refer to as "dealing with our feelings." We appropriately respond to our emotion. We examine the thoughts that go with it, and we accept them without repression or censorship.[+]

Then, we decide whether there is a next step. This is where we do our judging. This is where our moral code comes into play. We still don't judge ourselves for having the feeling. We decide what, if anything, we want to do about the feeling and the accompanying thought. We evaluate the situation, then choose a behavior in line with our moral code and our new ideal of self-care. Is there a problem we need to solve? Is our thinking off base? We may need to correct certain disaster-oriented thought patterns, such as: "I feel horribly afraid and sad because the car broke down, and it's the end of the world." It would be more accurate to say: "I feel sad that the car is broken." Is the problem something we can solve? Does it concern another person? Is it necessary or appropriate to discuss the feeling with that person? If so, when? Perhaps it is sufficient to merely feel the emotion and acknowledge the thought. If you are in doubt about what action to take, if the feeling is particularly strong, or if the action you decide to take is radical, I suggest waiting a day or so, until you are peaceful and your mind is consistent. In other words: detach.

Our feelings don't need to control us. Just because we're angry, we don't have to scream and hit. Just because we're sad or depressed, we don't have to lie in bed all day. Just because we're scared, doesn't mean we don't apply for that job. I am not in any way implying or suggesting we allow our emotions to control our behaviors. In fact, what I am saying is the opposite: if we don't feel our feelings and deal with them responsibly, they *will* control us. If we are dealing with our emotions responsibly, we submit them to our intellect, our reason, and our moral and behavioral code of ethics.[5]

Responding appropriately to our feelings also means we are liable for our feelings. Each person's feelings are his or her own. Nobody makes anyone feel; no one is ultimately responsible for our feelings except us, *no matter how much we insist they are.* People might help us feel, but they don't *make* us feel. People also cannot change the way we feel. Only we can do that. Furthermore, we are not responsible for anyone else's feelings, although we are responsible for choosing to be considerate of people's feelings. Responsible people choose to do that, at times. However, most codependents choose to overdo that. We need to be considerate of our feelings, too. Our feelings are reactions to life's circumstances. Thus, etiquette requires that when you discuss a feeling with someone, you say, "I feel such and such when you do such and such because . . ." not "You made me feel. . . ."[6]

However, we may want to make another decision about how to deal with our feelings. This is especially true if we are consistently reacting to someone's behavior with a great deal of emotional distress, and even after reporting this distress to the person he or she continues causing us pain. Maybe you don't need that much help to feel. Remember, feelings are indicators and motivators. Watch for patterns in our feelings. They tell us a great deal about ourselves and our relationships.

Sometimes, dealing with feelings means a change of thinking is needed. Many therapies acknowledge a direct correlation between what we think and what we feel.[7] There is a connection. What we think influences how we feel. Sometimes inaccurate, overreactive, or inappropriate thought patterns cause our emotions or cause them to remain longer than necessary. If we think something is awful, will never get better, and just shouldn't be, our feelings will be intense. I call this disaster thinking. That's why it is important, after we feel our emotions, to examine our thinking. Get it out in the light. If it's inappropriate, then we know what we have to do to solve our problem, don't we?

There are times when we may need to discuss our feelings and thoughts with other people. It is not healthy to live our lives in isolation. Sharing the emotional part of us with others creates closeness and intimacy. Also, being accepted by someone else for being who we are helps us accept ourselves. This is always a marvelous experience. Sometimes, we may want to discuss things with a friend who will just listen, while we air things and try to figure out what's going on. Things we lock inside can get too big and too powerful. Letting them out in the air makes them smaller. We gain perspective. It's always fun to share the pleasant feelings too: the joys, the successes, the "tickled-pinks." And if we want an intimate relationship with someone, we need to discuss our persistent feelings with him or her. It's called emotional honesty.

Caution: intense happy feelings can be as distracting and scary as intense sad feelings, especially to codependents who are not used to happy feelings, according to Scott Egleston. Many codependents believe happy feelings must always be followed by sad feelings, because that is the way it has usually happened in the past. Some codependents believe we can't, shouldn't, and don't deserve to feel happy. Sometimes we do things to create sad feelings after experiencing happy feelings, or whenever the possibility of a happy feeling exists. It's okay to feel happy. It's okay to feel sad. Let the emotional energy pass through, and strive for peace and balance.

There are times when we may need professional help to deal with our emotions. If we are stuck in any particular feeling we should give ourselves what we need. See a counselor, a therapist, a psychoanalyst, or a clergyperson. Take care of ourselves. We deserve it. We may also want to seek professional help if we've been repressing feelings for a long period of time or if we suspect what we've been repressing is intense.

Sometimes, it just takes only a little practice and awareness to awaken the emotional part of us. The following things help me get in touch with my feelings: physical exercise, writing letters I don't intend to send, talking to people I feel safe with, and spending quiet time in meditation. We need to make awareness of ourselves a habit. We need to pay attention to the "shouldn't feel that way" attitudes we tell ourselves; we need to pay attention to our level of comfortableness; we need to listen to what we're thinking and saying and the tone of voice we use; we need to keep an eye on what we're doing. We will find our way to and through our emotions, a way that works for us.

We need to invite emotions into our lives. Then make a commitment to take gentle, loving care of them. Feel our feelings. Trust our feelings and trust ourselves. We are wiser than we think.

ACTIVITY

1. Read through your journal writings. What emotions were squeaking or pouring out as you wrote?

2. Let's play a "what if" game. What if you could be feeling anything you wanted right now, and feeling that way wouldn't make you a bad person. What would you be feeling? Write about it.

3. Find someone who is safe, a good listener, accepting, and nonrescuing, and begin honestly and openly discussing your feelings with that person. Listen to that person's feelings without judgment or caretaking gestures. This is nice, isn't it? If you don't know anybody you feel safe doing that with, join a support group.

14

ANGER

"What is it about me that you hate so much?"
a man asked his wife six months into his sobriety.
"Everything!" she replied with a glare.

—Anonymous quote

For many years I rarely felt anger. I cried. I felt hurt. But anger? No, not me.

After I began my recovery from codependency, I wondered if I would ever *not* be angry.

Janet Woititz described me in this quote from *Marriage on the Rocks*: "You become rigid and mistrustful. Rage consumes you without a satisfying outlet. Anyone who walks into your house can feel the angry vibrations. There is no escape from it. Whoever thought you would turn into such a self-righteous witch?"[1]

Angry feelings are a part of almost everyone's life. Children feel anger; teenagers feel anger; adults feel anger. Sometimes, anger plays a small part in our lives and presents no particular problem. We blow off steam, and we're done with it. We go on with the business of living, and the problem is resolved.

That is usually not the case with codependents, particularly if we are involved with an alcoholic, an addict, or someone with a serious ongoing problem. Anger can become a large part of our lives. It can *become* our lives. The alcoholic is mad, we're mad, the kids are mad, and so is the dog. Everyone is mad, all the time. Nobody ever seems to blow off enough steam. Even if we aren't shouting, even if we're trying to pretend we're not angry, we're mad. We give looks and make little gestures that give us away. Hostility lurks just below the surface, waiting for a chance to come out in the open. The anger sometimes explodes like a bomb, but nobody ever gets done with it. The alcoholic says, "How dare you become angry with me? I'm the king. I'll get angry with you, but not the other way around." The codependent says, "After all I've done for you, I'll get angry any time I please." But silently, the codependent wonders: Maybe he or she is right. . . . How dare we get angry with the alcoholic? There must be something wrong with us for feeling this way. We deal another blow to our self-worth with a little guilt tacked on. Plus, the anger is still there. The problems don't get resolved; the anger doesn't blow over. It festers and boils.

Even with the gift of sobriety or recovery from any ongoing problem, the anger may and usually does linger.[2] Usually, it has reached a peak by the time the alcoholic gets help. Nobody, including the alcoholic, can stand the insanity any longer. Sometimes it gets worse. The codependent may learn for the first time that *it* isn't the codependent's fault. The codependent may even feel new anger for having believed for so long it was! It may be safe for the first time for the codependent to feel and express anger. Things may finally have calmed down enough for the codependent to realize how angry he or she was and is. This can cause more conflicts. The alcoholic may expect and want to start fresh—minus the dirty laundry from the past—now that he or she has begun a new life.

So the alcoholic says, "How dare you get angry now? We're starting over."

And the codependent replies, "That's what *you* think. I'm just getting started."

Then the codependent may add to his or her low self-worth and guilt another silent, torturing thought: "The alcoholic is right. How dare I be angry now? I should be ecstatic. I should be grateful. There's something wrong with *me*."

Then everyone feels guilty, because everyone feels angry. And everyone feels angrier because they feel guilty. They feel cheated and mad because sobriety did not bring the joy it had promised. It was not the turning point for living happily ever after. Don't misunderstand. It's better. It's a lot better when people become sober. But sobriety is not a magical cure for anger and relationship problems. The old anger burns away. New anger fuels the fire. The chemical or problem can no longer be blamed, although it frequently still is. The chemicals can no longer be used to medicate the angry feelings. Often, codependents can no longer even get the sympathy and nurturing we need from friends. We think it's wonderful that the alcoholic has quit drinking or the problem has been solved. What's wrong with us? we ask. Can't we forgive and forget? And once more the codependent wonders, What is wrong with me?

Anger may be a commonplace emotion, but it is tough to deal with. Most of us haven't been taught how to deal with anger, because people show us how they deal with anger; they don't teach us. And most people show us inappropriate ways to deal with anger because they're not sure either.

People may give us good advice. "Be angry, but do not sin; do not let the sun go down on your anger."[3] "Don't seek revenge." Many of us can't adhere to these mandates. Some of us think they mean: "Don't be angry." Many of us aren't sure what we believe about anger. Some of us believe lies about anger.

Frequently, codependents and other people believe the following myths about anger:

- It's not okay to feel angry.
- Anger is a waste of time and energy.
- Good, nice people don't feel angry.
- We shouldn't feel angry when we do.
- We'll lose control and go crazy if we get angry.
- People will go away if we get angry with them.
- Other people should never feel anger toward us.
- If others get angry with us, we must have done something wrong.
- If other people are angry with us, we made them feel that way and we're responsible for fixing their feelings.

- If we feel angry, someone else made us feel that way and that person is responsible for fixing our feelings.
- If we feel angry with someone, the relationship is over and that person has to go away.
- If we feel angry with someone, we should punish that person for making us feel angry.
- If we feel angry with someone, that person has to change what he or she is doing so we don't feel angry any more.
- If we feel angry, we have to hit someone or break something.
- If we feel angry, we have to shout and holler.
- If we feel angry with someone, it means we don't love that person any more.
- If someone feels angry with us, it means that person doesn't love us any more.
- Anger is a sinful emotion.
- It's okay to feel angry only when we can *justify* our feelings.[4]

Many people in programs such as Alcoholics Anonymous believe they should never feel angry in their recovery. The idea intended by recovery programs is that people learn to deal appropriately and immediately with anger, before it builds into harmful resentments.

As codependents, we may be frightened of our anger and other people's anger. Maybe we believe one or more of the myths. Or maybe we're frightened of anger for other reasons. Someone may have hit or abused us when he or she was angry. Some of us may have hit or abused someone else when we felt angry. Sometimes just the raw level of energy that accompanies someone's anger can be frightening, particularly if that person is drunk.

We react to anger, both ours and other people's. It is a provocative emotion. It can be contagious. And many of us have so much of it to react to. We have so much of the anger that accompanies grief. We have the anger that comes from the persecution stage of rescuing or caretaking. Many of us are stuck on that corner of the triangle. We have unreasonable anger feelings that may be unjustified and caused by reactive, disastrous thinking: the shoulds, awfuls, nevers, and always. We have justified anger—all the mad feelings anyone would feel if someone did *that* to him or her. We have the anger that covers up hurt and fear. Sad and scared feelings convert into anger, and many of us have so much hurt and fear. We have anger that comes from feeling guilty. Guilt, both earned and unearned, easily converts into anger.[5] Codependents have a lot of that too. Believe it or not, so do alcoholics. They're just more adept at converting it into anger.

And we have reactive anger. We get angry because the other person feels angry. Then they get angrier, and we get angrier because they got angrier. Soon everybody's angry, and no one is sure why. But we're all mad—and feeling guilty about it.

Sometimes, we prefer to stay angry. It helps us feel less vulnerable and more powerful. It's like a protective shield. If we're angry, we won't feel hurt or scared, at least not noticeably so.

Sadly, many of us have had no place to go with all that anger. We swallow it, bite our tongues, stiffen our shoulders, push it into our stomachs, let it rattle around in our heads, run from it, medicate it, or give it a cookie. We blame ourselves, turn anger into depression, put ourselves to bed, hope to die, and get sick because of it. Finally we ask God to forgive us for being such horrible people for feeling anger in the first place.

Many of us have been in a real dilemma with our anger, especially if we are living in a family system that says, "Don't feel; especially don't feel angry." The alcoholic certainly doesn't want to hear about how mad we feel. He or she probably thinks our anger is unreasonable anyway, and it may bother him or her when we discuss it. Our anger may push the alcoholic's guilt buttons. The alcoholic may even overpower us with his or her anger just to keep us guilty and repressed.

Frequently we can't or don't want to tell our parents how we feel. They may be mad at us for having a friendship with someone who has an alcohol or other drug problem. Or our parents may only see the good side of the alcoholic or addict and think we're unreasonable and unappreciative. Our friends may even become sick of hearing us complain.

Some of us may feel so ashamed that we believe we can't tell our pastor or priest how angry we are. The clergy would just call us sinners, and we don't need to hear any more of that. That's all we've been telling ourselves. Many of us wouldn't think of turning to our Higher Power and expressing how angry we are.

So what do we do with all this built-up steam? The same thing we do with almost everything that has to do with us: we repress it and feel guilty about it. Repressed anger, like other repressed emotions, causes problems. Sometimes our anger may leak out inappropriately. We scream at someone we didn't intend to scream at. We wrinkle up our faces, curl our lips, and help people feel like they don't want to be around us. We slam dishes around even though we can't afford to break anything of material value because we've already lost so much.

Other times our anger may show its face in different ways. We may find ourselves not wanting, unable, or refusing to enjoy sex.[6] We may find ourselves unable to enjoy anything. Then we add more self-hatred to our already heaping pile by wondering what is wrong with us and going on our hostile way. When people ask us what's wrong, we tighten our jaw and say, "Nothing. I feel just fine, thank you." We may even start doing little sneaky mean things or big sneaky mean things to get even with those we're angry at.

If anger is repressed long enough, it will ultimately do more than leak out. Unpleasant feelings are like weeds. They don't go away when we ignore them; they grow wild and take over. Our angry feelings may one day come roaring out. We say things we don't mean. Or, as usually happens, we may say what we really mean. We may lose control and unleash ourselves in a fighting, spitting, screeching, hair-pulling, dish-breaking rage. Or we may do something to hurt ourselves. Or the anger may harden into bitterness, hatred, contempt, revulsion, or resentment.

And we still wonder, "What's wrong with me?"

We can repeat it to ourselves as often as necessary: There's nothing wrong with us. Like the book title says, *Of Course You're Angry!*[7] Of course we're *that* angry. We're that steamed because anybody in his or her right mind would be that steamed. An excellent quote from *Marriage on the Rocks* follows:

"You cannot live with active alcoholism without being profoundly affected. Any human being who is bombarded with what you've been bombarded with is to be commended for sheer survival. You deserve a medal for the mere fact that you're around to tell the story."[8]

Anger is one profound effect of alcoholism. It is also an effect of many of the other compulsive disorders or problems codependents find themselves living with.

Even if we're not living with a serious problem or seriously ill person, it is still okay to feel anger when it occurs. Anger is one of the many profound effects life has on us. It's one of our emotions. And we're going to feel it when it comes our way—or else repress it. "I don't trust people who never get mad. People either get mad, or get even," says my friend Sharon George, who is a professional in the mental health field.

We have every right to feel anger. We have every right to feel as angry as we feel. So do other people. But we also have a responsibility—primarily to ourselves—to deal with our anger appropriately.

We're back to our original advice: Deal with our feelings. How do we deal with an emotion as potent as anger? How do we quit feeling that angry? When does it happen? Where does it go? Who can we talk to? Who would want to listen to all that? We probably don't even want to hear it ourselves. After all, the person we're mad at does have a disease. So shouldn't we be feeling compassion and all that good stuff? Is it really all right to be this mad at a sick person?

Yes, we have the right to be mad at a sick person. We didn't ask for the problem. Although the ideal feeling is compassion, we probably won't feel this until we deal with our anger. Somewhere between homicidal rage and biting our tongue because we feel sorry for that sick person is a way to get past our angry feelings—the old ones and the new ones. But I don't believe dealing with repressed emotions will happen overnight. It may not happen in a month or even a year. How long did it take us to get this angry? Dealing with a significant amount of repressed anger may take time and effort. Dealing with new anger takes practice.

Here are some suggestions for dealing with anger:

- *Address any myths we have subscribed to about anger.* Give ourselves permission to feel angry when we need to. Give other people permission to feel angry too.
- *Feel the emotion.* Even though it's anger, it's only emotional energy. It is not right or wrong; it calls for no judgment. Anger doesn't have to be justified or rationalized. If the energy is there, feel it. Feel any underlying emotions too, such as hurt or fear.
- *Acknowledge the thoughts that accompany the feeling.* Preferably, say these thoughts aloud.
- *Examine the thinking that goes with the feeling.* Hold it up to the light. See if there are any flaws in it. Watch for patterns and repetitive situations. We'll learn much about ourselves and our environment. Often, recovering alcoholics develop rancid thought patterns, known as stinking thinking, that can indicate the desire to start drinking again.
- *Make a responsible decision about what, if any, action we need to take.* Figure out what our anger is telling us. Is our anger indicating a problem in us or in our environment that needs attention? Sometimes while we're asking God to help us stop feeling angry, He's trying to tell us something. Do we need change? Do we need something from somebody else? Much anger comes from unmet needs. One quick way to resolve anger is to stop screaming at the person we're angry with, figure out what we need from that person, and ask him or her for that. If he or she won't or can't give it to us, figure out what we need to do next to take care of ourselves.
- *Don't let anger control us.* If we find ourselves being controlled by our angry feelings, we can stop ourselves. We don't have to continue screaming. Don't misinterpret; sometimes screaming helps. Sometimes, however, it doesn't. It's better if we decide, instead of letting our anger decide for us. We don't have to lose control of our actions. It's just energy, not a magical curse over us. Detach. Go to another room. Go to another house. Get peaceful. Then figure out what we need to do. We don't have to let other people's anger control us. I frequently hear codependents say, "I can't do this or that because he

(or she) will get angry." Don't jeopardize our safety, but strive to be free from anger's control—our anger or anyone else's. We don't have to react to anger. It's only emotional energy. We don't even have to react by becoming angry, if we don't want to. Try it sometime.

- *Openly and honestly discuss our anger, when it's appropriate.* But don't talk to a drunk when he's drunk. We can make good decisions about expressing our anger openly and appropriately. Beware of how we approach people, though. Anger frequently begets anger. Instead of venting our rage on the person, we can feel our feelings, think our thoughts, figure out what we need from that person, and then go back to him or her and express that need, instead of hollering.

- *Take responsibility for our anger.* We can say: "I feel angry when you do this because . . ." not, "You made me mad." However, I like to give people a little room in communication. We don't always have to say the words exactly right, as if we just walked out of a therapy group. Be ourselves. Just understand we are responsible for our angry feelings—even if they are an appropriate reaction to someone else's inappropriate behavior.

- *Talk to people we trust.* Talking about anger and being listened to and accepted really help clear the air. It helps us accept ourselves. Remember, we can't move forward until we accept where we are. And yes, people care. We may have to leave our house to find them, or go to Al-Anon meetings, but they are out there. If we have angry feelings that have hardened into resentments, we can talk them out with a clergyperson or take a Fourth and Fifth Step. Resentments may be hurting us a lot more than they're helping us.

- *Burn off the anger energy.* Clean the kitchen. Play softball. Exercise. Go dancing. Shovel the snow. Rake the yard. Build a condominium if necessary. Anger is extremely stressful, and it helps to physically discharge that energy.

- *Don't beat ourselves or others for feeling angry.* Don't let other people hit us or abuse us in any way when they feel angry. Don't hurt other people when we're angry. Seek professional help if abuse has occurred.

- *Write letters we don't intend to send.* If we feel guilty about anger, this really helps. Start the letter by asking: "If I could feel angry about anything, nobody would ever know, and it wasn't wrong to feel this way, what I would be angry about is this . . ." Once our anger is out on paper we can get past the guilt and figure out how to deal with it. If we are suffering from depression, this exercise may help too.

• *Deal with guilt.* Get rid of the unearned guilt. Get rid of all of it. Guilt doesn't help. God will forgive us for anything we have done. Besides, I bet He doesn't think we've done as much wrong as we think we have.

Once we begin dealing with anger, we may notice we feel angry much of the time. That's common. We're like kids with a new toy. We'll settle down with it. Be patient. We aren't going to deal with it perfectly. No one does. We'll make mistakes, but we'll also learn from them. The reason we're told to not seek revenge is because getting even is a common response to anger. If we've done or do some inappropriate things, deal with earned guilt and go on from there. Strive for progress.

We need to be gentle with ourselves if we've been repressing loads of angry feelings. Things take time. We may need to be that angry for now. When we don't need to be angry any more, we'll quit feeling angry if we want to. If we think we might be stuck in anger, get professional help.

Some people believe we never have to become angry; if we control our thinking and are appropriately detached, we will never react with or wallow around in anger. That's probably true; however, I prefer to relax and see what happens, rather than guard myself rigidly. And like my friend, I'm leery of people who smile and tell me they never get mad. Don't misunderstand—I'm not advising us to hang onto anger or resentments. I don't believe anger should become our focus in life, nor should we look for reasons to become angry to test ourselves. "It's not good to be angry all the time," says counselor Esther Olson. It's not healthy to act hostile. There is much more to life than anger.

But it's okay to feel anger when we need to.

ACTIVITY

1. What do you think would happen if you started feeling your angry feelings?

2. What do you believe deep inside about anger? What myths about anger have you subscribed to? If you need to subscribe to new beliefs about anger, do so. Attack the myths whenever they try to attack you.

3. How do the people in your current family situation deal with anger? How did your mother, father, brothers, and sisters deal with their anger? What's your pattern for dealing with anger?

4. If you have repressed anger, write about it in your notebook. You may need to buy a new notebook and devote it to anger.

5. If anger is a troublesome emotion for you, keep a pencil and paper handy and start writing about your anger as it occurs throughout the day.

15

YES, YOU CAN THINK

For God hath not given us the spirit of fear,
but of power, and of love, and of a sound mind.[1]

—II Timothy 1:7

"What do *you* think I should do?" a client, who was in the throes of her codependency, once asked me. The woman was facing a significant decision regarding her husband and children.

"What do *you* think?" I asked.

"You're asking *me*?" she asked. "It takes me fifteen minutes at the grocery store to decide if I want to buy the 59-cent or the 63-cent bottle of bleach. I can't make the tiniest decisions. How do you expect me to make a big, important one like this?"

As codependents, many of us don't trust our minds. We truly understand the horror of indecision. The smallest choices, such as what to order at the restaurant or which bottle of bleach to purchase, paralyze us. The larger significant decisions we face, such as how to solve our problems, what to do with our lives, and who to live with, can overwhelm us. Many of us simply give up and refuse to think about these things. Some of us allow other people or circumstances to make these choices for us.

This is a short chapter, but it's an important one. Throughout the book, I have been encouraging you to think about things, figure things out, decide what you need, decide what you want, and decide how to solve your problems. Some of you may be wondering if that's possible.

The purpose of this chapter is to tell you that you can think, you can figure things out, and you can make decisions—good, healthy decisions.

For a variety of reasons, we may have lost faith in our ability to think and reason things out. Believing lies, lying to ourselves (denial), chaos, stress, low self-esteem, and a stomach full of repressed emotions may cloud our ability to think. We become confused. That doesn't mean we *can't* think.

Overreacting may impair our mental functioning. Decisiveness is hindered by worrying about what other people think, telling ourselves we have to be perfect, and telling ourselves to hurry. We falsely believe we can't make the "wrong" choice, we'll never have another chance, and the whole world waits and rises on this particular decision. We don't have to do these things to ourselves.

Hating ourselves, telling ourselves we won't make good decisions, and then throwing in a batch of "shoulds" every time we try to make decisions, doesn't help our thinking process, either.

Not listening to our needs and wants, and telling ourselves that what we desire is wrong, cheats us out of the information we need to make good choices. Second-guessing and "what ifs" don't help either. We're learning to love, trust, and listen to ourselves.

Maybe we've been using our minds inappropriately, to worry and obsess, and our minds are tired, abused, and filled with anxious thoughts. We're learning to stop these patterns also.

Perhaps we lost faith in our ability to think because people have told us we can't think and make good decisions. Our parents may have directly or indirectly done this when we were children. They may have told us we were stupid. Or they may have made all our decisions for us. Maybe they criticized all our choices. Or they could have confused us by denying or by refusing to acknowledge our ability to think when we pointed out problems in the home.

Maybe we had difficulties with subjects in school when we were young; instead of doing what we needed to do to solve the problem, we gave up and told ourselves we couldn't think and figure things out.

People may have put down the intelligence of women, but that's non-sense. We're not stupid. Women can think. Men can think. Children can think. We may be living with people now who are telling us directly or indirectly that we can't think. Some of them may even be telling us we're crazy, but alcoholics do that to people they live with. Maybe we've started wondering if we are crazy! But don't believe any of it for one moment.

We can think. Our minds work well. We can figure things out. We can make decisions. We can figure out what we want and need to do and when it is time to do that. And we can make choices that enhance our self-esteem.

We're even entitled to opinions! And yes, we do have some of those. We can think appropriately and rationally. We even have the power to evaluate ourselves and our thoughts, so we can correct our thinking when it becomes disastrous or irrational.

We can evaluate our behavior. We can make decisions about what we need and want. We can figure out what our problems are and what we need to do to solve them. We can make little decisions and big decisions. We may feel frustrated when we try to make decisions or solve problems, but that's normal. Sometimes we need to become frustrated to make a breakthrough in our thinking. It's all part of the process.

Remember, decisions don't have to be made perfectly. We don't have to be perfect. We don't even have to be nearly perfect. We can just be who we are. We can make mistakes in our choices. We're not so fragile we can't handle making a mistake. It's no big deal! It's part of living. We can learn from our mistakes, or we can simply make another decision. The following quotation discusses decisiveness in the corporate world, but I believe it applies to other areas of life too.

"If you make a decision, you'll become a hero within the corporate culture. If 30 percent of your decisions are right, you're going to be a big hitter."[2]

We can even change our minds. Then change them again. Then again. Codependents vacillate.[3] As codependents, we are in the midst of upsetting situations. We may go back and forth a lot; we may throw the alcoholic out, then take him or her back. We may leave, then come back, then leave again. This is how we get to where we're going. It's okay. Let's take it one step further—it's normal and often necessary.

"But," a codependent may object, "you don't know my mind. Sometimes I think terrible thoughts. Sometimes I have unspeakable fantasies." We all do, and it's normal, especially if we're living with an alcoholic. We may have attended an alcoholic spouse's funeral 100 times in our minds. Our thoughts are keys to our feelings. Our feelings are keys to our thoughts. We don't have to repress. We need to let the thoughts and feelings pass through, then figure out what we need to do to take care of ourselves.

The following suggestions may help us gain confidence in our mental abilities:

- *Treat our minds to some peace.* Detach. Get calm. If we're facing a decision, big or small, get peaceful first, then decide. Wait until our minds are consistent. If we absolutely can't make a decision on a particular day, then it's obviously not time to make that decision. When it is time, we'll be able to do it. And do it well.

- *Ask God to help us think.* Every morning, I ask Him to give me the right thought, word, or action. I ask Him to send His inspiration and guidance. I ask Him to help me solve my problems.[4] I believe He does help. I know He does. But He expects me to do my part and think. Some days go better than others.

- *Quit abusing our minds.* Worry and obsession constitute mental abuse. Stop doing those things.

- *Feed our minds.* Give our minds information. Get the information we need about problems and decisions, whether that problem is overeating, alcoholism, relationships, or how to buy a computer. Give our minds a reasonable amount of data, then let them sort through things. We will come up with good answers and solutions.

- *Feed our minds healthy thoughts.* Indulge in activities that uplift our thoughts and give us a positive charge. Read a meditation book every morning. Find something that leaves us saying "I can," instead of "I can't."

- *Stretch our minds.* Many of us become so concerned about our problems and other people's problems that we stop reading newspapers, watching documentaries, reading books, and learning new things. Get interested in the world around us. Learn something new. Take a class.
- *Quit saying bad things about our minds.* Stop telling ourselves things like, "I'm stupid," "I can't make good decisions," "I'm really not very smart," "I've never been good at figuring things out," or "I'm not very good at decisions." It's just as easy to say good things about ourselves as it is to say negative things. And, we'll probably start believing the positive things and find out they're true. Isn't that exciting?
- *Use our minds.* Make decisions. Formulate opinions. Express them. Create! Think things through, but don't worry and obsess. We don't have to let anyone make our decisions for us, unless we're wards of the state. And even if we are, we can still think and make some of our choices. Letting people make our decisions for us means we're getting rescued, which means we're feeling like victims. We're not victims. Furthermore, it is not our business to make decisions for other adults. We can take possession of our power to think. And we can let others be responsible for their thinking. We will gain more confidence in ourselves, as we start feeling better and begin to make decisions, small and large. The people around us will grow, as they are allowed to make choices and mistakes.

We can become comfortable with our minds. Become acquainted with them. They're part of us, and they work. Trust them and our ability to think.

Activity

1. Who makes your decisions for you? How do you feel about that?

2. Did someone important in your life tell you that you couldn't think and make good decisions? Who?

3. Begin doing one thing every day to improve your mind: read an article in the newspaper and formulate an opinion. Later, you might really want to take a risk and tell somebody your opinion on that subject. You may even find yourself in a lively debate.

16

SET YOUR OWN GOALS

Believe that life is worth living and your belief
will create the fact. Be not afraid to live.

—William James

The most exciting idea I have discovered in my sobriety and my recovery from codependency is the magic in setting goals. Things happen. Things change. I accomplish important projects. I change. I meet new people. I find myself in interesting places. I make it through difficult times with a minimum of chaos. Problems get solved. My needs and wants get met. Dreams come true.

I am ecstatic about goal setting, and I hope I can transmit my enthusiasm to you. There is nothing in the world like going where we want to go, getting what we want, solving a problem, or doing something we always wanted to do.

Many codependents don't know this joy. It is new to me too. I spent many years of my life not even bothering to think about what I wanted and needed, where I wanted to go, and what I wanted to do. Life was to be endured. I didn't think I deserved good things. I didn't think most good things were within my reach. I wasn't that interested in my life, except as an appendage to other people. I didn't think about living my life; I was too focused on others. I was too busy reacting, rather than acting.

I am not suggesting we can control all the events in our lives. We can't. We don't have final say on much of anything; God does. But I believe we can cooperate with goodness. I believe we can plan, make requests, and start a process in motion.

"Desire, when harnessed, is *power*," writes David Schwartz in his best-seller, *The Magic of Thinking Big*. Failure to follow desire, to do what you want to do most, paves the way to mediocrity. "Success requires heart and soul effort and you can only put your heart and soul into something you really desire."[1]

Goals also give us direction and purpose. I don't get into my car, turn on the ignition, start driving, and hope I get someplace. I decide where I want to go or approximately where I would like to end up, then I steer the car in that general direction. That is how I try to live my life too. Sometimes things happen, and for a variety of reasons I may not end up where I wanted to go. If I change my mind or problems beyond my control interfere, I find myself doing something other than what I had planned to do. Timing and exact circumstances may vary. That's okay. I usually end up someplace better or someplace that is better for me. That is where acceptance, trust, faith, and letting go come in. But at least I'm not driving aimlessly through life. More of the things I want come to pass. I'm less worried about solving my problems, because I've turned my problems into goals. And I'm starting to think about and consider what *I* want and need.

Goals are fun. They generate interest and enthusiasm in life. They make life interesting and, sometimes, exciting.

". . . Surrender to desire and gain energy, enthusiasm, mental zip, and even better health. . . . energy increases, multiplies, when you set a desired goal and resolve to work toward that goal. Many people, millions of them, can find new energy by selecting a goal and giving all they've got to accomplish that goal. Goals cure boredom. Goals even cure many chronic ailments."[2]

There is magic in setting and writing down goals. It sets into motion a powerful psychological, spiritual, and emotional force. We become aware of and do the things we need to do to achieve and accomplish. Things come to us. Things begin to happen! Following is another excerpt from *The Magic of Thinking Big*.

Let's probe a little deeper into the power of goals. When you surrender yourself to your desires, when you let yourself become obsessed with a goal, you receive the physical power, energy, and enthusiasm needed to accomplish your goal. But you receive something else, something equally valuable. You receive the "automatic instrumentation" needed to keep you going straight to your objective.

The most amazing thing about a deeply entrenched goal is that it keeps you on course to reach your target. This isn't double-talk. What happens is this. When you surrender to your goal, the goal works itself into your subconscious mind. Your subconscious mind is always in balance. Your conscious mind is not, unless it is in tune with what your subconscious mind is thinking. Without full co-operation from the subconscious mind, a person is hesitant, confused, indecisive. Now, with your goal absorbed into your subconscious mind you react the right way automatically. The conscious mind is free for clear, straight thinking.[3]

What are our goals? What do we want to happen in our lives—this week, this month, this year, for the next five years? What problems do we want solved? What material things would we like to possess? What changes do we want to make in ourselves? What would we love to do for a career? What do we want to accomplish?

I'm not going to present a textbook lecture on exactly how you should set goals. Setting goals has been made too boring for too long. Following are some ideas I believe are important. Find a way that works.

• *Turn everything into a goal.* If we have a problem make its solution our goal. We don't have to know the solution. Our goal is solving this problem. Do we want something? A new waterbed, a red sweater, a new car, longer hair, longer nails? Turn it into a goal. Do we want to go someplace—Europe, South America, the circus? Do we want a loving, healthy relationship? Turn that into a goal. Is there something we've always wanted to do—go to school, work for a particular company, make $40,000 a year? Turn it into a goal. Do we need to decide

what we want to do for a career? Turn making a decision into a goal.
Do we want to grow closer to God, go to church every Sunday, or read
the Bible every day? Turn it into a goal. Do we want to change something about ourselves—learn to say no, make a particular decision,
resolve some anger? Turn it into a goal. Do we want to improve our
relationships with certain people—children, friends, spouse, a relative? Turn it into a goal. Do we want to form new relationships, lose
weight, gain weight, quit worrying, stop controlling? Do we want to
learn to have fun, learn to enjoy sex, achieve acceptance of some particular person or incident, forgive someone? I believe we can successfully turn every aspect of our lives into a goal. If it bothers us, make
it a goal. If we're aware something needs to be changed, make it a
goal. If we want it, make it a goal.

- *Omit the shoulds.* We have enough shoulds controlling our lives; we
  don't need them in our goals. Make it a goal to get rid of 75 percent
  of our shoulds.

- *Don't limit ourselves.* Go for all of it: everything we want and need, all
  the problems we want solved, all our desires, and even some of our
  whims. Don't worry. If we're not supposed to have it, we won't. If we
  are supposed to have it, I believe we'll stand an improved chance of
  getting it by turning it into a goal.

- *Write our goals on paper.* There is extraordinary power in jotting down
  goals, rather than storing them loosely in our minds. We worry less,
  we have less to think about, and it gives focus and organization to our
  goals. Recording our goals also helps us direct our energy and be in
  contact with our Higher Power. We don't have to write our goals neat-
  ly or perfectly, or use particular words or systems. Commit them to
  paper—all of them.

- *Commit our written goals to God.* Tell God these are the things we're
  interested in, ask for His help, then surrender humbly. It's called, "Thy
  will be done, not mine."

- *Let go.* Keep our goals close, where we can look at them as we need to
  but don't worry and obsess about how, when, if, and what if. Some
  people suggest we monitor our goals daily. I don't, except when I'm
  setting daily goals. But you can do it any way you choose. Once my
  goals are on paper, I try to not control or force.

- *Do what we can, one day at a time.* Within the framework of each 24-hour day, do what seems fitting and appropriate. Do God's will for us, that day. Do what we are inspired to do. Do what comes our way that needs to be done. Do it in peace and faith. Marvelous things can and do come to pass this way. Try it. We have to do our part. But I believe we can and will do our part best by doing it *one day at a time.* If it's time to do something, we'll know. If it's time for something to happen, it will. Trust ourselves and God.

- *Set goals regularly and as needed.* I like to do my annual goals at the beginning of each new year. It indicates to me that I am interested in living my life that particular year. I don't believe in New Year's resolutions; I believe in goals. I also write down goals as they occur to me throughout the year. If I am facing a problem, spot a need, feel a new want, I turn it into a goal and add it to my list. I also use goals to get me through crisis times, when I'm feeling shaky. Then, I write down all the things I want and need to accomplish on a daily, weekly, or monthly basis.

- *Check off the goals we reach.* Yes, we will start reaching our goals. Our wants and needs will get met. We will achieve certain things that are important to us. When this happens, cross off that goal, congratulate ourselves, and thank God. We will gain confidence in ourselves, in goal setting, in God, and in the rhythm of life this way. We will see for ourselves that good things do happen to us. Sometimes, we may experience a letdown when we reach a goal, if it's been an important goal that's required much energy or if we've done "magical thinking" about reaching it. (Magical thinking includes thoughts such as, "I will live happily ever after once this problem is solved" or "I will live happily ever after once I get a waterbed.") To avoid a letdown, it's important to have a long list of goals and avoid magical thinking. I've never yet reached a goal or solved a problem that has enabled me to live happily ever after. Life goes on, and I try to live happily and peacefully.

We may never be without a list of problems that we need to turn into goals. We will probably never be without wants and needs. But this process of goal setting, besides making life more enjoyable, helps develop a certain faith in the ebb and flow and general goodness of life. Problems arise. Problems get solved. Wants and needs come into awareness. Wants and needs get met. Dreams are born. Dreams are reached. Things happen. Good things happen. Then, more problems arise. But it's all okay.

- *Be patient.* Trust in God's timing. Don't take an item off the list if it's still important to us just because we didn't achieve or receive something when we thought we should have; the wretched shoulds infiltrate every area of our lives. Sometimes, my goals carry over for years. When I do my annual goal setting, I have looked at my sheet and thought, "Oh, this problem will never get solved. It's been on my list for years." Or, "This dream will never come true. It's the fourth year in a row I've written it down." Or, "I'll never be able to change this character defect of mine." Not true. It just hasn't happened yet. Here is one of the best thoughts I've ever encountered on patience. It is an excerpt from Dennis Wholey's book on alcoholism, *The Courage to Change.*

I've started to realize that waiting is an art, that waiting achieves things. Waiting can be very, very powerful. Time is a valuable thing. If you can wait two years, you can sometimes achieve something that you could not achieve today, however hard you worked, however much money you threw up in the air, however many times you banged your head against the wall. . . .[4]

Things happen when the time is right—when we're ready, when God is ready, when the world is ready. Give up. Let go. But keep it on our list.

We need to set goals for ourselves. Start today—when you finish this chapter. If you don't have any goals, make your first goal "getting some goals." You probably won't start living happily ever after, but you may start living happily.

ACTIVITY

1 Write your goals on a sheet of paper. Try to think of at least ten items such as wants, problems to be solved, and changes in yourself. Write as many goals as come to mind.

2 Review the checklist of "codependency characteristics" in Chapter Four. Make it a goal to change any of those characteristics that are a problem for you.

17

COMMUNICATION

When you're doing what's right for you, it's okay to say it once, simply, and then refuse to discuss anything further.[1]

—Toby Rice Drews

Read through the following conversations. You may identify with the dialogue, which appears in bold type, and the italicized interpretations, which explain the codependents' intentions and thought patterns.

*   *   *

Danielle is about to call Stacy on the telephone. Danielle wants Stacy to babysit Danielle's three children for the weekend, but she does not intend to ask Stacy to babysit; she intends to manipulate her into doing it. Pay attention to her techniques.

Stacy: **Hello.**

Danielle: **Hi** (mumbled). **Sigh.** *The sigh means, "Poor me. I'm just so helpless. Ask me what's wrong. Rescue me."*

Stacy: (After a long pause.) **Oh, hi, Danielle. Glad you called. How're you doing?** *During the long pause, Stacy thought, "Oh, no. Not her." Sighing and moaning again. "Good heavens, what does she want this time?"*

Danielle: **Sigh. Sigh. I'm doing about the same as always. Problems, you know.** *What Danielle is saying is: "C'mon. Ask me what's wrong."*

Stacy: (Again, after a long pause.) **What's the matter? You sound terrible.** *During the long pause this time, Stacy thought: "I'm not going to*

*ask her what's wrong. I won't get trapped. I refuse to ask her what's wrong."
Upon thinking this, Stacy felt angry, then guilty (the rescue feelings), then
went on to rescue Danielle by asking her what was wrong.*

Danielle: **Well, my husband just found out he's got to go out of
town this weekend on his job, and he's asked me to come with. I would
love to go with him. You know I never get to go anywhere. But I don't
know who I'd get to watch the kids. I hated to say no, but I had to turn
him down. He feels so bad. I hope he doesn't get too mad at me. Oh,
well, that's just the way things go, I guess. Sigh. Sigh.** *Danielle is laying
it on thick. She wants Stacy to feel sorry for her, guilty, and sorry for her husband.
Her words have been carefully chosen. Danielle, of course, told her husband she
could go. She told her husband she was going to get Stacy to babysit.*

Stacy: (Long, long pause.) **Well, I suppose I could see if I could
maybe help you out.** *During the pause this time, Stacy thought: "Oh, no.
No, no, no. I hate watching her kids. She never watches mine. I don't want to.
I won't. Darn her for putting me in this spot all the time. Rats. But how could
I say no? I should help people. Do unto others. And she needs me so much.
God, I don't want her to get angry at me. Besides, if I don't help her out, who
will? She leads such a pathetic life. But this is the last time. The last time
ever." The feelings were anger, pity, guilt, saintly, and back to anger. Notice
how she demeaned Danielle by labeling her helpless; notice her grandiose feelings of responsibility: "I'm the only person in the world who can help her."
Also, notice how she worded her response. She was hoping Danielle would
notice Stacy's lack of enthusiasm and rescue her by telling her to forget it.*

Danielle: **Would you really babysit? Thanks so much. You're the
greatest. I never dreamt you'd actually do this for me.** *"Ah, ha! Got
what I wanted."*

Stacy: **No problem. Glad to help.** *"I don't want to do this. Why does
this always happen to me?"*

✳   ✳   ✳

In the next conversation Robert wants his wife, Sally, to call his boss
and tell him Robert is sick. Robert was out drinking until 3 A.M. the

evening before. His alcoholism is causing increasing problems at home and on the job. During the conversation he feels sick, angry, guilty, and desperate. Sally feels the same way.

Robert: **Good morning, honey. How's my sweetie pie today?** *"Heaven help me, I feel awful. I can't go to work. She's mad. I can't face the boss. Better lather her up, get her to call in for me, and then I'll go back to bed. Better yet, I need another drink. Quick."*

Sally: **I'm fine.** (Said in a clipped, martyred voice after a cold stare, a dirty look, and a long silence.) *What Sally meant was: " I feel hurt. I feel angry. How could you do this to me? You were out again drinking last night. You promised not to do it anymore. Our lives are falling apart, and you don't care. Look at you: You're a mess. I can't stand this!"*

Robert: **Honey, I feel so sick today. I must be getting the flu. I can't even eat breakfast. Call my boss, okay? Tell him I'll be in tomorrow, if I'm better. Could you do that for the old dad? C'mon. Be my little sweetheart. I'm so sick.** *"I'm helpless, and I need you. Take care of me, and do it right now. I know you're angry at me, so I'll try to get you to feel sorry for me."*

Sally: **I really don't think I should call your boss. He likes to talk to you when you're not going to come in. He always has questions about things, and I can't answer them. Don't you think it would be better if you called? After all, you know what you want to say.** *"I hate calling his boss. I hate lying for him. But if I say no, he'll get angry. I'll try to act more helpless than he is."*

Robert: **What's with you, anyway? Can't you do that one little thing for me? Are you that selfish? I know you're mad at me. You're always mad at me. It's no wonder I drink, with a wife like you. Go ahead. Don't call. But if I lose my job, it's your fault.** *"How dare she refuse me?" he thinks. Then he decides it's time to get tough. He's got to get her to do this. He decides to throw a big portion of guilt at her, then top it off with a little fear. He knows she's worried about him losing his job. While he's at it, he lays the groundwork for today's drinking.*

Sally: **Fine. I'll do it. But don't you ever ask me to do it again. And if you drink one more time, I'm leaving you.** *Feeling trapped, Sally* *calls Robert's boss. Robert made his points well. He hit Sally on all her weak spots. She is afraid of being called selfish because she thinks it would be terrible if she was selfish; she feels guilty because she knows she is mad all the time; she feels responsible for Robert's drinking; and she is afraid of him losing his job. That business about leaving him if he drank again was an empty threat; she has made no decision to leave Robert. And the next time Robert asks her, she will call his boss again. After Sally makes the phone call she flies into a rage at Robert, persecuting him. She then ends up feeling sorry for herself and victimized. She also continues to feel extremely guilty, harboring the thought that there is something wrong with her for all her feelings and reactions, because Robert appears so powerful and she feels so weak and insecure.*

*   *   *

In this conversation, a counselor is talking to an alcoholic husband and his wife in a family therapy group. The couple appears to be the perfect couple. This is not their first time attending this group, but it is the first time the counselor focuses on them.

Counselor: **Steven and Joanne, I'm glad you're both here tonight. How are you doing?**

Steven: **We're doing great. Just great. Aren't we, Joanne?**

Joanne: (Smile). **Yes. Everything's fine.** (Nervous laugh.)

Counselor: **Joanne, you're laughing, but I sense something is wrong. It's okay to talk in here. It's okay to talk about your feelings, and it's okay to talk about your problems. This is what this group is for. What's going on underneath your smile?**

Joanne: (Her smile crumbles, and she begins crying.) **I'm so sick of this. I'm so sick of him hitting me. I'm so sick of being scared of him. I'm sick of the lies. I'm sick of the promises that are never kept. And I'm sick of being slapped around.**

*   *   *

Now that we've "listened" to some codependents' talk, let's consider the dialogue we use. Many codependents have poor communication skills. We carefully choose our words to manipulate, people please, control, cover up, and alleviate guilt. Our communication reeks of repressed feelings, repressed thoughts, ulterior motives, low self-worth, and shame. We laugh when we want to cry, we say we're fine when we're not. We allow ourselves to be bullied and buried. We sometimes react inappropriately. We justify, rationalize, compensate, and take others all around the block. We are nonassertive. We badger and threaten, then back down. Sometimes we lie. Frequently, we are hostile. We apologize a lot, and hint at what we want and need.

Codependents are indirect. We don't say what we mean, we don't mean what we say.[2]

We don't do it on purpose. We do it because we've learned to communicate this way. At some point, either in our childhood or adult family, we learned it was wrong to talk about problems, express feelings, and express opinions. We've learned it was wrong to directly state what we want and need. It was certainly wrong to say no, and stand up for ourselves. An alcoholic parent or spouse will be glad to teach these rules; we have been too willing to learn and accept them.

As John Powell asks in the title of his excellent book on communication: *Why Am I Afraid to Tell You Who I Am?* Why are we afraid to tell people who we are? Each of us must answer that question. Powell says it's because who we are is all we've got, and we're afraid of being rejected.[3] Some of us may be afraid because we're not sure who we are and what we want to say. Many of us have been inhibited and controlled by one or more of the family rules I discussed earlier in this chapter. Some of us have had to follow these rules to protect ourselves, to survive. However, I believe most of us are afraid to tell people who we are because we don't believe it is okay to be who we are.

Many of us don't like and don't trust ourselves. We don't trust our thoughts. We don't trust our feelings. We think our opinions stink. We don't think we have the right to say no. We're not sure what we want and need; if we do know, we feel guilty about having wants and needs and we're surely not going to be up front about them. We may feel ashamed for having our problems. Many of us don't even trust our ability to accurately identify problems, and we're more than willing to back down if somebody else insists the problem isn't there.

Communication is not mystical. The words we speak reflect who we are: what we think, judge, feel, value, honor, love, hate, fear, desire, hope for, believe in, and commit to.[4] If we think we're inappropriate to life our communication will reflect this: We will judge others as having all the answers; feel angry, hurt, scared, guilty, needy, and controlled by other people. We will desire to control others, value pleasing others at any cost, and fear disapproval and abandonment. We will hope for everything but believe we deserve and will get nothing unless we force things to happen, and remain committed to being responsible for other people's feelings and behavior. We're congested with negative feelings and thoughts.

No wonder we have communication problems.

Talking clearly and openly is not difficult. In fact, it's easy. And fun. Start by knowing that who we are is okay. Our feelings and thoughts are okay. Our opinions count. It's okay to talk about our problems. And it's okay to say no

We *can* say no—whenever we want to. It's easy. Say it right now. Ten times. See how easy that was? By the way, other people can say no, too. It makes it easier if we've got equal rights. Whenever our answer is no, start our response with the word *no,* instead of saying, "I don't think so," or "Maybe," or some other wavering phrase.[5]

Say what we mean, and mean what we say. If we don't know what we mean, be quiet and think about it. If our answer is, "I don't know," say "I don't know." Learn to be concise. Stop taking people all around the block. Get to the point and when we make it, stop.

Talk about our problems. We're not being disloyal to anyone by revealing who we are and what kinds of problems we're working on. All we're doing is pretending by not being who we are. Share secrets with trusted friends who won't use these against us or help us feel ashamed. We can make appropriate decisions about who to talk to, how much to tell them, and when the best time to talk is.

Express our feelings: openly, honestly, appropriately, and responsibly. Let others do the same. Learn the words: I feel. Let others say those words and learn to listen—not fix—when they do.

We can say what we think. Learn to say: "This is what I think." Our opinions can be different from other people's opinions. That doesn't mean we're wrong. We don't have to change our opinions, and neither does the other person, unless either of us wants to.

We can even be wrong.

We can say what we expect, without demanding that other people change to suit our needs. Other people can say what they expect, and we don't have to change to suit them, either—if we don't want to.

We can express our wants and needs. Learn the words: "This is what I need from you. This is what I want from you."

We can tell the truth. Lying about what we think, how we feel, and what we want isn't being polite—it's lying.

We don't have to be controlled by what other people say; we don't have to try to control them with our words and special effects. We don't have to be manipulated, guilted, coerced, or forced into anything. We can open our mouths and take care of ourselves! Learn to say: "I love you, but I love me, too. This is what I need to do to take care of *me*."

We can, as Earnie Larsen says, learn to ignore nonsense. We can refuse to talk to someone's illness, whether it is alcoholism or another compulsive disorder. If it doesn't make sense, it doesn't make sense. We don't have to waste our time trying to make sense out of it or trying to convince the other person that what he or she said didn't make sense. Learn to say, "I don't want to discuss this."

We can be assertive and stand up for ourselves without being abrasive or aggressive. Learn to say: "This is as far as I go. This is my limit. I will not tolerate this." And mean those words.

We can show compassion and concern without rescuing. Learn to say, "Sounds like you're having a problem. What do you need from me?" Learn to say, "I'm sorry you're having that problem." Then, let it go. We don't have to fix it.

We can discuss our feelings and problems without expecting people to rescue us too. We can settle for being listened to. That's probably all we ever wanted anyway.

One common complaint I hear from codependents is, "Nobody takes me seriously!" Take ourselves seriously. Balance that with an appropriate sense of humor and we won't have to worry about what anyone else is or isn't doing.

Learn to listen to what people are saying and not saying. Learn to listen to ourselves, the tone of voice we use, the words we choose, the way we express ourselves, and the thoughts going through our minds.

Talking is a tool and a delight. We talk to express ourselves. We talk to be listened to. Talking enables us to understand ourselves and helps us understand other people. Talking helps us get messages to people. Sometimes we talk to achieve closeness and intimacy. Maybe we don't always have something earth-shattering to say, but we want contact with people. We want to bridge the gap. We want to share and be close. Sometimes we talk to have fun—to play, enjoy, banter, and entertain. There are times when we talk to take care of ourselves—to make it clear that we will not be bullied or abused, that we love ourselves, and that we have made decisions in our best interests. And sometimes we just talk.

We need to take responsibility for communication. Let our words reflect high self-esteem and esteem for others. Be honest. Be direct. Be open. Be gentle and loving when that's appropriate. Be firm when the situation calls for firmness. Above all else, be who we are and say what we need to say.

In love and dignity, speak the truth—as we think, feel, and know it—and it shall set us free.

ACTIVITY

1. Read these books: *Why Am I Afraid to Tell You Who I Am?* by John Powell, and *How to Be an Assertive (Not Aggressive) Woman in Life, in Love, and on the Job,* by Jean Baer. *How to Be an Assertive Woman* is an excellent book for men, too.

18

WORK A TWELVE STEP PROGRAM

"How do the Twelve Steps work?"
"They work just fine, thank you."

—Anonymous A.A./Al-Anon quote

I detest the disease of alcoholism. Chemical dependency and other compulsive disorders destroy people—beautiful, intelligent, sensitive, creative, loving, caring people who do not deserve to be destroyed. The illnesses kill love and dreams, hurt children, and tear apart families. Alcoholism leaves in its wake sheared, fragmented, bewildered victims. Sometimes the early death it brings to the drinker causes far less pain than the wretched illness caused during his or her lifetime. It is a horrid, cunning, baffling, powerful, and deadly disease.

I unabashedly love Twelve Step programs. I have great respect for all of them: Alcoholics Anonymous, for people with a desire to stop drinking; Al-Anon, for people affected by someone else's drinking; Alateen, for teenagers affected by someone's drinking; Al-Atots, for children affected by someone's drinking; and Narcotics Anonymous, for people addicted to drugs.

Other Twelve Step programs that I respect include: Nar-Anon, for people affected by another's chemical addiction; Overeaters Anonymous, for people with eating disorders; O-Anon, for people affected by others' eating disorders; Families Anonymous, for people concerned about the use of chemicals and/or related behavioral problems in a relative or friend; Adult Children of Alcoholics, for adult children of alcoholics;

Emotions Anonymous, for people with a desire to become well emotionally.

Other good Twelve Step programs include: Sex Addicts Anonymous, for people with compulsive sexual behavior; Co-SA, for people affected by another person's sexual addiction; Gamblers Anonymous, for people with a desire to stop gambling; Gam-Anon, for people affected by another person's gambling; Parents Anonymous, for parents who are abusive, neglectful, or afraid of becoming so, or for adolescents who are encountering problems due to past or current abuse; and Sex Abusers Anonymous. There may also be other programs which I have either overlooked or which have sprung into origin since the writing of this book.

Twelve Step programs are not merely self-help groups that help people with compulsive disorders stop doing whatever it is they feel compelled to do (drinking, helping the drinker, etc.). The programs teach people how to live—peacefully, happily, successfully. They bring peace. They promote healing. They give life to their members—frequently a richer, healthier life than those people knew before they developed whatever problem they developed. The Twelve Steps are a way of life.

In this chapter I am going to focus on the programs for people who have been affected by another person's compulsive disorder, because this is a book on codependency and that's what codependency is about. I am going to refer specifically to the Al-Anon program, because that is one program I "work." (I will discuss that little piece of jargon, "working a program," later.) However, with a bit of creativity on your part, the information I present can be applied to any of the Twelve Step programs.

The Twelve Steps

The Twelve Steps are at the heart of the Twelve Step programs. The Steps, in their basic forms (following in italics), belong to various programs. But all of the programs adapted their Steps from those of Alcoholics Anonymous.

The interpretations following the Steps are my personal opinions and are not related to, endorsed by, or affiliated with any Twelve Step program. The programs also have Traditions, which guard the purity of the programs to ensure that they continue to operate effectively. The Eleventh Tradition in the Al-Anon program says, "Our public relations policy is based on attraction rather than promotion. . . ."[1] Please understand I am not promoting this program or any program. I am just saying what I think, and I happen to think highly of the Twelve Steps.

1. *We admitted we were powerless over alcohol—that our lives had become unmanageable.* This is an important Step. It must be taken first. That is why it is the First Step. Much of our struggle to accept whatever it is we must accept—a loved one's alcoholism or eating problem, for example, brings us to this door. My denial, my bargains, my efforts to control, my rescuing, my anger, my hurt, my grief propelled me to this place. Not once, but twice in my lifetime, I had tried to do the impossible. I tried to control alcohol. I had battled with alcohol in my own drinking and using days; I went to war again with alcohol when people I loved were using and abusing it. Both times, I lost. When will I learn to quit fighting lions? Both times, alcohol gained control of me—once directly, through my own imbibing; the second time, indirectly, through another person's use of the substance. It didn't matter, though, how it had gained control. It had. My thoughts, emotions, behaviors—my life—were regulated and directed by alcohol and its effects on another person's life. People were controlling me, but those people were being controlled by alcohol. Once the light was turned on, it wasn't difficult to see who was boss. The bottle was. Once I saw that, I could easily see my life had become unmanageable. Indeed, it had. Spiritually, emotionally, mentally, behaviorally, I was out of control. My relationships with people were unmanageable. My career was unmanageable. I couldn't even keep my house clean.

If this Step sounds like giving up, that's because it is. It is where we surrender to the truth. We are powerless over alcohol. We are powerless over the disease of alcoholism. We are powerless over another person's drinking and the effects of alcoholism in his or her life. We are powerless over people—what they do, say, think, feel, or don't do, say, think, or feel. We have been trying to do the impossible. At this point we understand this and make a rational decision to quit trying to do what we cannot ever do, no matter how hard we try. At this point we turn our eyes to ourselves—to the ways we have been affected, to our characteristics, to our pain. It sounds hopeless and defeatist, but it isn't. It is acceptance of what is. We can't change things we can't control, and trying to do that will make us crazy. This Step is appropriately humbling. It is also the bridge to the Second Step. For with our admission of powerlessness over that which we are truly powerless over, we receive the power which is appropriately ours—our own power to change ourselves and live our lives. When we quit trying to do the impossible, we are allowed to do the possible.

2. *Came to believe that a Power greater than ourselves could restore us to sanity.* If the First Step left us despairing, this Step will bring hope. I did not doubt for a minute that I was crazy, once I stopped comparing myself to the crazy people around me. The way I had been living was insane; the way I had not been living my life was insane. I needed to believe I could become sane. I needed to believe the pain I felt could somehow be lessened. Listening to, talking with, and actually seeing people who had been as upset as I was, and seeing they had found peace in circumstances sometimes worse than mine, helped me come to believe. There is no substitute for visualization. As someone once said, seeing is believing.

And, yes, this is a spiritual program. Thank God we aren't left to our own devices any longer. This is not a do-it-yourself program. This is not a do-it-yourself book. Do it yourself at your own risk. We are spiritual beings. We need a spiritual program. This program meets our spiritual needs. We are not talking about religion here; the word I used was *spiritual*. We select and come to terms with a Power greater than ourselves.

3. *Made a decision to turn our will and our lives over to the care of God as we understood Him.* I had turned my will and my life over to the care of alcohol and other drugs; I had turned my will and life over to the care of other human beings (usually alcoholics); I had spent many years trying to impose my own plan onto the scheme of things. It was time to remove myself from anyone or anything's control (including my own) and place myself in the hands of an extraordinarily loving God. "Take it," I said,

"All of it—who I am, what's happened to me, where I shall go, and how I'll get there." I said it once. I say it every day. Sometimes, I say it every half hour. This Step does not mean we resign ourselves to a bunch of shoulds and ought tos, and don our sackcloth. It in no way implies a continuation of martyrdom. The exciting thing about this Step is it means there is a purpose and a plan—a great, perfectly wonderful, usually enjoyable, and worthwhile plan that takes into account our needs, wants, desires, abilities, talents, and feelings—for each of our lives. This was good news to me. I thought I was a mistake. I didn't think there was anything of significance planned for my life. I was just stumbling around, trying to make the best out of being here when I learned this: We are here to live as long as we are alive, and there is a life for each of us to live.

4. *Made a searching and fearless moral inventory of ourselves.* We take our eyes off the other person and look at ourselves. We see just what we're working with, how we have been affected, what we are doing, what *our* characteristics are, and we write on a piece of paper what we see. We look fearlessly, not in self-hate and self-castigation, but in an attitude of love, honesty, and self-care. We may even discover that hating ourselves, not loving ourselves enough, has been a real moral problem. We root out any other problems, including earned guilt. We also look at our good qualities. We examine our hurts and angers. We examine ourselves and the part we have played in our lives. This Step also gives us an opportunity to examine the standards we judge ourselves by, choose those we believe to be appropriate, and disregard the rest. We are now on our way to dumping our earned guilt, getting rid of our unearned guilt, accepting the package we call ourselves, and starting on the path to growth and change.

5. *Admitted to God, to ourselves, and to another human being the exact nature of our wrongs.* Confession is good for the soul. There is nothing like it. We don't have to hide any longer. We tell our worst, most shameful secrets to a trusted person skilled in listening to the Fifth Step. We tell someone how hurt and angry we are. Someone listens. Someone cares. We are forgiven. Wounds begin to heal. We forgive. This Step is liberating.

6. *Were entirely ready to have God remove all these defects of character.* We realize some of the things we've been doing to protect ourselves have been hurting us and possibly others. We decide we're ready to take a risk, and let go of these outdated behaviors and attitudes. We become willing to be changed and to cooperate in the process of change. I use this and the next Step as daily tools to rid myself of any defects that come to my attention. I consider my low self-worth a defect, and I use this Step on it too.

7. *Humbly asked Him to remove our shortcomings.* From my experience, *humbly* seems to be the key here.

8. *Made a list of all persons we had harmed and became willing to make amends to them all. Willingness* is the important word here, although I suspect it's directly connected to humility. Don't forget to put ourselves on the list. Note that, as Jael Greenleaf writes: "The Eighth Step does not read 'Made a list of all persons we had harmed and became willing to feel guilty about it.' "[2] This is our chance to take care of our earned guilt. This is an important Step in a tool that will be available to us all our lives so we no longer have to feel guilty.

9. *Made direct amends to such people wherever possible except when to do so would injure them or others.* This is a simple Step in a simple program. Sometimes the simplest things help us feel happy.

10. *Continued to take personal inventory and when we were wrong, promptly admitted it.* We keep our eyes on ourselves. We continually and regularly evaluate our behavior. We figure out what we like about ourselves, what we've done right and good. Then we either congratulate ourselves, feel good about it, thank God, or do all three. We figure out what we don't like that we've been doing, then we figure out how to accept and take care of that without hating ourselves for it. Here's the difficult part: if *we're* wrong, we say so. If we have worked Steps Eight and Nine and dumped all our guilty feelings, we will know when we need to say "I'm wrong" and "I'm sorry." We will feel earned guilt, and we will be able to notice it. If, however, we are still feeling guilty all the time, it may be difficult to distinguish when we do something wrong because we're feeling guilty all the time and we don't feel any different. It's just one more

shovel of guilt thrown onto an already heaping pile. The moral of that story is: Dump guilt. If we get some, take care of it immediately.

11. *Sought through prayer and meditation to improve our conscious contact with God as we understood Him, praying only for knowledge of His will for us and the power to carry that out.* This Step, used daily and as needed, will successfully take us through our entire lives. This Step requires we learn the difference between *rumination* and *meditation*. It also requires us to decide whether we believe God is benevolent. We need to decide if we believe God "knows where we live," as another friend says. Get quiet. Detach. Pray. Meditate. Ask Him what He wants us to do. Ask to be given the power to do that. Then let go and watch what happens. Usually, His will is an appropriate, common-sense approach to life. Sometimes, we get surprises. Learn to trust this Higher Power to whom we have given the guardianship of our lives. Become sensitive to how He works with us. Learn to trust ourselves. He works through us too.

12. *Having had a spiritual awakening as the result of these steps, we tried to carry this message to others, and to practice these principles in all our affairs.** We will awaken spiritually. We will learn to spiritually take care of ourselves—not religiously, although that certainly is part of life. This program will enable us to love ourselves and other people, instead of rescuing and being rescued. Carrying the message does not mean we become evangelists; it means our lives become a light. We will learn how to shine. If we apply this program to all areas of our lives, it will work in all areas of our lives.

Working the Program

Now that we are familiar with the Steps, let's discuss what "working the program" and "working the Steps" mean. All over the world, "anony-

---

*The Twelve Steps printed here are those of Al-Anon, adapted from the Twelve Steps of Alcoholics Anonymous, found in *Alcoholics Anonymous*, A.A. World Services, New York, NY, pp. 59–60. Reprinted with permission.

mous" people meet at a variety of locations—churches, homes, and barber shops. They might meet once a day, twice a week, or seven nights a week. They don't preregister or register. They simply find out where a particular group meets that focuses on the problem these people are having troubles with. At the meeting, they don't have to identify their last names or where they or their spouse work; they don't have to say anything if they don't want to. They don't have to pay money, although they can make a donation of any amount to help pay for coffee and meeting room rent expenses—*if they want to.* They don't have to sign up. They don't have to fill out a card. They don't have to answer any questions. They just walk in and sit down. This is called going to a meeting. It is an essential part of working the program.

One nice thing about meetings is that people can be who they are. They don't have to pretend they don't have a particular problem, because everybody there has the same problem. If they didn't have that problem, they wouldn't be there.

Meeting formats vary with each particular group. Some groups sit around a table and the people who want to talk, discuss feelings or problems. Some meetings are speaker meetings, where one person gets up in front of everyone and talks about a Step or an experience. At some groups, the Steps are the theme and the people just put their chairs in a circle and each person gets a chance to say something about whatever Step is the theme that day. There are many meeting variations, but usually the meetings have something to do with the Steps, the Traditions, or topics related to the problem. People learn about the Steps at the meetings, and they learn what the Steps mean to other people. They also hear slogans. Al-Anon and A.A. slogans include such catchy little sayings as: *Let Go and Let God, Easy Does It,* and *One Day at a Time.* The reason these sayings have become slogans is because they are true. And even if people get sick of saying and hearing these slogans, they keep repeating and listening to them because they are so true. And the slogans help people feel better. After the meeting is over, people usually stay and chat or go out to a restaurant and have a soda or coffee. Learning the Steps and slogans, listening to other people's experiences, sharing personal experiences, and fellowship, are parts of working the program.

At the meetings, books, pamphlets, and literature are sold at cost. These books contain information on the problems common to that group. Some groups sell meditation books which contain suggestions for approaching each day. Reading the literature and reading the daily meditation books are parts of working the program. People have something to take home and do through the literature. They are reminded of what they learned at the meeting, and sometimes they learn new things.

During their daily routines, the people who go to these meetings think about the Steps and slogans. They try to figure out how the Steps and slogans apply to them, what they're feeling, what they're doing, and what's going on in their lives at that particular time. They do this regularly and when a problem arises. Sometimes, they call someone they met at the meeting and discuss a problem with that person or tell that person how they're doing that day. Sometimes, these people do the things a Step suggests they do, such as write out an inventory, make a list of people they have harmed, or make an appropriate amend. If these people think about and work these Steps enough, eventually the Twelve Steps may become habits—habitual ways of thinking, behaving, and handling situations—much the same as codependent characteristics become habits. When they become habits, the program becomes a way of life. This is called working the Steps and working the program.

That's all there is to working a program. Twelve Step programs are simple and basic. People don't graduate and go on to more complicated things—they stick with the basics. Twelve Step programs work because they are simple and basic.

I get excited about such simple things as going to meetings and working the Steps. I can try to explain, but words only convey a little bit of the important idea here. Something happens if we go to these meetings and work a program. A peace and a healing sets in. We start to change and feel better. The Steps are something we work on, but they also work on us. There is magic at these meetings.

We never have to do anything we are unable to do, truly find offensive, or don't want to do. When it is time to do or change a certain thing, we will know it is time and we will want to do it. There will be a rightness and an appropriateness to it. Our lives begin to work this way, too. Healing—growth—becomes a natural process. The Twelve Steps capture and are a formula for man's natural healing process.[3] Upon reading them, we may not think the Steps look like much and certainly not like enough to get as excited as I am about them, but when we work them something happens. They appear. Their power appears. We may not understand until it happens to us.

The best description of the Twelve Steps I have heard was the "invisible boat" story, told by a man at a meeting I attended recently. He was talking about A.A., but his story applies to Al-Anon and other groups. I have changed some of his words so his idea fits Al-Anon, but here is the essence of his analogy:

Picture ourselves standing on the shore. Way across the water is an island called serenity, where peace, happiness, and freedom exist from the despair of alcoholism and other problems. We really want to get to that island, but we've got to find a way to get across the water—that huge void that stands between us and where we want to be.

We have two choices. In the water is an ocean liner, a cruise ship that looks real posh and cozy. It's called treatment, therapy. Next to it, on the beach, sits a group of odd-looking people. They appear to be rowing a boat, but we can't see a boat, and we can't see the oars. We only see these happy people sitting on the beach, rowing an invisible boat with invisible oars. The invisible boat is called Al-Anon (or A.A. or any other Twelve Step program). The ocean liner honks, summoning us aboard the treatment and therapy cruise. We can see the people on board: they're happy and waving to us. Then there's these goofy people hollering at us to join them in their invisible boat. Would we choose the liner or the invisible boat? Of course, we'll get on the ocean liner, the luxury cruise. The next thing we know, we're heading toward that island of happiness.

The problem is about mid-way across the water, the ocean liner stops, turns around, and heads back to the shore where we started from. Then the captain orders everyone off the ship. When we ask, "Why?" he says, "Our cruise only goes so far. The only way you can ever get to that island is by getting in the invisible boat (called Al-Anon)."

So we shrug our shoulders and walk over to the people in the boat. "Get in!" they holler. "We can't see any boat to get into!" we holler back. "Get in anyway," they say. So we get in, and pretty soon they say, "Pick up an oar and start rowing (working the Steps)." "Can't see any oars," we holler back. "Pick 'em up and start rowing, anyway!" they say. So we pick up invisible oars and start rowing, and pretty soon we see the boat. Before we know it, we see the oars too. Next thing we know, we're so happy rowing the boat with the goofy people we don't care if we ever get to the other side.[4]

That is the magic of the Twelve Step programs—they work. I am not saying, implying, or suggesting treatment and therapy are not helpful. They are. For many of us, treatment or a little therapy is just what we need to get *started* on our journey. But that ride ends and if we have a compulsive disorder or love someone with a compulsive disorder, we may discover we need to get on the invisible boat with those happy people.

At the end of this chapter, I have included tests we can take to help determine if we are candidates for Al-Anon, Alateen, or O-Anon. I have also included further questions from Adult Children of Alcoholics (ACOA). Please understand that the "anon" and ACOA groups are not for people with the drinking problem; they are for people who have been affected by someone else's problem. People frequently misunderstand this. Also, many chemically dependent people who attend A.A. find they also need to go to Al-Anon or ACOA to deal with their codependent characteristics. If you believe you might be a candidate for any of the Twelve Step programs—if you even suspect you have a problem common to one of the groups I discussed at the beginning of this chapter—find a group and start going to meetings. It will help you feel better.

I know it's difficult to go to meetings. I know it's difficult to present ourselves to a group of strangers and hold up our problem for the world to see. I know many of us probably don't understand how going to meetings could help anything—especially if the *other person* has the problem. But it will help. I was so angry when I started attending Al-Anon meetings. I was already working a program for my alcoholism. I didn't want or need another program or another problem in my life to work on. Besides, I felt I had already done enough to help the alcoholics in my life. Why should *I* have to go to meetings? The alcoholics were the ones who needed help. At my first meeting, some cheery little woman walked up to me, talked to me for a few minutes, smiled, and said, "Aren't you lucky? You're a double winner. You get to work both programs!" I wanted to choke her. Now, I agree. I am lucky. I am a double winner.

Some of us may be reluctant to go to meetings because we feel we've already done enough for the *other people* in our lives. Well, we're right. We probably have. That's why it's important to go to our meetings. We're going for ourselves.

Others of us may want to go only to help the *other people,* and may feel disappointed that the meetings expect us to work on ourselves. That's okay, too. Health begets health. If we start working on ourselves, our good health may rub off on the other people, in the same fashion that their illness rubbed off on us.

Some of us may be embarrassed to go. All I could do at the first meetings I attended was sit and cry, and I felt terribly awkward. But for once, it was a good cry. My tears were tears of healing. I needed to sit and cry. When I stopped crying and looked around, I saw other people crying too. Al-Anon is a safe place to go and be who we are. The people there understand. So will you.

I've addressed most of the common objections I've heard to attending meetings. There may be other objections, but if we qualify for membership in a program, go anyway. I won't be talked down. The Twelve Steps are God's gift to people with compulsive disorders and to people who love people with compulsive disorders. If you're feeling crazy and reacting to people and things, go. If you don't like the first group you attend, find another meeting and go there. Each group has its own personality. Continue going to different groups until you find one that feels comfortable. If you used to go to meetings but stopped going, go back. If you start going, go for the rest of your life. Alcoholism is a lifetime illness that requires a lifetime of treatment. Our codependent characteristics become habits and may be tendencies we lean toward for the rest of our lives. Go whether the other people in your life get better or sicker.

Go until you feel grateful that you can go. In the words of one man, "Isn't it nice they have these meetings and they *let* me come to them? Nobody else wants me around when I get this crazy. The people here just smile, shake my hand, and say: 'We're glad you're here. Please come again.' "

Go until you see the boat and the oars and you get happy. Go until the magic works on you. And don't worry—if you go long enough, the magic will work.

ACTIVITY

1. Complete the tests or read over the list of characteristics on the following pages.

2. If you are a candidate for any of the programs discussed in this chapter, look in the phone book or call an appropriate human services organization in your community. Find out where and when meetings are being held, then go.

AL-ANON: IS IT FOR YOU?

Millions of people are affected by the excessive drinking of someone close. The following twenty questions are designed to help you decide whether or not you need Al-Anon.

1. Do you worry about how much someone else drinks?   Yes No

2. Do you have money problems because of someone else's drinking?   Yes No

3. Do you tell lies to cover up for someone else's drinking?   Yes No

4. Do you feel that drinking is more important to your loved one than you are?   Yes No

5. Do you think that the drinker's behavior is caused by his or her companions?   Yes No

6. Are mealtimes frequently delayed because of the drinker?   Yes No

7. Do you make threats, such as, "If you don't stop drinking I'll leave you"?   Yes No

8. When you kiss the drinker hello, do you secretly try to smell his or her breath?   Yes No

9. Are you afraid to upset someone for fear it will set off a drinking bout?   Yes No

10. Have you been hurt or embarrassed by a drinker's behavior?   Yes No

11. Does it seem as if every holiday is spoiled because of drinking?   Yes No

12. Have you considered calling the police because of drinking behavior?   Yes No

13. Do you find yourself searching for hidden liquor?   Yes No

14. Do you feel that if the drinker loved you, he or she would stop drinking to please you? Yes No

15. Have you refused social invitations out of fear or anxiety?   Yes No

16. Do you sometimes feel guilty when you think of the   Yes No
    lengths you have gone to to control the drinker?
17. Do you think that if the drinker stopped drinking,   Yes No
    your other problems would be solved?
18. Do you ever threaten to hurt yourself to scare the   Yes No
    drinker into saying, "I'm sorry" or "I love you"?
19. Do you ever treat people (children, employees,   Yes No
    parents, co-workers, etc.) unjustly because you are
    angry at someone else for drinking too much?
20. Do you feel there is no one who understands your   Yes No
    problems?

If you answered yes to three or more of these questions, Al-Anon or Alateen may help. You can contact Al-Anon or Alateen by looking in your local telephone directory.[5]

ARE YOU AN EATING DISORDER CODEPENDENT?

Use this questionnaire from *Fat Is a Family Affair* to evaluate the extent of your involvement with an under- or overeater.

Do you force diets?
Do you threaten to leave due to weight?
Do you check on the diet?
Do you make promises based on pounds lost or gained?
Do you hide food from an overeater?
Do you worry incessantly about an undereater?
Have you "walked on eggshells" so as not to upset the over/undereater?
Do you throw food away so the overeater won't find it?
Have you excused the erratic, sometimes violent, mood swings resulting from sugar binges?
Do you change social activities so the overeater won't be tempted?
Do you manipulate budgets to control spending on food and clothing?
Do you purchase and promote eating the "right" foods?
Do you promote gyms, health spas, and miracle cures?
Do you break into emotional tirades when you catch the overeater bingeing?
Are you constantly disappointed when you see relapse?
Are you embarrassed by the over/undereater's appearance?
Do you falsely console the over/undereater when he or she is embarrassed?
Do you set up tests of willpower to test the over/undereater?
Have you lowered your expectations of what you might like?
Does your weight fluctuate with your loved one's (you up, he or she down)?
Have you stopped attending to your own grooming?
Do you have many aches and pains, and preoccupation with health?
Are you drinking heavily or using sleeping pills or tranquilizers?
Do you bribe with food?
Do you talk about the eater's body to him or her or to others?

Do you feel life will be perfect if the over/undereater shapes up?

Are you grateful you aren't "that bad"?

Does his or her eating disorder give you license to run away?

Does his or her eating disorder give you an excuse to stay?

Do you "subtly" leave "helpful" literature around the house?

Do you read diet books though you have no weight problem?

Do you think you have the perfect home, except for the over/
undereater?

Do you use pills to get to sleep and escape worry?

Have you spent much time in your own therapy talking about the over/
undereater?

PROGRESSION OF A CODEPENDENT PERSONALITY

This is also from *Fat Is a Family Affair*. It is meant to be used as a checklist to monitor your own progression.

Early Stages

———— Often born of dysfunctional family and learned to "care" for others as measure of self-worth.

———— Failed to cure parents so will "cure" the over/undereater.

———— Finds over/undereater who is "needy" so controls.

———— Begins doubting own perceptions and wants to control eating to show decisiveness.

———— Social life affected. Isolated self from community to "help" over/undereater.

Obsession

———— Makes pleas and threats related to the eating behavior.

———— Judges self and feels the cause of eating/starving.

———— Hides food.

———— Attempts controlling eating, hiding food, idle threats, nagging, scolding.

———— Shows anger and disappointment regarding the over/undereater's promises.

Secret Life

———— Becomes obsessed with watching and covering up.

———— Takes over responsibilities of the over/undereater.

———— Takes pivotal role in communications, excluding contact between the over/undereater and others.

———— Expresses anger inappropriately.

Out of Control

_____ Makes violent attempts to control eating. Fights with the over/undereater.

_____ Lets self go physically and mentally.

_____ Has extramarital affairs such as infidelity, workaholism, obsession with outside interests.

_____ Becomes rigid, possessive. Appears angry most of the time and careful and secretive about home life.

_____ Has related illness and drug abuse: ulcers, rashes, migraines, depression, obesity, tranquilizer use.

_____ Constantly loses temper.

_____ Becomes sick and tired of being sick and tired.[6]

ADULT CHILDREN OF ALCOHOLICS

Are you an adult child of an alcoholic? Following are fourteen questions you may find relevant to your life and personality.

1. Do I often feel isolated and afraid of people, especially authority figures?

2. Have I observed myself to be an approval seeker, losing my own identity in the process?

3. Do I feel overly frightened of angry people and personal criticism?

4. Do I often feel I'm a victim in personal and career relationships?

5. Do I sometimes feel I have an overdeveloped sense of responsibility, which makes it easier to be concerned with others rather than myself?

6. Do I find it hard to look at my own faults and my own responsibility to myself?

7. Do I get guilt feelings when I stand up for myself instead of giving in to others?

8. Do I feel addicted to excitement?

9. Do I confuse love with pity and tend to love people I can pity and rescue?

10. Do I find it hard to feel or express feelings, including feelings such as joy or happiness?

11. Do I find I judge myself harshly?

12. Do I have a low sense of self-esteem?

13. Do I often feel abandoned in the course of my relationships?

14. Do I tend to be a reactor, instead of an actor?

THE TWELVE STEPS OF A.A.*

1. We admitted we were powerless over alcohol—that our lives had become unmanageable.

2. Came to believe that a Power greater than ourselves could restore us to sanity.

3. Made a decision to turn our will and our lives over to the care of God *as we understood Him.*

4. Made a searching and fearless moral inventory of ourselves.

5. Admitted to God, to ourselves, and to another human being the exact nature of our wrongs.

6. Were entirely ready to have God remove all these defects of character.

7. Humbly asked Him to remove our shortcomings.

8. Made a list of all persons we had harmed, and became willing to make amends to them all.

9. Made direct amends to such people wherever possible, except when to do so would injure them or others.

10. Continued to take personal inventory and when we were wrong promptly admitted it.

---

*The Twelve Steps are taken from *Alcoholics Anonymous,* published by A.A. World Services, New York, NY, pp. 59–60. Reprinted with permission.

11. Sought through prayer and meditation to improve our conscious contact with God *as we understood Him,* praying only for knowledge of His will for us and the power to carry that out.

12. Having had a spiritual awakening as the result of these Steps, we tried to carry this message to alcoholics, and to practice these principles in all our affairs.

19

Pieces and Bits

When Prince Charming does come along,
I'll probably be down at the pond kissing frogs.[1]

This chapter contains miscellaneous tidbits about codependency and self-care.

Drama Addicts

Many codependents become what some people call drama or crises addicts. Strangely enough, problems can become addicting. If we live with enough misery, crises, and turmoil long enough, the fear and stimulation caused by problems can become a comfortable emotional experience. In her excellent book, *Getting Them Sober, Volume II*, Toby Rice Drews refers to this feeling as "excited misery."[2] After a while, we can become so used to involving our emotions with problems and crises that we may get and stay involved with problems that aren't our concern. We may even start making troubles or making troubles greater than they are to create stimulation for ourselves. This is especially true if we have greatly neglected our own lives and feelings. When we're involved with a problem, we know we're alive. When the problem is solved, we may feel empty and void of feeling. Nothing to do. Being in crisis becomes a comfortable place, and it saves us from our humdrum existence. It's like getting addicted to soap operas, except the daily crises occur in our lives and the lives of our friends and family. "Will Ginny leave John?" "Can we save Herman's job?" "How will Henrietta survive this dilemma?"

After we have detached and begun minding our own business and our lives finally become serene, some codependents still occasionally crave a little of the old excitement. We may at times find our new way of life boring. We are just used to so much turmoil and excitement that peace seems bland at first. We'll get used to it. As we develop our lives, set our goals, and find things to do that interest us, peace will become comfortable—more comfortable than chaos. We will no longer need nor desire excited misery.

We need to learn to recognize when we are seeking out "excited misery." Understand that we don't have to make problems or get involved with others' problems. Find creative ways to fill our need for drama. Get enjoyable jobs. But keep the excited misery out of our lives.

Expectations

Expectations can be a confusing topic. Most of us have expectations. We entertain certain notions, on some level of consciousness, about how we hope things will turn out or how we want people to behave. But it is better to relinquish expectations, so we can detach. It is better to refrain from forcing our expectations on others or refrain from trying to control the outcome of events, since doing so causes problems and is usually impossible anyway. So where do we go with our expectations?

Some people strive to relinquish all expectations and live moment to moment. That is admirable. But I think the important idea here is to take responsibility for our expectations. Get them out into the light. Examine them. Talk about them. If they involve other people, talk to the people involved. Find out if they have similar expectations. See if they're realistic. For example, expecting healthy behavior from unhealthy people is futile; expecting different results from the same behaviors, according to Earnie Larsen, is insane. Then, let go. See how things turn out. Let things happen—without forcing. If we are constantly disappointed, we may have a problem to solve—either with ourselves, another person, or a situation.

It's okay to have expectations. At times, they are real clues to what we want, need, hope for, and fear. We have a right to expect good things and appropriate behavior. We will probably get more of these things (the good stuff and the appropriate behavior) if we consistently expect these things. If we have expectations, we will also realize when they are *not* being met. But we need to realize these are only expectations; they belong to us, and we're not always boss. We can make sure our expectations are realistic and appropriate and not let them interfere with reality or let them spoil the good things that are happening.

Fear of Intimacy

Most people want and need love. Most people want and need to be close to people. But fear is an equally strong force, and it competes with our need for love. More specifically, this force is fear of intimacy.

For many of us, it feels safer to be alone or in relationships where we are "unemotionally involved" than it does to be emotionally vulnerable, close, and loving. I understand that. In spite of the range of needs and wants that go unmet when we don't love, it may feel safer to not love. We don't risk the uncertainty and vulnerability of closeness. We don't risk the pain of loving, and for many of us love has caused a great deal of pain. We don't risk being trapped by ourselves in relationships that don't work. We don't risk having to be who we are, which includes being emotionally honest and the possible rejections of that. We don't risk people abandoning us; we don't risk. And we don't have to go through the awkwardness of initiating relationships. When we don't get close to people, at least we know what to expect: nothing. Denial of love feelings protects us from the anxiety caused by loving. Love and closeness often bring a sense of loss of control. Love and closeness challenge our deepest fears about who we are and whether it is okay to be ourselves, and about who others are and whether that is okay. Love and closeness—involvement with people—are the greatest risks a man or woman can take. They require honesty, spontaneity, vulnerability, trust, responsibility, self-acceptance, and acceptance of others. Love brings joy and warmth, but it also requires us to be willing to occasionally feel hurt and rejection.

Many of us have learned to run from closeness, rather than take the risks involved. We run from love or prevent closeness in many ways. We push people away or do hurtful things to them so they won't want to be close to us. We do ridiculous things in our minds to talk ourselves out of wanting to be close. We find fault with everyone we meet; we reject people before they have a chance to reject us. We wear masks and pretend to be something other than who we are. We scatter our energies and emotions among so many relationships that we don't get too close or vulnerable to anyone—a technique called "watering down the milk" by one person. We settle for artificial relationships, where we will not be expected nor asked to be close. We play roles instead of being a real person. We withdraw emotionally in our existing relationships. Sometimes, we prevent closeness by simply refusing to be honest and open. Some of us sit, paralyzed by fear, unable to initiate relationships or enjoy closeness in existing relationships. Some of us run; we physically remove ourselves from any situation where love, emotional vulnerability, and risk are or might be present. As a friend says, "We all have a pair of track shoes in our closet."

We run from intimacy for many reasons. Some of us, particularly those of us who grew up in alcoholic family situations, may never have learned how to initiate relationships and how to be close once a relationship begins. Closeness was not safe, taught, or allowed in our families. For many people, caretaking and chemical use became substitutes for intimacy.

Some of us allowed ourselves to get close once or twice, then got hurt. We may have decided (on some level) that it was better and safer not to get close, not to risk being hurt again.

Some of us learned to run from relationships that aren't good for us. But for some of us, running from or avoiding closeness and intimacy may have become a habit, a destructive habit that prevents us from getting the love and closeness we really want and need. Some of us may be tricking ourselves, so we're not even aware we're running or what we're running from. We may be running when it isn't necessary.

Closeness to people may look like scary, mind-boggling business, but it doesn't have to be that scary. And it's not that difficult. It even feels good, when we relax and let it happen.

It's okay to feel afraid of closeness and love, but it's also okay to allow ourselves to love and feel close to people. It's okay to give and receive love. We can make good decisions about who to love and when to do that. It's okay for us to be who we are around people. Take the risk of doing that. We can trust ourselves. We can go through the awkwardness and friction of initiating relationships. We can find people who are safe to trust. We can open up, become honest, and be who we are. We can even handle feeling hurt or rejected from time to time. We can love without losing ourselves or giving up our boundaries. We can love and think at the same time. We can take off our track shoes.

We can ask ourselves, are we preventing closeness in our existing relationship? How are we doing that? Is it necessary? Why? Do we know someone we want to be close to—someone who would be safe to be close to? Why don't we take steps to get close to that person? Would we like to initiate some new relationships? How could we do that? Are we needing and wanting more intimacy in our relationships but settling for less? Why?

Financial Responsibility

Some codependents become financially dependent on other people. Sometimes this is by agreement; for example, a wife stays home and raises the children while the husband works and provides the money. Sometimes this is not by agreement. Some codependents become so victimized that we believe we cannot take care of ourselves financially. Many codependents were, at one time, financially responsible, but as alcoholism or another problem progressed in a loved one we simply became too upset to work. Some of us just gave up: "If you don't care about the money, then neither do I."

Sometimes, codependents become financially responsible for other adults. I have frequently seen a codependent wife work two or even three jobs, while her husband brings home not one penny—yet he continues to eat, watch television, and live rent free.

Neither way is preferable. Each person is financially responsible for him- or herself as well as in all other ways. That does not mean housewives have to work at paying jobs to be financially responsible. Homemaking is a job, a heroic and admirable one. If that is what a man or woman chooses to do, then I believe that person is earning his or her share. Being financially responsible also does not mean all things have to be equal. Assuming financial responsibility for oneself is an attitude. It means figuring out exactly what our responsibilities are, then setting out to take care of those responsibilities. It also means we allow—even insist—other people be financially responsible for themselves. That includes becoming familiar with all areas of one's finances and deciding which task belongs to which person. Which bills need to be paid? When? When are taxes due? How much money has to last for how long? What's our part in all this? Are we doing less or more than our appropriate share? If it is not our responsibility to hold a salaried job, do we at least understand we may someday need to work? Do we feel financially responsible for ourselves? Or does this frighten us? Are the people around us assuming appropriate financial responsibility for themselves, or are we doing it for them?

Taking care of money is part of life. Earning money, paying bills, and feeling financially responsible is part of taking care of ourselves. Many codependents who have quit a job to control a spouse or who have otherwise centered their lives around a person and neglected their own careers, have discovered even a low-paying, part-time job does wonders for their self-esteem. We forgot we are worth money and someone will actually pay for our abilities. Many of us codependents, who have been financially dependent on a spouse, also like the freedom of having our own money. It's called a good feeling. It's something to think about as we begin living our own lives.

Being financially dependent on a person can trigger emotional dependency. Emotional dependency on a person can trigger financial dependency.[3] Becoming financially responsible for ourselves—however we accomplish that—can help trigger undependence.

Forgiveness

Compulsive disorders such as alcoholism twist and distort many good things, including the great principle of forgiveness. We repeatedly forgive the same people. We hear promises, we believe lies, and we try to forgive some more. Some of us may have reached a point where we cannot forgive. Some of us may not want to, because to forgive would leave us vulnerable to further hurt and we believe we cannot endure more pain. Forgiveness turns on us and becomes a painful experience.

Some of us may be truly trying to forgive; some of us may think we have forgiven, but the hurt and anger just won't disappear.

Some of us can't keep up with the things we need to forgive; the problems are happening so fast we barely know what's going on. Before we can register the hurt and say, "I forgive," another nasty thing has been dumped on us.

Then we feel guilty because someone asks, "Why can't you just forgive and forget?" People uninformed about the disease of alcoholism and other compulsive disorders frequently ask that. For many of us, the problem is not forgetting. Forgiving and forgetting feed our denial system. We need to think about, remember, understand, and make good decisions about what we are forgiving, what can be forgotten, and what is still a problem. And forgiving someone does not mean we have to let that person keep hurting us. An alcoholic doesn't need forgiveness; he or she needs treatment. We don't need to forgive the alcoholic, at least not initially. We need to step back so he or she can't keep stomping on our toes.

I am not suggesting we adopt an unforgiving attitude. We all need forgiveness. Grudges and anger hurt us; they don't help the other person much either. Forgiveness is wonderful. It wipes the slate clean. It clears up guilt. It brings peace and harmony. It acknowledges and accepts the humanness we all share, and it says, "That's okay. I love you anyway." But I believe we codependents need to be gentle, loving, and forgiving with ourselves before we can expect to forgive others. But I believe codependents need to think about how, why, and when we dole out forgiveness.

Also, forgiveness is closely tied into the acceptance or grief process. We cannot forgive someone for doing something if we have not fully accepted what this person has done. It does little good to forgive an alcoholic for going on a binge, if we have not yet accepted his or her disease of alcoholism. Ironically, the kind of forgiveness we often give to soothe an alcoholic's "morning after" remorse may help him or her continue drinking.

Forgiveness comes in time—in its own time—if we are striving to take care of ourselves. Don't let other people use this principle against us. Don't let other people help us feel guilty because they think we should forgive someone, and we are either not ready or believe forgiveness is not the appropriate solution. Take responsibility for forgiveness. We can dole out forgiveness appropriately based on good decisions, high self-esteem, and knowledge of the problem we are working on. Don't misuse forgiveness to justify hurting ourselves; don't misuse it to help other people continue hurting themselves. We can work our program, live our own lives, and take the Fourth and Fifth Steps. If we are taking care of us, we will understand what to forgive and when it's time to do that.

While we're at it, don't forget to forgive ourselves.

The Frog Syndrome

There is an anecdote circulating through codependency groups. It goes like this: "Did you hear about the woman who kissed a frog? She was hoping it would turn into a prince. It didn't. She turned into a frog too."

Many codependents like to kiss frogs. We see so much good in them. Some of us even become chronically attracted to frogs after kissing enough of them. Alcoholics and people with other compulsive disorders are attractive people. They radiate power, energy, and charm. They promise the world. Never mind that they deliver pain, suffering, and anguish. The words they say sound so good.

If we don't deal with our codependent characteristics, probabilities dictate we will continue to be attracted to and kiss frogs. Even if we deal with our characteristics, we may still lean toward frogs, but we can learn not to jump into the pond with them.

Fun

Fun does not go hand in hand with codependency. It is difficult to have fun when we hate ourselves. It is difficult to enjoy life when there is no money for groceries because the alcoholic has drunk it all up. It is almost impossible to have fun when we are bottled up with repressed emotions, worried sick about someone, saturated with guilt and despair, rigidly controlling ourselves or someone else, or worried about what other people are thinking about us. However, most people aren't thinking about us; they're worried about themselves and what we think of them.

As codependents, we need to learn to play and enjoy ourselves. Arranging for and allowing ourselves to have fun is an important part of taking care of ourselves. It helps us stay healthy. It helps us work better. It balances life. We deserve to have fun. Fun is a normal part of being alive. Fun is taking time to celebrate being alive.

We can schedule fun into our routine. We can learn to recognize when we need to play and what kinds of things we enjoy doing. If we don't do this, we can make "learning to have fun" an immediate goal. Start doing things just for ourselves, just because we want to. It might feel uncomfortable at first, but after a while it'll feel better. It'll become fun.

We can let ourselves enjoy life. If we want something and can afford it, buy it. If we want to do something that is legal and harmless, do it. When we're actually involved with doing something that is recreational, don't find ways to feel bad. Let go and enjoy life. We can find things we enjoy doing, then let ourselves enjoy doing them. We can learn to relax and enjoy the things we do daily, not just the recreational activities. Martyrdom can interfere with our ability to feel good long after the alcoholic has stopped helping us feel miserable. Suffering can become habitual, but so can enjoying life and being good to ourselves. Try it.

Limits/Boundaries

Codependents, it has been said, have boundary problems. I agree. Most of us don't have boundaries.

Boundaries are limits that say: "This is how far I shall go. This is what I will or won't do for you. This is what I won't tolerate from you."

Most of us began relationships with boundaries. We had certain expectations, and we entertained certain ideas about what we would or wouldn't tolerate from those people. Alcoholism and other compulsive disorders laugh in the face of limits. The diseases not only push on our boundaries, they step boldly across them. Each time the disease pushes or steps across our limits we give in. We move our boundaries back, giving the disease more room to work. As the disease pushes more, we give in more until we are tolerating things we said we would never tolerate and doing things we said we would never do.[4] Later, this process of "increased tolerance" of inappropriate behaviors may reverse. We may become totally intolerant of even the most human behaviors. In the beginning, we make excuses for a person's inappropriate behavior; toward the end, there is no excuse.

Not only do many of us begin tolerating abnormal, unhealthy, and inappropriate behaviors, we take it one step further: we convince ourselves these behaviors are normal and what we deserve. We may become so familiar with verbal abuse and disrespectful treatment that we don't even recognize when these things are happening. But deep inside, an important part of us knows. Our *selves* know and will tell us if we will listen. Sometimes living with subtle problems, such as a nondrinking alcoholic who is not in any recovery program, can be harder on our *selves* than the more blatant problems. We sense something is wrong. We start feeling crazy, but we can't understand why because we can't identify the problem.

Codependents need boundaries. We need to set limits on what we shall do to and for people. We need to set limits on what we will allow people to do to and for us. The people we relate to need to know we have boundaries. It will help them and us. I am not suggesting we become tyrants. I also advise against absolute inflexibility, but we can understand our limits. As we grow and change, we may want to change our boundaries too. Here are some examples of boundaries common to codependents who are recovering:

- I will not allow anyone to physically or verbally abuse me.
- I will not knowingly believe or support lies.
- I will not allow chemical abuse in my home.
- I will not allow criminal behavior in my home.
- I will not rescue people from the consequences of their alcohol abuse or other irresponsible behavior.
- I will not finance a person's alcoholism or other irresponsible behavior.
- I will not lie to protect you or me from your alcoholism.
- I will not use my home as a detoxification center for recovering alcoholics.
- If you want to act crazy that's your business, but you can't do it in front of me. Either you leave or I'll walk away.
- You can spoil your fun, your day, your life—that's your business— but I won't let you spoil my fun, my day, or my life.

Sometimes it is necessary to set a certain boundary that applies to a particular relationship, such as, "I won't baby-sit Mary Lou's children anymore, because I don't want to and she takes advantage of me in that area."

Set boundaries, but make sure they're our boundaries. The things we're sick of, can't stand, and make threats about, may be clues to some boundaries we need to set. They may also be clues to changes we need to make within ourselves. Mean what we say, and say what we mean.

People may get angry at us for setting boundaries; they can't use us any-more. They may try to help us feel guilty so we will remove our boundary and return to the old system of letting them use or abuse you. Don't feel guilty and don't back down. We can stick to our boundaries and enforce them. Be consistent. We will probably be tested more than once on every boundary we set. People do that to see if we're serious, especially if we haven't meant what we said in the past. As codependents, we have made many empty threats. We lose our credibility, then wonder why people don't take us seriously. Tell people what our boundaries are—once, qui-etly, in peace. Watch our level of tolerance, so the pendulum doesn't swing too far to either extreme.

Some codependents, particularly those of us in the latter stages of a relationship with an alcoholic, may find we have a difficult time setting and enforcing limits with children, as well as with the troubled adults in our lives. Setting limits takes time and thought; enforcing limits takes energy and consistency.

But boundaries are worth every bit of time, energy, and thought re-quired to set and enforce them. Ultimately, they will provide us with more time and energy.

What are our limits? What boundaries do we need to establish?

Physical Care

Sometimes in the latter stages of codependency, we codependents neglect our health and grooming. It's okay to look the best we possibly can! We can get our hair styled or cut, for example. That's a normal part of living. We can dress in a manner that helps us feel good about our-selves. Look in the mirror; if we don't like what we see, fix it. If we can't fix it, we can stop hating ourselves and accept it.

Don't abandon the importance of exercise. If we're sick, go to a doc-tor. If we're overweight, figure out what we need to do to take care of ourselves. The less we care for our bodies, the worse we will feel about ourselves. Sometimes, doing little things can help us feel a lot better. Get in touch with the physical parts of us. Listen to them. Give them what they need. Taking care of ourselves means taking care of our bodies and grooming. Make both a daily practice.

Taking care of our emotional selves is also connected to our bodies. The more we take care of our emotional selves—the more we get our needs met—the less we find ourselves sick. If we refuse long enough to take care of ourselves, our bodies will rebel and become sick, forcing us and the people around us to give us the caretaking we need. It's easier to take care of ourselves before we get sick.

Professional Help

We need to seek professional help if:

- We are depressed and thinking about suicide.
- We want to do an intervention and confront an alcoholic or other troubled person.
- We have been the victim of physical or sexual abuse.
- We have been physically or sexually abusing somebody else.
- We are experiencing problems with alcohol or other drugs.
- We can't seem to solve our problems or get "unstuck" by ourselves.
- For any other reason, we believe we might benefit from professional help.

We can remember to trust ourselves when we go to professionals and pay attention to our feelings. If we are not comfortable with the agency or person we're working with, if we don't agree with the direction the counseling is taking, or if we in any way don't trust the help we are receiving or not receiving, find another professional. We may be experiencing a normal resistance to change, but it could be the person we're working with is not right for us. Not all professionals are able to work well with codependency, compulsive disorders, or chemical dependency.

One woman sought help from a private therapist because her daughter's chemical dependency and behavioral problems were disrupting the family. The therapist pulled the whole family into counseling, then began devoting most of the session time to trying to convince the parents that the reason the daughter was misbehaving was because the parents smoked cigarettes. The therapist had a prejudice against smoking. The goal of therapy switched from "daughter behaving" to "Mom and Dad stopping smoking." The parents were a little baffled and not entirely comfortable with the setup, but they were desperate for help. And they assumed the therapist knew more than they did. After spending three months and $50 a week on this nonsense, the parents finally realized they were going nowhere and the trip was costing them a lot of money. I'm not saying it's not good to stop smoking—but it was not the problem this family sought help for.

If we seek help and it doesn't seem right for us, seek different help. If we honestly make an effort to try something and it doesn't work, try something else. We don't have to give up our power to think, feel, and make good decisions to anyone—including someone with a Ph.D. after his or her name.

We can get ourselves the best care possible.

Strokes

I'm not talking about heart problems; *strokes* is a Transactional Analysis term that caught on in therapy circles years ago. Most of us need people. Most of us have at least a few relationships. When we are with these people, we can either generate warm, loving feelings; no feeling; or cold, hostile feelings. We can say honest, tender, appreciative things, and they can say those things back to us. We can lie, and people can lie back to us. We can talk about unimportant, superficial stuff, and others can do the same. Or we can say nasty things, and they can respond in the same way. Most of us do a little of all those things from time to time.

The idea is to strive for good relationships. If we don't have people to be honest, tender, loving, and appreciative with, find some. If people say mean things to us, causing us to retaliate, stop retaliating and try to get the person to quit talking that way. If we can't get this person to change, find someone else to talk to. We need to be treated nicely. It helps us grow, and it feels good.

Strive for good physical treatment too. We don't ever have to let people hit us. And we don't have to hit people. Hug them instead. Or, if a hug isn't appropriate, touch them in gentle, loving ways that communicate positive energy. For those who think hugging is a waste of time or an unnecessary activity indulged in by overly-sentimental people, read the following excerpt from *Fat Is a Family Affair* and think again:

> . . . In the early 1970s, doctors began studying a mechanism within the nervous system which produces a morphine-like effect helping to alleviate pain and subduing trauma and shock.
>
> These morphine-like substances are called endorphins and they are secreted to soothe pain, take the edge off, and promote general well-being. Some research indicates that overeaters and alcoholics produce fewer of these endorphins than normal people. . . . Since you produce fewer endorphins, you often feel on a raw edge. Eating sugar increases endorphin production, so when you eat, the rawness vanishes. . . .
>
> If anorexic, you get the same kind of soothing from the "high" of not eating. That exuberant feeling comes from the endurance high of pushing yourself beyond your limits, much like the "runner's high" . . . there is an alternative method to increased endorphin production. . . . It involves hugging. That's right, hugging. When you turn to a fellow human being and you put your arms around one another, this starts the endorphins flowing and the raw edges are removed by the warmth of a loving friend. Your dog is no dummy when he jumps up for a rub on the chest or a pat on the head. He's getting his endorphins up and keeping himself mellow.[5]

Codependents also frequently have difficulties accepting compliments—positive strokes. We can stop fighting the fact that we are good people with good qualities. If someone tells us something good about ourselves, we can accept it unless instinct tells us the person has ulterior motives. Even if he or she is trying to manipulate us, take the compliment and refuse to be manipulated. Let it go all the way down to the heart and let the warm glow come. We deserve compliments. We need them. We all need them. They help us believe what we are working so hard to believe: we are good people. The beauty of compliments is, the more good things we believe about ourselves, the better we get.

We can also pass out compliments and spread around some positive energy. We can share what we like about people and say what we appreciate in them. Make it honest, but make it good.

We can learn to recognize when we need to give a stroke. Learn to recognize when we need to be around people and get some strokes. Choose friends that can give us the good stuff. Sometimes codependents get involved with friends who see them as victims, helpless people who can't take care of themselves. These friends give sympathy, which is probably better than nothing, but it's not the same as strokes. Real love says, "You're having problems. I care, and I'll listen, but I won't and can't do it for you." Real friendship says, "I think so highly of you that I'll let you figure out how to do it for yourself. I know you can."

Trust

Codependents frequently aren't certain whom or when to trust. "Harvey's been in treatment for alcoholism two weeks. He's lied to me 129 times. Now he's mad at me because I say I don't trust him. What should I do?"

I've repeatedly heard variations of this from codependents. My answer is usually the same: There's a difference between trust and stupidity. Of course you don't trust Harvey. Quit trying to make yourself trust someone you don't trust.

Throughout the book I have repeated this phrase, and I will say it again: we can trust ourselves. We can trust ourselves to make good decisions about whom to trust. Many of us have been making inappropriate decisions about trust. It is not wise to trust an alcoholic to never drink again if that alcoholic has not received treatment for the disease of alcoholism. It is not even wise to trust an alcoholic never to drink again if he or she has received treatment—there are no guarantees on human behavior. But we can trust people to be who they are. We can learn to see people clearly.

Figure out if people's words match their behaviors. Is what they *say* the same as what they *do*? As one woman puts it, "He's looking real good, but he's not acting any better."

If we pay attention to ourselves and the messages we receive from the world, we will know whom to trust, when to trust, and why to trust a particular person. We may discover we've always known whom to trust—we just weren't listening to ourselves.

Sex

In one breath, a codependent will tell me her marriage is falling apart. In the next breath, she will ask if it's normal to have sexual problems when things get that bad.

Yes, it's normal to have sexual problems. Many people have problems with sex. Many codependents experience sexual problems. Alcoholism and the whole range of compulsive disorders attack all areas of intimacy.[6] Sometimes, the physical expression of love is the last and final loss we suffer—the blow that tells us the problem won't go away, no matter how long we close our eyes.

Sometimes the alcoholic has the problem. He becomes impotent, or she loses her sexual desire. This can happen both before and after recovery. Frequently, it is the codependent who has problems with sex. There is a range of difficulties that can be encountered in the bedroom. We may be unable to achieve orgasm, fear loss of control, or lack trust in our partner. We may withdraw emotionally from our partner, be unwilling to be vulnerable with our partner, or lack desire for our partner. We may feel revulsion toward our partner, or we don't get needs met because we're not asking to get these needs met. The relationship probably isn't going to be much better in bed than it is outside the bedroom. If we're caretaking in the kitchen, we'll probably be caretaking in the bedroom. If we're angry and hurt before we make love, we'll probably feel angry and hurt after we make love. If we don't want to be in the relationship, we won't want to have sex with that person. The sexual relationship will echo and reflect the overall tone of the relationship.

Sexual problems can sneak up on people. For a while, sex can be the salvation of a troubled relationship. Sex can be a way of making up after an argument. Talking seems to clear the air, and sex makes it all better. After a certain point, though, talking may no longer clear the air. Talking just fogs it up more, and sex stops making it better. Instead, sex can make things worse.

For some, sex may become a purely clinical act that provides approximately the same emotional satisfaction as brushing one's teeth. For others, it can become a time of humiliation and degradation: another chore, another duty, something else we should do but don't want to. It becomes one more area that isn't working, that we feel guilty and ashamed about, that we try to lie to ourselves about. We have one more area in our lives that causes us to wonder, "What's wrong with me?"

I am not a sex therapist. I have no cures or technical advice—just some common sense. I believe taking care of ourselves means we apply the same principles in the bedroom as we do in any other area of our lives. First, we stop blaming and hating ourselves.

Once we understand that, we get honest with ourselves. We stop running, hiding, and denying. We gently ask ourselves what we are feeling and thinking, then we trust our answers. We respectfully listen to ourselves. We don't abuse and punish ourselves. We understand the problem we are experiencing is a normal response to the system we have been living in. Of course we're having that problem—it's a normal part of the process. It would be abnormal to not feel revulsion, withdrawal, lack of trust, or other negative feelings. There's nothing wrong with us.

After we have sorted things out, we get honest with our partner. We tell him or her what we are thinking and feeling, and what we need from him or her. We explore possibilities, negotiating and compromising when appropriate. If we cannot solve our problems by ourselves, we seek professional help.

Some of us may have sought comfort in extramarital affairs. We need to forgive ourselves and figure out what we need to do to take care of ourselves. Take the Fourth and Fifth Steps; talk to a clergyperson. We can try to understand our actions were common reactions to the problems we have been living with.

Some of us may be trying to run from our problems by having a series of unsatisfactory sexual relationships. That frequently occurs during the denial stage, when compulsive behaviors tend to set in. We don't have to continue doing that. We can face and solve our problems in other ways. We can forgive ourselves and quit hurting ourselves.

Some of us may be looking for love and coming up with sex instead. Understand what we need and figure out how to best meet our needs.

Some of us may need to start asking for what we need. Others may need to learn to say no. Some of us may be trying to force love back into a dead relationship by trying to force sexual enjoyment. That technique may not work. Sex isn't love; it is sex. It doesn't make love exist if the love wasn't there to start with. Sex can only express the love that already exists.

Some of us may have given up and decided sex isn't that important. I happen to believe sex is important. It's not the most important thing in life, but it's an important part of my life.

Sex is a powerful force, a great source for intimacy and for pleasure. We can take care of ourselves if our sex life isn't working the way we would like it to. We are responsible for our sexual behavior—for our enjoyment or lack of pleasure in bed. We can ask ourselves, what are our sex lives telling us about our relationships?

20

LEARNING TO LIVE AND LOVE AGAIN

*At least I don't run around actively
seeking my own demise any more.*

—Al-Anon member

Originally I planned to separate the material in this chapter into two chapters: Learning to Live Again and Learning to Love Again. However, I decided separately addressing living and loving was not the issue. The problem many codependents encounter is learning to do both at the same time.

According to Earnie Larsen and others, the two deepest desires most people have are: to love and be loved, and to believe they are worthwhile and know someone else believes that also.[1] I have also heard this phrased more simply, with one item added: To be happy we need someone to love, something to do, and something to look forward to.

I am not going to split hairs over whether those desires are needs or wants. I think they're important. Whether we have been aware of these desires or not, they probably have been driving forces in our lives. Most of us have been trying, on some level of consciousness, to meet these needs. To protect ourselves, some of us may have blocked or shut off these needs. They are still there, whether we acknowledge or repress them. Understanding ourselves and our desires is powerful information. What we, as codependents, need to learn to do is fulfill these desires, needs, and wants in ways that don't hurt ourselves or other people, in ways that allow maximum enjoyment of life.

For many of us, that means we need to do things differently, because the ways we have gone about getting our needs met haven't worked. We've talked about some concepts that will help us do that: detachment, a nonrescuing approach to people, not controlling the object of our attention, directness, paying attention to ourselves, working a Twelve Step program, and becoming undependent. I believe as we get healthier, love will be different. I believe love will be better, perhaps better than ever before, if we let it and if we insist on it.

I don't think love has to hurt as much as it did in the past. I don't think we have to allow love to hurt us as much as it has. We certainly don't have to let it destroy us. As one woman so aptly phrases it, "I'm sick of being addicted to pain. I'm sick of being addicted to suffering. And I'm sick of letting men work out their unfinished business in my life!" It's not God's will that we stay miserable and stay in miserable relationships. That's something we've been doing to ourselves. We don't have to stay in relationships that cause us pain and misery. We are free to take care of ourselves.

We can learn to recognize the difference between relationships that do and don't work. We can learn to leave destructive relationships and enjoy the good ones. We can learn new behaviors that will help our good relationships work better.

I believe God allows certain people to come into our lives. But I also believe we are responsible for our choices and behaviors in initiating, maintaining, and discontinuing these relationships when appropriate. We may want and need love, but we don't need destructive love. And when we believe that, our message will come across clearly.

I believe our professional lives can be different and better. We can learn to take care of ourselves and our needs on the job. And if we are not so absorbed in other people and their business, if we believe we are important, we are free to set our own goals and reach our dreams. We are able to capture a vision for our own lives. That's exciting because good things can, do, and will happen to us if we allow those things to happen and if we are open to and believe we deserve those things. The good things probably won't happen without some struggle and pain, but at least we will be struggling and stretching for something worthwhile, instead of simply suffering.

It's okay to succeed, to have good things, and to have loving relationships that work. These things may not come easily or naturally. We may struggle and kick and want to hide our heads in the sand along the way. That's okay. That's how growth feels. If it feels too comfortable, too natural, or too easy, we're not growing and we're not doing anything dif ferent. We're doing the same things we always have, and that's why it feels so comfortable.

Learning to live and love again means finding a balance: learning to love and, at the same time, living our own lives; learning to love without getting so emotionally entangled with the object of our affection; and learning to love others without forfeiting love for ourselves. We need to learn to live, love, and have fun so each activity does not unreasonably interfere with any of the others.

Much of recovery is finding and maintaining balance in all areas of our lives. We need to watch the scales so they do not tip too far to either side as we measure our responsibilities to ourselves and to others. We need to balance our emotional needs with our physical, mental, and spiritual needs. We need to balance giving and receiving; we need to find the dividing line between letting go and doing our part. We need to find a balance between solving problems and learning to live with unsolved problems. Much of our anguish comes from having to live with the grief of unsolved problems, and having things not go the way we hoped and expected. We need to find a balance between letting go of our expectations and remembering we are important, valuable people who deserve to lead decent lives.

Getting Started

Frequently I am asked, where do I start? How do I get started? How do I even get my balance?

I've discussed many suggestions and ideas in this book, and some of us may feel overwhelmed

For some of us, getting our balance may seem impossible. We may feel like we are lying flat on the floor of a dark cellar, and we cannot possibly crawl out. We can. Alcoholics Anonymous and Al-Anon offer a simple three-part formula for doing this. It's called "HOW": Honesty, Openness, and Willingness to try. Earlier, I wrote change begins with awareness and acceptance. The third step in changing human behavior is assertive action. For us that means doing things differently. Get honest, keep an open mind, and become willing to try to do things differently, and we will change.

Choose one behavior to work on and when that becomes comfortable go on to another item. I have heard we need to repeat an action 21 times to make it a habit. That's a rule of thumb to keep in mind. The checklist in Chapter Four may provide some clues about where to start. The activities at the end of the chapters may give us some ideas. Figure out where we want to start and begin there. Start where we're at. If we can't figure out where to start, start by going to Al-Anon meetings, or another appropriate group. If we're in the basement, start crawling out. We'll learn to walk; we'll get our balance.

Getting started is both difficult and fun. When I began my recovery from codependency, I felt hopelessly trapped in myself and my relationships. Gloom surrounded me, and depression seemed to have permanently confined me to my bed. One morning, unhappy about being alive and awake, I dragged myself into the bathroom to get dressed and comb my hair, when my son insisted I follow him to another part of the house. I discovered a raging fire was consuming my bedroom. It had spread to the curtains, the ceiling, and the carpet. As in the past, I thought I could handle things myself; I thought the fire was not the disaster it appeared to be, so I grabbed a fire extinguisher and emptied it on the flames. Too little, too late. The fire raged on as we left the house.

My house was gutted by the time the fire department arrived. It was two weeks before Christmas, and my family and I had to move into a small apartment minus most of our clothing and the most basic of comforts. I hit my peak of despondency and anxiety. I had already lost so much, including myself. My home had been my nest, my remaining source of emotional security, and now I had lost that too. I had lost everything.

As the weeks passed, life began to require a little activity from me. Insurance inventories, negotiations, cleanup, and rebuilding plans demanded my attention. I felt anxious and insecure, but I had no choice. I had to think. I had to get busy. I had to do certain things. Once the actual reconstruction began, I had to do even more. I made choices about how to spend thousands of dollars. I worked hand in hand with the crews, doing everything I was able to do to help cut costs and expedite the project. That included physical activity, a part of my life that had become nonexistent. The busier I got, the better I felt. I began to trust my decisions. I worked off lots of anger and fear. By the time my family and I moved back into our home, my balance had been restored. I had begun living my own life, and I wasn't going to stop. It felt good!

The important concept here is, get started. Light a fire under yourself.

Growing Forward

Once we have gotten started, moving forward will become a natural process, if we continue to move. Sometimes, we will take a few steps backward. That's okay too. Sometimes it's necessary. Sometimes it's part of going forward.

Some of us may be facing tough decisions, decisions about ending relationships that are miserable and destructive. According to Earnie Larsen, if the relationship is dead, bury it. We can take our time, work on ourselves, and we will be able to make the right decision when the time is right.

Some of us may be trying to repair damaged but still alive relationships. Be patient. Love and trust are fragile, living entities. They do not automatically regenerate upon command if they have been bruised. Love and trust do not automatically reappear if the other person gets sober or solves whatever problem he or she had.[3] Love and trust must be allowed to heal in their own time. Sometimes they heal; sometimes they don't.

Some of us may be without a special person to love. That can be difficult, but it is not an impossible situation. We may want and need someone to love, but I think it helps if we love ourselves enough. It's okay to be in a relationship, but it's also okay to not be in a relationship. Find friends to love, be loved by, and who think we are worthwhile. Love ourselves and know we are worthwhile. Use our time alone as a breather. Let go. Learn the lessons we are to be learning. Grow. Develop. Work on ourselves, so when love comes along, it enhances a full and interesting life. Love shouldn't be the concern of our whole life or an escape from an unpleasant life. Strive toward goals. Have fun. Trust God and His timing. He cares and knows about all our needs and wants.

Whatever our situation, we can go slowly. Our hearts may lead us where our heads say we shouldn't go. Our heads may insist we go where our hearts don't want to follow. Sometimes our attraction to frogs may take us where neither our hearts nor heads choose to be. That's okay. There are no rules about whom we should or shouldn't love and relate to. We can love whomever we love, however we want to. But slow down and take the time to do it in a way that doesn't hurt us. Pay attention to what's happening. Love from our strengths, not from our weaknesses, and ask others to do the same. Make good decisions each day about what we need to do to take care of ourselves. Between our Higher Power and ourselves, we will be able to figure out what to do. I hope we will find people we enjoy loving—people who enjoy loving us and challenge us to grow. I hope we find enjoyable work that challenges us to grow.

A word of caution. From time to time, we may lose our balance. We may start running, skipping, and jumping, then suddenly find ourselves with our noses on the cement. All the old crazy feelings come rushing in. Don't be frightened. This is normal. Codependent characteristics, ways of thinking, and feelings become habits. Those habitual feelings and thoughts may surface on occasion. Change (even good change), certain circumstances reminiscent of alcoholic insanity, and stress, may provoke codependency. Sometimes the craziness returns unprovoked. See it through. Don't be ashamed and don't hide. We can pick ourselves up again. We will get through it. Talk to trusted friends; be patient and gentle with ourselves. Just keep doing the things we know we need to do. It will get better. Don't stop taking care of *us* no matter what happens.

Getting our balance and keeping it once we have found it is what recovery is all about. If that sounds like a big order, don't worry. We can do it. We can learn to live again. We can learn to love again. We can even learn to have fun at the same time.

EPILOGUE

I am not a teacher, but an awakener.

—Robert Frost

I wanted to write this book many years before I began it.

Originally, I wanted to write a book about codependency because when I was in so much pain with my codependency, I couldn't find a book that explained what had happened. I wanted to write a book for other hurting people that would explain codependency, help them understand, and ease their pain.·

That motive got squelched when I was "beaten to the punch." Other people began writing about codependency. Also, some literature had been available; I just hadn't found it.

Later, my motive for writing this book changed. I not only wanted to ease other people's pain; I wanted to redeem my suffering. It was a bargain I was trying to strike on my somewhat extended path to acceptance: If I write a book about this, then that part of my life won't be such a loss.

That motive was squelched too. Before I wrote the book, I accepted what had happened to me. It was okay, whether I did or didn't write about it. I also realized I had gained more than I had lost. Through my experience with codependency, I found my *self*. Everything from our pasts has prepared and propelled us to this moment; today prepares us for tomorrow. And it all works out for the good. Nothing's wasted.

By the time I actually sat down to write this book, my motive was about the same as it had been originally. I wanted to write something that would help codependent people, and I thought I had a few worthwhile ideas to pass along. However, this book is just an opinion, and my thoughts and ideas are just that—thoughts and ideas. To illustrate this point, let me quote Garrison Keillor. He was discussing fiction, but his statement applies to nonfiction, self-help books, as well:

"It's tough to tell the truth especially when . . . we're not absolutely sure of the truth. You're looking for the truth, and you are just putting out some markers."[1]

I hope this book has marked some truth for you. I hope I have helped awaken you to your *self*.

NOTES

Introduction

1. Janet Geringer Woititz, "Co-Dependency: The Insidious Invader of Intimacy," in *Co-Dependency, An Emerging Issue* (Hollywood, FL: Health Communications, 1984), 59.

2. Toby Rice Drews, *Getting Them Sober* (South Plainfield, NJ: Bridge Publishing, 1980), vol.1, xv.

Chapter 3

1. Paraphrase based on a quote by Joan Wexler and John Steidll (teachers of psychiatric social work at Yale University), quoted by Colette Dowling, *The Cinderella Complex: Women's Hidden Fear of Independence* (New York: Pocket Books, 1981), 145.

2. Robert Subby, "Inside the Chemically Dependent Marriage: Denial and Manipulation," in *Co-Dependency, An Emerging Issue* (Hollywood, FL: Health Communications, 1984), 26.

3. Robert Subby and John Friel, "Co-Dependency: A Paradoxical Dependency," in *Co-Dependency, An Emerging Issue*, 31.

4. Al-Anon Family Group, *Al-Anon Faces Alcoholism* (New York: Al-Anon Family Group Headquarters, 1977).

5. Al-Anon protects the anonymity of its members and keeps no official record of membership data. However, the Minneapolis Intergroup office agreed this figure was probably accurate.

6. Terence T. Gorski and Merlene Miller, "Co-Alcoholic Relapse: Family Factors and Warning Signs," in *Co-Dependency, An Emerging Issue*, 78.

7. Earnie Larsen; Subby, "Inside the Chemically Dependent Marriage."
8. Subby and Friel, "Co-Dependency."
9. Charles L. Whitfield, "Co-Dependency: An Emerging Problem Among Professionals," in *Co-Dependency, An Emerging Issue*, 53; Joseph L. Kellermann, *The Family and Alcoholism: A Move from Pathology to Process* (Center City MN: Hazelden Educational Materials, 1984).
10. Wayne W. Dyer, *Your Erroneous Zones* (New York: Funk and Wagnalls, 1976); Theodore I. Rubin with Eleanor Rubin, *Compassion and Self-Hate: An Alternative to Despair* (New York: David McKay Company, 1975).

Chapter 4

1. Nathaniel Branden, *Honoring the Self: Personal Integrity and the Heroic Potentials of Human Nature* (Boston: Houghton Mifflin Company, 1983), 162.
2. Dennis Wholey, *The Courage to Change* (Boston: Houghton Mifflin Company, 1984), 207.
3. Judi Hollis, *Fat Is a Family Affair* (San Francisco: Harper/Hazelden, 1986), 55.
4. *Ibid.*, 53.
5. Robert Subby and John Friel, "Co-Dependency: A Paradoxical Dependency," in *Co-Dependency, An Emerging Issue* (Hollywood, FL: Health Communications, 1984), 32.

Chapter 5

1. This quote is excerpted from a handout entitled "Detachment," which contains a collection of writings by anonymous Al-Anon members.
2. Wayne W. Dyer, *Your Erroneous Zones* (New York: Funk and Wagnalls, 1976), 89.
3. Al-Anon Family Group, *One Day at a Time in Al-Anon* (New York: Al-Anon Family Group Headquarters, Inc., 1976).
4. Judi Hollis, *Fat Is a Family Affair* (San Francisco: Harper/Hazelden, 1986), 47.
5. Terence Williams, *Free to Care: Therapy for the Whole Family* (Center City, MN: Hazelden Educational Materials, 1975).
6. Hollis, *Fat Is a Family Affair*.

7. Carolyn W., *Detaching with Love* (Center City, MN: Hazelden Educational Materials, 1984), 5.

8. Lois Walfrid Johnson, *Either Way, I Win: A Guide to Growth in the Power of Prayer* (Minneapolis: Augsburg, 1979).

9. Earnie Larsen does a similar meditation exercise at the end of his seminars.

Chapter 6

1. William Backus and Marie Chapian, *Telling Yourself the Truth* (Minneapolis: Bethany Fellowship, 1980).

Chapter 7

1. Eda LeShan, "Beware the Helpless," *Woman's Day*, 26 April 1983.

Chapter 8

1. Claude M. Steiner, *Scripts People Live* (New York: Grove Press, 1974).

2. *Ibid.*; Claude M. Steiner, *Games Alcoholics Play* (New York: Grove Press, 1971); and Claude M. Steiner, *What Do You Say After You Say Hello?* (New York: Grove Press, 1972).

Chapter 9

1. Penelope Russianoff, *Why Do I Think I'm Nothing Without a Man?* (New York: Bantam Books, 1982); Theodore I. Rubin with Eleanor Rubin, *Compassion and Self-Hate: An Alternative to Despair* (New York: David McKay Company, 1975), 278.

2. Janet Geringer Woititz, "Co-Dependency: The Insidious Invader of Intimacy," in *Co-Dependency, An Emerging Issue* (Hollywood, FL: Health Communications, 1984), 56.

3. Rubin, *Compassion*, 196.

4. Colette Dowling, *The Cinderella Complex: Women's Hidden Fear of Independence* (New York: Pocket Books, 1981).

5. *Ibid.*, 152–53.

6. *Ibid.*

7. Russianoff, *Why Do I Think I'm Nothing.*

8. Dowling, *The Cinderella Complex*, 22.

9. Kathy Capell-Sowder, "On Being Addicted to the Addict: Co-Dependent Relationships," in *Co-Dependency*, 23. See also Stanton Peele and Archie Brodsky, *Love and Addiction* (New York: New American Library, 1975).

Chapter 10

1. Nathaniel Branden, *Honoring the Self: Personal Integrity and the Heroic Potentials of Human Nature* (Boston: Houghton Mifflin Company, 1983), 53.

2. Theodore I. Rubin with Eleanor Rubin, *Compassion and Self-Hate: An Alternative to Despair* (New York: David McKay Company, 1975), 65.

3. *Ibid.*

Chapter 11

1. Theodore I. Rubin with Eleanor Rubin, *Compassion and Self-Hate: An Alternative to Despair* (New York: David McKay Company, 1975); Nathaniel Branden, *Honoring the Self: Personal Integrity and the Heroic Potentials of Human Nature* (Boston: Houghton Mifflin Company, 1983).

2. Robert Subby and John Friel, "Co-Dependency: A Paradoxical Dependency," in *Co-Dependency, An Emerging Issue* (Hollywood, FL: Health Communications, 1984), 40.

3. Rubin, *Compassion*.

4. *Ibid.*

5. Branden, *Honoring the Self*.

6. *Ibid.*, 76.

7. Wayne W. Dyer, *Your Erroneous Zones* (New York: Funk and Wagnalls, 1976).

8. Toby Rice Drews, *Getting Them Sober* (South Plainfield, NJ: Bridge Publishing, 1980), vol. 1, xxi.

9. Branden, *Honoring the Self*, 1–4.

Chapter 12

1. Joseph L. Kellermann, *A Guide for the Family of the Alcoholic* (New York: Al-Anon Family Group Headquarters, 1984), 8–9.

2. Janet Geringer Woititz, "Co-Dependency: The Insidious Invader of Intima-
    cy," in *Co-Dependency, An Emerging Issue* (Hollywood, FL: Health Commu-
    nications, 1984), 55.

3. *Ibid.*, 59.

4. Harold A. Swift and Terence Williams, *Recovery for the Whole Family* (Cen-
    ter City, MN: Hazelden Educational Materials, 1975).

5. Nathaniel Branden, *Honoring the Self: Personal Integrity and the Heroic Poten-
    tials of Human Nature* (Boston: Houghton Mifflin Company, 1983), 62–65.

6. Elisabeth Kübler-Ross, *On Death and Dying* (New York: MacMillan Publish-
    ing, 1969).

7. Melody Beattie, *Denial* (Center City, MN: Hazelden Educational Materials,
    1986).

8. Claudia L. Jewett, *Helping Children Cope with Separation and Loss* (Harvard,
    MA: The Harvard Common Press, 1982), 29.

9. *Ibid.*, 23, 29.

10. John Powell, *Why Am I Afraid to Tell You Who I Am?* (Allen, TX: Argus Com-
    munications, 1969), 116–17.

11. Kübler-Ross, *On Death and Dying*, 99–100.

12. Judi Hollis, *Fat Is a Family Affair* (San Francisco: Harper/Hazelden, 1986),
    80.

13. Donald L. Anderson, *Better Than Blessed* (Wheaton, IL: Tyndale House Pub-
    lishers, 1981), 11.

Chapter 13

1. John Powell, *Why Am I Afraid to Tell You Who I Am?* (Allen, TX: Argus Com-
    munications, 1969), 155.

2. Jael Greenleaf, "Co-Alcoholic/Para-Alcoholic: Who's Who and What's the
    Difference?" in *Co-Dependency, An Emerging Issue* (Hollywood, FL: Health
    Communications, 1984), 9.

3. Scott Egleston; Powell, *Why Am I Afraid*; Toby Rice Drews, *Getting Them
    Sober* (South Plainfield, NJ: Bridge Publishing, 1980), vol. 1.

4. Nathaniel Branden, *Honoring the Self: Personal Integrity and the Heroic Poten-
    tials of Human Nature* (Boston: Houghton Mifflin Company, 1983).

5. Powell, *Why Am I Afraid*.

6. *Ibid.*
7. Albert Ellis and Robert A. Harper, *A New Guide to Rational Living* (Holly-wood, CA: Wilshire Book, 1975); William Backus and Marie Chapian, *Telling Yourself the Truth* (Minneapolis: Bethany Fellowship, 1980).

Chapter 14

1. Janet Geringer Woititz, "The Co-Dependent Spouse: What Happens to You When Your Husband Is an Alcoholic," in *Co-Dependency, An Emerging Issue* (Hollywood, FL: Health Communications, 1984), 90.
2. Gayle Rosellini and Mark Worden, *Of Course You're Angry* (San Francisco: Harper/Hazelden, 1986).
3. Ephesians 4:26 RSV.
4. Toby Rice Drews, *Getting Them Sober* (South Plainfield, NJ: Bridge Publishing, 1980), vol. 1; Rosellini and Worden, *Of Course You're Angry*; and Scott Egleston.
5. Frederick S. Perls, *Gestalt Therapy Verbatim* (New York: Bantam Books, 1969).
6. Claude M. Steiner, *Scripts People Live* (New York: Grove Press, 1979).
7. Rosellini and Worden, *Of Course You're Angry*.
8. Woititz, "The Co-Dependent Spouse," 83.

Chapter 15

1. 2 Timothy 1:7 New Scofield Reference Bible.
2. Aron Kahn, "Indecision Decidedly in Vogue," *St. Paul Pioneer Press and Dispatch* (1 April 1986, sec. C).
3. Toby Rice Drews, *Getting Them Sober* (South Plainfield, NJ: Bridge Publishing, 1980), vol. 1.
4. Paraphrase of material in *Alcoholics Anonymous,* 3d ed. *"The Big Book"* (New York: Alcoholics Anonymous World Services, 1976).

Chapter 16

1. David J. Schwartz, *The Magic of Thinking Big* (New York: Cornerstone Library, 1959), 162–63.

2. *Ibid.*, 163–64.

3. *Ibid.*, 164.

4. Dennis Wholey, *The Courage to Change* (Boston: Houghton Mifflin Company, 1984), 39.

Chapter 17

1. Toby Rice Drews, *Getting Them Sober* (South Plainfield, NJ: Bridge Publishing, 1980), vol. 1, 77–78.

2. *Ibid.*, 76.

3. John Powell, *Why Am I Afraid to Tell You Who I Am?* (Allen, TX: Argus Communications, 1969), 12.

4. *Ibid.*, 8.

5. Jean Baer, *How to Be an Assertive (Not Aggressive) Woman in Life, in Love, and on the Job* (New York: New American Library, 1976).

Chapter 18

1. Al-Anon Family Group, *Al-Anon's Twelve Steps and Twelve Traditions* (New York: Al-Anon Family Group Headquarters, 1981), 131.

2. Jael Greenleaf, "Co-Alcoholic/Para-Alcoholic: Who's Who and What's the Difference?" in *Co-Dependency, An Emerging Issue* (Hollywood, FL: Health Communications, 1984), 15.

3. George E. Vaillant, *The Natural History of Alcoholism* (Cambridge, MA: Harvard University Press, 1983).

4. Warren W. told this story in Minneapolis 23 August 1985, borrowing it from circuit speaker Clancy Imislund who operates the Midnight Mission and lives in Venice, CA.

5. Al-Anon Family Group, *Al-Anon: Is It for You?* (New York: Al-Anon Family Group Headquarters, 1983). Reprinted by permission of Al-Anon Family Group Headquarters, Inc.

6. Judi Hollis, *Fat Is a Family Affair* (San Francisco: Harper/Hazelden, 1986), 49–52.

Chapter 19

1. Paraphrased quote based on a greeting card and poster sold years ago; author is unknown.

2. Toby Rice Drews, *Getting Them Sober* (South Plainfield, NJ: Bridge Publishing, 1983), vol. 2, 52.

3 Penelope Russianoff, *Why Do I Think I'm Nothing Without a Man?* (New York. Bantam Books, 1982).

4. Kathy Capell-Sowder, "On Being Addicted to the Addict: Co-Dependent Relationships," in *Co-Dependency, An Emerging Issue* (Hollywood, FL: Health Communications, 1984), 20–21.

5. Judi Hollis, *Fat Is a Family Affair* (San Francisco: Harper/Hazelden, 1986), 30–31.

6. Ideas discussed in this section are drawn from several articles in *Co-Dependency, An Emerging Issue* (Hollywood, FL: Health Communications, 1984); Janet Geringer Woititz, "The Co-Dependent Spouse: What Happens to You When Your Husband Is an Alcoholic"; Gerald Shulman, "Sexuality and Recovery: Impact on the Recovering Couple"; Marilyn Mason, "Bodies and Beings: Sexuality Issues During Recovery for the Dependent and Co-Dependent"; and Janet Geringer Woititz, "Co-Dependency: The Insidious Invader of Intimacy."

Chapter 20

1. Abraham H. Maslow, ed., *Motivation and Personality*, 2d ed. (New York: Harper & Row, 1970); Benjamin Wolman, ed., *International Encyclopedia of Psychiatry, Psychology, Psychoanalysis, & Neurology* (New York: Aesculapius Publishers, 1977), vol. 7, 32–33.

2. Nathaniel Branden, *Honoring the Self: Personal Integrity and the Heroic Potentials of Human Nature* (Boston: Houghton Mifflin Company, 1983), 162.

3. Janet Geringer Woititz, "Co-Dependency: The Insidious Invader of Intimacy," in *Co-Dependency, An Emerging Issue* (Hollywood, FL: Health Communications, 1984), 59.

Epilogue

1. Michael Schumacher, "Sharing the Laughter with Garrison Keillor," *Writer's Digest* (January 1986), 33.

BIBLIOGRAPHY

Books:

Alcoholics Anonymous World Services. *Alcoholics Anonymous "The Big Book"* 3d ed. New York: Alcoholics Anonymous World Services, 1976.

Al-Anon Family Group. *Al-Anon: Is It for You?* New York: Al-Anon Family Group Headquarters, 1983.

—— *Al-Anon's Twelve Steps and Twelve Traditions* New York: Al-Anon Family Group Headquarters, 1981.

—— *Al-Anon Faces Alcoholism* New York: Al-Anon Family Group Headquarters, 1977.

—— *One Day at a Time in Al-Anon* New York: Al-Anon Family Group Headquarters, 1974.

—— *The Dilemma of the Alcoholic Marriage* New York: Al-Anon Family Group Headquarters, 1971.

Anderson, Donald L. *Better Than Blessed* Wheaton, IL: Tyndale House Publishers, 1981.

Backus, William, and Marie Chapian. *Telling Yourself the Truth* Minneapolis: Bethany Fellowship, 1980.

Baer, Jean. *How to Be an Assertive (Not Aggressive) Woman in Life, in Love, and on the Job* New York: New American Library, 1976.

Branden, Nathaniel. *Honoring the Self: Personal Integrity and the Heroic Potentials of Human Nature* Boston: Houghton Mifflin Company, 1983.

DeRosis, Helen A., and Victoria Y. Pellegrino. *The Book of Hope: How Women Can Overcome Depression* New York: MacMillan Publishing, 1976.

Dowling, Colette. *The Cinderella Complex: Women's Hidden Fear of Independence* New York: Pocket Books, 1981.

Drews, Toby Rice. *Getting Them Sober, Volume 1* South Plainfield, NJ: Bridge Publishing, 1980.

———*Getting Them Sober, Volume 2* South Plainfield, NJ: Bridge Publishing, 1983.

Dyer, Wayne W. *Your Erroneous Zones* New York: Funk and Wagnalls, 1976.

Ellis, Albert, and Robert A. Harper. *A New Guide to Rational Living* Hollywood, CA: Wilshire Books, 1975.

Fort, Joel. *The Addicted Society: Pleasure-Seeking and Punishment Revisited* New York: Grove Press, 1981.

Hafen, Brent Q., with Kathryn J. Frandsen. *The Crisis Intervention Handbook* Englewood Cliffs, NJ: Prentice-Hall, 1982.

Hazelden. *Day by Day* San Francisco: Harper/Hazelden, 1986.

———*Twenty-Four Hours a Day* San Francisco: Harper/Hazelden, 1985.

Health Communications. *Co-Dependency, An Emerging Issue* Hollywood, FL: Health Communications, 1984.

Hollis, Judi. *Fat Is a Family Affair* San Francisco: Harper/Hazelden, 1986.

Hornik-Beer, Edith Lynn. *A Teenager's Guide to Living with an Alcoholic Parent* Center City, MN: Hazelden Educational Materials, 1984.

Jewett, Claudia L. *Helping Children Cope with Separation and Loss* Harvard, MA: The Harvard Common Press, 1982.

Johnson, Lois Walfrid. *Either Way, I Win: A Guide to Growth in the Power of Prayer* Minneapolis: Augsburg Publishing House, 1979.

Kimball, Bonnie-Jean. *The Alcoholic Woman's Mad, Mad World of Denial and Mind Games* Center City, MN: Hazelden Educational Materials, 1978.

Kübler-Ross, Elisabeth. *On Death and Dying* New York: MacMillan Publishing, 1969.

Landorf, Joyce. *Irregular People* Waco, TX: Word, 1982.

Lee, Wayne. *Formulating and Reaching Goals* Champaign, IL: Research Press Company, 1978.

Maslow, Abraham H., ed. *Motivation and Personality* 2d ed. New York: Harper & Row, 1970.

Maxwell, Ruth. *The Booze Battle* New York: Ballantine Books, 1976.

McCabe, Thomas R. *Victims No More* Center City, MN: Hazelden Educational Materials, 1978.

Perls, Frederick S. *Gestalt Therapy Verbatim* New York: Bantam Books, 1969.

Pickens, Roy W., and Dace S. Svikis. *Alcoholic Family Disorders: More Than Statistics* Center City, MN: Hazelden Educational Materials, 1985.

Powell, John S. *Why Am I Afraid to Tell You Who I Am?* Allen, TX: Argus Communications, 1969.

Restak, Richard M. *The Self Seekers* Garden City, NY: Doubleday and Company, 1982.

Rosellini, Gayle, and Mark Worden. *Of Course You're Angry* San Francisco: Harper/Hazelden, 1986.

Rubin, Theodore I. *Reconciliations: Inner Peace in an Age of Anxiety* New York: The Viking Press, 1980.

Rubin, Theodore I., with Eleanor Rubin. *Compassion and Self-Hate: An Alternative to Despair* New York: David McKay Company, 1975.

Russianoff, Penelope. *Why Do I Think I Am Nothing Without a Man?* New York: Bantam Books, 1982.

Schwartz, David J. *The Magic of Thinking Big* New York: Cornerstone Library, 1959.

Steiner, Claude M. *Games Alcoholics Play: The Analysis of Life Scripts* New York: Grove Press, 1971.

———— *Healing Alcoholism* New York: Grove Press, 1979.

———— *Scripts People Live* New York: Grove Press, 1974.

———— *What Do You Say After You Say Hello?* New York: Grove Press, 1972.

Vaillant, George E. *The Natural History of Alcoholism: Causes, Patterns and Paths to Recovery* Cambridge, MA: Harvard University Press, 1982.

Vine, Phyllis. *Families in Pain: Children, Siblings, Spouses and Parents of the Mentally Ill Speak Out* New York: Pantheon Books, 1982.

Wallis, Charles L., ed. *The Treasure Chest* New York: Harper & Row, 1965.

Wholey, Dennis. *The Courage to Change* Boston: Houghton Mifflin Company, 1984.

Woititz, Janet Geringer. *Adult Children of Alcoholics* Hollywood, FL: Health Communications, 1983.

Wolman, Benjamin B., ed. *International Encyclopedia of Psychiatry, Psychology, Psychoanalysis & Neurology*, vol. 7 New York: Aesculapius Publishers, 1977.

York, Phyllis and David, and Ted Wachtel. *Toughlove* Garden City, NY: Doubleday and Company, 1982.

Pamphlets:

Beattie, Melody. *Denial* Center City, MN: Hazelden Educational Materials, 1986.

Burgin, James E. *Help for the Marriage Partner of an Alcoholic* Center City, MN: Hazelden Educational Materials, 1976.

Emotions Anonymous International Services. *The Enormity of Emotional Illness: The Hope Emotions Anonymous Has to Offer* St. Paul, MN: Emotions Anonymous International Services, 1973.

H., Barbara. *Untying the Knots: One Parent's View* Center City, MN: Hazelden Educational Materials, 1984.

Harrison, Earl. *Boozlebane on Alcoholism and the Family* Center City, MN: Hazelden Educational Materials, 1984.

Hazelden Educational Materials. *Teen Drug Use: What Can Parents Do?* Center City, MN: Hazelden Educational Materials. (Reprinted with permission of Department of Public Instruction, Bismarck, ND, Drug Abuse Education Act of 1970.)

——— *No Substitute for Love: Ideas for Family Living* Center City, MN: Hazelden Educational Materials. (Reprinted with permission of Special Action Office for Drug Abuse Prevention, Executive Office of the President, Washington, DC, in conjunction with the Drug Abuse Prevention Week in 1973.)

——— *Step Four: Guide to Fourth Step Inventory for the Spouse* Center City, MN: Hazelden Educational Materials, 1976.

——— *Learn about Families and Chemical Dependency* Center City, MN: Hazelden Educational Materials, 1985.

Kellermann, Joseph L. *The Family and Alcoholism: A Move from Pathology to Process* Center City, MN: Hazelden Educational Materials, 1984.

——— *A Guide for the Family of the Alcoholic* New York: Al-Anon Family Group Headquarters, 1984.

Nakken, Jane. *Enabling Change: When Your Child Returns Home from Treatment* Center City, MN: Hazelden Educational Materials, 1985.

Schroeder, Melvin. *Hope for Relationships* Center City, MN: Hazelden Educational Materials, 1980.

Scientific Affairs Committee of the Bay Area Physicians for Human Rights. *Guidelines for AIDS Risk Reduction* San Francisco: The San Francisco AIDS Foundation, 1984.

Swift, Harold A., and Terence Williams *Recovery for the Whole Family* Center City, MN: Hazelden Educational Materials, 1975.

Timmerman, Nancy G. *Step One for Family and Friends* Center City, MN: Hazelden Educational Materials, 1985.

———— *Step Two for Family and Friends* Center City, MN: Hazelden Educational Materials, 1985.

W., Carolyn. *Detaching with Love* Center City, MN: Hazelden Educational Materials, 1984.

Williams, Terence. *Free to Care: Therapy for the Whole Family of Concerned Persons* Center City, MN: Hazelden Educational Materials, 1975.

Articles:

Anderson, Eileen. "When Therapists Are Hooked on Power" *The Phoenix*, vol. 5, no. 7, July 1985.

"Author's Study Says CoAs Can't Identify Their Needs" *The Phoenix* (from Family Focus, published by the U.S. Journal of Drug and Alcohol Dependence), vol. 4, no. 11, November 1984.

Bartell, Jim. "Family Illness Needs Family Treatment, Experts Say" *The Phoenix*, vol. 4, no. 11, November 1984.

Black, Claudia. "Parental Alcoholism Leaves Most Kids Without Information, Feelings, Hope" *The Phoenix*, vol. 4, no. 11, November 1984.

Hamburg, Jay. "Student of Depression Sights a Silver Lining" *St. Paul Pioneer Press and Dispatch (Orlando Sentinel)*, 23 September 1985.

Jeffris, Maxine. "About the Word Co-Dependency" *The Phoenix*, vol. 5, no. 7, July 1985.

Kahn, Aron. "Indecision Decidedly in Vogue" *St. Paul Pioneer Press and Dispatch*, 1 April 1986.

Kalbrener, John. "We Better Believe That Our Children Are People, Says Children Are People" *The Phoenix,* vol. 4, no. 11, November 1984.

LeShan, Eda. "Beware the Helpless" *Woman's Day,* 26 April 1983.

Ross, Walter S. "Stress: It's Not Worth Dying For" *Reader's Digest,* January 1985, 76.

Schumacher, Michael. "Sharing the Laughter with Garrison Keillor" *Writer's Digest,* January 1986, 33.

Strick, Lisa Wilson. "What's So Bad About Being So-So?" *Reader's Digest,* August 1984, 78 (reprinted from *Woman's Day,* 3 April 1984).

Miscellaneous:

"Adult Children of Alcoholics," handout, author unknown.

"Detachment," handout written by anonymous Al-Anon members.

Jourard, Sidney, with Ardis Whitman. "The Fear That Cheats Us of Love," handout.

Larsen, Earnie. "Co-Dependency Seminar," Stillwater, MN, 1985.

Wright, Thomas. "Profile of a Professional Caretaker," handout.

Beyond
Codependency

AND GETTING BETTER ALL THE TIME

One night, in a dream, I saw a group of people. These people were deserving, lovable people. The problem was, they didn't know it. They were stuck, confused—reacting to some crazy stuff that happened long ago.

They were running around in adult bodies, but in many ways they were still children. And they were scared.

These people were so busy protecting themselves and trying to figure out what everything meant, they didn't do what they most needed to do: relax, be who they were, and allow themselves to shine.

They didn't know it was okay to stop protecting themselves. They didn't know it was okay to love and be loved. They didn't know they could love themselves.

When I awoke, I realized I was one of them.

This book is dedicated to us, the recovering adult children and code-pendents. May we each awaken to the beauty of ourselves, other people, and life.

For helping make this book possible, I thank God, Nichole, Shane, Mom, John, Becky, Terry, Ruth, Scott, Lee, Linda, Carolyn, and my readers. Some encouraged and inspired me to write; some had to put up with me while I did.

CONTENTS

ACKNOWLEDGMENTS

First, I want to acknowledge the recovering people who shared their stories with me. They brought life to my work.

I also want to acknowledge the contributions of Timmen Cermak, M.D., a founding member and first president of the National Association for Children of Alcoholics, and Bedford Combs, M.Ed., LMFT, Founding President of the South Carolina Association for Children of Alcoholics. Their work helped me understand the recovery process, and they helped me grow.

INTRODUCTION

*"Have you been writing any personal experience
articles lately?" the woman asked the writer. "No,"
replied the writer. "I've been busy having them."*
— Ruth Peterman[1]

This is a book about recovery.

Actually, this is a book about continuing our recoveries.

I wrote it for people recovering from the ways they've allowed themselves to be affected by other people and their problems. I wrote it for people recovering from codependency, chemical dependency, and adult children issues. I wrote it for people struggling to master the art of self-care.

Codependent No More, my last book, was about stopping the pain and gaining control of our lives. This book is about what to do when the pain has stopped and we've begun to suspect we have lives to live. It's about what happens next.

We'll look at recovery, relapse, doing our family of origin work, and what to do about it after we've done it. We'll talk about relationships. We'll talk about concepts like surrender and spirituality too.

We'll talk about many ideas: dealing with shame, growing in self-esteem, overcoming deprivation, sharing recovery with our children, and getting beyond our fatal attractions long enough to find relationships that work.

When I began this manuscript, I had a long list of scattered bits of information I wanted to parlay. I wasn't certain how these ideas would fit together. When I stopped trying to control, the book took on, as some do, a unique and occasionally surprising life of its own.

Codependent No More was about beginning our recoveries. This book is about the core issues of recovery: working on the nuts and bolts, and fine-tuning.

In retrospect, it has emerged primarily as a book about growing in self-love, and our ability to affirm and nurture ourselves. A serendipity of that process is growing in our capacity to love others and to let them, and God, love us.

This book is based on research, my personal and professional experiences, and my opinion. Throughout, I'll attempt to attribute all ideas, theories, and quotes to appropriate sources. Sometimes it's difficult to do that in the recovery field because many people say many of the same things.

The case histories I use are true. I've changed names and details to protect people's privacy.

I've included activities at the end of some chapters. You can explore your answers in a separate journal or notebook.

Also, this book is not about how to change or help the other person. It's about knowing it's okay for us to continue helping ourselves, to better lives and improved relationships.

An old adage says, "When the student is ready, the teacher will appear." Another, however, says, "You teach what you most need to learn."

Writers, they say, are teachers.

"It is possible," wrote Lawrence Block, "to see everything we write as a letter to ourselves, designed to convey to one portion of ourselves the lesson that another portion has already learned."[2]

I have learned from writing this book. I hope you gain as much from reading it.

Section I:

RECOVERY

*Recovery is when
fun becomes fun;
love becomes love;
and life becomes worth living.*

1

THE RECOVERY MOVEMENT

I started taking care of myself and it feels so good
I'm not going to stop, no matter what.

—Anonymous

Something exciting is happening across the land. Let's take a look.

Carla's Story

Two years ago, Carla thought she was crazy and her schedule was normal.

"Well, almost normal," said Carla, an elementary school teacher and the thirty-five-year-old daughter of a well-groomed, professional family.

From 6 to 8 A.M., Carla worked at a day-care center. From 8:30 A.M. to 12:30 P.M., she taught grade school. From 2 to 6 P.M., she taught at an after-school latchkey program.

To save a woman from being sent to a nursing home, Carla had moved in with an Alzheimer's victim. So at 12:30, Carla rushed home to make lunch for her roommate. At supper time, Carla rushed home again to make supper for her roommate.

Several years earlier, while working at the state prison, Carla had befriended, then fallen in love with, an inmate (a phenomenon peculiar to many people who identify with codependency). After washing the supper dishes, Carla hurried to the prison to visit him. At 9 P.M., Carla dashed home to put her roommate to bed.

In her spare time, Carla volunteered forty hours each month to the county mental health center. And she taught Sunday school.

Besides those volunteer activities, Carla had offered use of her home, rent-free, to a family she met at the prison visiting room. She was able to do this because she had left her home standing empty when she moved in with the Alzheimer's patient.

"I thought I was doing everything right. I was doing everything people expected of me. I was being good to people. I was being a good Christian. One thing I couldn't understand was why everyone was mad at me," Carla says. "The other thing I couldn't understand was why I felt crazy and wished I was dead.

"The relatives of the woman I lived with got angry at me for telling them how sick she was and how much care she needed. My boyfriend was mad at me. My bosses were upset because I kept getting sick and missing work. And the woman living in my house got angry because when she began working, I started asking for rent money.

"I didn't know how I felt," Carla says. "For as long as I can remember, I couldn't remember feeling joy, sorrow, anything! I knew I was physically sick. My legs and feet were swollen so badly I couldn't walk some days. But I didn't go to the doctor because I didn't want to bother him.

"I didn't want to bother the doctor," she says, shaking her head. "Things were crazy, but they were about to get crazier."

The woman living in Carla's house became so indignant about paying rent she moved out. Carla moved back into her home. Within days, the furnace went out, the sewer pipe collapsed, the basement flooded, and gophers chewed through the gas line and the house almost blew up. A neighbor selling his property used the wrong land description and instead sold Carla's house, and a pheasant flew through the bay window, decapitated itself, and ran through the house like a dead chicken.

"Just like me," Carla recalls.

Soon, Carla's boyfriend, an alcoholic, was released from prison. Within two weeks he started drinking and disappeared from her life. "I bottomed out. This was the culmination of over thirty years of failure," Carla says. "I felt like a failure professionally and personally. I had gone from one hundred fifteen pounds to over two hundred pounds. I had been married and divorced twice, both times to successful professional men who physically or verbally abused me. Now, I had been rejected by a prison inmate. This was it. This was the end! I hadn't drank for fifteen years, but I started drinking two quarts of vodka a day. I wanted to die."

Carla didn't die. Instead, someone handed her a book about codependency. From reading it, she learned that although her behaviors were a little crazy, she wasn't. She was battling codependency. She also learned a recovery program was available to her, one that promised to change her life.

Although she's worked at recovery for only a year and a half, Carla has worked hard at it. She regularly attends both Al-Anon and Alcoholics Anonymous meetings. She goes to workshops on codependency, shame, and self-esteem. She also works with a therapist experienced with codependency recovery issues.

"I got mad at the therapist," Carla recalls. "I was a professional; he was a professional. I went to him expecting him to do his job: fix me. He told me he couldn't do that. I learned there wasn't a magic cure. I learned I had to do my own recovery work."

Although she didn't find a magic cure, Carla describes the changes in her life in eighteen months as "dramatic."

"I've done a lot of grieving, but at least I'm feeling. I'm feeling feelings for the first time in my life. I'm feeling sad, and I'm feeling happy.

"I'm still busy, but I'm not running around like a chicken with its head chopped off. I'm choosing to do the things I'm doing, instead of feeling like I have no choices. I'm setting and reaching goals. That feels good," Carla says.

Carla is still struggling to undo the financial chaos connected to her codependency. "But at least I'm struggling for and toward something. I now have money in my checkbook. I can take myself out to eat. And I've even started buying myself new clothes. That's different. I used to shop at secondhand stores and deliberately chose the worst items there, the things I thought nobody else would want. I didn't want to take any clothing away from the poor people," she explains, "the ones who really needed it."

Carla has made other advances too. She's learning to say no. She's learning to stick up for herself and her rights, instead of fighting only for the rights of others. She's beginning to look back to discover the origins of her codependency (family of origin work).

"My family wasn't bad or awful," Carla says. "They were good, smart, professional people. Although my father abused prescription drugs for about two years, my parents weren't obviously addicted or dysfunctional. They were close. We had some fun times.

"But there were subtleties," Carla adds. "I learned how to be a martyr. I always felt I needed to be perfect. I never felt good enough. I didn't know how to deal with feelings. We lived in a small community. During one phase of my childhood, my parents' political stance caused us to be ostracized by the town. I felt so rejected. And I learned how to reject *myself*. I started believing something was wrong with me."

Besides looking back, Carla has begun to look around. She's noticing how codependency has permeated her life.

"I have two groups of friends: other codependents who want to complain about being victims, and the people who want to use and mistreat me. I'm working at changing my friendships. I'm also reevaluating my professional life. My codependency influenced my career choices. Most of my jobs demanded a lot and gave me little in return. Of course, I gave and gave on my jobs, then got angry because I felt used. Now, I'm learning to set boundaries at work. Some people are getting mad at me for changing, but I'm not feeling so used.

"I'm learning to stop asking why people are doing this to me,"

Carla says. "I've started asking why I'm allowing them to do this to me."

Relationships with men are still a weak spot in Carla's recovery. "I'm still attracted to the sickest man in the room, the one who needs me the most," Carla admits. "But at least I've started to get red flags. That's new. I always used to get green lights."

She says she has much work left to do on self-esteem but has begun to accept herself. "I do a lot of work with affirmations. I've got my bathroom mirror pasted full of them. That helps. It really does.

"Sometimes I still let other people control me. Sometimes I'm not sure when it's okay to want approval from people, and when it's a codependent behavior. I'm not always sure when it's okay to give, and when I'm doing caretaking stuff. And sometimes I get scared.

"But the best thing that's happened to me is I've begun to feel peaceful," Carla says. "For the first time in my life I want to live, and I believe there's a purpose for my life.

"My relationship with my Higher Power, God, has improved. I'm not in control of my life, but by working my program, it's become manageable. I know Someone is caring for me and helping me care for myself.

"And," Carla adds, "I'm proud of my recovery."

Recently, while paging through a photo album, Carla found one of the few pictures taken of her when she was a child. She rarely allowed people to photograph her because she hated the way she looked.

"I was surprised when I saw this picture," Carla says. "I wasn't ugly. There wasn't anything so terribly wrong with me, like I thought there was. It's sad I've spent so many years of my life believing there was."

The other day, when Carla walked into the student bathroom at the grade school where she works, she found a sobbing fourth-grade girl curled up behind the trash can. The girl, a beautiful child with long dark hair, had tried to smash the bathroom mirror.

Carla asked what was wrong. The girl said she hated herself, she hated the way she looked, and she wanted to die. Carla gently scooped up the child, carried her into the office, and referred her to the school psychiatrist.

"I cried for her, and I cried for me. But it wasn't all tears of sadness," Carla says. "I cried because I felt relieved. At last we have hope."

Our Stories

That's the good news, and that's what this book is about: hope for Carla, hope for the little girl who hates herself, hope for you, and hope for me. This book is about hope for continued recovery from this problem we've come to call codependency.

Many of us have found that hope. By the numbers, we're flocking to Twelve Step meetings, workshops, and therapists—to get help for ourselves. We're demanding (well, "inquiring about," at least initially) our birthright, our right to be, our right to live, and our right to recover.

Celebrities are publicly declaring themselves adult children of alcoholics. Men, women, and young children (not just adult children) are beginning their searches for hope. I've heard from older people who have just begun their recoveries. "I'm seventy-five years old and I feel like I'm just learning to live," said one woman. "But at least I'm learning."

Codependent jokes have emerged. Did you hear about the codependent wife? Each morning, she wakes her husband and asks him how she's going to feel that day.

Codependency even made the pages of *Newsweek* magazine.[1]

The important idea here is we've lost our invisibility. We're recognizing ourselves, and others are recognizing us too. More help and hope has become available to us—from teddy bears that tell us it's okay to feel what we feel, to in-patient codependency treatment programs where we can deal with our inner child (the part of us that feels, plays, and needs to be nurtured) and where we can address our family of origin issues (our messages from the past that control what we do today—like a computer program). And we're taking advantage of it.

We're part of a groundswell movement, a tremendous movement that's come into its own time. We're saying, simply and clearly, enough is enough, and we've suffered enough. It's time to do things differently.

For years, we called chemical dependency and other disorders "family diseases." Now, we're believing our own words. At last, as Carla said, we have hope. Practical hope. The word *codependency* may label a problem, but to many of us it also labels the solution: recovery.

Many of us have suffered, and are still suffering to some degree, from a relationship with a dysfunctional person. Sometimes that person appeared in our childhoods, sometimes in our adult lives. Usually, we've had relationships with more than one dysfunctional person; this pattern began in childhood and repeated itself as we grew older.

Discovering that many of us have suffered to some extent from codependency has affirmed one of my earlier beliefs: it's okay to be codependent. It has to be; there are so many of us. But it's even better to be recovering.

Some of us have been recovering for a long time; others are just beginning the recovery experience. Some of us are working on dual or multiple recovery programs; for instance, recovery from codependency and chemical dependency, or recovery from codependency and an eating disorder. We may not always be certain what it means to be recovering or where our recovery programs will take us, but we're going there anyway.

We may be codependent "not as much" while we're striving to be codependent no more, but we're getting better all the time. And that's good enough.

What does the future hold?

The word *codependency* may disappear. Media and public attention may subside. But no matter what we call it, recovery from code-pendency is more than a fad. We've started the journey of self-care and self-love. Although there may be a few detours and resting places along the way, we're not going to stop now.

Let me wrap up this chapter with an anecdote about my son, Shane, who loves video games. Recently, he got involved playing a particular game. This game offered about forty levels of skill, each deeper and more complicated than the last, to those who could overcome the obstacles, avoid the pitfalls, stay empowered by the power source, and not get killed by the enemy.

Shane was playing well enough, but couldn't get past a certain level of play. No matter how hard he tried, he couldn't go any further. After a while, he stopped believing it was possible to go further.

Then one day a friend stopped by, and my son watched her play the game. She'd been playing longer; she'd watched an older brother play; she'd learned a few tricks. She could jump, hop, and scurry her way down to the deepest levels.

Watching her was all it took. After that, with confidence and ease, my son began to play at increasingly deeper levels. He got unstuck. He broke through.

That's what this book is about: believing we can go further than we've ever gone before. Let's love ourselves for how far we've come. Let's see how far we can go. And let's go there together. We each have to do our own work, but doing it together is what makes it work.

2

RECOVERY

What's a codependent? The answer's easy.
They're some of the most loving, caring people I know.

—Lonny Owen[1]

In spite of the emergence of the word *codependency,* and so many people recovering from it, it is still jargon. No standard definition exists. We haven't agreed on whether codependency is a sickness, a condition, or a normal response to abnormal people. We still haven't agreed on whether it's hyphenated: *codependency* or *co-dependency?*

What most people have decided is this: whatever codependency is, it's a problem, and recovering from it feels better than not.

If codependency is so common, why bother to call it anything? Why not just call it normal? Because it hurts. And recovery means learning how to stop the pain. In this chapter, we'll explore what it means to do that.

To explain recovery, let me indulge in a metaphor. In 1982, a fire nearly destroyed my home. I learned some truths then about fires.

The fire's not over when the fire truck leaves. Repairing fire damage can involve an extensive, sometimes frustrating rehabilitation process.

A fire can smolder for a long time before it bursts into flames. The fire in my home smoldered quietly, but dangerously, in a mattress for hours before it became apparent. I had been in the room minutes before flames erupted, and the room looked "fine."

Although we physically survive a fire, we can be affected—trauma-tized—mentally and emotionally. For years after my fire, each time I saw a fire truck speeding to a fire, each time I heard sirens, or saw a burning house on the news, I panicked. My chest tightened. My breath quickened. My hands trembled. When leaving home, I checked and double-checked to make certain no hazards existed. *I no longer felt safe.*

These same truths apply to another fire, the one we've come to label codependency. It can require an extensive, sometimes frustrating rehabilitation process. It can smolder for a long time before it bursts into flames. And, though we've survived the fire, many of us have been traumatized.

Let's explore these ideas.

The Fire's Not Out When the Fire Truck Leaves

Many good definitions of codependency have surfaced.

In 1987, a handout at a week-long training seminar on chemical dependency and the family, sponsored by the Johnson Institute of Minneapolis, described codependency as "a set of maladaptive, compulsive behaviors learned by family members to survive in a family experiencing great emotional pain and stress. . . . Behaviors . . . passed on from generation to generation whether alcoholism is present or not."

Earnie Larsen, the recovery pioneer from Minnesota, calls codependency "those self-defeating learned behaviors or character defects that result in a diminished capacity to initiate, or participate in, loving relationships."

A friend, and recovering woman, defines codependents as "people who don't take care of themselves, whether or not they are, or have ever been, in a relationship with an alcoholic."

And in *Codependent No More* I called a codependent "a person who has let someone else's behavior affect him or her, and is obsessed with controlling other people's behavior."

These definitions refer to behaviors—today's self-defeating, learned survival behaviors. Certainly, recovery means extinguishing any fires blazing in our homes and lives today. But the heart of recovery is the sometimes grueling, extensive reconstruction process of acquiring new behaviors. In recovery, we stop enduring life and begin to live it.

Instead of obsessively trying to control others, we learn to detach. Instead of allowing others to hurt and use us, we set boundaries. Instead of reacting, we learn to relax and let things settle into place. We replace tunnel vision with perspective. We forego worrying and denial, and learn constructive problem solving skills. We learn to feel and express feelings; we learn to value what we want and need; we stop punishing ourselves for other people's problems, nonsense, and insanity. We stop expecting ourselves to be perfect, and we stop expecting perfection of others.

We stop reacting to the powerfully dysfunctional systems so many of us have been affected by. We stop getting tangled up in craziness. We acquire the art of removing ourselves as victims.

We stop compulsively taking care of other people and we take care of ourselves. We learn to be good to ourselves, to have fun, and to enjoy life. We learn to feel good about what we've accomplished. We stop focusing on what's wrong and we notice what's right. We learn to function in relationships. We learn to love ourselves, so we can better love others.

Recovery also means addressing any other issues or compulsive behaviors that have cropped up along the way. Codependency is sneaky and deceptive. It's also progressive. One thing leads to another, and often things get worse.

We may become workaholics, or busy freaks. We may develop eating disorders or abuse mood-altering chemicals. We may develop compulsive sexual behaviors or become compulsive about spending, religion, achievement, or appearance.

Other complications can emerge too. We can become chronically depressed, develop emotional or mental problems, or stress-related illnesses.

"We hear a lot about how alcoholism is terminal for the alcoholic," says one recovering man. "We don't hear enough about how codependency can be terminal too. So many of us wind up thinking about, or trying to, kill ourselves."

Recovery means dealing with the entire package of self-defeating, compulsive behaviors, and any other problems that may have emerged. But we don't deal with these behaviors or problems by thinking we're bad for having them. We address ourselves, and recovery, with a sense of forgiveness and a certain gentleness toward ourselves. We begin to understand that the behaviors we've used were survival tools. We've been coping. We've been doing the best we could. We've been protecting ourselves. Some recovery professionals suggest these behaviors may have saved our lives.

"If we hadn't protected ourselves, we may have given up or developed a fatal illness and died," says Bedford Combs.[2]

Whether it's a compulsion to caretake, control, work, or eat pecan pies, compulsive behaviors initially are about stopping the pain.[3] We begin to realize what we've been doing: trying to stop the pain. But we begin to understand something else too. Although compulsive behaviors may help us temporarily avoid feelings or problems, they don't really stop the pain. They create more. They may even take on a habitual and problematic life of their own.

So we acquire new behaviors, gradually, sometimes with reluctance, and usually with a great deal of experimentation and forward and backward movement.

We don't change perfectly or completely. Sometimes, in recovery, we still protect ourselves with survival behaviors. Sometimes we need to do that. Sometimes we regress, and that's okay too. Sometimes, we turn our behaviors around and let them work for us, instead of against us. For instance, in recovery, many of us have used our ability to endure deprivation to *help ourselves* get through college.

In recovery, we still give to people. We continue to care about people. But we learn we are responsible for our behaviors, and our behaviors have consequences. We learn some behaviors have self-defeating consequences, while others have beneficial consequences. We learn we have choices.

We also learn we don't change by ourselves, or by exerting greater amounts of willpower. Intertwined with this process of changing our behaviors is a Higher Power, God, as we each understand Him. Paradoxically, we change most during those tremendous moments when we run out of willpower.

Recovery means acquiring, living by, and sometimes living and recovering *because of* spiritual principles. We learn to do intangible things like "Let Go and Let God," "surrender," and "accept" while we're doing the more tangible behaviors such as making decisions and setting boundaries.

Changing today's self-defeating behaviors is an important part of recovery. It's where most of us begin. It's what most of us need to work on for the duration. But recovery is more than that.

The Smoldering Coals

When I first began my recovery from codependency, I assumed my codependency started when I formed relationships with the alcoholics in my life. I now believe my codependency was the reason I had so many alcoholics in my life.

A fire had been smoldering for many years in me, probably since I was a child. That fire burst into flames in my thirties, when I bottomed out and wanted to end my life.

Some of the smoldering coals in that fire were the rules, *the codependent rules.*

Robert Subby, a codependency and adult children recovery professional, talks about codependency being "an emotional, psychological, and behavioral condition that develops as a result of an individual's prolonged exposure to, and practice of, a set of oppressive rules."[4]

These rules say:

- Don't feel or talk about feelings.
- Don't think.
- Don't identify, talk about, or solve problems.
- Don't be who you are—be good, right, strong, and perfect.
- Don't be selfish—take care of others and neglect yourself.
- Don't have fun, don't be silly or enjoy life.
- Don't trust other people or yourself.
- Don't be vulnerable.
- Don't be direct.
- Don't get close to people.
- Don't grow, change, or in any way rock this family's boat.[5]

These rules probably weren't pasted on the refrigerator next to "clean up your room" and "take out the garbage," but they might as well have been.

More coals in that fire were the *other messages* I interpreted while growing up. These messages included beliefs such as:

- I'm not lovable.
- I don't deserve good things.
- I'll never succeed.

And for many of us, the smoldering fire contains other coals too. Included among these are *feelings from our childhood*, feelings that hurt too much to feel. Many of us denied these feelings, then lived out situations that recreated the same feelings we were denying from our childhoods. The smoldering fire is a past buried alive, according to Earnie Larsen.

"I always knew my dad was an alcoholic," says a recovering woman. "It wasn't until recently I realized I was an adult child of an alcoholic. It wasn't until recently I realized how I felt about him being an alcoholic. It wasn't until recently I realized how much I had been affected by the disease."

Codependency is about the ways we have been affected by other people and our pasts.

Some of us grew up in powerfully dysfunctional family systems. Some of us lived in those systems as children, then recreated the experience as adults. We may have spent much of our lifetimes being affected by, and reacting to, systems too powerful to budge.

We may have spent lifetimes wondering what was wrong with us when the other person, or the system, was "what was wrong." Many of us have surpassed being "affected." Many of us have been, to some degree, traumatized.[6]

In his writings about codependency and the adult child syndrome, Timmen Cermak calls this "Post Traumatic Stress Disorder." According to Cermak, it can happen to people who chronically live through or with events "outside the range of what is considered to be normal human experience."[7]

The symptoms of stress disorder in codependency are similar to the symptoms of stress disorder in war veterans. The symptoms are comparable to the way I was affected by the fire that burned my home.

We may, without warning, reexperience the feelings, thoughts, and behaviors that were present during the original traumatic event.[8] Codependent feelings and behaviors—fear, anxiety, shame, an overwhelming need to control, neglecting ourselves, and focusing on others—may suddenly emerge when something in our environment, something innocuous, reminds us or our subconscious of something noxious that happened before.

These reactions may have been entirely appropriate when we went through the original experience, but these reactions may be inappropriate, confusing, and self-defeating today.

After the fire, events that triggered a stress reaction in me were: hearing sirens, seeing fire trucks speeding by, watching a home burn on the news. After living with an alcoholic, or living through another kind of trauma, many events can be "triggers."

"For children from chemically dependent families, the trigger can be almost anything," Cermak writes, "the sound of ice clinking in a glass, an expression of anger or criticism, arguing, the sensation of losing control. . . ."[9]

Another symptom of stress disorder is *psychic numbing.* Cermak describes this as suspending feelings in favor of taking steps to ensure our safety, or splitting between one's self and one's experience.[10] To protect ourselves, to keep things going, to keep ourselves going, we disconnect from our feelings—our *selves.* We go into "freeze" or "survival" mode.

Still another symptom of stress disorder is *hypervigilance,* an inability to feel comfortable unless we're continually monitoring our surroundings. "They remained on edge," Cermak writes, "always expecting the worst, unable to trust or feel safe again."[11]

Cermak is describing Vietnam veterans, but his statement applies to many of us. We stay on guard. We watch, listen, and worry, wondering when the other shoe will drop. We no longer feel safe.

Finally, in discussing this syndrome, Cermak talks about survivor guilt. "Whenever they begin to experience the fullness that life has to offer, they immediately feel as if they are betraying those who never had the chance." He's describing people who survived a war that others didn't. "It seems somehow wrong to go away and be healthy when those who are left behind are still suffering."[12]

Recovery means changing today's self-defeating, learned survival behaviors. Recovery means putting out the smoldering coals. And recovery means dealing with any ways we may have been traumatized.

We reconnect with ourselves. We learn to give ourselves some love and concern. We learn to make ourselves feel safe. We know, really know, it's okay for us to be as healthy as we can become.

We're not crazy. We're codependent. And recovery means putting out the fire.

In the next chapter, we'll look at how that happens.

3

THE PROCESS

*I can tell you what it was like, and I can tell you what it's like now
but I'm still not sure what happened.*

—Anonymous

Recovery is a process. Recovery is a process. How many times have
we heard that? We've heard it so many times because it's true. Recovery is a process, a gradual one of awareness, acceptance, and
change. It's also a healing process. Yet, recovery often feels more like
"being processed."

Both ideas are true. Recovery is a process by which we change,
and by which we become changed. The important ideas here are
learning when it's time to do something, and when it's time to let
something happen.

Although our recovery experiences are unique, there are similar-
ities. Timmen Cermak and other professionals have identified certain
recovery stages.[1] In this chapter, we'll explore those stages which are:

- survival/denial
- reidentification
- core issues
- reintegration
- genesis

Survival/Denial

In this pre-recovery stage, denial operates unbidden (borrowing a line from Robin Norwood),[2] and we're using our coping behaviors to survive. We don't see things too painful to see; we don't feel emotions too painful to feel. We don't realize our coping behaviors are self-defeating. In fact, we're often proud of our gestures.

"Look at all the people I'm taking care of," we tell people. "See what I did to control him!" We may take pride in our ability to deprive ourselves or stifle feelings.

"It's not that bad," we tell others and ourselves. "Things will be better tomorrow." "I'll get my reward in heaven." Or, "Everything's fine. Baby's back in my arms again!" We may smile and say, "Things are fine," but things aren't fine.[3] We've lost touch with ourselves. We're existing, not living.

Then something happens. Maybe it's one big problem. Maybe it's several smaller problems, or many large ones. Maybe it's the same problem that's happened so many times before. What changes is our reaction. We become fed up. We run out of willpower. We run out of ourselves.

We realize, on some level, that our lives have become unmanageable. Regardless of what the other person is or isn't doing, we know our lives aren't working. We've been enduring life, not living it. And we become ready to be changed. Although we may not be sure *what,* we know *something* has to change. Something does. We move on to the next stage.

Reidentification

Two important events take place here.

We reidentify ourselves and our behaviors. I become Melody, a recovering codependent (or adult child or Al-Anon). Instead of taking pride in our coping behaviors, we begin to see them as self-defeating.

And we surrender. We wave the white flag. We accept our powerlessness over other people, their problems, our pasts, our messages from the past, our circumstances, sometimes ourselves and our feelings, or any other appropriate area. We begin to establish, as Timmen Cermak puts it, "a realistic relationship with willpower."[4]

Some people, like Carla from the first chapter, feel immensely relieved upon getting to this point in the journey. "I was so glad to find out I wasn't crazy; I was codependent," she says.

Others feel angry. "I was furious when I discovered I had a problem with codependency," recalls one man. "I was mad at God, mad at life, and mad because I had to wait until I was fifty-five years old to find out why my life wasn't working."

Besides feeling angry or relieved, we start feeling many of the feelings we've been freezing. We thaw out. We do this when we feel safe enough to do this. We begin to feel all the sadness and pain we've been working so hard to avoid. We begin our grief work. Some of us have more loss to face than others.

"My recovery began when I left my home and my sex addict husband, in an ambulance headed for a psychiatric ward," says Sheryl. "I wanted to commit suicide, but I didn't. I wanted to leave my husband, but I couldn't bring myself to do that either. I asked God to get me out if He wanted me out, and my answer came the day the ambulance took me away. I was released from the hospital six weeks later, but I never went back to my husband.

"For the first year, I cried every day for hours," Sheryl recalls. "I faced the financial chaos created by my destructive relationship. I had borrowed and borrowed to live a lifestyle we couldn't afford. I was barely able to work. I had to take a job under my usual level. I felt suicidal, and the emotional pain was overwhelming. I took antidepressants, went to support groups four nights a week, and almost lived at the psychiatrist's office. I was scared, hopeless, and shaken to the bone. I felt," Sheryl says, "like a wounded deer.

"Things are better now. I still miss my ex-husband from time to time, but I don't want him back. I'm still struggling financially, but I've paid off some bills. I've taken a better job, and I'm living in a nicer apartment. In fact, I'm living. I've got my brains and my life out of hock and no matter where I go, I intend to take them with me. It's been a long haul and I don't ever want to go back. I'm not willing to. And the good thing is, I don't have to."

Some recovering people seek professional help during this stage. Some go on antidepressant therapy for a time. And, like Sheryl, some take jobs beneath their usual level of competence. This can be necessary, but frustrating.

"I'm a dentist. My boyfriend is an alcoholic and a womanizer," explains another woman. "He left me. Now he's living with another woman. He's working. I'm so depressed I can't work. I lay on my couch eating chocolates and turning into the great white whale. I'm so mad. He can go on with his life, and mine has stopped. It's not fair."

This stage of recovery can be confusing. We're just recouping from hitting our lowest point. Our grief work may take much of our energy. And, though we've begun recovering, we haven't yet acquired new living tools.

Now is when we begin experimenting with recovery concepts like detachment, not reacting as much, and letting go. It is a time for diligent evaluation of those things we cannot control. It is a time for acceptance. In this stage, we begin connecting with other people who are recovering. In this stage, we establish, or reestablish, our relationship with a Higher Power. We begin connecting, or reconnecting, with ourselves.

This is a time to remember that we are more than our pain and more than our problems. It's a time to cling to hope. The healing process has begun. Like healing from a physical condition, it hurts most the day after surgery.

Core Issues

This stage can be fun, occasionally overwhelming, but fun.

Here, the lights come on. We see and understand more about

ourselves and our behaviors. We become aware. And aware. And aware . . . Often, we feel uncertain about what to do with all this awareness.

We look back and see how long we've been using our self-defeating behaviors. We look around and see how codependency has permeated our lives. But, we're looking and moving forward too.

We begin setting goals. We begin experimenting with new behaviors. We get better at detachment. We learn different ways of caring for and nurturing ourselves. We begin setting boundaries. We get better at dealing with feelings, including anger. We may tenuously take first steps toward learning how to have fun. We start practicing new relationship and living skills. We may try something new, get scared, and go back to our old ways for a while. We may end relationships, get scared, then go back to check those out for a time too.

We may stay stuck in a state of awareness—knowing we're doing a particular thing, but feeling unable to do much about it.

Within a short time span, we may feel scared, excited, hopeless, and hopeful. Some days, we wonder if anything is happening. Other days, we're certain too much is happening. Some days, we wake knowing all, indeed, is well.

In this stage, recovery begins to have less to do with coping with "the other person." It becomes more of a personal affair—a private journey of finding and building a "self" and a life. We may start to dream and hope again, but our hopes usually center on our own dreams, not someone else's. We may get protective of the new life and self we're building.

Throughout, we're working a program. We're going to our meetings, working with a therapist (if that's appropriate), and connecting with healthy, supportive friends.

This is a time of experimentation and growth. It's a time of becoming more comfortable with new behaviors, and less comfortable with old ones. Our newly-formed beliefs about what we can and cannot change grow stronger. It's a time when we start to figure out what it means to take care of ourselves. We try, fail, try, succeed, try some more, fail some more, and through it all, make a little progress.

It's a time to be patient.

Reintegration

Since we started this journey, we've been struggling with power issues: powerlessness and finding a Higher Power. Now comes the exciting and paradoxical part of this journey. Through powerlessness and surrender we find our personal power. We become empowered to do the possible—live our own lives. Owning our power is as important as learning to accept powerlessness.

In this stage, we discover ourselves as complete, healthy, imperfect but lovable and certainly adequate. We become comfortable with ourselves. We come back home to live with ourselves.

We learn to respect and love ourselves. We find ourselves loving others too, and allowing them to love us in healthy ways that feel good. We accept the fact that we're good enough.

We are neither running around spewing feelings, nor are we repressing them. We're feeling feelings and knowing that's okay. We make mistakes but we know that's okay, and we try to learn from them as best we can. Although a tendency to control may still be our instinctive response to situations, detachment becomes a secondary reaction—for by now, we're certain we can't control others.

Sometimes, we slip into caretaking, shame, and martyrdom. But we get out. We may still feel guilty when we say no, set a boundary, or refuse to take care of someone, but we know the guilt will pass. We've gained the confidence that taking care of ourselves is in everyone's best interests. We've learned we can take care of ourselves. And what we can't do, God can and will do for us.

By this time, we've accepted the premise that problems are an ongoing part of life. We don't dwell on this, but we've gained a degree of confidence in our problem-solving skills. Our messages from the past haven't disappeared, but we develop a keener ear for identifying when these messages are trying to sabotage us.

Our relationships with ourselves, our friends, our family, and our Higher Power have improved. Intimacy becomes a reality.

We have become more comfortable with applying the four recovery power concepts: accepting powerlessness, finding a Higher Power, owning our personal power, and learning to share the power by participating in relationships.

We still feel frightened sometimes. We still have gray days. But they're gray, not black. And we know they'll pass.

When we reach this stage, life becomes more than something to be endured. At times, it's still tough. But sometimes it's downright peaceful and other times it's an adventure. And we're living it, all of it.

"I'm learning anything can happen," says one woman. "And 'anything' doesn't necessarily mean 'something bad' anymore."

Fun becomes fun; love becomes love; life becomes worth living. And we become grateful.

"Eight years ago, I went to a treatment center to get help for my alcoholic husband. Instead of helping my husband, the counselor told me to start helping myself," says Lisa.

Lisa started working on her recovery, and she worked hard at it. She went to her Al-Anon meetings. She put herself through college. She learned how to take care of herself.

"When I went to that counselor eight years ago, I was a mess. Living through my husband's alcoholism was the worst thing that ever happened to me. But it was also the best," Lisa says. "If it hadn't been so bad, I wouldn't have gotten off dead center and found a life for myself. And for that, I'm grateful."

During this stage of recovery, we continue our involvement with Twelve Step programs. We still need to ask for help sometimes, and we still need understanding and acceptance. But the healing process is well under way.

Genesis

This isn't the end. It's a new beginning. We're no longer carrying around "imprisoned" selves. Nor are we indulging in all our whims and desires. Discipline has found its place in our lives too. Like butterflies broken loose from a cocoon, our selves are "flying free," yet surrendered to a loving, caring Higher Power. We've found a new way of life—one that works.

This is the recovery process. It's a fluid process, with carryovers and crossovers to the different stages. There isn't a fixed time frame for moving through these stages.

It begins through the grace of God. It continues in the same manner, assisted by our commitment to the process. Recovery is many things. It's a gradual process, a healing process, and a predictable process. But it's also a spiritual process.

What's our part?

- Attending Twelve Step meetings or other appropriate support groups.
- Applying the Steps and other recovery concepts in our lives.
- Working with a therapist, if appropriate.
- Attending seminars and workshops.
- Maintaining an attitude of honesty, openness, and willingness to try.
- Struggling through the frustration, awkwardness, and discomfort of change.
- Connecting with other recovering people.
- Reading meditation books and other helpful literature.
- Continuing to surrender.

Our part means having the courage to feel what we need to feel, and do what we need to do. Our part is doing our own recovery work. If we cooperate, to the best of our ability, with this process, we'll know what to do and when to do that. Recovery isn't something we do perfectly or at once. Neither concept applies here.

"I'm still real controlling, but at least I recognize when I'm doing it," says one woman.

"I'm going right home and ask for what I want and need," says another, "just as soon as I figure out what that is."

These comments represent recovery as much as any tremendous "before and after" tale. Struggling is okay. Backstepping is okay. Small bits of progress are not only okay, they're admirable.

People who have been recovering for a while may become more comfortable dealing with certain situations because they've encountered similar situations so many times before, but they still struggle.

Some days, my feelings flow freely through me. Self-acceptance comes naturally, as though it has always been my friend. I don't even feel shame about feeling ashamed. I simply acknowledge it, then move harmoniously into the next circumstance. I am part and parcel of the universe; there is a place for me, and I find delight, peace, and intimacy in that place. My life has been planned by a Loving Friend, and all I need do is show up.

Other days, I can't tell a feeling from a manhole cover. As one friend says, "I'm certain God has forgotten where I live."

Anne Morrow Lindbergh, in *Gift from the Sea,* writes:

> Vague as this definition may be, I believe most people are aware of periods in their lives when they seem to be "in grace" and other periods when they feel "out of grace," even though they may use different words to describe these states. "In the first happy condition, one seems to carry all one's tasks before one lightly, as if borne along on a great tide; and in the opposite state one can hardly tie a shoestring. It is true that a large part of life consists in learning a technique of tying the shoestring, whether one is in grace or not. But there are techniques of living too; there are even techniques in the search for grace. And techniques can be cultivated.[5]

Much of recovery means learning to tie our shoestrings, whether we feel in grace or not, while we're cultivating recovery techniques. Some days go better than others.

A man approached me at a workshop one day. "I'm thirty-eight years old, and I've been recovering for three years," he said. "I'm dropping all the behaviors and coping mechanisms that have gotten me through this far in my life. I want so badly for the second half of my life to be as good as the first half has been miserable. The pain has stopped, but now I'm scared."

Well, I get scared too. I want the second half of my life to be as good as the first half was miserable. I get scared it won't be, and sometimes I get scared it will be. Sometimes, I'm just frightened. But I keep working at recovery anyway. I believe if we really want our lives to be different and better, and if we work toward that, our lives will be different and better.

Codependency is a progressive process, one of reaction, inaction, and malefaction.[6] One thing leads to another and things get worse. Recovery is also a progressive process—of action. If we take certain steps, we get better and so do things. Codependency takes on a life of its own, but so does recovery.

Recovery is a process, and we can trust that process. In spite of its ups and downs, back and forths, and blind spots, it works.

We can do our part, then let go and let ourselves grow.

ACTIVITY

1. What stage of the recovery process are you in?

2. What steps have you taken to do your part in the recovery process? Do you have a self-care plan? Do you go to Twelve Step meetings or other support groups? How often? Do you read a meditation book regularly? Are you seeing a therapist, or are you involved with another kind of therapy group? Do

you go to seminars or workshops? Do you read recovery books? Do you spend time with other recovering people?

3. If you've been recovering for a while, what are some of the things you did early in your recovery that helped you feel good? Are you still doing these things?[7]

4. What is the most recent action you've taken to do your part in your recovery? What did you gain from that?

4

YOUR STORY AND MINE

Give us gladness in proportion to our former misery . . .
favor us and give us success.

—Psalm 90:15–17[1]

My Story

There are many different stories of recovery. I have one.

Several members of my extended family had trouble with alcohol. My mother, a single parent, raised me, and raised me well. I was sent to the best private schools money could buy. I went to church, Sunday school, and summer Bible camp.

When I was five years old, I was abducted and molested by a man in an abandoned church on the block where I lived.

I started drinking to get drunk when I was twelve. The pain of being me was intense. I had been depressed since age four. As an adolescent, my memories of hating myself went as far back as I could remember.

By age thirteen, I was having blackouts. I graduated from high school on the Twin Cities honor roll, almost a straight A student. I was a good writer. I was also a chronic overachiever and perfectionist. I loved my studies, but no matter how well I did, I never did "good enough." Once, I had dreams of someday becoming a writer and newspaper reporter, but by the time I graduated from high school, I stopped expecting anything good from myself or life.

While growing up, on several occasions, prolonged childhood illnesses forced me to bed for a long time. I had one friend for several years, and another for several months, but no close friends. I didn't know how to be close to people. I had deliberately turned my back on God, certain He had done the same to me.

By my twentieth birthday, I was a heroin addict. My relationships with men amounted to a series of victimizations and crazy entanglements with other heroin users. By the time I was twenty-three, I was on the methadone program, a government program that doled out a synthetic substitute for heroin. By the time I was twenty-six, I was committed by the State of Minnesota to the chemical dependency ward of a state hospital. I had a failed marriage and a failed life. I didn't want to stop using chemicals; I wanted to stop living.

Then, something unexpected happened. I decided to give God another chance. He decided to give me another chance. I surrendered. I accepted my powerlessness over chemicals. I saw the unmanageability in my life. I got honest. And I got sober.

I didn't get the program, but it got me.

After eight months, I left the state hospital with much fear, a little hope, and a set of instructions: ask God each morning to help you stay straight that day, thank Him for doing that when you go to bed at night, wait at least two years before going to work in the chemical dependency field, and wait a year to have "a relationship."

I complied with the first three rules. Since my "relationship" didn't work out, I figured I did okay on that one too.

I stayed straight, and in many ways my life improved. Two years after getting sober, I went to work as a chemical dependency and family counselor. I also got married and started having babies.

Seven years after I became sober, my career, relationships, and life stopped working. It didn't matter how long I waited to have a relationship, I didn't know how to have one. I was surrounded by alcoholics. I worked with them; I loved them; I even had some living in my attic. (They didn't want to go to a detoxification center. Could they please learn to stop drinking by living at my house?)

I felt like a perpetual victim. Sobriety became, as a speaker at the Gopher State Round-Up 1986 called it, "a long dark tunnel through which I plodded. And each year a trap door opened and a cake fell through."

I became depressed. One day, I called the local suicide hotline and told a stranger I was thinking about ending my life. I told the counselor I wouldn't really kill myself, because too many people needed me. But I got scared. I had been given a second chance at life, and I didn't know if I wanted it. I didn't know if it was worth living. I didn't know what was wrong. It felt like everyone, including God, had abandoned me. I wondered if I was crazy.

Then, something happened. I learned I wasn't crazy. I learned that, without touching a drop of alcohol, I had been affected by the disease of alcoholism in ways so powerful and baffling it would take me years to fully understand. I stopped resisting and started attending meetings for people affected by alcoholism.

I didn't like it. I resented all those peppy little women running around with smiling faces. But I was there. I started crying. I got honest. And I didn't get the Twelve Step program. But it got me.

I accepted my powerlessness over other people's alcoholism, over other people, over the entire mess my life had become. I saw the unmanageability in my life.

I surrendered. I waved the white flag. I didn't start living happily ever after, but I started living my own life. And that life started to get better.

For years, I trudged through my recovery from codependency, feeling afraid and uncertain about where I was going. But I had faith I was going somewhere different than I had ever before been. I struggled and worked at changing my behaviors—the caretaking, the controlling, the low self-esteem.

I watched myself in relationships and learned how to behave in ways that would leave me feeling less victimized. I learned how to identify what I wanted and then considered that important. I worked on letting go and practicing detachment. I wallowed around in feelings, especially anger, as I came alive emotionally. I learned how to terminate and initiate relationships. I learned how to have fun. I had to make myself do that. It took years.

I've made many mistakes. But I've learned that mistakes are okay too. I learned how to communicate, to laugh, to cry, to ask for help. I'm learning to react less, and act more, quietly confident that who I am is okay.

I've learned to own my power. I've also learned I must constantly return to the act of surrendering to do that.

Recovery from codependency has been the most exciting journey I've taken.

I've learned that self-care isn't narcissistic or indulgent. Self-care is the one thing I can do that most helps me and others too.

My relationships have improved with family, friends, other people, myself, and God. The most difficult matter I've had to face in my recovery was the end of my marriage. Right now, I'm working on the toughest lesson I've ever had to master. I'm learning how to let others love me, and how to allow the "good stuff" to happen in my life. I'm learning how to let God love me. And I'm learning to love, really love, myself.

I can see the many ways I've spent my life sabotaging intimacy, relationships, and myself. I'm changing my behaviors. I'm changing my rules, the powerful messages from the past that control what I do or don't do today. I work aggressively with affirmations. I'm dealing with the host of ways I have been affected by other people and their problems. Sometimes, that means bowing to simple acceptance of what is.

And I'm becoming changed.

Recently, during a radio interview, the host asked me if my life was better now. Of course, I answered, "Yes." But driving home after the interview, I became aware of what I really wanted to say. I wanted to tell him this: "I have many good days. I have some difficult days. But I'm living my life. Is that better? You bet it is. For the first time in my life, I have a life!"

Your Story

Throughout this book, I'll share other people's stories with you. One important story is missing, though. That story is yours.

Twelve Step programs have developed a simple format for telling our story. What was it like? What happened? What's it like now?

People who stop drinking can point to a day on the calendar and say, "There. That's the day I stopped drinking." It's not as easy for us to grab a calendar and say, "There. That's the day I stopped taking care of other people and started taking care of myself!" But try, anyway. How and when did your recovery begin? What got you to that point?

Think about the changes you've made and the changes that have happened to you. What insights have you had? Do you feel good about your progress?

Give some thought to how you've worked at recovery. Which behavior have you struggled with? Name the most difficult thing you've had to deal with in your recovery and tell how you got through that. What's the best thing that happened to you in your recovery? List the things you're working on now. What rewards have you gained? Tell how your life is better and different now.

In the last chapter, I called recovery a process. I said we can trust that process. I want to follow that thought with another one. Not only can we trust the process, we can trust where we're at in it.

Recovery is a healing and a spiritual process. It's also a journey, not a destination. We travel a path from self-neglect into self-responsibility, self-care, and self-love. Like other journeys, it's one of moving forward, taking detours, backtracking, getting lost, finding the way again, and occasionally stopping to rest. Unlike other journeys, we can't travel it by forcing the next foot forward. It's a gentle journey, traveled by discipline, and by accepting and celebrating where we are in that journey today.

Where we are today is where we're meant to be. It's where we need to be to get where we're going tomorrow. And that place we're going tomorrow will be better than any we've been before.

ACTIVITY

1. Write your story. At an appropriate time and place, share your story with someone safe.

2. Pat yourself on the back for what you've accomplished.

Section II:

RELAPSE

Maybe we shouldn't call relapse "recycling."
Maybe we should call it "cycles of growth."
Or maybe we should just call it
"growth."

5

RECYCLING: THE RELAPSE PROCESS

"Tell me about the reality of recovery," I said. "Oh, that," she replied.
"You mean two steps forward and one step back."

—Anonymous

"I did it again," Jan confided. "And I did it ten years after I began my recovery from codependency.

"Steve and I are divorced. He hasn't paid child support in six months because he's drinking and not working, and I handed him $250 of my hard-earned money—probably to get drunk on.

"I'm furious! I can't believe I let him do that to me. I know better. I didn't want to do it. I let him bully and guilt me out of the money."

Jan took a deep breath and continued. "Afterward, I drove over to his apartment and demanded the money back. I made a fool of myself, screaming and stomping around.

"I feel angry, depressed, and ashamed. Sometimes I think I don't know anything about recovery. I called my sponsor and whined to her. All those meetings! All that therapy! All that work! Didn't it mean anything? I was still caretaking. Still allowing people to use me. And still stomping around acting crazy."

I asked Jan what her sponsor said. "She said at least I was asking why I was allowing people to use me, instead of asking why they were doing this to me," Jan said. "And she said at least I could recognize when my behavior was crazy."

Over the years, I've seen people use different diagrams to represent the recovery or growth process. I've seen recovery portrayed as a zig-zagging line moving upward and forward, with each zig forming a higher peak than the last. (See Diagram 1, page 41.)[1] I've seen recovery drawn as a circular line moving inward in smaller circles until an inner core of stability is reached; an inner core large enough to permit continued growth. (See Diagram 2.)[2] I've seen recovery diagramed as a line moving upward and forward, making repetitively-spinning circles on the way, cyclical but forward-moving. (See Diagram 3.)[3] One diagram I haven't seen drawn to represent recovery is a straight line upward and forward. (See Diagram 4.) Recovery is not this.

Recovery is a process. Within that process is another one called relapse. Regression, reverting, slips—whatever we call it—any diagram we use to represent growth needs to accommodate it.

In spite of our best efforts to stay on track, we sometimes find ourselves reverting to old ways of thinking, feeling, and behaving, even when we know better.

Relapse can sneak up on us, linger, and become as confusing as our original codependency. Or it can be brief. Sometimes, we're reacting to other people's craziness. Sometimes, we're reacting to ourselves. Sometimes, we're reacting to the years of training we've had in how to be codependent. Sometimes, we're just reacting.

For many reasons, we can find ourselves using coping behaviors we thought we had outgrown. We start neglecting ourselves, taking care of others, feeling victimized, freezing feelings, overreacting, trying to control, feeling dependent and needy, guilty, afraid, obligated, depressed, deprived, undeserving, and trapped. The codependent crazies come back, and we feel neck deep in shame.

No need to feel shame. I've questioned thousands of recovering people. No one claimed a perfect recovery.

"I thought something awful was wrong with me," recalls Charlene. "I kept threatening to leave my boyfriend, but I didn't leave him. I felt disconnected from people—all alone in the world. I got irrita-

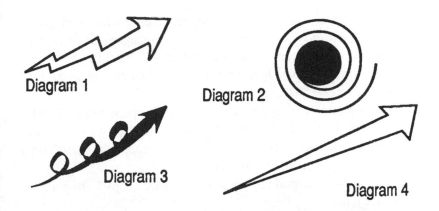

Diagram 1

Diagram 2

Diagram 3

Diagram 4

ble, depressed, and couldn't sleep. I thought I was dying. I went to the doctor. He said I was fine, but I didn't feel fine. This went on for months before I realized it was my codependency. I got really scared. It took some work, but now I'm back on track again."

Jack tells this story: "Last weekend my friend's wife called me. I'm recovering from chemical addiction and codependency. My friend is still drinking, and his wife is still thinking about going to Al-Anon. She planned to leave town for the weekend and asked me to stay with her husband while she was gone. She said *he* really wanted to stay sober that weekend and *he* wanted to go fishing with me. I agreed. When I arrived, I realized her husband had no intention of going fishing. He wanted to go drinking. She set me up to be his baby-sitter for the weekend. I felt tricked and trapped. It was one of the most miserable weekends I've had in my two years of recovery. And I couldn't open my mouth and get out. I had a big slip, a codependency slip."

Marilyn tells this story: "I was recovering for five years when I moved in with Bob, a recovering alcoholic. One year later, I found myself living with a nondrinking alcoholic who had stopped attending his recovery meetings. I started feeling crazy again. I felt guilty, insecure, needy, and resentful. It happened gradually. I just slid into it. I stopped setting boundaries. I quit asking for what I wanted and needed. I stopped saying, 'No!' I stopped taking care of myself. I couldn't figure out what was wrong. Then one day, when I was considering ending the relationship, I found myself thinking, *No! I can't do that. I can't live without him.* That thought jolted me into awareness and action. I know better than that!"

Relapse happens to many of us. Relapse happens to people who have been recovering for ten months or ten years. It happens not because we're deficient or lackadaisical. Relapse happens because it's a normal part of the recovery process.

In fact, it's so normal I'm not going to call it relapse. I'm going to call it "recycling."[4]

Relapse, according to the New World Dictionary, means to slip or fall back into a former condition after improvement or *seeming* improvement.[5] *Recycle* means to recover; or to pass through a cycle or part of a cycle again for checking or treating.[6]

"Relapse sounds like going all the way back to where we started from—square one on the game board," explains my friend, Scott Egleston, who is also a therapist. "We don't go all the way back. When we finish a recycling process, we move to a progressed location on our recovery journey."

Recycling is more than a normal part of recovery. Sometimes, it's a necessary part. For example, in the beginning of this chapter, Jan talked about allowing her ex-husband to bully her out of money. Her story has an epilogue. About four months after the incident, Jan was having coffee with her sponsor. Her sponsor asked Jan if she had learned anything from the incident.

"By then, I had learned something from it," Jan said, "something valuable. That incident was part of a larger, important lesson I was in the midst of learning. Financially, I was finally getting on my feet, and I was starting to leave behind the sick people in my life. I was standing up to the bullying, and I was letting go of the guilt about becoming healthy. The lesson I was learning involved the idea that I could feel compassion for people without acting on it."

All our recycling incidents can have epilogues. We can gain from them when they happen. Recycling is a chance to do our recovery work. It's a way to discover what we need to work on and work through. It's one way we figure out what we haven't yet learned, so we can start to learn that. It's a way to solidify what we've already learned, so we continue to know that. Recycling is about learning our lessons so we can move forward on our journey.

ACTIVITY

1. What would a diagram of your recovery look like?

2. As you progress through this book, you may want to start accumulating a list of affirmations. Some suggestions for affirmations on recycling would be:

   • My recovery history is okay. All my experiences are necessary and valuable.
   • I am learning what I need to know. I will learn what I need to when the time is right.
   • I am right where I need to be.

6

COMMON RECYCLING SITUATIONS

"Thank you for writing Codependent Once More. *Oops! Freudian
slip. I mean,* Codependent No More.*"[1]*

Society is filled with invitations to be codependent, Anne Wilson
Schaef once said.[2] And, if we don't get invited, we may invite ourselves. In this chapter, we'll explore some of these situations.

Recycling on the Job

We can recycle at work for many reasons. Sometimes, we bring
our behaviors with us. If we're still trying to control people at home,
we may be doing the same at work. If we're not setting boundaries at
home, we may not be doing it at work either. Sometimes, we've acquired self-care skills at home and in personal relationships, but we
haven't learned how to take care of ourselves on the job and in professional relationships.

Other times, issues at work can point to a larger issue we need
to address. "I haven't been happy about my job," says Alice, who has
been recovering from codependency for many years. "I've been complaining and whining about it. So I decided to go see a counselor, and
during counseling a new awareness struck me.

"I don't like my job. I took it because it met my parents' standards. I've stayed because they wouldn't approve of me leaving. I can

hear them: 'All those benefits? All that seniority? You're going to walk away and leave all that?'

"Yes," Alice says, "that's exactly what I'm going to do."

Sometimes, we find ourselves working with an alcoholic or other troubled person. An addicted person can inflict as much chaos at work as he or she can at home.

When a prestigious hospital offered Marlyss a job, she was delighted. She had put herself through nursing school in mid-life. Eight years ago, she began recovering from codependency, and developing her career was a big part of that. But two and a half years after she started working at the hospital, Marlyss was feeling crazy again.

"I finally figured out what was happening," she says. "I had been promoted to a supervisory position. My supervisor was a practicing alcoholic. The nurses under my supervision were reacting to my alcoholic supervisor and the crazy system. I was reacting to everyone—my supervisor and the nurses I supervised. I was in my familiar role of peacemaker and caretaker, feeling responsible for everyone and everything. It was like the family system at home used to be. And I felt like I used to—real codependent."

Marlyss began to practice detachment at work. After a while, she found a different job. She's worked there three years now. "I love it," Marlyss says. "Moving on was one of the best moves I ever made."

Some people may find themselves employed by abusive or abrasive people. "My boss treated me so nasty," Ella says. "He was verbally abusive. He made sexual innuendos. I had been recovering from codependency for several years, and it still took me months to realize I wasn't doing something wrong; he was."

Jerry, a recovering codependent and alcoholic who owned his own business, had the following experience. "I hired a secretary. She was great, at first," Jerry recalls. "She was willing to learn and work hard. Before long, I discovered she was married to an alcoholic. At first I felt sorry for her, then I got mad. Whenever he was doing too much drinking, she didn't want to stay home. She worked late and weekends, and charged me overtime. It was taking her longer than it should to get her work done. She was making a lot of mistakes at my expense.

"I didn't say much at first. I suggested she go to Al-Anon, but she wasn't ready. I felt ashamed about getting angry. She really did have it hard, married to an alcoholic. But I could also see how she kept setting herself up to be used by the guy. I got angrier and angrier, then the pieces started to fit. I've stopped feeling sorry for her and started taking care of myself. I know it's a myth that codependents are sicker than alcoholics. I know how much codependents hurt; I am one. But I'm also beginning to see how difficult it can be to deal with one. You can get just as codependent on a codependent as you can on an alcoholic."

A family is a system with its own rules, roles, and personality. And employment settings can be similar. Sometimes a person in that system is dysfunctional. Sometimes, the system is dysfunctional, either covertly or overtly.

"I had been recovering for about two years when I went to work for a radio station," says Al, an adult child of an alcoholic. "I really wanted the job. I still do. But boy, did it hook my codependency. We're a small station on a small budget with a small staff and a large mission—doing all we can to save the city.

"After I'd been working there a couple of months, I noticed many of my codependency symptoms reappearing. This time it wasn't about my relationship; it was about my job. I was working sixty hours a week, neglecting myself, feeling like no matter how much I did it wasn't enough. I was feeling irritable, angry, and guilty because I couldn't do more. Whenever I considered setting boundaries or taking care of myself, I felt more guilt. How could I be so selfish? Who would do it, if I didn't? What about our mission? There wasn't enough of me to go around. Now, I'm figuring out how to take care of myself in this organization."

Sally found herself in a difficult employment situation. She took a management position in a sales force several years after beginning recovery from chemical dependency and codependency. Within six months, she started feeling "nuts" again. "Just like in the old days," Sally says.

"Company policy surpassed high-pressure selling. It involved unethical practices. The company used people—employees and customers. I didn't feel comfortable following company policy. For a while, I tried to pretend I did. Then, pretending got too hard. I talked to my supervisor. He understood, but company policy was company policy. By then, I had learned you can't change other people. Now, I was learning you can't change a corporation either. The only thing left was to change myself. I did. I changed jobs."

For years, Earnie Larsen, a respected author and lecturer on recovery issues, has preached that some systems demand sick behavior from the people in it. He was talking about families, but employment systems can be just as demanding.

Sometimes, recycling at work is a clue to something we need to work on or through. Other times, it's an indicator of how much we've grown. We often choose relationships that are about as healthy as we are and meet our current (but changing) needs; we often choose jobs in the same way. We can grow out of relationships; we can grow out of jobs.

"I took a job during the first year of my recovery from codependency," Kelly says. "I was devastated at the time, crushed by a sick relationship that had gone on for years. At first, the job felt good. It was a safe place to be. The work wasn't demanding, but it kept me busy. And the people were nice. I felt like I fit in."

After about eighteen months, Kelly's feelings about her job changed. She felt out of place. She started repressing feelings, going numb at work.

"I don't know how or when it happened, but I realized I no longer fit in. The healthier I became, the more I saw many of my co-workers were victims. And they wanted me to be a victim. As I grew and did more things to take care of myself, they got angry at me. I felt torn. I wanted to fit in and be part of the crowd. But I didn't want to be a victim."

Although Kelly has decided to stay at her job for a while, she says she suspects she'll soon move on. She's been recovering long enough to know change isn't necessarily bad. It can bring us to our next plateau of growth.

Other systems besides employment settings can invite us to behave codependently. We can recycle at church, in recovery groups, and in social, professional, or charitable associations. Wherever people gather, the possibility of us using our codependent coping behaviors exists.

"I went to church on Sunday feeling good. I left feeling ashamed. I never felt good enough, no matter what I did," says Len, a recovering codependent. "I constantly felt pressured into volunteering for things. I couldn't tell if I was giving money because I wanted to or because I felt guilty. I was fine all week. But I felt crazy in church.

"I've since switched churches. I need to hear God loves me, not that He's waiting to punish me. I've lived with fear and condemnation all my life. Looking back, I think that church was as shame-based as my family. I just didn't realize it until I got healthier."

We can recycle in therapy or support groups too. "I knew I was an alcoholic and needed A.A. I also knew I was codependent and needed Al-Anon," says Theresa. "But members of my A.A. group started giving me a hard time. They said if I was really working a good A.A. program, I wouldn't need Al-Anon.

"I dropped out of Al-Anon, and started feeling real crazy again. Then I realized the people in my A.A. group didn't have to approve of me dealing with my codependency. Either they didn't understand, or they were uncomfortable with my attendance in Al-Anon. I didn't need to figure them out; my job was to take care of myself."

Taking care of ourselves may mean finding another job, church, or group. Or, it may mean figuring out how to function in the job, church, or group we're in. Theresa has continued attending the same A.A. group. She also continues to attend Al-Anon.

Recycling in Relationships

Recycling is possible and fairly predictable in any relationship. We can give up our power and get crazy with people we've known for years and with strangers. We can start reacting to people we love and people we're not certain we like.

We can start feeling guilty, as if we are at fault, when others behave inappropriately. Sometimes, we recycle without any help from them at all.

Sometimes we need to learn to use certain recovery skills that we've acquired in one kind of relationship—for instance, our special love relationship—in another kind of relationship—for instance, a friendship.

"I can set boundaries with my husband and children. I'm lousy at setting boundaries with friends," says one woman.

We can react to new people in our lives—people whose addiction or problem catches us off guard. Or we can react to people whose addiction or dysfunction we know all too well.

"I can be going along just fine," says Sarah. "But after ten minutes on the phone with my ex-husband, I'm a basket case again. I still try to trust him. I still go into denial about his alcoholism. I still get hooked into shame and guilt when I talk to him. It's taken me a long time, but I'm finally learning I don't have to talk to him. The same thing happens each time."

Sometimes, past relationships hold important lessons. We may need to go back long enough to realize we don't want to stay.

Family reunions, holidays, and other family gatherings can challenge our recovery. Besides triggering a reaction to whatever is happening that day, it can trigger old feelings.

Dealing with family members, whether they're in recovery or not, can be provocative. "I get trapped on the phone with family members," explains Linda. "I can feel myself going through the whole process, feeling enraged, guilty, then going numb. They're not in recovery. They go on and on. I tell them I have to go, but they don't listen. Short of hanging up, I don't know what to do!

"Sometimes it leaves me feeling drained for hours. I get so angry. My family is important to me. I'd like to tape record those conversations and make them listen to themselves for endless hours, like I do.

"I've been recovering from codependency for eight years. I know the answer isn't making other people listen to themselves and 'see the light.' The solution is me listening to myself and me 'seeing the light.' Sometimes I can cope with my family, but sometimes, I still get tangled up with them."

We may find ourselves periodically, or cyclically, reacting to certain people in our lives. "I've noticed my recycling in relationships comes in cycles. I'm fine for a few months, then it feels like crazy people come crawling out of the woodwork. It's usually the same people, and they seem determined to inflict their insanity on me, all at the same time," says one woman. "I don't understand it. But I do understand this: it becomes time to detach and take care of myself."

Dealing with children can challenge our recovery. "I'm good at taking care of myself with the rest of the world. But with my kids, I feel guilty when I say no. I feel guilty when I feel angry at them. I feel guilty about disciplining them. I allow them to treat me terribly, then I'm the one who feels guilty!" says one woman.

"My son has admitted he deliberately uses guilt-producing tactics on me. In his weaker moments, he calls it 'the guilt trap.' He's admitted he compares me to other mothers and lies about what they're letting their kids do to control me. My kids know what they're doing. It's about time I learn what I need to do," she concludes.

"Setting boundaries with my children is harder for me than setting limits at work, with friends, or with my girlfriend," says a divorced man. "I feel so guilty when I do, and so victimized when I don't."

Dealing with other people's children can be more difficult than dealing with our own. I've asked recovering people, "What's the hardest part of your relationship?" Many people in relationships involving children from past marriages say, "Dealing with the children."

But the greatest challenge to our recoveries still seems to be our special love relationships. "I don't know how to be in love and not be codependent," says a recovering woman. "I was friends for over a year with a man. The minute we moved in together, we both stopped taking care of ourselves and tried to control each other. It really got nuts. When I'm in love, anything goes. And what usually goes first is my recovery behaviors."

We can't get uncomfortable when a relationship gets too close and too good. Crisis and chaos may not feel good, but those things can feel comfortable. Sometimes, we get so anxious waiting for the formidable other shoe to drop that we take it off and toss it ourselves.

"I'm in a good relationship, one with tremendous potential," says a recovering woman. "We get along great, but whenever things get too good, I create a problem. At first, I couldn't see this was my pattern. I thought things just got good, then bad. Now, I'm starting to see my part."

There are many reasons for recycling in relationships. Sometimes the relationship is over, but we're not ready to end it. Sometimes the relationship needs to be enjoyed, but we're too frightened to do that. Sometimes we're making chaos to avoid intimacy. Sometimes falling in love can resemble codependency; as boundaries weaken, we focus on the other person and have a sense of loss of control. Sometimes what we call "codependent behaviors" are a normal part of intimate or close relationships.

Relationships are where we take our recovery show on the road. Taking good care of ourselves doesn't mean we avoid relationships. The goal of recovery is learning how to function in relationships. The task during recycling is to relax and let ourselves learn whatever we need to learn.

Other Recycling Situations

Many other circumstances can provoke our codependency. Sometimes we begin denying that codependency is real and recovery is our responsibility. We may neglect our recoveries and stop taking care of ourselves. Sometimes we neglect ourselves before a recycling incident; sometimes we do it after we begin recycling, making things worse.

"How long do I need to keep working at recovery?" asks one woman. "All my life, I guess," she says, answering her own question. "Whenever I stop taking my recovery seriously, my life gets crazy again."

Sometimes our old reactions appear for *no reason*.

Sometimes recycling is part of the experimental process we go through as we struggle to acquire new behaviors and shed old, self-defeating ones.

Getting sick or becoming overly tired can trigger codependent reactions in us. Stress—from today and yesterday—can trigger our codependency. Our instinctive reaction to stressful situations can be to neglect ourselves.

Innocuous events that remind us of past traumatic events can also trigger our codependency.

"Once a person has been overwhelmed by traumatic events, he or she is susceptible to the sudden reemergence of the feelings, thoughts, and behaviors that were present during the trauma," Cermak writes in *Diagnosing and Treating Co-Dependence*. "This reemergence is most likely to occur when the individual is faced with something which symbolically represents the original trauma—a 'trigger.' "[3]

Triggers remind our subconscious of a traumatic event, causing codependent feelings and behaviors to emerge. This can include

- feeling anxious or afraid;
- freezing feelings, or "going numb";

- focusing on others and neglecting ourselves;
- attempting to control things, events, and people;
- experiencing sudden low self-worth;
- or any of the codependent behaviors or feelings we did or felt during the actual event.

We automatically start reacting and protecting ourselves.

We each have our own triggers. If it was connected to something frightening or distressing that happened before, it can be a trigger now.

Almost anything can be a trigger:

- conflict;
- the threat of someone leaving us, even if we want him or her to leave;
- confrontation;
- paying bills;
- or hearing a certain song.

Anything connected with, resembling, or representing a past traumatic experience can be a trigger. Falling in love can resemble codependency; it can trigger it too.

Understanding our triggers may not make these sudden resurgences of codependency disappear, but understanding can help us get out more swiftly.

"Paying bills is a trigger for me," says Carol. "I've got enough money now. That's not the problem. The problem is all the years I was married to an alcoholic, and there wasn't enough money. Before I learned about my triggers, I felt anxious and distressed the day I paid the bills. Now, I recognize what's happening. I still get skittish, but I tell myself it's okay. There's enough money now. And there's going to be enough."

Problems and trauma aren't the only matters that can provoke codependency. Success, in any area of our lives, can cause us to start controlling and caretaking again.

"I know how to cope with emergencies, tragedy, and disappointment," confides a recovering woman. "I don't know how to deal with success, peace, and loving relationships. Those things are uncomfortable. I get scared. I wonder what bad thing is going to happen next. Some terrible thing always did in the past. It's difficult for me to believe I deserve good things. It's even harder for me to believe good things can last."

Changing circumstances can cause us to recycle. Changing jobs, moving, ending a relationship, the threat of ending a relationship, a change in finances, or a shift in routine can be unnerving. Even desirable change brings a sense of loss. Most of us have been through so much change and loss that we don't want to go through any more.

About six months after *Codependent No More* was released, my life began to change. I was working for a newspaper and doing freelance writing on weekends and evenings. Requests for me to speak began filtering in. I was shuffling all this into the routine of being the single parent of two young children. I was also trying to stay involved in my own recovery process and find time to have fun.

My life kept filling up with new activities. I kept trying to hang on to the old ones and make room for the new. I kept waiting for things to go back to normal. What I didn't realize was normal had changed.

Then I got sick with double pneumonia. I learned of the diagnosis twenty-four hours before I was scheduled to speak in Joplin, Missouri. I thought it would be inappropriate to cancel that close to the event, so I pushed myself through. When I returned to Minnesota, I had several stories due at the paper. I told myself I couldn't cancel that either.

I spent a day struggling to grind out a story that ordinarily would have taken me three hours. After eight hours, I hadn't yet produced the first paragraph. I stayed late, hoping the quiet would help me think more clearly. By eight o'clock that night, I had wrestled out four or five paragraphs.

When I went to the lounge to take a break, I heard that still voice within me. It said: *It's time to take care of yourself.* I was running around the country, preaching those words. I had written a book carrying that message. Now, it was time to listen to myself.

When we start feeling the codependent crazies again, we know what time it is. It's time to take care of ourselves.

Whether we recycle or not, we can benefit by putting extra attention into self-care during these circumstances. And whether we're reacting to a crazy system, a person, ourselves, our pasts, or just reacting, taking care of ourselves remains a "no-fault" issue. It's our responsibility.

Somewhere between our first response—shaking our finger at the other person and saying, "It's your fault"—and our second reaction—pointing that finger at ourselves and wondering, *What's wrong with me?*—there's a lesson to learn. That lesson is ours to learn.

ACTIVITY

1. Did any recycling incidents come to mind as you read this chapter? How did you take care of yourself in that situation?

2. Do any people in your life seem to particularly trigger your codependency? Who? What happens? What are some ways you can start taking care of yourself with these people?

3. As you go through your daily routine, watch for your "triggers." What things seem to engage those old codependent feelings "for no reason"? Look for the reason, the connection to the past. When that happens, what can you tell yourself to help yourself feel better?

7

GETTING THROUGH THE CYCLE

I still have bad days, but that's okay. I used to have bad years.

—Anonymous

Recycling can mean a momentary lapse into our old behaviors. Or recycling can lead to more serious problems: depression, use of mood-altering chemicals to cope, or physical illness. Codependency is progressive; recycling can be too. We can get stuck, spin our wheels, then discover we've gotten ourselves more deeply entrenched in the muck.

Whether our recycling experience lasts six minutes or six months, our instinctive reaction is usually one of denial, shame, and self-neglect. That's not the way out. That's the way in more deeply.

We get out of, or through, a recycling process by practicing acceptance, self-compassion, and self-care. These attitudes and behaviors may not come as effortlessly as denial, shame, and neglect. We've spent years practicing denial, shame, and neglect. But we can learn to practice healthier alternatives, even when it feels awkward. Some suggestions for doing that follow.

Practicing Healthier Alternatives

The first step toward getting through a recycling situation is identifying when we're in it. Here are some warning signs.[1]

Emotions Shut Down. We may go numb and begin freezing or ignoring feelings. We return to the mind set that feelings are unnecessary, inappropriate, unjustified, or unimportant. We may tell ourselves the same things about wants and needs.

Compulsive Behaviors Return. We may begin compulsively eating, caretaking, controlling, working, staying busy, spending money, engaging in sexual behaviors, or anything else we compulsively do to avoid feeling.

Victim Self-Image Returns. We may start feeling, thinking, talking, and acting like a victim again. We may begin focusing on others, or resort to blaming and scapegoating. A good clue that I'm "in it" is when I hear myself whining about how someone is doing this or that to me, or how awful something is. My voice begins to grate on my nerves.

Self-Worth Drops. Our level of self-esteem may drop. We may get stuck in self-hatred or shame. We may become overly critical of ourselves and others. Perfectionism and feelings of not being good enough may return.

Self-Neglect Starts. Neglecting the small and large acts of self-care that are a regular part of our recovery routine may indicate we're close to a recycling situation. Abandoning our daily routine is another sign.

The Crazies Return. All the old crud can come back. This includes: return of anxiety and fear; feeling disconnected from people and our Higher Power; problems sleeping (too much or too little); mind-racing; feeling overwhelmed by confusion (or just overwhelmed); difficulty thinking clearly; feeling angry and resentful; feeling guilty because we feel that way; feeling desperate, depressed, deprived, undeserving, and unloved. We may get into the "overs": overtired, overworked, overcommitted, overextended, overly sensitive; or the "unders": underpaid, underappreciated, underspent, underfed, and under-the-weather.

A continuing physical condition can be a warning sign that something is nagging at our minds and emotions. We may begin withdrawing from and avoiding people. A return to martyrdom or the "endurance mode" is another warning sign. This would include resuming the belief that we can't enjoy life or have fun today, this week, or this month; life is something to be "gotten through," and maybe next week or next year we can be happy.

The Behaviors Return Too. Once we're into a recycling situation, any or all the coping behaviors may return.

Trapped! Feeling trapped, believing we have no choices, is a highly suspect attitude.

Not That Again. It's possible to progress to the danger zone during recycling. Symptoms here include chronic physical illness, chemical dependency, chronic depression, or possible fantasies about suicide.

After we've identified a return to our old ways, the next step is simple. We say, "Oops! I'm doing it again." This is called *acceptance and honesty.* It's helpful to return to concepts like powerlessness and unmanageability at this time. If we're working a Twelve Step program, this is a good time to work Step One. This is called "surrender." Now comes the potentially difficult part. We tell ourselves, *It's okay, I did it again.* This is called "self-compassion."

Recycling Myths

Believing any of the following myths about recycling may make recovery more difficult than necessary.

- I should be further along than I am.
- If I've been recovering for a number of years, I shouldn't be having problems with this anymore.
- If I was working a good program, I wouldn't be doing this.
- If I'm a professional in the recovery, mental health, or general helping field, I shouldn't be having this problem.
- If my recovery was real, I wouldn't be doing this.
- People wouldn't respect me if they knew I thought, felt, or did this.

- Once changed, a behavior is gone forever.
- I couldn't possibly be doing this again. I know better.
- Oh, no! I'm back to square one.

These are myths. If we believe them, we need to try to change what we believe. It's okay to have problems. It's okay to recycle. People who work good programs and have good recoveries recycle, even if they're professionals. It's okay to do "it" again, even when we know better. We haven't gone all the way back to square one. Who knows? We may learn from it this time.

If we insist on blaming or feeling ashamed, we can give ourselves a limited time to do that. Five to fifteen minutes should be enough.

Taking Care of Ourselves

After we've accepted ourselves and given ourselves a hug, we ask ourselves two questions.

- "What do I need to do to take care of myself?"
- "What am I supposed to learn?"

Often, the self-care concepts we need to practice are basic:

- acceptance,
- surrender,
- realistic evaluation of what we can control,
- detachment,
- removing the victim,
- dealing with feelings,
- taking what we want and need seriously,
- setting boundaries,
- making choices and taking responsibility for them,
- setting goals,
- getting honest,

- letting go, and
- giving ourselves huge doses of love and nurturing.

Consciously focusing on our recovery program, talking to healthy people, plying ourselves with meditations and positive thoughts, relaxing, and doing fun activities help too. We need to get our balance back.

Taking care of ourselves at work may require some different considerations than caring for ourselves at home. Certain behaviors may be appropriate at home but could result in loss of our job. We may not want to tell the boss how mad we are at him. Self-care is self-responsibility.

Codependency is a self-defeating cycle. Codependent feelings lead to self-neglect, self-neglect leads to more codependent feelings and behaviors, leading to more self-neglect, and around we go. Recovery is a more energizing cycle. Self-care leads to better feelings, healthier feelings lead to more self-care, and around that track we travel.

I don't know precisely what you need to do to take care of yourself. But I know you can figure it out.

Another thing I don't know is what lesson you're learning. It's all I can do to learn my own. I can't tell you how to make sense of the particular experiences in your life, but I can tell you this: between you and your Higher Power, you will figure that out too.

Don't worry. If you don't understand, or if you aren't ready to learn your lesson today, that's okay. Lessons don't go away. They keep presenting themselves until we learn them. And we'll do that when we're ready and the time is right.[2]

Recycling Tips

Although I don't have a formula for self-care and learning life's lessons, I've collected some tips that may help during recycling.

- If it feels crazy, it probably is. Often when we run into a crazy system, our first reaction is still to wonder what's wrong with us. We can trust some people, but we can't trust everyone. We can trust ourselves.
- If we're protecting ourselves, something may be threatening us. Maybe a trigger is reminding us of the old days or an old message is sabotaging us. Sometimes, someone in our present is threatening us, and we're trying to pretend they're not. If we're protecting ourselves, it helps to understand who or what is scaring us, and what we're protecting ourselves from.
- When one method of problem solving fails, try another. Sometimes, we get stuck. We encounter a problem, decide to solve it a certain way, fail, then repeatedly, sometimes for years, try to solve that problem in the same way, even though that way doesn't work. Regroup and try something else.
- Self-will doesn't work any better during recovery than it did before. Surrendering does work. Sometimes in recycling, we're going through the process of denying a problem that's creeping into our awareness. We're struggling to avoid it or overcome it by exerting greater amounts of self-will. When self-will fails, try surrender.
- Feelings of guilt, pity, and obligation are to the codependent as the first drink is to the alcoholic. Watch out for what happens next.
- Feeling sad and frustrated because we can't control someone or something is not the same as controlling.[3]
- Trying to recoup our losses generally doesn't work. "If I look back and stare at my losses too long, they gain on me," says one man. "I've learned to take them and run."
- We cannot simultaneously set a boundary and take care of the other person's feelings.[4]
- Today isn't yesterday. Things change.
- We don't have to do more today than we can reasonably do. If we're tired, rest. If we need to play, play. The work will get done.
- When depressed, look to see if anger, shame, or guilt is present.[5]
- If we're not certain, we can wait.

- It's hard to feel compassion for someone while that person is using or victimizing us. We'll probably feel angry. First, we stop allowing ourselves to be used. Then, we work toward compassion. Anger can motivate us to set boundaries, but we don't need to stay resentful to keep taking care of ourselves.
- If we listen to ourselves, we'll probably hear ourselves say what the problem is. The next step is acceptance.
- We never outgrow our need for nurturing and self-care.
- If everything looks black, we've probably got our eyes shut.

When all else fails, try gratitude. Sometimes, that's what we're supposed to be learning. If we can't think of anything to be grateful about, be grateful anyway. Will gratitude. Fake it if necessary. Sometimes in recycling, we need to change something we're doing. Sometimes things are being worked out in us, important intangibles that may not be clear for months or years, things like patience, faith, and self-esteem.

"I've had a lot of ups and downs, a lot of pain, and a lot of loss," says one woman. "I'm still not sure what everything's been about, but I've learned a few things. I've learned where I live, what I wear, and where I work isn't me. I'm me. And no matter what happens, I can land on my feet."

Come to think of it, maybe we shouldn't call relapse "recycling." Maybe we should call it "cycles of growth." Or maybe we should just call it "growth."

Recycling, getting stuck, bad days, whatever we call it, can be tough, especially if we've had a taste of better days. We can frighten ourselves, worrying that all the old stuff is back again, maybe to stay. We don't have to worry. We don't have to go all the way back. The old stuff isn't here to stay. It's part of the process, and in that process, some days go better than others. We can count them all for joy.

Lonny Owen[6] and I conducted a ten-week workshop and support group for "advanced codependents" (those of us who know better, but do it anyway). All the participants had previously identified themselves as codependents; all had been actively involved in recovery for at least a year. Most had been working at recovery much longer. We bypassed the business of "Am I codependent? Maybe I'm not? What is codependency anyway?" We got down to the core of the matter: "Where am I stuck in my recovery? What am I stuck on? And what do I need to do to improve my life and my relationships?"

The workshop required much vulnerability from the participants. They were asked to expose themselves, to be honest about who they were when they had been recovering that long. The group also required some vulnerability from Lonny and me. This time we weren't working with "beginning" codependents. We were working with people who had a good deal of information about the subject we were teaching. In other words, we were scared too.

It was the most challenging group I've facilitated in my thirteen-plus years in and around the recovery field. It was also the most exciting. I saw more growth accomplished in ten weeks than I've seen in any similar group.

Want to know how we did it? First, let me tell you what we didn't do. We didn't criticize, judge, condemn, confront, blame, or shame. Of course, the participants' commitment and courage to grow made their growth possible. But the growth in that group happened because we stuck to concepts like honesty, acceptance, nurturing, affirmation, approval, empowerment, and love.

That's how we did our work. You can too.

ACTIVITY

1. What are your patterns of self-neglect when you get into a recycling situation? For example, mine include: eliminating fun activities, neglecting proper nutrition, and pushing harder when the problem is I've pushed too hard.

2. What are some of your favorite acts of self-care, activities that help you feel good about yourself? What are some things you

enjoyed doing for yourself when you began your recovery from codependency that you've stopped doing? What is your rationale for not doing those things anymore?[7]

3. Look over the recovery checklist that follows. This checklist can help you determine your strengths and weaknesses in recovery. It can also be helpful in setting your recovery goals.

RECOVERY CHECK LIST [8]

_____ Maintaining appropriate daily routine
_____ Setting and achieving daily and long-term goals
_____ Personal care
_____ Setting and sticking to limits with children and others
_____ Constructive planning
_____ Appropriate decision-making and problem-solving efforts
_____ Choosing behaviors
_____ Well-rested
_____ Resentment-free
_____ Accepting (versus denying)
_____ Not controlling others nor feeling controlled by them
_____ Open to appropriate criticism and feedback
_____ Free of excessive criticism of self and others
_____ Gratitude versus self-pity and deprivation
_____ Responsible financial decisions (not over- or underspending)
_____ Appropriate nutrition (not over- or undereating)
_____ Not escaping or avoiding through work or sex
_____ Self-responsibility (versus scapegoating and blaming)
_____ Valuing wants and needs
_____ Free of victim self-image
_____ Free of fear and anxiety
_____ Free of guilt and shame
_____ Free of worry and obsession

_____ Not feeling excessively responsible for others

_____ Faith in Higher Power

_____ Trusting and valuing self

_____ Making appropriate decisions about trusting others

_____ Maintaining recovery routine (attending support groups, et cetera)

_____ Mind clear and peaceful; logical thinking; free of confusion

_____ Feeling and dealing appropriately with feelings, including anger

_____ Appropriately disclosing

_____ Reasonable expectations of self and others

_____ Needing people versus NEEDING them

_____ Feeling secure with self; self-affirming

_____ Communicating clearly, directly, and honestly

_____ Balanced mood

_____ Maintaining contact with friends

_____ Feeling connected and close to people versus lonely and isolated

_____ Healthy perspective; life looks worth living

_____ Not using alcohol and medication to cope

_____ Having fun, relaxing during leisure activities, enjoying daily routine

_____ Giving appropriate positive feedback to self and others

_____ Getting—and allowing self to believe—positive feedback

Section III:

HISTORY AND CURRENT EVENTS

We go back . . . and back . . . and back . . .
until we discover the exuberant, unencumbered, delightful
and
lovable child that was, and still is, in us.
And once we find it, we love and cherish it,
and never, never let it go.

8

COMING TO TERMS WITH OUR
FAMILY OF ORIGIN

*"Does anyone need anything more from the group?" the therapist
asked. "Yes," replied a woman. "Could you all come with me to a
family reunion this weekend so I don't lose my mind?"*

For years, I thought about doing family of origin work. For years, I
didn't do it. The idea brought several images to mind. I envisioned a
patient lying on a psychiatrist's couch, endlessly reminiscing about
childhood. I pictured thousand-page family genealogy books.

I tried to do the Transactional Analysis version: Draw three circles for each family member. Stack the circles vertically (like a stick
figure of a snowman), then run arrows from each person's circles to
another's. Along the arrows, write the psychological messages received from that circle. To find these messages, answer a questionnaire. "Mom always . . . (fill in the blank). Dad usually . . . (fill in the
blank). The front of my sweatshirt says . . . The back of my sweatshirt says . . ."

Well, Mom always did different things. Dad usually did too. I
was always worried I'd write the wrong answer, so I usually didn't fill
in anything. And I didn't own a sweatshirt until I was thirty-three
years old, when I bought one at a garage sale. The front of it read, "St.
Cloud State University." The back of it was blank, except for a small
hole.

With due respect to Sigmund Freud, family trees, and Transactional Analysis, I considered family of origin work expensive, boring, and complicated. The past is over and done with, I thought. Just forget about it. Besides, how could *that* be affecting me *now*? I've since changed my mind. My question has become: How could that *not* be affecting me now?

For many years, therapists have understood the value of doing historical work. They understood its profound influence on current events. Yesterday's smoldering coals—the unresolved feelings and unexamined messages—create today's fires. We work it out, or live it out. What we deny from yesterday, we'll be blind to today. And we'll have many opportunities to deny it because we'll continue to recreate it. Unfinished business may be buried, but it is alive and breathing. And it may have control of our lives.

In recent years, family of origin work has emerged as a significant part of recovery from codependency and the adult child syndrome. Doing our historical work is recognized as one way we can stop allowing ourselves to be affected by other people and their issues.

Many methods for doing historical work have emerged too.

"Moving Through Unfinished Business"

Bedford Combs, founding president of the South Carolina Association for Children of Alcoholics, uses an experiential process in his workshop, "Moving Through Unfinished Business: The Recovery Journey from Codependency."

In a gentle voice, Combs encourages us to get comfortable. Then he plays *The Rose* on a cassette recorder:

Some say love it is a river . . .
When the night has been too lonely . . .

When the room feels safe, Combs talks about families. He talks about control-release systems, where periods of controlling are balanced by times of acting out or releasing. He talks about other families, where times of self-care and nurturing are balanced by periods of creativity and experimentation.

Then Combs draws a picture of our memory center on the blackboard. Maybe we had an alcoholic parent, he said. And to survive, we had to take care of that parent as well as other people in our family. We couldn't be a child, and that hurt. Instead of feeling the hurt, we froze it. He draws a frozen nugget of pain in the memory center. Maybe someone abused us and we froze that pain. Maybe we were so angry at our parents we thought we hated them. And we felt guilty about feeling that way, so we froze that.

Combs talks about overwhelming feelings, feelings that hurt too much to feel. He talks about different coping behaviors we use to stop the pain. He says it was okay we did those things; protecting ourselves helped us survive. But he also says those frozen feelings and coping behaviors may now be blocking us from ourselves and others. He talks about people who have the courage to face those feelings. The reward is great, he says, because the scars from the pain turn into an ability to love and be loved.

He talks about family of origin work—experiential style.

Other Methods of Dealing with the Past

Earnie Larsen, a recovery professional, has developed another method for doing family of origin work. What undesirable consequence are we experiencing today? What behavior are we doing to create that consequence? What's the rule or message from the past that generates the behavior?[1]

Some people use a family geneagram to do historical work.[2] A geneagram is a family tree drawn with little square boxes, one for each family member. Squares on the top line represent grandparents. Underneath, we draw squares representing Mom and Dad. On the next line, we draw squares for ourselves, our brothers and sisters. We include any significant people, such as Great Aunt Helen, the woman who really raised Father.

After we put each person's name in a box, we add descriptive phrases. The phrases can characterize the person, how we felt about or around a person, or what others said about him or her. We don't have to wring our subconscious or our hands to do this. We write whatever comes to mind, and we keep it simple. If we remember Grandpa was scary, mean, laughed a lot, or never noticed us, we write it down. If we remember double messages—Grandpa said he was glad to see us but ignored us for the rest of the visit—we write both. We mention addictions and other problems. For example, we might write that Dad drank a lot, worked all the time, couldn't hold a job, never worked up to his potential, gambled, was overweight, or had affairs.

We write the "bad" and the "good." We mention family roles. Role descriptions describe how people got their attention. For instance, sister Mabel got all her attention by taking care of people; acting naughty; or being smart, cute, or funny. Or, nobody noticed sister Mabel. She didn't get any attention.

We describe our relationships with the people. Maybe a relationship was characterized by someone neglecting us while we waited, hoping someday to be noticed. Maybe someone tried to control us, and we rebelled. Maybe we turned ourselves inside out to get approval from someone who never gave us approval. Maybe we had to play an inappropriate role with a parent.

"My mother never had a fulfilling relationship with my father or anyone else," recalls one man, a recovering adult child of an alcoholic. "She looked to me to meet her needs: her need to be close, to share feelings, to go places with. She never touched me sexually, not once, but it was an incestuous relationship. I wasn't her child," he says, "I was her husband."

We draw a picture of our family, using boxes and words. We remember, and say, what happened. We do this without guilt, because it's okay to talk about things now. Writing it down is important; we gain insights from writing we can't from contemplation.

These are only three of many possible approaches to family of origin work. Some counselors specialize in family of origin work. We can use the Transactional Analysis version. Or we can use the Fourth and Fifth Steps of Twelve Step programs.

Some of us do historical work when we begin recovery. Some of us aren't ready for a while. Some of us tackle the entire business in one clump; others of us string it out, doing it naturally and gradually as issues and insights surface.

However and whenever we do it, we don't do it to blame or disrespect our families. Nor is the purpose to stay entrenched in yesterday's muck. The goal is to forget the past—after we *remember* what happened. The goal is to become free of its destructive or self-defeating influences.

In the following pages we'll discuss the elements that can help us break free of the past. These include

- feelings
- messages
- patterns
- people

Feelings

One part of historical work is feeling and releasing frozen, denied feelings. I'm a controlling person. I've spent many years trying to make people be who they weren't and do things they didn't want to. I've also tried to control my feelings by willing them away. One way I've done this is by going numb, freezing feelings. In my freezer of feelings, I have a full shelf from childhood. I didn't deal with feelings then, but they didn't go away. They're in storage. Some are big; some are little. Some have been stored so long they have freezer burn. They're stored in body tissue, in messages, and behaviors.

Remembering events is one way to expose these feelings. We recall an event, then follow it to an emotional conclusion. What was the feeling we had during or after an event? Did we feel it or freeze it? How we felt about an experience—rather, *what we didn't feel but needed to*—is as important as what happened. We're safe now. We let ourselves feel the fear, shame, rage, hurt, and loneliness we didn't feel safe enough to feel then. We may even want to play with fantasy, to go back and pretend we had better ways to protect ourselves. We're ten feet tall; we've got a shield and a sword; we have whatever we need to protect ourselves. Then we come back to reality. We know we're grown up now and can take care of ourselves.[3]

This work isn't to be done casually. Many of us have frozen big wounds. If we open them, we need to know we're doing it with someone who can help us properly close the incisions. A good rule of thumb is: If you can't close it, don't open it. Some people find complete blocks to the past. Denial is a necessary safety device.[4] We use it to protect ourselves. If that protective device is taken from us, we need other protection.

Not having any recollection of certain times in our lives may be a key to historical work. Or, repeatedly thinking or talking about certain past events can indicate unfinished business. Resolving it will help dissolve it. Unfinished business remains in the air, in us, and in our lives. We will be attracted, drawn, compelled to what is unfinished in us. Experiencing and releasing the feelings completes the transaction.

"These feelings can be overwhelming and scary," says therapist Scott Egleston, who works with juveniles. "Some of the kids in my program tell me they're afraid they'll disappear if they feel all that pain."

The child in us may fear the same thing. Don't worry. We won't disappear. Once we feel and release those emotions, we'll appear.

Messages

Another important goal of family of origin work is decoding and changing the self-defeating messages we picked up as children. The message is the meaning we interpreted from what happened. It's our frame of reference—our filing catalog for life's events.[5] Our messages may be related to the codependent rules:

- It's not okay for me to feel.
- It's not okay for me to have problems.
- It's not okay for me to have fun.
- I'm not lovable.
- I'm not good enough.
- If people feel bad or act crazy, it's my fault.

"When we're young, we don't have the experienced frame of reference adults have to make sense of things," Egleston says. "When someone, especially someone we love, behaves inappropriately or treats us badly, we don't see the behavior connected to a person's problem or addiction. We don't understand that it's *their* issue. Our only frame of reference is, 'It must be me. There must be something wrong with me.' "

We each have our own set of messages unique to our circumstances and to us. Each person can interpret entirely different messages from the same event.[6]

Messages control, or generate, our behaviors. Some messages are good and allow us to do certain things without thinking too much about them: "Be a good student." "Pay your bills on time." "Don't get into the car with strangers." Other messages may be neutral: "Go to your room if you're going to cry." It can be interesting to decode these messages, but we don't need to be overly concerned with them. It's the destructive ones, the "It's not okay to be who I am" or "I'm not lovable" messages we want to change. Those generate self-defeating behaviors.

One way to understand our messages is to use Earnie Larsen's approach:

- What is today's undesirable consequence?
- What behavior is causing the consequence?
- What's the rule (yesterday's message) that generates the behavior?

"One consequence was that I never had any money, no matter how much I earned," says one man. "I used Larsen's formula. The behavior was that I spent money the second I got it. The rule or message was that I wasn't financially responsible; I didn't know the value of a dollar, and I didn't deserve to have money."

Another way to uncover our messages is to start listening to ourselves. If we listen closely, with an ear toward understanding, we'll hear the message. It's right there, under the behavior.

Once we've decoded our messages, we give ourselves new, more constructive ones. It's a big job, but so are the rewards from doing it.

Patterns

Another goal of historical work is to understand and change self-defeating patterns, including our patterns of intimacy or intimacy avoidance. What keeps happening, over and over? What do I keep doing, over and over? What do other people keep doing to me, over and over? Why do I need this to happen? How and why do I attract it? How do the characteristics of today's relationships connect to my past relationships?

"I continually found myself in relationships with men who said they loved me, but they couldn't show that love or be close to me because they were addicted," says one woman. "My idea of intimacy was me waiting endlessly for something that wasn't going to happen. Then I realized this was the same pattern I had, and still have, with my brother and father."

"The men in my family were sex addicts," says another woman.

"I spent my childhood feeling scared and uncomfortable around men, and wondering what was wrong with me for feeling that way. Then I went on to create the same patterns in my adult life."

"As a child, I was surrounded by very negative, controlling people. Guess what kind of people I attracted when I grew up? The same," reported a third woman.

Some of us may have more than one pattern. "I find myself alternating patterns. In one relationship, I create my pattern with my father; in the next, my pattern with my mother," explains a fourth woman.

We also examine our roles. How did we get our attention as children? How do we get our attention today?

The feelings, messages, patterns, and roles are connected, interwoven like a tapestry.

People

An important part of family of origin work is resolving our relationships with the people in our families. This means acknowledging and releasing any intense feelings about family members, so we are free to love and grow. That can mean running a gamut of emotions from denial, hate, rage, disappointment, frustration, rejection, disillusionment, wishful thinking, resentment, and despair to acceptance, forgiveness, and love. Many adult children wish circumstances and people could have been, or would be different. They weren't and aren't. And although our feelings toward family members and our childhoods are valid, these feelings can block our growth if we don't resolve them.

We have our family of origin issues, and so do other family members. Often, our parents have more severe family of origin issues than we do. In recovery, we learn to accept the darker side of ourselves. In family of origin work, we learn to accept the darker side of our parents too.[7]

"We forget our parents were people before and after they became parents," says Egleston.

In *You Can Heal Your Life*, one of the best books I've read on self-love, Louise Hay suggests a powerful visualization exercise to help achieve compassion and forgiveness for our parents.

> Begin to visualize yourself as a little child of five or six. . . . Now let this little child get very small, until it is just the size to fit into your heart. Put it there so whenever you look down you can see this little face looking up at you and you can give it lots of love.
>
> Now visualize your mother as a little girl of four or five, frightened and looking for love and not knowing where to find it. Reach out your arms and hold this little girl and let her know how much you love her. . . . When she quiets down and begins to feel safe, let her get very small, just the size to fit into your heart. Put her there, with your own little child.
>
> Now imagine your father as a little boy of three or four, frightened, crying, and looking for love. . . . Let him get very small, just the size to fit into your heart. Put him there so those three little children can give each other lots of love and you can love them all.[8]

Besides dealing with our feelings about family members, we learn to function in relationships with them, when possible. Some people have an easy time dealing with family. Others have a difficult time. Some have an awful struggle. For those of us in the last two categories, the solution means practicing self-care and basic recovery principles the best we can, one day at a time. We can't change others, but we can change ourselves. We don't have to take other people's behaviors personally. If they have no love or approval to give us, it isn't our fault. They may not have any to give anyone, including themselves.[9] Some say family of origin work means accepting that one or both of our parents didn't love us. Others, and I agree, say it means accepting our parents couldn't show their love for us in ways we wanted, but loved us the best they could, and maybe more than we thought.

Some people need to take a break from certain family members until they (the recovering people) feel more equipped to deal with these relationships.

"I've really struggled with family relationships," says one woman. "My father molested me for years. My mother knew. I've tried going home and pretending nothing happened. I've tried getting them to deal with the abuse. They weren't ready. Sometimes, I've needed to stay away. Some people recommended that I stay away forever, but I don't want to," she admits. "They're the only mom and dad I'll ever have. My family is important to me. For years, I used their treatment of me to justify punishing them emotionally and blackmailing them financially. What I'm working on now is trying to forgive them and still take care of myself. I'm working at changing my behaviors with them. I visit them when I feel good, when I want to, and when I can handle it. I'm working at taking responsibility for me."

"My dad is still drinking, and my mom's still a martyr," explains a man recovering from codependency. "For many years I needed to back off from them. Now, I can go home. I can do things with my parents. I can let them be who they are, enjoy what's good, let the rest go, and take care of myself when I need to."

We go back to our families when we're ready. When we go back, we go back differently. We're not part of the system anymore. We have a new system of self-care, self-love, and self-responsibility.

Also, just because we have an insight doesn't mean other family members will be ready to hear or appreciate that insight. In fact, discussing our issues with them may trigger their defenses. We each deal with our secrets and issues when we're ready. The purpose of family of origin work is to benefit us; it's not to change other family members. The best way to help people, including family members, is to keep doing our own work.[10]

The pull and demands of a dysfunctional family are strong. Listen, can you hear the disease singing in the background?[11] Can you understand that diseases like chemical dependency and intergenerational abuse create victims of everyone? Do you know it's not your fault? It's probably not your parents' fault, either. Do you know you have a right to become as healthy as you want, no matter what your family does or doesn't do? Do you know you can love people anyway? Do you know that you're lovable?

Like recovery, family of origin work is a process. It's a healing process, an awareness process, a forgiveness process, and a process of changing and becoming changed. It's a grief process, in which we mourn the things we lost or never had. We deny, get angry, bargain, feel the pain, then finally accept what was and is. After we accept, we forgive. And we take responsibility for *ourselves*. We'll do this when we're ready, when it's time, and when we've worked through the other emotions. When we can do this, the good will shine through if we let it and look for it. The process starts with willingness.

We go back to the house we grew up in. We walk around to each dark room, turn on the lights, and look around. We expose the secrets, the problems, the addictions, the messages, the patterns, and the feelings. We look at events and people. We look at roles and survival behaviors. We see what we're denying today because we denied it yesterday. We see what needs weren't met yesterday and how we may still be reacting to that deprivation. Then after we've stared at our childhood and felt what we needed to feel, we release our feelings. We let go, so we can appreciate what was and is good. We do this courageously, fearlessly, and with compassion—for others and for ourselves—when we're ready to do this.

We go back long enough to see what happened and how that's affecting us now. We visit yesterday long enough to feel and be healed. We come back to today knowing we're free to make choices. We go to war with the messages, but we make peace with the people because we deserve to be free.

We go back . . . and back . . . and back . . . through the layers of fear, shame, rage, hurt, and negative incantations until we discover the exuberant, unencumbered, delightful, and lovable child that was, and still is, in us.

And once we find it, we love and cherish it, and never, never let it go.

ACTIVITY

1. What are some significant events from your past that you find yourself repeatedly thinking or talking about? Have you dealt with your feelings about those events?

2. As a start toward accomplishing family of origin work, you may want to try the family geneagram approach described in this chapter. With a friend or in group, draw a picture of your family, using boxes and words.

3. What are some messages you've uncovered? How have you worked at changing those?

4. When you're ready, write a letter to family members, telling them everything you like and think is good about them. You don't have to mail it, but you can if you want.

9

BREAKING FREE

"How does one become a butterfly?" she asked pensively.
"You must want to fly so much that you are willing
to give up being a caterpillar."

—Trina Paulus
Hope for the Flowers

"Eureka! The rules are real! They're a living entity."

That light went on one dark night, while I lay in bed confused by a previously unexplained funk of several months. I'd been recovering from codependency for several years. I'd heard and *taught* about the codependent rules.[1] But in that moment, I finally gave the rules the respect they deserved.

The rules position themselves in our control center. They jam things up and take over. They direct our behaviors, and sometimes our lives. Once situated, they program us to do things that leave us feeling miserable, stuck, and codependent.

That's what happened to me. The rules had crept back in and I hadn't noticed. Actually, I had lived with them so long they felt comfortable. But I felt crazy because I was doing what they instructed:

- Don't feel or talk about feelings.
- Don't think, figure things out, or make decisions—you probably don't know what you want or what's best for you.

- Don't identify, mention, or solve problems—it's not okay to have them.
- Be good, right, perfect, and strong.
- Don't be who you are because that's not good enough.
- Don't be selfish, put yourself first, say what you want and need, say no, set boundaries, or take care of yourself—always take care of others and never hurt their feelings or make them angry.
- Don't have fun, be silly or enjoy life—it costs money, makes noise and isn't necessary.
- Don't trust yourself, your Higher Power, the process of life or certain people—instead put your faith in untrustworthy people; then act surprised when they let you down.
- Don't be open, honest, and direct—hint, manipulate, get others to talk for you, guess what they want and need and expect them to do the same for you.
- Don't get close to people—it isn't safe.
- Don't disrupt the system by growing or changing.[2]

People don't make these rules. Addictions, secrets, and other crazy systems make these rules to protect the addictions and secrets and keep the crazy systems in place. But people follow these rules. And people mindlessly pass them on from generation to generation. The rules are the guardians and protectors of the system—the crazy system.

Many of us have lived with and learned these rules. Experts like lecturer Robert Subby say that above all else, even beyond living with a drinking alcoholic, these rules are the tie that binds most of us together in this trap called codependency.[3] Following these rules keeps us locked into codependency; breaking them is a key to recovery.

When you were a child, what happened when you felt sad, angry, or frightened? What happened when you told someone about your feelings? Were you criticized, ignored, told "Hush" or "Don't feel that way"? How did family members deal with feelings? Were you allowed to make decisions? What did others say about your choices?

What happened when you pointed out a problem? Were you told you could solve your problems? Were things explained in a way that made sense? Was denial a way of life? Was conflict allowed, then resolved?

Did you know it was okay to be who you are, and that you're good enough? Did anybody teach you how to take care of yourself? Did you have fun? Did people in your family enjoy life? Were you encouraged to trust yourself, God, and life?

Did people in your family talk openly, honestly, and directly? Or was the air thick with tension while people smiled and said, "Fine"? Did you learn how to be close to people? What happened when you tried to grow, change, or step outside the system? Did someone in the family agitate, complain, develop a problem or crisis, or otherwise make such a loud noise you came back? What happens in your family now?

Some, all, or variations of the rules may be operating. We may have more rules than these. Since hearing author Bedford Combs lecture on "lookin' good" families—families that look good but feel crazy because feelings and problems aren't allowed—I've added another possible rule: Always *look* good, no matter how you feel or what you have to do.

We may have been taught directly or indirectly to follow these rules. Powerful methods such as shame, disapproving looks, or role modeling may have enforced them. Once we learn the rules, they govern silently but surely. We begin to feel a feeling. The "don't feel" rule gets triggered. We automatically stop the process of feeling. We decide to do something special for ourselves. The idea or act triggers the "don't be selfish" mandate.

Thinking about or doing a behavior that violates the rules may trigger the rule. Being around a person or system that follows the rules can also activate our rules. Once the rules become our messages, they operate unbidden. They keep us "in line" by dishing out negative consequences of guilt, shame, and fear if we break them without consciously giving ourselves permission to do that.

"An old friend, a recovering alcoholic, called me to borrow money," recalls Sandy, who's recovering from codependency. "Something didn't feel right about it, but when I thought about saying no, I felt waves of guilt and shame. How could I be so selfish? I loaned him the money, and two weeks later learned he'd been drinking again—for over a month. Now I can clearly see how the message 'don't be selfish' clicked in and kept me from doing what I wanted. I'm trying to learn to recognize the messages when they pop up, instead of two weeks later."

Many of us are attracted to and feel comfortable around people and systems with rules similar to ours.[4] If the system or person has different rules, we'll catch on soon. Rules are powerful, quick to make themselves known.

It's Okay to Change the Rules

Over time, in recovery, we make new rules. Gradually, we learn—from people in our support groups, counselors, healthy friends, and recovery literature and tapes—that it's okay to break the rules. But if we try to change our behaviors without changing the rules, we may find ourselves in conflict with our control center.

Instead of being in conflict or waiting for time and happenstance to give us new rules, why not consciously change the rules? Like the other coping behaviors we *used* to use, the rules were only valuable as a protective device when we had no other way to protect ourselves. We had to get along and survive then. We can choose now.

When I first began detaching from the alcoholics in my life, when I made a conscious choice to give other people's lives back to them and reclaim my own, I had such a puny sense of self that I felt like a deflated balloon. Living in close proximity to active alcoholism contributed to that. My active codependency contributed to that. But following the rules for over thirty years contributed to it all—my weak sense of self, living in close proximity to alcoholics, and my codependency. The rules don't allow for *self*. The rules didn't let me be a healthy person. They didn't allow me to be, much less be me.

The rules strip us of our God-given personal power—our human, mental, emotional, physical, and spiritual rights. We don't have to forfeit our personal power to these messages. We can give ourselves new rules once we've accepted—surrendered to—the old ones. Surrender usually precedes empowerment. (In my life, surrender usually precedes everything.) And how much we're willing to surrender is usually how much we'll be empowered.

Here's our first new rule: It's okay to change the rules. We have the power, the ability, and the right. Whether we've been recovering for ten minutes or ten years, it's never too early or too late to assertively—even aggressively—change the rules. We can take back our personal power. We'll be empowered. And when we change the rules, our behaviors will change.

My new rules are:

- It's okay to feel my feelings and talk about them when it's safe and appropriate, and I want to.
- I can think, make good decisions, and figure things out.
- I can have, talk about, and solve my problems.
- It's okay for me to be who I am.
- I can make mistakes, be imperfect, sometimes be weak, sometimes be not so good, sometimes be better, and occasionally be great.
- It's okay to be selfish sometimes, put myself first sometimes, and say what I want and need.
- It's okay to give to others, but it's okay to keep some for myself too.
- It's okay for me to take care of me. I can say no and set boundaries.
- It's okay to have fun, be silly sometimes, and enjoy life.
- I can make good decisions about who to trust. I can trust myself. I can trust God, even when it looks like I can't.
- I can be appropriately vulnerable.

- I can be direct and honest.
- It's okay for me to be close to some people.
- I can grow and change, even if that means rocking a bunch of boats.
- I can grow at my own pace.
- I can love and be loved. And I can love me, because I'm lovable. And I'm good enough.

We've lived with the old rules for a long time. Breaking them and following new messages may not feel comfortable at first. That's okay. We can do it anyway. As I said earlier, the old rules probably weren't pasted on the refrigerator, but they might as well have been. If we've been following them all our lives, they're glued in our minds. It may take more than once, twice, or a hundred times to make the new rules stick. And we may want to paste the new ones on the refrigerator.

We can think. We can feel. We can figure things out. We can solve our problems and let go of those we can't solve. We can stop taking care of other people and start taking care of ourselves. We can enjoy life. We can be close, trust, grow, change, and love. It's okay to do all those things. And it's our responsibility to give ourselves permission.

If we're in a relationship with someone who follows the old rules, that person may react when we break the rules. He or she may feel all the feelings we feel when a rule tries to enforce itself: fear, guilt, shame, and anxiety. He or she may want us to feel that way too. But we don't have to feel that way. If we do feel that way, we don't have to let our feelings stop us. Living by new messages, we can gently but powerfully give people around us permission to live by new rules.

Break free by surrendering. Break free by breaking the rules. Work at enforcing new rules. Work at them until they become as powerful and alive as the old rules. Work at them until you've reclaimed yourself and your life. Then work at them some more.

When you get stuck, when the old stuff comes back, when people tell you "you shouldn't," when you start to wonder if they're right, redouble your efforts. When the guilt and fear and shame come rushing in, pound the new rule into your conscious mind. Ask your Higher Power to help. Surround yourself with people who'll support you in your efforts, people striving to live by new rules. Support them in their efforts too. It's called recovery.

Rules are rules, but some rules are made to be broken.

ACTIVITY

1. What are your old rules? What new rules do you want to start living by? Write down the rules you want to break, then draw a line through them. Cross them out. Now, write down the new rules of your choosing.

2. Learn to recognize when an old message is trying to control your behavior. Pay attention to how you feel. Use those times to consciously affirm your new rule.

3. Visualization work can help us change rules. We know the behaviors the old rules generate; what behaviors will the new ones generate? Imagine what it would look like following the new rules. What, specifically, will you do differently when you're following a new rule? What will that look like? Feel like? Sound like?

10

BREAKING THROUGH THE SHAME BARRIER

I'm pore, I'm black, I may be ugly and can't cook,
a voice say to everything listening. But I'm here.

—Celie, from *The Color Purple,*
by Alice Walker

"You don't have to be ashamed about wanting to be in a relationship,"
I told the audience. "If you were unemployed, you wouldn't feel
ashamed about looking for a job, would you?"

"I would," mumbled a man in the fifth row.

"I went to a dance," said Marcie, a thirty-four-year-old woman recovering from adult children and incest issues. "All I could do was
hang my head and stare at my feet."

"You don't ever have to apologize for being who you are. And
you don't have to be ashamed of who you are," I told her.

"Well," she replied hesitantly, "maybe sometimes I do."

"I've been recovering from codependency and chemical dependency for years," said one woman. "For many of those years, my
sponsor told me she's never seen such a discrepancy between a person's potential, intelligence, and talent and what that person believes
about her potential, intelligence, and talent. I'm finally beginning to
see what she means. I've never believed in myself! I've never given
myself any credit! It's like keeping a high-performance car idling or
in park, then complaining because it won't move forward."

Whether we call it "shame bound," "shame based," or "shame

faced,"[1] shame can be a burden and problem for many of us. Shame can hold us back, hold us down, and keep us staring at our feet. We may not understand shame technically. We may not be able to label it. We may call it other things: fear, confusion, guilt, rage, indifference, or the other person's fault.[2] But if we're recovering from codependency or adult children issues, we've probably been profoundly influenced by shame.

Shame is the trademark of dysfunctional families. It comes with addictive families, where one or more people were addicted to alcohol, drugs, food, work, sex, religion, or gambling. It comes with families with problems and secrets. It comes with families whose parents, grandparents, or even great-grandparents had addictions, problems, or secrets.[3] Shame adds fuel to the addictive fire. It's used to protect secrets and keep them in place. It's used to keep us in place. And often it's passed from generation to generation, like a fine piece of porcelain, until it rests on the mantel in our living room.

Shame on you. The words are a curse, a spell others cast on us. It's a spell we learn to cast on ourselves. The creepy, crawling muck drips like black ink from our heads to our toes. Whether the spell is cast with a look, certain words, a tone of voice, or an old message inside our heads, it's there until we do something about it. The spell says, "What you did isn't okay, who you are isn't okay, and nothing you do will change that." *Shame on you.*

Shame has its roots in our childhood and its branches in our lives today. Shame is a form of control, a tool used by parents and societies probably since the beginning of time. Shame is the feeling we get when we do something that disappoints people we love. Used properly, it can help instill ethics and a conscience.[4] It is externally-applied guilt.

Appropriate shame tells us certain behaviors are inappropriate, and it separates our behaviors from who we are. "Stop that Johnny!" the mother scolds. "I don't ever want to see you hitting someone again. It's not okay to hit."[5] In this case, Johnny learns it's not okay to hit, but it's okay to be Johnny. That's not the kind of shame I'm talking about in this chapter. I'm talking about the malignant kind, the shaming that says, "Stop that Johnny. And you're a bad, bad person for doing it in the first place."

In this case, Johnny learns it's not okay to hit, and it's not okay to be Johnny. The externally-applied guilt becomes guilt for being. In some of our families, we are shamed for healthy, appropriate behaviors too, such as thinking, feeling, having fun, loving and being loved, making mistakes, and taking care of ourselves. We may have developed a sense of shame about our bodies, or certain parts of our bodies, or our sexuality.

Sometimes, we become shame based because of what others did to us. Victims of abuse are often plagued by shame, even though they weren't responsible for the inappropriate behavior.

How Shame Can Control Us, If We Let It

For many of us, shame expands from being the feeling we get when we disappoint someone we love to a feeling we get when we provoke anyone's disapproval, even a stranger's disapproval.

"My children were in a restaurant lobby playing with some other children they didn't know. They got into some kid stuff together— making faces at each other, sticking their tongues out," says one recovering woman. "Then the other children's mother got involved. I told her I didn't want to get involved with the children's argument; I had learned both sides usually played a part. She started harping about how bad my kids were, and no wonder because I was a bad mother. I froze. I folded up and died inside. It took me half a day to work through the shame. I let a total stranger put it on me!"

People can control us through our areas of shame. That's what shame is—a tool for controlling behavior. Being vulnerable to shame makes us vulnerable to being controlled. The thought of people disapproving of us—*casting the spell*—can become enough to stop us. Shame can almost paralyze us.

"Shame binds and blocks the flow of energy," says therapist Scott Egleston.

Let me give an example. Some time ago, I had a problem being late for church. For many reasons, mostly because I was leaving home late, I was arriving late at church. And I began to feel ashamed. What were others thinking of me? What kind of person was I, if I couldn't get myself and the children to church on time? And if I didn't care enough to be on time, why was I even bothering to come at all? I began sneaking into a back pew, berating myself during the entire service instead of listening. Nobody was disapproving of me. I was doing it to myself.

The more ashamed I became, the more I vowed to be on time and the later I was each Sunday. One week, everything went wrong from the time I got up to the time the children and I got to the church sanctuary. Nobody could find the right clothes. Someone spilled their cereal. We were arguing. I felt frantic, and my feelings were spilling over on the entire family. The issue wasn't that it was preferable to arrive on time. The issue had become I wasn't okay if I got to church late. We arrived almost fifteen minutes late.

I stood in the foyer outside the sanctuary. *What an awful person I am,* I thought. *How dare I walk in this late!* Nobody paid any particular attention to me, but I could just see the entire congregation turning to look at me, judging and frowning.

I couldn't walk into the sanctuary. I couldn't move my feet forward. I was paralyzed by shame. I grabbed the children, and whisked them out the door vowing it would never happen again.

The next week I got up, left the house early, and got to church five minutes early. Everybody was getting into their cars and leaving. The service was over. We had gone on daylight savings time that day, and I didn't set the clock forward. I was almost an hour late. I surrendered, and the issue has since become manageable.

The point of the story is this: Shame can stop us from acting. If we grew up in a system that attached shame to healthy behaviors like thinking, feeling, and taking care of ourselves, shame may be stopping us from doing those things. Each time we have a feeling, a thought, have some fun, get close, or just let go with some spontaneous "being," shame can spoil it. Shame can stop us from setting boundaries. And shame can keep us entrenched in our mistakes.

"I became involved with some inappropriate sexual behaviors," recalls one man. "I fell into a situation, and did some things I didn't feel good about at all. Later, I felt so guilty and ashamed. I felt like trash. I didn't know how to deal with all those awful feelings. I didn't know how to forgive and accept myself. The only thing that promised to make me feel better was to do the same thing again. I started a compulsive behavior that went on for several months, until I finally surrendered and forgave myself. I couldn't change the behavior when I hated myself. I could only change when I started loving myself—unconditionally."

Even Opus, the little penguin in the *Bloom County* cartoon strip, had his experience with shame. Some members of the community found Opus reading certain magazines. They charged him with penguin lust, and banished him from the Bloom County kingdom. Hanging his head, the exiled Opus shuffled off to far corners of the world. Sometime later, he accepted employment as a male penguin stripper, the only job he felt worthy of. "I am suffering," Opus said, "from chronically and fatally low self-esteem."

Shame can affect each choice we make: choice of spouse, friends, home, job, or car; how we spend our money; and what we do with our time. Shame can prevent us from seeing our good choices, because we don't believe we deserve the best. If we believe who we are isn't good enough, each encounter with life will prove what we believe, no matter how much good we do. We may seek out or create experiences to reinforce that belief. Sometimes, it will cause us to destroy what's good.

One recovering man tells the following story. "I always wanted a Mercedes," he says. "One day, I bought one. I ordered the car, picked it up, and immediately the worst feeling flooded through me. Whenever I went someplace, I parked a block or two away. I didn't tell anybody I got the car. I felt like wearing a paper bag over my head when I drove it. I didn't know what was wrong; I just knew I felt uncomfortable about the car. One week later, I took it to another car lot and started to trade it for a car of far less value. I was going to lose money! Then it hit me. What was wrong was shame. I didn't believe I deserved that car.

"I kept the car," the man says. "I'm working on my shame. I'm working at changing what I believe about myself, and my right to have nice things."

Shame can make us feel crazy and do crazy things. It hurts to believe it's not okay to be who we are. To protect ourselves from that pain, we may avoid shame by turning it into other feelings that are safer and easier to handle: rage; indifference; an overwhelming need to control; depression; confusion; flightiness; or an obsession to use our drug of choice, whether that "drug" is alcohol, a pill, food, sex, or money. We may transform shame into blame, numbness, or panic. Or we may deal with it by running away.[6]

We may not understand that shame is causing us or others to do these things. It's confusing to be in a relationship with a shame-based person.[7] We see the running, blaming, or rage, and may not understand why we or the other person is doing these things.

I had a dream one night. I was in an underground prison. Other people were in that prison with me. All my choices had to be made from the people and things in that underground prison. When I awoke, I realized that the prison represented shame and low self-esteem. I also realized the door to that prison wasn't locked; it was open. All I had to do was walk through.

In the following pages I'll discuss some ideas to help you start walking through that door. These points include

- switching from a shame-based system to one of self-love and acceptance,
- exposing shame,
- treating shame like a feeling,

- tracking shame to its roots,
- changing what's needed,
- releasing shame, and
- knowing your rights and your rules.

Switch from a Shame-Based System to One of Self-Love and Acceptance

A shame-based system means we operate from the underlying belief that who we are *and* what we do isn't okay. In recovery, we decide who we are is okay. We love and accept ourselves unconditionally. When we do something that's inappropriate we separate the behavior from our identity. What we did may not be okay, but we're okay. Then we take steps to correct our behavior. This is the basic goal in recovery. It's the essence of Twelve Step programs, and it's what working the Steps can accomplish for us.[8]

This healthy system believes if we're working at recovery and connected to our Higher Power, we have an internal moral code that will send signals when it's violated. This system says we can trust ourselves, recovery, and our Higher Power. And it tells us we're okay if we make mistakes, because that's how we learn and grow.

Expose Shame

Learn to recognize the difference between shame and guilt. Guilt is believing that what we did isn't okay. Authentic guilt is valuable. It's a signal that we've violated our own, or a universal, moral code. It helps keep us honest, healthy, and on track. Shame is worthless. Shame is the belief that whether what we did is okay or not, who we are isn't.[9] Guilt is resolvable. We make amends for what we did, learn from our mistake, and attempt to correct our behavior. Shame isn't resolvable. It leaves us with a sense that all we can do is apologize for our existence, and even that falls short of what's needed.

We may have mild, medium, or severe shame attacks. We may

live in a constant state of shame. We can learn to recognize and identify shame: how it feels, the thoughts it produces, and what it makes
us do. Do you run, hide, blame, freeze, fly into a rage or try to control? Learn to detect when shame is at the core of these behaviors.
Hold a light to shame and call it what it is: a nasty feeling dumped on
us to impose rules—usually someone else's rules.

Treat Shame Like a Feeling

Shame is a powerful force. For lack of a better word, let's call it a
feeling. When it appears, treat it like any other feeling. Talk about it.
At least acknowledge it to yourself. Sometimes, I "Gestalt" my way
through shame: I hang my head, cover my face with my hands, and
say, "I'm so ashamed." Other times, I simply say, "Yes. That's shame."
The basic "dealing with feelings etiquette" applies to shame: it's our
feeling and our responsibility. Become aware of it. Then accept it.
Shame is like any other feeling: denying it won't make it go away; it'll
make it get bigger.

Actually, I don't mind those moments when I feel ashamed. I
used to feel that way most of the time. Now, I usually have enough
self-esteem and good feelings to notice when shame creeps back in.

Track Shame to Its Roots

Why are you feeling ashamed? Who have you disappointed?
Whose rules are you breaking? Someone else's, or your own? Maybe
we're doing something that's causing us to feel legitimately guilty.
Maybe we're violating our own moral code, and guilt has become intertwined with shame. Sometimes, shame is a clue to something we
legitimately need to change, but we probably won't change until we
get rid of the shame.

Sometimes, shame creeps in about our pasts—something that
can't be changed.

Other times, shame indicates we've broken a family rule. We

each have our own messages, and shame will be bonded to the messages. Dealing with shame can help us understand our messages. One woman shared the following experience with me.

"Whenever I talked to men, I became flooded with shame," she says. "It didn't matter if it was men friends or a man I was interested in dating. Then, I realized what was happening. When I was an adolescent, my family had some real taboos about being sexual. Whenever my father caught me talking to a boy, he shamed me. The words he used were, 'You ought'a be ashamed. You're acting just like a tramp.'

"I was thirty-five years old, I lived in a different city than my father, but his words were still in my head. The shame was still inside me, each time I talked to a man. Understanding this helped. I've been able to give myself new messages, and the shame is disappearing."

"I felt ashamed each time I left the house without the children," explains another woman, a mother of three children. "Once I stopped running from my shame, I uncovered the message: A good mother always puts her children first. Once I uncovered it, I could change it. My new message is: A good mother takes care of herself too."

Change What's Needed

If we feel ashamed because we've done something we feel guilty about, we convert shame to guilt, then make any appropriate amends and change our behavior. If we decide shame is trying to enforce an unhealthy, inappropriate message on us, we change the message. If we feel ashamed about something we cannot or need not change, we surrender to the situation and give ourselves a big hug.

Release Shame

Once we accept shame's presence, find a way to make it disappear. Talk back to it. Get mad at it. Tell it to go away. Feel it intensely.

Make friends with it. Let it go. Work Step Six and Step Seven of the Twelve Step program. Work Step Six by getting ready to have the shortcoming of shame removed, and work Step Seven by asking God to remove it.[10] Handle it however it works for you, but continue with the course of action you choose, and let go of the shame feeling.

Know Your Rights and Your Rules

Many of us grew up with shame bonded to basic human rights and needs.[11] It helps to know our rights and our new rules. Then, we can deal with the shame when it tries to enforce the old rules. We have the right to say no or yes, be healthy, feel safe, and take care of ourselves. We have the right to set limits, be free from abuse, grow at our pace, make mistakes, have fun, and love and be loved. We have the right to our perceptions, observations, opinions, and feelings. We have the right to become as healthy and successful as we can.

We have other rights too. I discovered them the day I discovered my shame "base." I was driving to an appointment I had at a local college with a vocational counselor. I didn't have to take a test. I didn't have to pass an exam. I had nothing to win or lose. I just needed to gather a few pamphlets and get some information. Yet I felt anxious and frightened, which was the way I usually felt. Then I realized what was going on. I felt anxious most of the time because I didn't feel appropriate to life. The situation or circumstance didn't matter. I didn't feel good enough. I wasn't enough.

I made a decision that day. I was here, I was me, and I was enough in spite of my past, my present, my future, my weaknesses, my foibles, my mistakes, and my humanness.

We're good, and we're good enough. Sometimes we make big mistakes; sometimes we make little mistakes. But the mistake is what we do, not who we are. We have a right to be, to be here, and be who we are. If we're not certain who we are, we have a right to make that exciting discovery. And we don't ever have to let shame tell us any differently.

ACTIVITY

1. As you go through your daily activities, keep a record of your shame attacks. Then, look for patterns. In what areas are you most vulnerable to shame: Talking about feelings? Your body? Fun activities? Making mistakes and being imperfect? Your past? Which people seem most prone to trigger your shame?

11

FROM DEPRIVED TO DESERVING

I will take a long look at where I am today and be grateful for my place. It's right for me now, and is preparing me for the adventure ahead.

—from *Each Day a New Beginning*

The psychiatrist showed Jason a sketch.[1] "What does this look like?"

Jason, a middle-aged man with dusty brown hair, said it looked like a bird.

"Good," said the psychiatrist. He flipped to the next picture. "And this one?"

Jason said it looked like a tree. The doctor nodded, and showed Jason the next sketch.

"A butterfly."

"And this one?" the doctor asked.

Jason stared. He examined the picture from all angles. "I don't know what that is," Jason said.

The psychiatrist showed Jason the next sketch and the one after that. Neither of those reminded Jason of anything either. After those three sketches, Jason identified the rest of the pictures in the test.

"Why couldn't I recognize those pictures?" Jason asked, when the psychiatrist finished.

"It's not surprising that group of sketches didn't make sense to you," the psychiatrist said. "They represent a father's love. You'd only be able to recognize the pictures if you had experienced a father's love. The pictures were blank because that's a blank spot in your development."

Jason started talking. He talked about being the youngest of nine children born to a farm family during the depression. He rehashed his fifteen-year battle with alcoholism. He mentioned two failed marriages to women who treated him as his father had—coolly and with rejection. He talked about unceasing efforts to do things for people and not feeling appreciated. Toward the end of the session, Jason paused. When he spoke again, he looked and sounded more like a nine-year-old boy than a fifty-year-old man.

"Why didn't he ever hold me on his lap, or hug me, or tell me he thought I was special?" Jason asked. "Why didn't he ever tell me he loved me?"

"Either he wasn't capable of it, or he didn't know how to show love," the psychiatrist said quietly.

Jason stood up. He had tears in his eyes, but a new strength in his face. "You mean it wasn't me?" Jason said. "It wasn't my fault? I'm not unlovable?"

"No," the doctor said. "You're not unlovable. You were just deprived of love."

The Quest for Normal

Many of us were deprived as children. We may have been so deprived of good feelings that we believed life wasn't worth living. We may have been so deprived of love that we believed we weren't worthwhile. We may have been so deprived of protection and consistency that we believed people were untrustworthy. Our parents may have been so wrapped up in their problems and pain, so deprived themselves, they couldn't give us what we needed. We may have been deprived of material items: toys, candy, clothing, food, or a decent home.

Some of us were deprived of childhood.

It's been said that adult children from dysfunctional families don't know what "normal" is. That's because many of us haven't had much of that either.

My quest for normal has been an enormous undertaking. What's fun? What's love? How does it feel and what does it look like? What's a good relationship? How do you form an opinion? What do you do on your day off? How do you buy clothes? How do you make friends? What do you do with them when you get them? What's crazy? What's sane? How do you make yourself feel better when you hurt? What's the good stuff in life? Is there any? How much can I have?

For many of us, life is a big store. This store has two departments: the main floor, holding display after display of good stuff, much of which we can't label because we've never seen it; and the bargain basement, the room with the leftovers and irregulars. The room where we shop.

Listen to the following conversation between two women. One woman is recovering from adult children issues and a marriage to an alcoholic. The other is of fairly normal descent.

"I can't decide whether to break up with my boyfriend or not," says a woman.

"What are his good points?" asks her friend.

"Well, he works every day. He usually does what he says he's going to do. He's kind. And he's never hit me."

"No," says her friend. "You don't understand. What are his good points? The things you listed are givens."

"Oh," says the woman. "I didn't know that."

Which of the two women do you think is the adult child?

Losses are tough. It hurts to have something, then lose it. Deprivation runs deep. It creates blank spots in us.

"I never had a healthy, loving, present father figure," says one recovering woman. "I had an alcoholic father who left home when I was two; and an uninvolved stepfather for two years, when I was a teenager.

"When I grew up, I had several unsuccessful relationships with those same kinds of men: alcoholic or uninvolved. I didn't know there was anything else. If you've never had ice cream and haven't heard much about it, ice cream isn't part of your world. It's not a choice. Well, healthy, loving men weren't part of my world. They weren't a choice.

"One day, on a bus ride across the state, I sat next to an elderly gentleman. We chatted, and he told me about his wife, and how lonely he felt because it was the first time in years they had traveled separately. He told stories about his children. He recalled most incidents with happiness. He talked about an incident when his son had asked him to do something, and he was too busy to respond. He said he felt guilty about it for years, until one day he mentioned it to his son and his son couldn't even remember.

"What he didn't say that I heard anyway was he was there for his family in some substantive ways. He was present emotionally, physically, mentally, and financially. He cared about them and was healthy enough to show that.

"My eyes opened to something for the first time," she explains. "I didn't know that kind of man—that kind of husband, father, person, or family—existed in real life. For a moment, sadness flooded through me. I had done some grief work before, but how could I grieve something I didn't know I had lost? I felt sad that I hadn't known that kind of fatherly or family love. Then, I put that information into my reality. That kind of love, that kind of man, was out there."

We need to fill in the blank spots. Many things could be options for us:

- healthy love,
- an identity,
- an underlying feeling of safety,
- a norm of feeling good,
- the ability to resolve conflicts,
- good friends,

- fulfilling work,
- enough money, and
- the unconditional love and protection of a Higher Power.

Many of us were deprived as children, but many of us have carried that deprivation into adulthood. Deprivation creates deprived thinking. Deprived thinking perpetuates deprivation.

We can fall into the trap of short supply thinking: there's good stuff out there, but there isn't enough for us. We may become desperate, scrambling to get what we can and holding tightly to it, whether it's what we want or is good for us. We may become resentful and jealous of people who have enough. We may hoard what we have or refuse to enjoy it, fearing we'll use it up. We may give up and settle for less. Deprivation becomes habitual. We may continue to feel afraid and deprived, even when we're not.

"I buy fifty-two rolls of toilet paper at a time," says one woman, an adult child of an alcoholic who's been married to two alcoholics. "I buy fifty-two rolls of toilet paper at a time because for many years there wasn't enough toilet paper or money to buy more. And I don't ever want to run out again. For the past three years, I've earned over $25,000 a year. There's enough money to buy more. But there doesn't feel like there's enough, or like there's going to be enough."

We may react to deprivation in many ways. We may insist life, and the people in our lives, make up for all we never had. That's unfair, and those expectations can wreck what's good today.

Deprived, negative thinking makes things disappear. We're grumbling about the half-empty water glass, so focused on what we don't have that we fail to appreciate the half-full glass of water, the glass itself, or being alive and well enough to drink the water. We become so afraid that we might not get more, or we're so sour about only having half a glass to drink, we may not drink it. We let it sit on the table until it evaporates. Then we have nothing, which is what we thought we had anyway. It's an illusion! We can drink the water if we're thirsty, then go to the tap and get more.

Perhaps the most profound effect of deprivation is we may decide we don't deserve the good things in life. That isn't true, but our belief will make it true. What we believe we deserve, what we really believe deep inside, will be about what we get.

Deprived, negative thinking can prevent us from seeing what's good in our lives today, and it can stop the good stuff from happening. It hurts to be deprived. It hurts to walk through life believing there's not enough. It's painful to believe we're undeserving. So, stop. Now. You can fill in the blanks with "there's enough" and "I deserve." There's enough for you. There's enough for the person next door too. You deserve the best, whatever that means to you.

The Gratitude Principle

Deprived thinking turns good things into less or nothing. Grateful thinking turns things into more.

Many years ago, when I started rebuilding a life shattered by my chemical use, I dreamt of getting married and raising a family. I also dreamt of owning a house, a beautiful home to be our little castle. I wanted some of the things other people had. I wanted "normal," whatever that was.

It looked like I was about to get it. I got married. I got pregnant. I had a baby girl. Now, all I needed was the home. We looked at all sorts of dream homes—big dream homes and in-between dream homes. The home we bought didn't turn out to be one of those, but it was the one we could afford.

It had been used as rental property for fifteen years, had been standing vacant for a year, and was three stories of broken windows and broken wood. Some rooms had ten layers of wallpaper on the walls. Some walls had holes straight through to the outdoors. The floors were covered with bright orange carpeting with large stains on it. And we didn't have money or skills to fix it. We had no money for windows, curtains, paint. We couldn't afford to furnish it. We had three stories of a dilapidated home, with a kitchen table, two chairs, a high chair, a bed, a crib, and two dressers, one of which had broken drawers.

About two weeks after we moved in, a friend stopped by. We stood talking on what would have been the lawn if grass had been growing there. My friend kept repeating how lucky I was and how nice it was to own your own home. But I didn't feel lucky, and it didn't feel nice. I didn't know anyone else who owned a home like this.

I didn't talk much about how I felt, but each night while my husband and daughter slept, I tiptoed down to the living room, sat on the floor and cried. This became a ritual. When everyone was asleep, I sat in the middle of the floor thinking about everything I hated about the house, crying, and feeling hopeless. I did this for months. However legitimate my reaction may have been, it changed nothing.

A few times, in desperation, I tried to fix up the house, but nothing worked. The day before Thanksgiving I attempted to put some paint on the living and dining room walls. But layers of wallpaper started to peel off the minute I put paint on them. Another time, I ordered expensive wallpaper, trying to have faith I'd have the money to pay for it when it came. I didn't.

Then one evening, when I was sitting in the middle of the floor going through my wailing ritual, a thought occurred to me: *Why don't I try gratitude?*

At first I dismissed the idea. Gratitude was absurd. What could I possibly be grateful for? How could I? And why should I? Then, I decided to try anyway. I had nothing to lose. And I was getting sick of my whining.

I still wasn't certain what to be grateful for, so I decided to be grateful for everything. I didn't feel grateful. I willed it. I forced it. I faked it. I pretended. I made myself think grateful thoughts. When I thought about the layers of peeling wallpaper, I thanked God. I thanked God for each thing I hated about that house. I thanked Him for giving it to me. I thanked Him I was there. I even thanked Him I hated it. Each time I had a negative thought about the house, I countered it with a grateful one.

Maybe this wasn't as logical a reaction as negativity, but it turned out to be more effective. After I practiced gratitude for about three or four months, things started to change.

My attitude changed. I stopped sitting and crying in the middle of the floor and started to accept the house—as it was. I started taking care of the house as though it were a dream home. I acted as if it were my dream home. I kept it clean, orderly, as nice as could be.

Then, I started thinking. If I took all the old wallpaper off first, maybe the paint would stay on. I pulled up some of the orange carpeting and discovered solid oak floors throughout the house. I went through some boxes I had packed away and found antique lace curtains that fit the windows. I found a community action program that sold decent wallpaper for a dollar a roll. I learned about textured paint, the kind that fills and covers old, cracked walls. I decided if I didn't know how to do the work, I could learn. My mother volunteered to help me with wallpapering. Everything I needed came to me.

Nine months later, I had a beautiful home. Solid oak floors glistened throughout the house. Country-print wallpaper and textured white walls contrasted beautifully with the dark, scrolled woodwork that decorated each room.

Whenever I encountered a problem—half the cupboard doors are missing and I don't have money to hire a carpenter—I willed gratitude. Pretty soon, a solution appeared: tear all the doors off and have an open, country kitchen pantry.

I worked and worked, and I had three floors of beautiful home. It wasn't perfect, but it was mine and I was happy to be there. Proud to be there. Truly grateful to be there. I loved that home.

Soon the house filled up with furniture too. I learned to selectively collect pieces here and there for $5 and $10, cover the flaws with lace doilies, and refinish. I learned how to make something out of almost nothing, instead of nothing out of something.

I have had the opportunity to practice the gratitude principle many times in my recovery. It hasn't failed me. Either I change, my circumstances change, or both change.

"But you don't know how deprived I am!" people say. "You don't know everything I've gone without. You don't know how difficult it is right now. You don't know what it's like to have nothing!"

Yes, I do. And gratitude is the solution. Being grateful for what we have today doesn't mean we have to have that forever. It means we acknowledge that what we have today is what we're supposed to have today. There is enough, we're enough, and all we need will come to us. We don't have to be desperate, fearful, jealous, resentful, or miserly. We don't have to worry about what someone else has; they don't have ours. All we need to do is appreciate and take care of what we have today. The trick is, we need to be grateful first—before we get anything else, not afterward.

Then, we need to believe that we deserve the best life has to offer. If we don't believe that, we need to change what we believe we deserve. Changing our beliefs about what we deserve isn't an overnight process. Whether we're talking about relationships, work, home, or money, this usually happens in increments. We believe we deserve something a little better, then a little better, and so on. We need to start where we're at, changing our beliefs as we're capable. Sometimes things take time.

Believing we deserve good things is as important as gratitude. Practicing gratitude without changing what we believe we deserve may keep us stuck in deprivation.

"I earned $30,000 a year and every morning I got into my ten-year-old car with a busted heater and thanked God for it. I was so grateful," says one woman who's recovering from codependency. "My kids would encourage me to buy a new car and I'd say no; I was just grateful to have my old one. Then one day, when I was talking to someone about deprivation, it hit me that I could afford to have a new car if I really believed I deserved one. I changed my mind about what I deserved, then went out and bought a new car."

There are times in our lives when depriving ourselves helps build character, renders us fit for certain purposes, or is part of "paying our dues" as we stretch toward goals. There is a purpose as well as a beginning and an end to the deprivation. Many of us have carried this too far. Our deprivation is without purpose or end.

In an Andy Capp cartoon strip, Andy's wife came to him one day grumbling about her tattered coat. "That coat of mine is a disgrace. I'm ashamed to go out in it. I'll really have to get a new one," she said.

"We'll see, we'll see," he replied.

"Roughly translated," she said, scrunching up her face, "you never know what you can do without until you try."

Well, we never know what we can have until we try. And we may not know what we already have until we get grateful. Be grateful and believe you deserve the best. You may have more today than you think. And tomorrow might be better than you can imagine.

ACTIVITY

1. To help determine what you believe you deserve, complete each of the following statements. Write as many completions as come to your mind for each statement. Write until you ferret out your bottom-line beliefs. Write free-association style, putting down whatever comes to mind. This isn't a test. It's to increase self-awareness. Once you identify any negative beliefs, change them to positive "I deserve" statements. Here is an example of possible answers to the first questions.

I can't or don't have a healthy, loving relationship because:

John wouldn't stop drinking.
There aren't any good men out there.
I don't have time.
It's no use.
Men always leave me.
I give up.

I'll never find love.
I don't know how.
Nobody could love me.

Here's another example:

I can't, or don't have, a job I like because:

I don't have a college degree.
Nobody would hire me.
I don't have a good work history.
I never learned how to do anything.
I'll never amount to anything anyway.
All the good jobs are taken.
I might as well settle for what I've got; it's better than nothing.
Who cares?

Write as many completions to these statements as you can think of.

- I can't, or don't have, a healthy, loving relationship because:
- I can't, or don't have, a job I like because:
- I can't, or don't have, enough money because:
- I can't, or don't have, a comfortable home or apartment because:
- I can't, or don't have, a happy, safe life because:
- I can't, or don't, love myself unconditionally because:
- I can't, or don't have, enough friends because:
- I can't, or don't, have fun because:
- I can't, or don't, accept God's love for me because:
- I can't, or don't, have good health because:
- I can't be successful because:
- I can't be smart enough because:
- I can't be good looking enough because:
- I can't enjoy life because:

12

AFFIRM YOURSELF

It's what we all wanted when we were children—
to be loved and accepted exactly as we were then,
not when we got taller or thinner or prettier . . .
and we still want it . . . but we aren't going to get
it from other people until we can get it from ourselves.

—Louise Hay[1]

I used to think affirmations were, well, silly. I have since changed my mind—and my life. I changed my mind because affirmations are a tool that helped change my life. Besides Twelve Step programs and our Higher Power, affirmations may be the most important recovery tool we can embrace.

To "affirm" means to say positively, declare firmly, or assert to be true.[2] In recovery, the concept of using affirmations is closely connected to another term, *empowerment*. To "empower" means to give ability to, enable, or permit.[3]

In the last four chapters we've examined a host of sources for negative messages. Through family of origin messages, living with the "rules," being shamed, and deprivation, many of us have developed a repertoire of negative ideas about ourselves, other people, and life. We may have said, thought, and believed these messages for years. We may have a disciplined ritual for chanting these messages. Many of us have repeated these beliefs so long we've internalized them. The negative messages have become embedded in our subconscious and have manifested themselves in our lives. They've become our premises, our truths, and therefore our reality.

In recovery, we develop a repertoire of positive ideas about ourselves, other people, and life. We develop a disciplined ritual for chanting these messages. We repeat these beliefs so often we internalize them. The positive messages become embedded in our subconscious, and manifest themselves in our lives. They become our premises, our truths, and therefore our reality. That's what affirmations are. We change the energy in ourselves and our lives from negative to positive. Affirmations are how we charge our battery.

Most of us have spent much of our lives asserting and emphasizing certain ideas about ourselves, others, and life. The issue in recovery is choosing what we want to affirm.[4]

"I've done my family of origin work," says one woman. "I know my messages. I know my patterns. But what do I do about it?"

Affirmations and empowerment are "what we do about it." Affirmations are how we change the rules, change the messages, deal with shame, and travel the road from deprived to deserving. We assert new beliefs to be true, give ourselves new permissions, make new messages, and endow ourselves with new abilities. We empower the good and the positive in ourselves and life. Affirmations aren't optional. They are the core of our recovery work. If negative messages have contributed to this havoc, imagine what positive messages can help create!

Affirmations aren't silly little sayings or wishful thinking. They're the antidote to all the negative garbage we've been feeding ourselves for years. Affirmations open the door to good things coming our way, and to the good already there.

The connection between thoughts, feelings, beliefs, physical well-being, and reality has been in the spotlight lately. Books like Louise Hay's *You Can Heal Your Life*[5] and Bernie Siegel's *Love, Medicine & Miracles*[6] have climbed to the top of best-seller charts with good reason. They're making sense. What we think, say, and believe can affect what we do, who we meet, who we marry, how we look, how we feel, the course of our lives, and even, some say, how long we live.[7] Our beliefs can influence the kinds of diseases and ailments we get, and whether we recover from those ailments.

Affirmations Help Create Reality

Affirmations create space for reality to happen in.[8] The concept of using affirmations in recovery means replacing negative messages with positive ones: we change what we say so we can change what we see. If we emphasize and empower the good in ourselves, we will see and get more of that. If we empower the good in others, we will get more of that too.

The power and responsibility to change our messages and beliefs—to affirm and empower ourselves—lies with each of us. During certain times in our lives we may need to rely on others to empower and affirm us. When I began recovering from codependency, certain people affirmed and empowered me, and it was a gift from God. I try to pass this gift on. I still need people to believe in me and empower me. It's good to do this for each other. But when we begin affirming and empowering ourselves, we'll make giant strides forward.

Recovery is a process, and it's a spiritual one. But aggressively working with affirmations is one of our parts in the process.

To empower means to give power to.[9] What have we been giving power to? The terrible way we look? How bad we feel? Our problems? Another person's problem? Our lack of money, time, or talent? The awfulness of life? Next question: Do we really want to feed and nurture negative ideas—knowing those attitudes will likely create more negative ideas and negative reality? Do we want to empower the problem or the solution?

If our relationships have worked out badly, we may believe that relationships don't work, there aren't any healthy people out there, and people always use us. We may joke about it. We may say it seriously. Or we may keep this thought to ourselves. But it becomes what we believe and expect. If we want to change what happens, we change what we believe and expect. We surrender to what was and is. We let go of our need to have these negative circumstances happen,[10] and we change our behaviors. We accept our present circumstances, but we create space for something different to happen in our lives.

There are good people out there. I am attracted to healthy, loving people, and they to me. A healthy relationship is on its way. We don't obsess about this thought. We don't watch for it to happen. But we may want to think this new thought five times a day or whenever an old, negative thought occurs to us. Then we let go of the results. Whether anything happens today, tomorrow, or next week, we decide this will be our belief. If something contrary to our new belief happens, we don't use the incident to prove our old belief was really true.

We change our family of origin rules and messages from negative to positive. For instance, we change: *I'm not lovable* and *I can't take care of myself* to *I'm lovable* and *I can take care of myself.* We overpower the negative with an equally powerful positive message.

If shame is an issue for us, we might want to focus on the message: *It's okay to be who I am. Who I am is good, and I'm good enough.* We change what we believe we deserve too. From the activity at the end of the last chapter, we can uncover a list of negative ideas begging to be changed to positive assumptions. What we want to affirm is dealer's choice. If we have believed that there are not enough good jobs, good men, money, or love to go around, we start claiming prosperity in those areas.

Our goal in using affirmations isn't to eliminate every negative thought and sad feeling from our lives. That's not healthy nor desirable. We don't want to turn into robots. Feeling sad and angry is sometimes as important as feeling happy and peaceful.

What Affirmations Are and Are Not

Using affirmations doesn't mean we ignore problems. That's denial. We need to identify problems, but we need to empower solutions. Affirmations won't eliminate problems from our lives; affirmations will help solve them.

Affirmations aren't a substitute for accepting reality. They aren't a form of control. They need to be used with heavy doses of surrender, spirituality, and letting go.

Often, it feels awkward and uncomfortable when we start the process of changing negative messages to positive ones. Things may temporarily get worse. Our old ways of thinking surface into conscious awareness. That's good. It's clearing out of our subconscious and making room for the new.[11] A room always looks dirtier when we start to clean it. We pull the unwanted items and trash out of the nooks and crannies. Cleaning intensifies the disorder, until a new order can be created.

It's normal to resist affirmations and positive thoughts. If you've been feeding yourself negative ideas for ten, twenty, or thirty years, of course the positive will feel strange for a while. Give yourself five or ten years of diligently and assertively affirming the good. It won't take that long to manifest itself in your life, but give it time anyway. Be patient. Don't give up. Don't let whatever problems or issues that arise reinforce your old, negative thought patterns.

You'll probably be tested when you turn negative beliefs into positive ones. Often, when I change a belief, a big tidal wave sweeps into my life to try to wash away my new belief. It's as if life is saying, "There! Now what do you *really* believe?" Let the storm roar. Hold fast to your new affirmations. Let them be your anchor. When the storm passes, you'll see you're on solid ground with new beliefs.

Actions That Affirm

Many actions and activities are affirming. In the next pages I've listed some of these.

• Regularly attending Twelve Step support groups and applying those Steps to our lives affirms us and our recoveries.

- Reading meditation books and concentrating on uplifting thoughts is affirming.
- Prayer is an affirmation.
- Listening to audiotapes helps. The self-help audiotape market is rapidly expanding. Subliminal tapes are also becoming popular. On subliminals, only our subconscious hears the affirmations, bypassing any conscious resistance to the positive messages.
- Attending a church we feel comfortable in is an affirmation.
- Attending seminars, workshops, and lectures affirms us.
- The concept of "acting as if" is an affirmation. Another phrase for this concept is "faking it 'til we make it." This doesn't imply a negative use of pretense. It means treating ourselves as if we were already the person we want to become.[12] This is a powerful way to create space for a new reality.
- Written goals are an affirmation.
- Using imagery or visualization is another method for inviting the positive. We create mental images of what we want to happen; we see ourselves as we want to be.
- Positive self-talk is a basic way to affirm ourselves. We force ourselves to think positively. We give ourselves new rules, new messages, and new beliefs. We look in the mirror and talk aloud to ourselves: we look ourselves in the eye and tell ourselves we love us and we're great. It may feel awkward at first, but we'll absorb it as certainly as we absorbed all the negative ideas we've ingested. Looking at old pictures of ourselves and talking positively to those pictures is another helpful technique. We talk positively and lovingly to ourselves at every age and time in our lives. We give ourselves all the good stuff we want and need.
- Written affirmations are helpful too. Many people like to tape positive messages in the bathroom, bedroom, work area, or any place they want a positive focus.
- Surrounding ourselves with friends who believe in us is affirming. What people say, think, and believe about us can have a significant impact on what we believe.

- Affirming others—believing in, supporting, and empowering them—will help us too. If we give some away, we'll have more to keep. Believing in the positive enough to give it away will reinforce and remind us of what we believe.
- Relaxation and fun is affirming.
- Work can be an affirmation of who we are, our abilities, and our creative talents.
- Celebrating our successes and achievements is affirming.
- Giving and receiving compliments is an affirmation.
- Exercise and proper nutrition is an affirmation.
- Therapeutic massage is a form of affirmation that's growing in popularity. Many people recovering from codependency, abuse, and the adult child syndrome have disowned their bodies. Disowning our bodies, splitting from our physical selves, may have been a protective device. To survive physical or emotional pain, we may have frozen our emotions and we may have frozen or numbed our bodies too.[13] The energy supply to certain parts of our bodies may be blocked. Therapeutic massage—nurturing, nonsexual touch—can restore the energy flow and bring needed healing. Our physical selves are as much "us" as our minds, emotions, and spiritual selves.
- Reading positive literature, even watching movies with a positive theme, can be affirming.
- Being grateful is a tremendous way to say yes to the good.
- Hugs help too.
- Love is affirming. Affirmations are love.

The more of our senses we involve with the affirmation process, the more powerful our affirmations will be. Speaking, seeing, hearing, thinking, and positive touch are ways to do this. We inundate ourselves with positive energy. Affirmations are more than little slips of paper we paste to our mirrors—although those slips of paper are important. Affirming ourselves means developing a lifestyle that's self-affirming, instead of self-negating.

Nurturing Ourselves

We develop a way of life that embraces and blends the concepts of self-nurturing and self-discipline. We love ourselves in all the ways we need and deserve to be loved; we discipline ourselves in ways that will be in our own best interests. We become our own best friend and parent.[14]

How do we nurture ourselves? Of all the blank spots we have, this one is often the blankest. If we've never seen, touched, tasted, or felt it, how could we know what nurturing is? Nurturing is an attitude toward ourselves—one of unconditional love and acceptance. I'm talking about loving ourselves so much and so hard the good stuff gets right into the core of us, then spills over into our lives and our relationships. I'm talking about loving ourselves no matter what happens or where we go.

In the morning and throughout our day, we lovingly and gently ask ourselves what we can do for ourselves that would feel good. We ask ourselves what we need to do to take care of ourselves. When we hurt, we ask what would help us feel better.[15] We give ourselves encouragement and support. We tell ourselves we can do it, we can do it good enough, and things will work out. When we make a mistake, we tell ourselves that's okay. We wait a moment, until we get our balance back, and then we ask ourselves if there's something we can learn from our mistake, or if there's some way we can improve our conduct in the future, or if there's an amend we need to make.

We tell ourselves we love and accept ourselves. We tell ourselves we're great and we're special. We tell ourselves we'll always be there for us. We make ourselves feel safe and loved. We do all those wonderful things for ourselves that we wish someone else would have done for us.

If we don't believe we're lovable, why would anyone else? If I don't believe I'm lovable, I can't even believe my Higher Power loves me. If I don't believe I'm lovable, I don't let people, or God, love me. If we love ourselves, we become enabled to love others.

We stop criticizing and lambasting ourselves with harshness. Instead we make a conscious effort to nurture and praise ourselves, because it brings out the best in us.

"I've pushed myself all my life," says Arlene. "If I work hard, I tell myself to work harder. When I get tired, I push myself some more. I do and say all the critical things to myself that my mother did and said to herself and me."

Arlene worried that if she nurtured herself, the work wouldn't get done. She feared if she gave in to her needs, she'd get lazy. She decided to nurture herself anyway, and she was amazed.

"It was my day off. I was exhausted, but I was pushing myself to clean the house. Then I made a decision to nurture myself. I asked myself what would help me feel better, and I decided a nap would. I rested for two hours. When I woke up, I felt like doing the housework. I got it finished, and even had time to go out that night. Nurturing myself didn't make me lazy or ineffective. It made me energized and more effective."

Nurturing is how we empower and energize ourselves. When we love, accept, and nurture ourselves, we can relax enough to do our best. A bonus is, when we love, accept, and nurture ourselves, we're able to do the same for others. We can help them love themselves, and they're more apt to react to us with love and acceptance. It starts a great chain reaction.

Loving and accepting ourselves unconditionally doesn't mean we negate our need to change and grow. It's how we enable ourselves to love and grow.

"Criticism locks us into the very pattern we are trying to change," writes Louise Hay. "Understanding and being gentle with ourselves helps us to move out of it. Remember, you have been criticizing yourself for years and it hasn't worked. Try approving of yourself and see what happens."[16]

There isn't a set of instructions for nurturing ourselves. But if we ask ourselves what would help us feel better or what we need, then listen, we'll hear the answer.

Developing Self-Discipline

Discipline is an individual process. Discipline means we don't always talk about feelings. Sometimes it's not appropriate, or sometimes we need to wait. Discipline means we go through the motions of recovery behaviors on the gray days, the days we're uncertain whether anything is happening or if we're going anywhere on this journey. Discipline means we believe in our Higher Power and His love for us, even when it might not look or feel like He loves us. Discipline means we understand the cause and effect nature of things and choose behaviors that generate the consequences we desire. Discipline is self-control, but not the kind of control many of us have lived with. It's the kind we would teach a child we love very much, because we know that child needs to do certain things in life to live a good life.

When will we become lovable? When will we feel safe? When will we get all the protection, nurturing, and love we so richly deserve? We will get it when we begin giving it to ourselves.

Before I began working with affirmations, my first thought in the morning was "Oh, no. Not another day." It was downhill from there, until I dropped into bed at night, closed my eyes, and said, "Thank God that's over."

Now, when I open my eyes in the morning, I dwell on this thought for a moment: *This is the day the Lord has made. I will rejoice and be glad in it.*[17]

A short time later, I say my morning prayers. While I'm brushing my teeth and putting on my makeup, I tell myself *out loud* that I love myself, I'll be there to take care of myself, God loves me and is taking care of me, I'm good at what I do, and all I need today shall be provided.[18]

During morning break, I read from a meditation book. On my office desk are several cards with uplifting sayings. I have a regular schedule for attending support groups. At least every other day, I talk to a recovering person to give and receive support, encouragement, and acceptance.

Throughout the day, I force-feed positive thoughts into my mind. When I feel ashamed, I tell myself it's okay to be who I am. When I have a feeling, I tell myself it's okay to feel. When I worry about money, I focus on this thought: *My God shall supply all my needs according to His riches in glory.*[19]

I focus on a positive thought whenever a negative, fear-producing thought strikes. I also focus on positive thoughts during those odd moments when I would otherwise be concentrating on negative messages. If I feel panicky or desperate, I ply my mind with positive thoughts. I promise myself I'm safe.

I regularly write goals. I write down what I believe I deserve. I spend an hour a week listening to meditation tapes. I spend a few minutes a week visualizing the good I want to happen. I see what it will look and feel like when it happens. I go in for a therapeutic massage regularly, and work on affirmations during that time. And I will gratitude for almost everything.

This is my regular routine. In times of stress, I intensify efforts. If this sounds like overkill, it isn't. Overkill was all the years I spent focusing on negative, destructive messages.

To discover what you need to work on, spend a day or two listening to your thoughts. Listen to what you say. Listen to the problems and negative qualities you empower in yourself and others. Look in the mirror and notice what you think and say. Sit down to pay bills and listen to your thoughts then. Go to your job and listen to what you think about your work, abilities, and career prospects. Hold your special person in your arms and listen to your thoughts. Listen to how you react to your problems. Listen to what you say to and about your children. What are you giving power to? What are you creating space for? Are you feeding what you want to grow? Change what's needed and make it good. Declare all-out war on your destructive thought patterns.

Many of us have spent years negating ourselves out of existence. Now we're learning to love ourselves into a life of our own.

ACTIVITY

1. Spend some time researching your present assertions, beliefs, and premises. Listen to what you say and think. Do this as though you were a detached observer. What do you think and say about yourself, your abilities, your looks, finances, relationships? Is what you're emphasizing what you want to see more of? What problems are you affirming?

2. Write a set of personalized affirmations for yourself. Write loving, empowering affirmations that feel good when you read them. Spend time each day reading these, saying them aloud. You may want to change these as your needs change.

3. Take time, when you're looking in the mirror, to tell yourself you love you, you're beautiful, you're good at what you do. Tell yourself you're going to take care of you, and your Higher Power is caring for you too.

4. Develop a routine of self-care that includes nurturing. You may want to include a daily time for using meditation books, a regular time for attending support groups, a regular program for writing goals, relaxation time, time with friends, and some time for pampering yourself. Choose from any options listed in this chapter, or any others you've discovered. Give yourself the freedom to experiment with different ways of doing this until you find a way that works for you.

Section IV:

RELATIONSHIPS

We accepted powerlessness.
We've found a Higher Power.
We're learning to own our power.
Now we can share the power.

13

IMPROVING OUR RELATIONSHIPS

*. . . it is neither cynical nor glib to describe love,
like all of nature, as having its season. Even the
loveliest living things regularly leave for a time . . .
and with equal reliability return.*

—Martin Blinder, M.D.[1]

Relationships are where we take our recovery show on the road. In this section, we'll explore some ideas for improving relationships. Much of the focus will be on special love relationships, but the ideas apply to all our relationships. Many of them can grow into special love relationships too.[2]

Actually, the entire book explores ideas for improving relationships. All our recovery work—dealing with shame, doing our historical work, believing we deserve the best, breaking the rules, learning to affirm and empower ourselves, learning to believe we're lovable—affects our relationships.

There's more to recovery than learning to terminate or avoid relationships. Although some of us may call time-out from certain relationships for a while, recovery isn't done apart from relationships. And relationships aren't done apart from recovery. Recovery is learning to function in relationships.[3] And we learn to function in relationships by participating in relationships.

At a workshop I facilitated, I asked participants how many had failed relationships. Everyone raised both hands. "I didn't know you were going to do jokes," responded one woman.

Many of us have had failed relationships. Many of us are struggling with relationships now. "Kate and I have been married six years," Del says. "We're both from moderately dysfunctional families, and we were both working on recovery years before we married. Sometimes we've worked hard on the relationship. Sometimes we've backed off and worked on ourselves. Sometimes we've been too busy to work on anything. Sometimes we know we really love each other; sometimes it's a real struggle. I never knew relationships were so difficult."

In spite of our struggles, many of us still believe in marriage, family, and love. In spite of our failures, many of us want a loving, committed, fulfilling relationship. We may be afraid and cautious, but, whatever our circumstances, most of us want our relationships to be the best possible. The subject of this chapter, this section, this book, and recovery *is* improving our relationships. The purpose of this chapter is to tell us we can.

Since the beginning of time, people have been struggling to live with, or without, someone they love. Some elements of relationships have changed over the years. We've progressed from a time when people had few choices about choosing a mate, getting a divorce, or living a certain lifestyle, to an age when it's possible to become paralyzed by options. Women have traveled the road from culturally mandated dependency to feminism and a liberation that includes the choice of traditional values. For some people, relationship roles have changed dramatically.

"I don't know what women want or expect anymore," said one man.

"Don't feel bad," I responded. "We're not always sure either."

People are hungry for information about relationships. We want to learn more about how we can make them work, make them work better, and avoid past mistakes. We want to understand and gain insight. In recent years, we've been bombarded with books about relationships. We have relationship enrichment courses, counseling, seminars, and intimacy training. Working on relationships has become one of our many choices about relationships.

"I used to think people just met someone, fell in love, and got married," Hank says. "After recovery, I got into 'a relationship' and discovered I was expected to 'work' on it. I didn't even know what the term meant! Even the word 'relationship' was new to me. We used to call it 'finding a girl friend,' or 'getting married.' "

Nurturing Relationships

We've discovered certain behaviors and attitudes nurture relationships and help them grow. Healthy detachment, honesty, self-love, love for each other, tackling problems, negotiating differences, and being flexible help nurture relationships. We can enhance relationships with acceptance, forgiveness, a sense of humor, an empowering but realistic attitude, open communication, respect, tolerance, patience, and faith in a Higher Power.

- Caring about our own and each other's feelings helps.
- Asking instead of ordering helps.
- Not caring, when caring too much hurts, helps too.
- Being there when we need each other helps.
- Being there for ourselves, and doing our own recovery work helps.
- Having and setting boundaries and respecting other people's boundaries improves relationships.
- Taking care of ourselves—taking responsibility for ourselves—benefits relationships.
- Being interested in others and ourselves helps.
- Believing in ourselves and the other person is beneficial.
- Being vulnerable, and allowing ourselves to get close helps.
- Giving relationships energy, attention, and time helps them grow.

- Initiating relationships with people who are capable of participating in relationships helps.[4]

On the other hand, certain behaviors and attitudes harm relationships. Low self-esteem, taking responsibility for others, neglecting ourselves, unfinished business, and trying to control other people or the relationship can cause damage. Harm can also be caused by being overly dependent, not discussing feelings and problems, lying, abuse, and unresolved addictions. Certain attitudes such as hopelessness, resentment, perpetual criticism, naivete, unreliability, hardheartedness, negativity, or cynicism can ruin relationships.

- Being too selfish, or not selfish enough, can hurt relationships.
- Too little or too much tolerance can harm relationships.
- Having expectations too high or too low can hurt relationships.
- Looking for all our good feelings, excitement, or stimulation from our relationships can damage them.
- Not learning from our mistakes can cause us to repeat the same mistakes.
- Being too hard on ourselves for our mistakes can hurt relationships.
- Expecting other people, ourselves, or our relationships to be perfect can damage relationships.
- Not examining a relationship enough can damage it; so can holding it under a microscope.

Relationships and love have a life of their own.[5] Like other living things, they have a birth, death, and some activity between—a beginning, middle, and end.[6] Some run the course in twelve hours; some span a lifetime. Like other living things, relationships are cyclical, not static. We have cycles of passion and boredom, ease and struggle, closeness and distance, joy and pain, growth and repose.[7]

Sometimes as the cycles or seasons of relationships change, the boundaries and dimensions of relationships change. We can learn to be flexible enough to go through and accept these changing seasons.

We've identified many types of relationships. We label some "healthy" and some "unhealthy." The energy between two people can be positive or negative. Relationships can be formed out of our deficiencies, our strengths, or out of loneliness. Some are based on chemistry. Most combine these characteristics and are formed for many reasons—many of which are unknown to people at the time and become clear only in retrospect. Usually, two people simply believe they love each other and the relationship seems to fit.[8] The relationship meets both people's needs at the time.[9]

In his lectures and writing, Earnie Larsen has identified three relationship states: "in," "out," or "wait." And there can be no relationship if one person calls "out," says Larsen.

No particular state of being "in or out of a relationship" indicates recovery. Recovery is indicated by each of us making our own choices about what we want and need to do, and what's important to us. Perhaps no area of our lives expresses our uniqueness as much as our relationships—our relationship history, present circumstances, and goals.

When Sheryl began recovering from codependency, she divorced her husband, who she calls "a practicing sex addict and alcoholic." Now, two and one-half years later, she dates only occasionally.

"It wouldn't be fair to me or a man to get into a relationship yet. I'm not ready. Besides, I don't know anyone I want to be involved with. I want a good relationship someday," Sheryl says. "In the meantime, I'm working on myself."

Many years ago, Sam's wife, Beth, went through treatment for chemical addiction, and he began attending Al-Anon. They've been married for twenty-five years, and plan to stay married the rest of their lives.

"The crazy behavior stopped. Things got better. We don't have a fantastic relationship, but we want to hold the family structure together. Our children have thanked us for doing that. I'm glad we've done that," Sam says. "It isn't a perfect relationship, but it's workable. And it's what we both want. If we had our lives to live over, we probably would choose someone else. But we chose each other, and we're going to honor our commitment."

After three years in Al-Anon, Marianne divorced her husband Jake, a practicing alcoholic.

"We have three children. I was scared about being on my own, and I felt guilty about getting a divorce. I don't believe in divorce. Sometimes I feel sad about losing our natural family. Sometimes I miss the good things we had together. But I don't regret breaking up our unhappy home. It was hurting the children and me," Marianne says.

Jan and Tom have been married for twenty-five years. For the past ten years, Jan has attended Al-Anon. For the last eight years, Tom has attended Alcoholics Anonymous.

"Some days I don't think much of this marriage; other days I know I still love Tom as much as I did the day I married him. Sometimes we've grown together, sometimes apart," says Jan. "We've changed a lot, but in some ways we're still the same. What has changed is this: I'm with Tom today because I'm choosing to be with him, not because I think I don't have a choice."

I've heard many relationship stories. Some recovering people are happily married, some unhappily married, some in so-so marriages, and some fluctuate. Some people are divorced, some single and looking, some single and avoiding relationships. Some people are dating, some living together and very committed, some are together one day at a time. Some people formed successful relationships after they began recovering; some didn't. Some couples are working on salvageable relationships from pre-recovery days.

Some relationships last a lifetime; some don't. Many of us have decided to call the ones that don't last "learning experiences." Unless we refuse to learn from our mistakes, most relationships are an improvement over past ones. Martin Blinder, who was quoted at the beginning of this chapter, writes:

Most of us, as part of growing up, fall in and out of love over and over again. . . . While some few people fall in love at seventeen and remain enamored of the same person for the rest of their lives, most of us move through a series of shorter relationships, repeatedly leaving one lover in favor of another who matches our ever-increasing level of maturation. Each new partner usually combines characteristics of our previous lovers and our ultimate ideal, representing, in effect, a recycling of the old enriched with nuances of the new. Familiar conflicts may reemerge but are resolved more quickly and with less pain. Mistakes may still be made, choices be less than optimum, but by and large we learn and profit from past experience. In the long run, our newer relationships are frequently a vast improvement over earlier ones.[10]

Despite our discoveries about relationships, we probably still know as much about controlling the course of love as we do about curing the common cold. The age-old advice many of us have heard still encompasses much wisdom. "If it's meant to be, it'll be." "If you love it set it free; if it comes back to you, it's yours." And "to find the right person, be the right person." These sayings did not reach the lofty state of cliche-hood without passing the tests of truth and time.[11] The idea that our relationships are about as healthy as we are is still the bottom line.[12]

Perhaps the greatest relationship failure we can have is invalidating our relationship history or present circumstances by becoming cynical, hopeless, embittered, or ashamed.[13] Our histories aren't a mistake. Our present circumstances aren't a mistake. We may have made choices that need correcting. We may want to make new decisions as we grow. We may discover patterns that need unraveling. But we can learn and gain from each relationship we've encountered. Our relationships are a reflection of our growth, and often our relationships have contributed to that growth.

Although some may be healthier than others, there is no such thing as the perfect person or perfect relationship. Much writing and teaching is done about ideals, but relationships don't happen that way and people don't behave that way. The fact is, some people are easier to live with than others.

On this recovery journey, you are where you need to be, and you're with the people you need to be with—today. You've been with the people you've needed to be with to get this far. It's okay to not be in a relationship. It's okay to walk away if it's dead. It's okay to stay. It's okay to want a relationship—even if you've had one or some that didn't work. You deserve another chance—whether that's a chance to form a new relationship or improve a current one.[14]

You can find love that lasts. You can practice your recovery behaviors with the people in your life today. You can improve, sometimes tremendously, the quality and energy of your relationships. Perhaps you've started to practice new relationship behaviors and have already seen improvement. You deserve the best love has to offer. But the process of getting the best from love begins within you.

Indeed, as Earnie Larsen drills, "Nothing changes if nothing changes." And the only person you can ever change is yourself. But sometimes, by doing that, you'll change more than you can imagine.

Let's look at how you can help turn learning experiences into loving experiences.

ACTIVITY

1. Write a relationship history. Include any significant people—friends, family members, boyfriends, girlfriends, spouses, et cetera. For those other than family members, how did the relationship begin? If it's over, how did it end? What needs has each relationship met? How have you learned, or gained, from each relationship?

2. Are you harboring any negative feelings about past relationships? Can you become willing to let go of these feelings? Can you accept your relationship history?

14

OVERCOMING FATAL ATTRACTIONS

*I am not telling you to settle! . . . I'm telling you
to go for the gold, not for a cheap imitation.*

—Nita Tucker[1]

In 1987, the movie *Fatal Attraction* drew blockbuster crowds. The
title drew me in. It summed up my forty-year relationship history in
two words.

"I can walk into a room of 500 men, 499 of whom are successful
and healthy, spot the one unemployed felon in the bunch, and find
him catching my eye," says Christy.

"When I met my ex-husband, a raving sex addict and alcoholic,
my first thought was, *This guy looks like trouble.* My second thought
was, *Let me at him!*" says Jan.

"There's something compelling about a woman who looks like
she might 'do me wrong,' " says Don. "I've been recovering for years,
and that's the kind of woman I'm still drawn to."

Many of us have lived with this phenomena of being instinctively and powerfully attracted to people who aren't in our best interests. For years I mistakenly called it "falling in love" and "God's
will." In this chapter, we'll explore getting beyond our if not fatal,
then disastrous, attractions and learning to be attracted to people
who are good for us. Listen closely. I didn't say "boring." I said "good
for us." Boring is five, ten, fifteen, or more years of living in close

proximity to an alcoholic, an abuser, or a sex addict. Nita Tucker writes:

> I'm not saying you should have a relationship with someone to whom you're not physically attracted. I'm saying that you may not always know how attracted you are to someone right off the bat. . . . Maybe your mother tells you your expectations are too high. I'm not telling you that. I'm telling you they're inaccurate. . . . I'm telling you there's something far more exciting, romantic, spine-tingling, and satisfying than chemistry. It's when you've been with someone for five years, ten years, or forty years, and the passion is still deepening.[2]

This chapter is about learning to initiate that kind of relationship, a relationship that has the possibility of working, lasting, being satisfying, and what we want. Recovery is about more than terminating relationships. It's about some good beginnings. Many of the ideas in this chapter are based on the best book I've read on the subject: *Beyond Cinderella: How to Find and Marry the Man You Want*, by Nita Tucker.

On Your Mark

First, let's legitimize the process of initiating relationships. It's okay to want to be in a relationship, and it's okay to be looking for one. Acknowledge and accept your desire to be in a relationship. It's a normal, healthy, human desire.

Next, consider what kind of relationship you want. Any kind? A satisfying, fulfilling, loving, and lasting one? A temporary relationship? The kind you've been in before?

Once you clarify what kind of relationship you *want* to be in, discern what kind you *need* to be in. The two may be different.[3] You may want to be in a healthy, loving relationship but if you haven't done your homework (family of origin work) and changed your messages, you may "need" to be (or end up) in a relationship that's abusive, caretaking, or similar to past ones.

Our underlying needs will be connected to our unfinished business, and to what we believe we deserve. The people we meet will prove what we believe about men, women, and what *always happens* in relationships. If we have unresolved anger at men or women, our relationships will likely justify that anger.

We can let go of, or begin working toward ridding ourselves of, our destructive needs or past feelings. We change what we believe so we can change what we see.

The next concept to consider is this business about "our type."[4] For years, I've entertained notions about "my type." When I looked for a relationship, I looked for men I was attracted to. I knew "my type." He stood a certain way, walked a certain way, talked a certain way, had a certain look in his eyes, and a certain history that created that look. By "attracted to," I mean that explosive chemistry I'd experience before I even met the person. I wouldn't consider getting involved with men who weren't my type. On the other hand, I'd enter a relationship solely on the strength of that initial attraction.

Never, not once have I been able to maintain a working relationship with "my type." I could make and win bets that any man I was powerfully and initially attracted to had a serious flaw that would prevent us from having a compatible relationship. On the other side of this coin were the many men I didn't notice. If I did see them, I wouldn't bother to get to know or date them. Maybe they wore their hair a certain way, wore polyester pants, or had a beard.

I am forty years old and have finally learned one lesson: It's much easier to get a man to shop for trousers at a different store or shave his beard than it is to get him to stop drinking. My type wasn't really my type. He was my "drug of choice."

"Who are you dating now?" I asked a recovering friend.

"Oh, you know," she said. "He's got a different name and face, but essentially he's the same man I have been dating all my life."

Many of us have allowed this fatal attraction phenomena to con-

trol our relationships. Many of us have overlooked people with
whom we really could have a successful relationship. It's possible to
broaden our ideas about our type. Chemistry is important in a relationship, but so are other things. That initial attraction isn't love,
doesn't guarantee love, and usually precludes love. We can become
attracted to and develop a better chemistry with people who aren't
our type—but really are. It may not be as powerful immediately, but
it will become powerful and last much longer.

In a course Nita Tucker teaches, called "Connecting," she gives
participants an assignment: interview happily married couples about
their relationships. "One of the things people are instructed to ask
each couple about is their initial encounter," Tucker writes. "Eighty
percent of those interviewed so far (that's more than a thousand people) reported they did *not* feel an immediate attraction to each other
when they first met."[5]

It may feel awkward to initiate relationships without being propelled by that initial chemistry.[6] That's okay. It'll feel better later. You
may discover you feel more comfortable with people who aren't your
type.

"I was attracted to this man. It took eight dates and many talks
with my sponsor to see that though I was attracted to him, I didn't
like being with him. I didn't feel comfortable about our time together.
There were serious problems from the start. All we had in common
was this attraction," says one woman.

This leads to our next consideration: *the availability factor.*[7] There
are several *facts* that make a person unavailable to participate in an
intimate, loving relationship. That person may be married or cur-
rently involved in another love relationship. The person may be so
recently divorced, or so recently out of another relationship that he
or she is unavailable. The person may not want to be in a healthy, loving relationship, or perhaps the person may not want to be in a relationship with *you.*

Active chemical dependency, sex addiction, or other unresolved
issues make a person unavailable to participate in a relationship.

Practicing alcoholics, sex addicts, and gamblers aren't available to participate in healthy, loving relationships. Repeat after me: practicing alcoholics, sex addicts, and gamblers aren't available to participate in healthy, loving relationships. People who need to be in recovery from anything, but aren't, aren't available to participate in relationships.

Other factors that may signal unavailability are

- being so tied to a past family that the person hasn't the material or emotional resources to participate in a current relationship;
- being a compulsive worker or so busy the person hasn't the time to devote to a relationship;
- living in another city or state, causing the person to be unavailable to meet the relationship's needs.

Trying to initiate a relationship with someone who's unavailable can trigger the codependent crazies in us. The unavailability factor isn't to be taken personally. We don't need to use it to prove negative beliefs about men, women, or relationships. A person's availability is a fact, and facts need to be accepted and taken into account. Many of us have spent much of our lives beating our heads against the cement and wailing because we were trying to make a relationship work with someone who wasn't available to do that from the day the relationship began. Many of us have spent our lives being attracted to our type when the compelling factor causing that person to be our type was his or her unavailability.

We can learn to screen for availability. Often, it can be determined in the first few minutes, but sometimes it takes longer. "Hi. Are you in the program?" "Where do you work?" "Are you married?" "How long have you been divorced?"

While on the subject of availability, many of us may want to consider our own. Are you still entangled in a past relationship? Are you recovering sufficiently to be available? Do you have time and energy to devote to a relationship? Are you emotionally available? If you're with someone you don't want to be in a permanent, committed relationship with, you're unavailable.

Who we've been dating and the people we've been having relationships with is a statement about our availability.[8] Our prejudices about people and relationships is also a statement about our availability. If you date and form relationships only with unavailable people, and if you have negative beliefs about people and relationships, you may be unavailable until you change.

Affirmations can help here. We can change what we believe about the kind of people we attract and are attracted to. New affirmations might be:

- I'm attracted to healthy, loving, available people, and they're attracted to me.
- I'm attracted to people who are good for me.

If we've been asserting scarcity, we can change "There aren't any good men (or women) out there" to "There are enough good men (or women) out there. I'm finding and meeting healthy, loving people." We can change any negative beliefs about men, women, or relationships.

A prince (or princess) is a man (or woman) with whom you can have a satisfying and lasting relationship, writes Nita Tucker. A frog is a person with whom, for one reason or another, you can't have a lasting and satisfying relationship.[9] Many of us have spent lifetimes kissing frogs and hoping they'll turn into princes, or, as one woman said, "kissing princes and watching them deteriorate into frogs." Some frogs are nicer than others, but a frog is a frog.[10] We may forever feel a tingle in our spine when we see a frog, but we don't have to jump into the pond with it.

What do you want to happen in your relationships? What do you need to happen? What do you believe you deserve? You can begin making space for the good by affirming the good, and by taking responsibility for your behavior in the relationship initiation process. Fatal attractions aren't love. They aren't God's will, so stop blaming Him. They aren't necessarily destiny. And they don't have to be deadly.

Get Set

If we've done our homework, we're ready to do the legwork. We can start meeting people, and selecting those we would like to get to know better. There are three key words in the last sentence: *meeting, people,* and *selecting.*

We're not out duck hunting. We're not out to bag a catch before the season ends at the stroke of midnight. We're not out to get sucked in by chemistry. We're out to meet people. And we're learning to connect with them in a better way.[11]

How do you meet people? Socialize. Go places where people go. Therapy groups and Twelve Step meetings aren't a good place to meet people to date. The primary purpose of groups is recovery. We can sabotage an important part of our support system by playing the dating game there. Places to meet people include: church; sporting events (as a participant or observer); parties; classes; shopping for clothes, food, or "toys"; cultural events; charitable or fund-raising events; volunteer activities; political activities; marinas; dances; restaurants; decent nightclubs; the zoo; trade shows or organizations; single's clubs; and quality dating services.[12]

If we're serious about meeting people, we need to socialize regularly. We need to look and feel our best. That means extra effort goes into our appearance. That means extra effort also goes into self-care, self-nurturing, and self-esteem. The most attractive people are those who love themselves and live their own lives.

Then, we learn to smile and say, "Hi!"[13] Otherwise people won't know we want to meet them. We may have to fend off the suitors and the unavailables, but it's better than the alternative. Besides, it'll be good practice. We'll have many chances to say no—and some opportunities to say yes. The concept of accessibility, of being warm and friendly, may be an obvious one, but it's often overlooked.

"I tried to meet people for months," says one woman. "I would go to events, than stand in the corner like a statue. One day, the lights came on. I was at some gathering when I spotted a man I thought I'd like to meet. I wondered if he'd notice me. I wondered if he'd speak to me. I hoped he would, but feared he wouldn't. It was all the stuff I went over in my head each time I saw someone I was interested in. Then, it occurred to me. Why didn't I just go over, smile, and say, 'Hi!' I didn't have to be aggressive. I just needed to be friendly. I wasn't out to 'get' him; I just wanted to meet him. I did it. The relationship never got off the ground. After talking to him briefly, I decided he wasn't right for me. But I learned a lesson. If I want to meet someone, I can probably do that by smiling and saying, 'Hi!' "

The more fully we're living our lives, the more people we'll meet. The more people we meet, the greater our chance of meeting someone who is available and really our type. We can be selective, but we can select on a more accurate criteria. Stop ruling out people who may not be our type; stop automatically ruling in people because we're attracted to them. Tucker advocates dating someone three times before ruling out.[14] Take the time to find out if we've met someone we want to get to know better.

We don't have to abandon reason in favor of emotion. Someone may "feel" right for us, but if that person isn't available, he or she isn't right. On the other hand, we don't have to abandon emotion in favor of reason. We may think someone is right for us, but if no feelings emerge *after we've gotten to know the person,* that person isn't right for us—even if he or she is healthy and available.

Let Go

Now that we're on our toes and ready to sprint into the love of a lifetime, take a deep breath . . . and let go.

"I'm out looking for a relationship," says one woman. "I am absolutely wild, totally out of control, and if I can't do something with myself soon, I'm going to put myself back in therapy."

I reassured this woman that the process of initiating relationships tends to bring out the beast in many of us. There are things we can do, however, to make ourselves more or less available for a good relationship. One thing most of us need to do is surrender.

If we are unhappy without a relationship, we'll probably be unhappy with one as well. A relationship doesn't begin our life; a relationship doesn't become our life. A relationship is a continuation of life. While a special love relationship may meet certain needs that only a special love relationship can meet, it won't meet all our needs and it won't "make us happy." If we can't achieve happiness in this moment, we probably won't find it in the next. It's called *acceptance,* the blissful state from which all things can change for the better.

There's a difference between accepting that we want to be in a relationship, and being desperate to be in one. Hungry people make poor shoppers. Desperate people frighten others away. They attract people who may not be good for them. They make second-best choices.

"What if I am desperate?" one woman asks. "I'm so starved for a loving relationship. I've been waiting so long, I feel desperate. What can I do about that?"

I'll answer her question with another woman's story. "Each time I end a relationship, I panic," Karen says. "I worry I'll never meet anyone again, and I'll never be in love again. The truth is, I'm thirty-six years old and the longest I've not been in a relationship since I've been fifteen is six months."

Desperation is like panic. Whenever we feel either one, we need to deal with it separately.[15] Desperation may be connected to fear and our need to control. Desperation may be signaling unresolved or hidden dependency issues. Often, underneath the desperation lie some negative beliefs: about scarcity, about what's coming our way, about what we deserve, and about whether we'll ever get that. If we do find a relationship when we're desperate, it may turn out to be one that proves our negative beliefs. Change what we believe. Apply heavy doses of self-love, nurturing, and self-care. Find other ways of getting needs met. Act as if we're not desperate, until we really aren't.

Don't take rejection personally. Don't give up, become hopeless, negative, or cynical. A key to determining what you really believe you deserve is how you react when a relationship fails in the initiation stages. What does that prove? That nothing good will ever happen to you? That you're unlovable? That you'll never find love? You can feel your hurt or disappointment, but you need to check out what life is proving to you. If a relationship fails or you're rejected, all that really proves is that you haven't yet found the love of your life.

Be gentle with yourself. Sometimes, the only way to surrender is to experience and work through the desperation. You'll make mistakes. You may go a little crazy, at times. But no matter what your age or history, you can find love, if that's what you want. If you're willing to wait and work at it, you'll even be able to find the kind of love you want.

True Closeness Takes Time

A word of warning: Don't go to bed with someone too soon. Going to bed too soon and particularly on the first date, which is always too soon, wrecks relationships. Besides supremely important moral and health concerns (AIDS, herpes, et cetera), there's another reason not to do this: Sex is a powerful form of intimacy. If we have sex with someone before we achieve an emotional, mental, and spiritual connection, the imbalance will probably be greater than at least one person can handle. And, apart from casual sexual encounters (not the subject of this chapter), no matter what people say, one person usually expects something after sex. *That's normal.* But it's your responsibility to wait until you're assured those expectations will be met.[16]

We can handle the awkwardness of feeling sexually attracted to someone without acting on the feelings. Going to bed with someone doesn't tell us if we want to be in a relationship with that person. The intimacy we're striving to build isn't immediate. Get close in other ways first to see if you even want to be close to that person. Let the chemistry emerge slowly. Give yourself time to develop a mental, emotional, and spiritual bond before sexual intimacy.

Don't Ever Stop Taking Care of Yourself

So often we say, "I want a good relationship. Until then, I'll keep doing my own work and taking care of myself." Why "until then"? Self-care is a lifetime commitment and responsibility. It doesn't end when a relationship begins. That's when we need to intensify efforts.

"I can't tell if a person is unhealthy (addicted, unavailable, dysfunctional) until it's too late," many people complain.

"Too late for what?" I ask.

A characteristic of many failed relationships is that it looks good . . . until we get "in." It looks like needs are going to be met. It looks like the other person is healthy and cares. We let down our guard, become vulnerable, emotionally involved, and things immediately change. The system switches to a destructive or crazy one and we stand there scratching our heads.[17] We don't have to forfeit our ability to take care of ourselves because we're emotionally involved.

"I met a man. Things were great, for about two months," says one woman. "Then things changed. He stopped going to support meetings and started drinking. Things were awful for the next year. I kept waiting for things to go back to the way they used to be. It finally dawned on me that this is the way it is. I'd been waiting for something that wasn't going to happen."

It's possible to get into relationships slowly. And we can get out if it gets crazy. It's never too late or too soon to take care of ourselves.

"What about this business that the minute we let go of our desire to be in a relationship, we find one," a man once asked me. "I've been letting go for a while now, and nothing has happened."

I'm not going to flippantly suggest we "Let Go and Let God." I'm going to seriously suggest we do that, *and* we need to also examine doing our part:

- doing our family of origin work,
- changing our messages,
- affirming that we deserve and will get the best, and
- taking action steps to meet people.

Along with doing our part, we need to let the rest happen, in its own time. We need to combine our actions with surrender and letting go. In spite of our best efforts, relationships usually happen when and where we least expect. Louise Hay writes:

> Love comes when we least expect it, and when we are not looking for it. Hunting for love never brings the right partner. It only creates longing and unhappiness. Love is never outside ourselves; love is within us.
>
> Don't insist that love come immediately. Perhaps you are not ready for it, or you are not developed enough to attract the love you want.
>
> Don't settle for anybody just to have someone. Set your standards. What kind of love do you want to attract? List the qualities you really want in the relationship. Develop those qualities in yourself and you will attract a person who has them.
>
> You might examine what may be keeping love away. Could it be criticism? Feelings of unworthiness? Unreasonable standards? Movie star images? Fear of intimacy? A belief that you are unlovable?
>
> Be ready for love when it does come. Prepare the field and be ready to nourish love. Be loving, and you will be lovable. Be open and receptive to love.[18]

Looking for a relationship? Enjoy the process. Do your part, then "Let go and Let God." Have some fun. Meet people, but don't stop caring for yourself. Learn from your successes and failures. Be open. You may know less about who your type is than you think. You may have some pleasant surprises in store. Talk to people you trust about what you're doing, so you're not initiating relationships in isolation from your support system.

There are healthy men out there. There are healthy women out there. There is such a thing as a relationship that works. You can learn to initiate relationships that work. You can learn to attract and enjoy love that's good for you. Affirm yourself and your prospects. Affirm that you deserve the best, and that it's coming to you because if you begin to believe that, it will.

ACTIVITY

1. Describe your type. Be as specific as possible. Is unavailability one characteristic of your type? Have you ever been able to have a successful relationship with your type?

2. If you are looking for a relationship, where are you looking? What places do you regularly go to meet people? What are some new places you could go to meet people?

3. Are you available for a relationship? Do you have a history of dating and trying to form relationships with unavailable people? What are your prejudices and beliefs, about men, women, or relationships? What do men or women *always* do, and *always do to you*? What do you believe always happens in relationships? What do you believe you deserve in a relationship?

4. Write goals and begin affirming what you want to happen in your love life.

5. Find some positive friends willing to support you as you look for a relationship. Talk openly to them about what you are doing, thinking, and feeling.

15

BOUNDARIES

*I'm forty-two years old and I've finally figured out
what I don't want. Now all I have to do is figure
out what I want.*

—Anonymous

I was on assignment for the newspaper when I spotted the sign on
the lecture room wall in the U.S. Air Force base in Panama City,
Panama. The sign made a statement about American foreign policy
on Soviet expansion in Latin America, but it also made a statement
about my new policy. "No ground to give."

I'm no longer willing to *lose* my self-esteem, self-respect, my children's well-being, my job, home, possessions, safety, credit, my sanity, or *myself* to preserve a relationship. I'm learning how to
appropriately, and with a sense of high self-esteem, *choose* to give. I'm
learning I can occasionally decide to *give up* something during conflict negotiations. But I'm no longer willing to mindlessly lose everything I have for the sake of relationships, appearance, or in the name
of love.

For years, I entered relationships with an all-or-nothing attitude.
What usually happened was I lost all I had and ended up with nothing. I thought a willingness to lose and give everything was manda-
tory in love. The only place that works is in the movies, and it doesn't
work well there either.

Here's the scenario: The man is running around with a smoking gun and fifteen police departments on his tail. He's hostile, bitter, staring out the window of a darkened apartment. His girl friend embraces him and whispers, "I'm with you all the way, baby."

All the way where? A few scenes later, the man is either on Death Row, waiting for his turn in the electric chair, or lying dead on the street. He's gone. She's alone—crying—and the movie's over. It was *his* story. When she finishes grieving for him, she'll really have something to cry about. Besides losing the relationship, she's lost her job, apartment, and furniture. Her credit is shot. Her friends and family are mad at her. And after all the rotten publicity, she's lost her reputation.

The moral of this story and chapter is boundaries. We don't have to be willing to lose everything for love. In fact, setting and sticking to reasonable, healthy limits in all our relationships is a prerequisite to love and relationships that work. We can learn to make appropriate choices concerning what we're willing to *give* in our relationships—of ourselves, time, talents, and money. We can learn to choose to give up certain things while negotiating conflict and working on relationships.

Having boundaries doesn't complicate life; boundaries simplify life. We need to know how far we'll go, and how far we'll allow others to go with us. Once we understand this, we can go anywhere.

What Are Boundaries?

I asked a recovering friend to tell me about boundaries, using her own words.

"How can you tell someone, without using jargon, that you've been allowing people to trample on you all your life?" she replied.

The New World Dictionary defines *boundary* as "any line or thing marking a limit," or a "border."[1]

In recovery, we use the phrase *boundary issues* to describe a primary characteristic of codependency. By this we mean a person has a difficult time defining where he or she ends and another person begins. We have an unclear sense of ourselves. For instance, we may find it difficult to define the difference between our feelings and someone else's feelings, our problem and someone else's problem, our responsibility and someone else's responsibility. Often, the issue isn't that we take responsibility for others; it's that we feel responsible for them. Our ability to define and appropriately distinguish ourselves from others is blurred. The boundaries surrounding ourselves are blurred. People with weak boundaries seem to "pick up" or "absorb" other people's feelings—almost like a sponge absorbs water.[2]

"I went to visit my family. My sister's acting pretty crazy," says Kate. "She's not recovering from codependency, but she needs to be. She's allowing herself to be abused. And she's got a lot of intense, un-resolved feelings going on.

"I was around her for one hour and I started feeling all those crazy feelings. It took me a day to get peaceful and get my balance back. At first I couldn't figure out what happened. Now, I know. I picked up her feelings. Those weren't my feelings; they were hers."

The word *boundary* is also used in recovery circles to describe an action, as in "setting a boundary." By this, we mean we've set a limit with someone. Often, when we say this, we're saying we've decided to tell someone he or she can't use us, hurt us, or take what we have, whether those possessions are concrete or abstract. We've decided to tell them they can't abuse us, or otherwise invade or infringe on us in a particular way.

In geography, boundaries are the borders marking a state, a country, or a person's land. In recovery, we're talking about the lines and limits establishing and marking our personal territory—our *selves*. Unlike states on maps, we don't have thick black lines delin-eating our borders. Yet, each of us has our own territory. Our bound-aries define and contain that territory, our bodies, minds, emotions, spirit, possessions, and rights. Our boundaries define and surround all our energy, the individual self that we each call "me." Our borders are invisible, but real. There is a place where I end and you begin. Our goal is learning to identify and have respect for that line.

What Happened to My Boundaries?

"Nobody is born with boundaries," says Rokelle Lerner, a therapist and author on adult children issues. "Boundaries are taught to us by our parents. . . . Some of us have no sense of boundary, others have built walls instead of boundaries, and others have boundaries with holes in them."[3]

Some people are fortunate enough to emerge into adulthood knowing who they are, and what their rights are and aren't. They don't trespass on other people's territory, and they don't allow others to invade theirs. They have healthy boundaries and a solid sense of self.

Unfortunately, many of us emerged into adulthood with damaged, scarred, or nonexistent boundaries. Or we may have constructed such a thick turtle shell around us people can't get close.

Many events contribute to this. It happens when healthy boundaries aren't role modeled or taught to children, when children's boundaries and rights are invaded or violated, and when children are forced into inappropriate roles with those around them.[4] Diseases like chemical dependency or other compulsive disorders play hell with boundaries.

Children may have weak or nonexistent boundaries if they were emotionally or physically neglected or abandoned. Their boundaries also may be weak if they weren't nurtured or didn't grow up with appropriate discipline and limits. They may not develop a self, an identify, or a healthy sense of self-esteem. It's difficult for a "self" to form in a void.

Abuse, humiliation, or shame damages boundaries. It leaves gaping holes where the violation occurred.[5] If we were emotionally, physically, or sexually abused as children, we may grow up without healthy borders around that part of our territory. As adults, we'll be vulnerable to invasion in that area until we repair and strengthen that part of our border.

Inappropriate generational roles among family members, and inappropriate roles between our family and other families, can damage boundary formation.[6] We may not have learned to identify or respect other people's territory or our own territory.

If we had to take care of someone who was supposed to be our caregiver, we may believe other people's thoughts, feelings, and problems are our responsibility. If we lived with someone who encouraged us to be overly dependent on him or her, we may not have learned we had a complete self of our own. We may have entered adulthood feeling like we were half of something, and needed another person to be complete. Caretaking, whether it involves other people taking responsibility for us or us taking responsibility for them, damages boundaries. It leaves us with an unclear sense of ourselves and others—of who we and others are.

Controlling people invade territory.[7] They trespass, and think it's their right to do that. If we lived with someone who tried to control our thoughts, bodies, or feelings, our boundaries may have been damaged. If our rights to our emotions, thoughts, bodies, privacy, and possessions weren't respected, we may not know we have rights. We may not know others do too.

Our original bond with our primary caregiver determines how we bond with others.[8] Our boundaries determine how we fit or bond with those around us. If we have weak boundaries, we may get lost in other people's territory. If we have holes or gaps in our borders, we're vulnerable to invasion. If our borders are too thick and rigid, we won't let people get close to us.

Without boundaries, relationships will cause us fear. We're vulnerable to losing all we have, including ourselves.

With too many boundaries, we won't have any relationships. We won't dare get too close, because it'll be a long time before we see our *selves* again. People may run from us.

People feel most comfortable around people who have healthy boundaries. It's uncomfortable to be around people with too many or too few boundaries. It's uncomfortable to be around trespassers, although if we've lived with certain kinds of invaders and trespassers all our lives, we may not realize how uncomfortable it feels to be around them.

The goal in recovery is to develop healthy boundaries, not too pliable nor too rigid. And we patch any chinks in our borders. Developing healthy boundaries is our responsibility. We cannot afford to put the responsibility for taking care of ourselves, or looking out for our best interests, in anyone's hands but ours and our Higher Power's.

As we develop healthy boundaries, we develop an appropriate sense of roles among family members, others, and ourselves. We learn to respect others and ourselves. We don't use or abuse others or allow them to use or abuse us. We stop abusing ourselves! We don't control others or let them control us. We stop taking responsibility for other people and stop letting them take responsibility for us. We take responsibility for ourselves. If we're rigid, we loosen up a bit. We develop a clear sense of our self and our rights. We learn we have a complete self. We learn to respect other people's territory as well as our own. We do that by learning to listen to and trust ourselves.

What hurts? What feels good?[9] What's ours and what isn't? And what are we willing to lose?

How Can I Get Some Boundaries?

"I lived with an alcoholic father and a controlling mother. Then I left home and married my own alcoholic," says Diane. "When I began recovering from codependency, I had no idea of what boundaries were. My life proved that.

"I thought I had to do everything people asked. If anyone had a problem, I thought it was my responsibility to solve it. I let people use me, then felt guilty because I didn't like being used. My husband manipulated me, lied to me, and verbally abused me. I felt guilty because I didn't like the way he treated me. My children walked all over me. They talked any way they wanted to me. They refused to respect or follow my rules. I felt guilty when I became angry at them for treating me that way.

"I've been recovering from codependency for eight years now," Diane continues. "Gradually, I've learned to recognize the difference between appropriate and inappropriate treatment. I've come to believe I deserve to be treated well and with respect by people, including my children. I know I don't have to allow people to use me or talk ugly to me. I don't have to do everything people ask or tell me to do. I don't have to be touched when I don't want to be touched. I don't have to feel the way others tell me to feel. I don't have to let people use me. I can say 'No,' and 'Stop that.' I can make my own decisions about what I want and need to do in particular situations. I can stand up for *myself*.

"I've learned to stop incessantly controlling and taking care of others. I've learned to respect people, their individuality and rights, especially the rights of family members.

"I've learned that if what others do hurts me or feels wrong, I can walk away or figure out how to take care of myself. I've developed clearer ideas about what is and isn't my responsibility. But," Diane says, "I have to work at this, and sometimes I have to work hard at it."

That's the proverbial good and bad news. We can learn to have and set boundaries, but we may have to work harder at it than others. To live with what many of us have, we may not immediately know what hurts and feels good. We may not instinctively know what's ours and what's not. We may be uncertain about our rights. It may be difficult to hear ourselves because we may have abandoned ourselves.

To survive living with hurtful incidents, abuse, and crazy behavior, we learn to deny pain and craziness. If we've lived in systems that have a "no boundaries" rule (don't take care of yourself), we may feel shame each time we consider setting a boundary.

"I've been recovering for six years," says one man, who was physically abused as a child. "I'm good at setting boundaries once I realize something is hurting me, but it still takes me a long time to recognize when something hurts."

Many of us have developed a high tolerance for pain and insanity. Just as experts say alcoholics develop a high alcohol tolerance that will remain high whether the alcoholic drinks or not, we may develop a high tolerance for pain, abuse, mistreatment, and boundary violation. Sometimes it's difficult to discern when someone is hurting us, when we're hurting them, or even when we're hurting ourselves. Sometimes it has to hurt long and hard before we know it's hurting. And many of us don't have a frame of reference for what is normal and appropriate.

How can we tell someone to stop hurting us if we're not sure it hurts? How can we identify it as inappropriate if that's all we've ever lived with? To us, it's normal. How can we know what we want if nobody ever told us it's okay to want something?

We have to work at it. We may have to work harder at it than others. We may have to work at it all our lives. To do that, we need to come home to live—in ourselves.

"Boundaries are not just a thought process," says Lerner.

We need to listen to our body to know where our boundaries are. If we were raised with addiction, a lot of us had to leave our body, to abandon our self, in order to survive. If we were raised by someone who was sexually abusive, we had to ignore it when our skin crawled, or our stomach tied up in knots. We needed to ignore our bodies in order to survive.

Then all of a sudden as adults we are expected to set boundaries. Without being inside our body, we can't do it. We need to learn how to come home to ourself again, to learn to listen to our body.[10]

Setting boundaries is not an isolated process.[11] It is intertwined with growing in self-esteem, dealing with feelings, breaking the rules, and developing spiritually. It's connected to detachment. Shame is connected to boundaries. We may feel ashamed when we allow people to invade or trespass on our boundaries. Shame may try to block us from setting boundaries we need to set.[12]

Our boundaries *and* selves develop and emerge as we grow in self-confidence, interact with healthy people, and gain clearer ideas about what's appropriate and what isn't. The more we grow in recovery, the better we'll become at setting boundaries.

- Setting boundaries is about learning to take care of ourselves, no matter what happens, where we go, or who we're with.
- Boundaries emerge from deep decisions about what we believe we deserve and don't deserve.
- Boundaries emerge from the belief that what we want and need, like and dislike, is important.
- Boundaries emerge from a deeper sense of our personal rights, especially the right we have to take care of ourselves and to be ourselves.
- Boundaries emerge as we learn to value, trust, and listen to ourselves.

The goal of having and setting boundaries isn't to build thick walls around ourselves. The purpose is to gain enough security and sense of self to get close to others without the threat of losing ourselves, smothering them, trespassing, or being invaded. Boundaries are the key to loving relationships.

When we have a sense of self, we'll be able to experience closeness and intimacy. We'll be able to play, be creative, and be spontaneous. We'll be able to love and be loved.

Intimacy, play, and creativity require loss of control. Only when we have boundaries and know we can trust ourselves to enforce them and take care of ourselves, will we be able to let go enough to soar. These same activities help develop a sense of self, for it is through love, play, and creativity that we begin to understand who we are and become reassured we can trust ourselves. Having boundaries means having a self strong, nurtured, healthy, and confident enough to let go—and come back again intact.[13]

Tips for Setting Boundaries

We don't have to construct a blockade to protect our territory; we don't have to become hypervigilant. We need to learn to pay attention. Here are some tips for strengthening boundary-setting skills.

When we identify we need to set a limit with someone, do it clearly, preferably without anger, and in as few words as possible. Avoid justifying, rationalizing, or apologizing. Offer a brief explanation, if it makes sense to do that. We will not be able to maintain intimate relationships until we can tell people what hurts and what feels good.[14] The most important person to notify of our boundary is ourselves.

We cannot simultaneously set a boundary (a limit) and take care of another person's feelings. The two acts are mutually exclusive. I listed this tip earlier, but it bears repeating.[15]

We'll probably feel ashamed and afraid when we set boundaries. Do it anyway. People may not know they're trespassing. And people don't respect people they can use. People use people they can use, and respect people they can't use. Healthy limits benefit everyone. Children and adults will feel more comfortable around us.

Anger, rage, complaining, and whining are clues to boundaries we need to set. The things we say we can't stand, don't like, feel angry about, and hate may be areas screaming for boundaries. Recovery doesn't mean an absence of feeling angry, whining, or complaining. Recovery means we learn to listen closely to ourselves to hear what we're saying. These things are indicators of problems, like a flashing red light on the dashboard. Shame and fear may be the barrier we need to break through to take care of ourselves. Other clues that we may need to set a boundary are feeling threatened, "suffocated,"[16] or victimized by someone. We need to pay attention to what our bodies are telling us too. And, as I said before, we may need to get angry to set a boundary, but we don't need to stay resentful to enforce it.

We'll be tested when we set boundaries. Plan on it. It doesn't do any good to set a boundary until we're ready to enforce it. Often, the key to boundaries isn't convincing other people we have limits—it's convincing ourselves. Once we know, really know, what our limits are, it won't be difficult to convince others. In fact, people often sense when we've reached our limit. We'll stop attracting so many boundary invaders. Things will change. A woman went to her counselor and recited her usual and regular tirade of complaints about her husband. "When will this stop?" the woman finally asked her counselor. "When you want it to," the counselor said.

Be prepared to follow through by acting in congruence with boundaries. Our boundaries need to match our behavior. What we do needs to match what we say. If you say your boundary is not to let other people drive your car, but you continue to let people take your car, then whine about it, it's not a boundary yet. Consequences and ultimatums are one way to enforce boundaries. For instance, if your boundary is you won't live with active alcoholism and a drinking alcoholic is living with you, you can give him or her an ultimatum— an either/or. Either that person stops drinking and starts recovering or you move. I've often heard people complain, "I've set a boundary, but Henry won't respect it." Boundaries are to take care of ourselves, not to control others. If we set a boundary not to be around practicing alcoholics, it isn't to force Harvey to stop drinking. Harvey can choose to drink or not drink. Our boundary gives us a guideline to make our choice—whether we want to be around Harvey.

Some people are happy to respect our boundaries. The problem hasn't been what they've been doing to us; it's what we've been doing to ourselves. Some people may get angry at us for setting boundaries, particularly if we're changing a system by setting a boundary where we previously had none. People especially become angry if we've been caretaking them, or allowing them to use or control us, and we decide it's time to change that.

We'll set boundaries when we're ready, and not a minute sooner. We do it on our own time, not someone else's—not our sponsor's timing, our group's timing, nor our counselor's timing. That's because it's connected to *our* growth.

A support system can be helpful as we strive to establish and enforce boundaries. It can be valuable to have feedback about what's normal and what's not, what our rights are and aren't. A cheering squad is very helpful as we strive to assert these rights.

There's a fun side to boundary setting too. Besides learning to identify what hurts and what we don't like, we learn to identify what we like, what feels good, what we want, and what brings us pleasure.[17] That's when we begin to enhance the quality of our lives. If we're not certain who we are, and what we like and want, we have a right to those exciting discoveries.

Boundaries are a personal issue. They reflect and contribute to our growth, our *selves,* our connection to ourselves, to our Higher Power, and other people. Paying attention to what we like, to what we want, to what feels good and what hurts, doesn't take us away from our Higher Power or God's plan for our lives. Listening to ourselves and valuing ourselves moves us into God's will for our lives: a rich, abundant plan for good. As we take risks and learn more about who we are, our boundaries and selves will emerge. As we go through different circumstances, we'll be faced with setting new boundaries about what hurts, what feels good, what we like and don't like. Setting boundaries is an ongoing process of listening to ourselves, respecting ourselves and others, understanding our rights, and caring for ourselves.

Strive for balance. Strive for flexibility. Strive for a healthy sense of self and how you deserve to be treated. Healthy living means you give to people from time to time, but there's a big difference between giving, and being robbed.[18]

I've listed some "tips," but there isn't a guidebook for setting boundaries. Each of us has our own guide inside ourselves. If we continue to work at recovery, our boundaries will develop. They will get healthy and sensitive. Our *selves* will tell us what we need to know, and we'll love ourselves enough to listen.

Ask yourself, *What hurts?* Listen and stop the pain. Ask yourself, *What feels good?* If it feels good, you've got a winner. Ask yourself, *What's mine?* If it's yours, you can have it; if it isn't, don't put it in your pocket.[19] Ask yourself, *What am I willing to lose?* You may have no ground to give.

ACTIVITY

1. What are some boundaries you've set early in recovery? What are some boundaries you've set recently? Can you remember how you felt before and after you set that boundary? Were you called on to enforce it? What are the most difficult kind of boundaries for you to set and enforce?

2. Is somebody in your life using you, or not treating you appropriately or respectfully now? Are you now complaining, angry, whining, or upset about something? What's preventing you from taking care of yourself? What do you think will happen if you do? What do you think will happen if you don't?

3. How do you feel when you're around people with rigid boundaries—too many rules and regulations? How do you feel when you're around people with few, or no, boundaries?

4. In the past, what have you been willing to lose for the sake of a particular relationship? What are you willing to lose now? What are you not willing to lose?

16

INTIMACY

"Do you want intimacy in this relationship, or not?"
she finally blurted. "Sure," he said. "What is it?"

—Anonymous

As I've traveled across the country speaking to groups of recovering people, I've done some informal surveys. I've asked how many people are doing recovery perfectly. I've asked how many have a perfect relationship. I've asked another question too.

"How many of you saw intimacy and closeness role modeled in your families?"

In audiences ranging from two hundred to nine hundred people, rarely do more than two or three people raise their hands to answer "yes" to the last question. (No one answers yes to the first; about two in fifteen thousand answer yes to the second, but I haven't interviewed their spouses.)

A few of us have been lucky enough to see what intimacy looks like. Most of us have lived in families where intimacy and closeness didn't exist. Behaviors such as controlling, caretaking, dishonesty, and sometimes the more painful issues of abuse, may have made intimacy and closeness impossible. The rules—don't trust, don't be close, don't talk about feelings, don't be vulnerable—may have made intimacy and closeness highly improbable.

My friend Chad announced his engagement to a group of

friends. Later in the evening he asked Veronica, one of his friends, if she and her boyfriend intended to get married.

"No," Veronica said. "We have no plans."

Chad looked at her. "Your boyfriend would have to be a fool not to marry you," he said.

"What you don't understand," Veronica said, "is if he wasn't a fool, I wouldn't be in a relationship with him. I have a limited capacity for intimacy, and anyone who wants a warm, loving relationship has no business being in one with me."

Veronica's comment expressed a problem common to many of us. Most of us want intimacy and closeness, but few of us know what these concepts look or feel like. Even fewer of us have been taught how to have these things. Most of us have been taught how not to have intimacy and closeness.

I used to think *intimacy* was jargon. I didn't understand intimacy because I hadn't experienced it. How did it happen? What did it look and feel like?

I wondered if intimacy had something to do with sex. Then I decided it meant staying awake all night sharing feelings: his guilt and my anger. Once, in a group of people, I felt a powerful, universal bonding with the group. It happened while one person was talking and I was listening. It scared me because I felt out of control. I wondered if that was intimacy. I tried to figure out if intimacy was the same thing John Powell called "peak communication" in his book, *Why Am I Afraid to Tell You Who I Am?*[1]

Intimacy and closeness seemed mysterious and elusive. Yet, I yearned for both.

I can remember sitting in a car with a friend. We were on our way to a garage sale. I realized I had never let my guard down enough with her, or anyone else, to be close.

I can recall walking into the living room one evening and having the sudden and profound awareness that I was too frightened and nervous to be close to my children. I knew how to stay in the "Mom" role. I knew how to take care of and control them. But I didn't know how to relax and be close.

I can remember lying in bed at night with my ex-husband, longing for an emotional and spiritual connection with him and not having the foggiest notion of how to do that.

In the years since I began recovering from codependency and adult children issues, I've had more moments of intimacy and closeness than I had in all my life before I began recovering. I'd blamed others, complained about not having closeness, and wondered if I ever would. But when I got serious about achieving close, intimate relationships, and combined that with recovery, I started having intimate relationships.

Someone has yet to tell me everything I've wanted to know about intimacy. But this is what I've learned.

Achieving Intimacy

Closeness happens when our boundaries soften and touch another's borders. Closeness feels good. It's a comfortable, relaxed experience. We can have many hours and days of closeness, if we allow ourselves to do that and have someone to do it with. Closeness is something we have some control over. I believe it has a lot to do with attitudes—concern, honesty, openness, willingness, safety, and availability. Closeness can be nurtured, developed, and sustained. We can merge our energy and soften our boundaries with inanimate objects too: a diamond ring, our work, a pet.[2] Sometimes, this is okay. The key is choosing.

Intimacy is the great energy connection. It's transcendental. Our borders and barriers break down and we merge *temporarily and usually momentarily* with another. Intimacy can be emotional, mental, sexual, spiritual, or a stimulating and mysterious combination. Although intimacy can't be examined, weighed, or compared, the most profound experiences are multidimensional energy connections. Intimacy is such a powerful connection that it can't be sustained. It's a gift, a cherished guest that arrives and departs unexpectedly and on its own schedule. The moment we become aware it's there, it disappears.[3]

Closeness and intimacy are like happiness. They're difficult to describe. We've either got 'em or we don't. We know when we've got 'em and we know when we don't. Closeness and intimacy happen when and where we least expect them. They can't be manufactured, forced, or bought. They come as by-products of living a certain way. That "way" is called recovery—taking care of and loving ourselves. Recovery makes us available for these activities. It increases our capacity for intimacy and closeness.

"Intimacy begins when individual (usually instinctual) programming becomes more intense, and both social patterning and ulterior restrictions and motives begin to give way," writes Eric Berne in *Games People Play.*[4]

We can have close or intimate moments, and we can have close, intimate relationships—relationships with an overall tone of intimacy.

Closeness and intimacy can look like two people sitting down, having coffee, talking; three people sitting around the dinner table chatting; two people cooking dinner together or painting a room; two people fishing; one person praying; a couple dancing together; or two people silently holding hands while riding in the car or watching the sunset. These activities aren't necessarily acts of intimacy and closeness, but they can be. So can sex.

For closeness to exist, both people have to want it to be that. We need to be present and available for closeness. We have to desire it and be willing to have it. We have to drop pretense and fear, and shed games and protective devices. Intimacy and closeness can involve doing something or just being together, but the "being" is of prime importance. So is "wanting to be together." We have to spend time together to accomplish that.

Then, we let down our guard for a while. We soften our borders, the line distinguishing and separating us from the other person. And we surrender—which is in itself no small task—to the relationship, each other, and the moment. We become vulnerable.⁵

To do this feat of letting go in our relationships, we need healthy boundaries. We need to be safe, strong, and nurtured enough to be able to surrender. We need to know we can let down our guard. Our boundaries need to be healthy and firm before we can choose where and with whom to soften them.⁶

To momentarily merge with another in the experience we call intimacy, we must be able to emerge again. Otherwise it's not intimacy and closeness—it's fusion and dependency. We need a healthy sense of self so we can count on ourselves to take care of ourselves. The other person needs to know we'll leave his or her territory when that's appropriate. Both people need the reassurance that when we blend territories, no invasion, shaming, humiliation, trespassing, or overextended stays will occur.

For that delightful, exuberant, lovable child in us to come out and play and show his or her beautiful face in moments of intimacy and closeness, that child first has to be found. Secondly, that child must know that if he or she comes out to play he or she will be protected, valued, cherished, and cared for. That the child in us must feel this way isn't optional: it's essential and a prerequisite to intimacy.

Barriers to Intimacy

To be intimate or close, we have to let go, for the moment, of our need to control. Controlling and caretaking prevent intimacy and closeness. They are substitutes for, and barricades to, closeness. We can't be close if we're trying to control or caretake. Controlling and caretaking are ways to connect with people. They're not as satisfying as closeness and intimacy, but for some of us, those are the only ways we learned how to connect with others.

Other behaviors can become intimacy substitutes: gossip, blaming, punishing, fight-picking, nit-picking, judging, and self-pity. These are protective devices, but they're not intimacy or closeness.

Being obsessed with the past, future, or present will prevent closeness because being obsessed prevents us from being present.

Unfinished business, unresolved anger, blocks to our past and thus blocks to us, prevent intimacy. If we haven't tackled our historical work, if our old messages are driving us, we may be unable to attain intimacy and closeness. If we haven't finished our grief work and accepted our present circumstances and the people in our present circumstances, we may be unable to be present enough to achieve intimacy and closeness. Unresolved anger and resentments, either at the person we're with or the people that person represents from other times in our lives, can block intimacy and closeness.

"I had been victimized by men for most of my life," says Jane. "Several years into my recovery, when I tried to have a healthy relationship, I became aware of how angry I was at men. I had never dealt with how full of rage I was at the men who had mistreated me. I rationalized my anger. I denied my anger. But it was there. Of course it was! But I hadn't acknowledged or accepted it. Instead, I used my anger to punish the current man in my life and prove all men were creeps. One way I punished men was not allowing them to get close to me."

Another ploy that will prohibit intimacy and closeness is expecting intimacy and closeness to happen with people who are incapable of either. That brings us back to the availability or unavailability factor in relationships. Active addictions, serious unresolved historical or current issues, abuse, and lying absolutely prohibit intimacy and closeness. Intimacy won't happen with people with these problems or in relationships with these issues. We can wait until the sky turns purple, but we won't be able to get close to or intimate with someone who's actively addicted, someone who we believe is lying to us, or someone who we fear might verbally, physically, or emotionally injure us.

Someone abusing, lying, or acting out his or her addiction isn't capable at the moment of the honesty and surrender, acceptance, self-responsibility, disclosure, and exposure necessary for intimacy and closeness. These people aren't present for themselves and won't be present for the relationship. And, we'll know, deep inside where it counts, that it isn't safe for us to surrender and be vulnerable. Our territory is at risk—high risk—of invasion and attack.

Shame can preclude intimacy. If it's not okay to be who we are, we won't show or expose ourselves to another. Intimacy and closeness require self-acceptance. We need to be intimate with ourselves before we can be intimate with another.

The difference between intimacy and the "games" we play as a substitute can be described in the following manner. It's a "game" when I punish you because I'm angry at you. It's intimacy when I tell you I'm hurt, angry, and want to punish you. But it's intimacy only if my tone of voice is soft and I claim responsibility for my feelings and behaviors. It's intimacy if I'm willing to be vulnerable, and am confident you'll care about how I feel.

True Intimacy

In *Leaving the Enchanted Forest: The Path from Relationship Addiction to Intimacy,* authors Stephanie Covington and Liana Beckett listed three more factors essential to intimate relationships.[7]

- *The relationship must be mutual.* That means both people are free to either stay or leave, and both are now in the relationship because they *choose* to be, not because they *need* to be or feel they *have* to be.
- *Reciprocal empathy must be present.* This means both people are willing to try to understand and care about the other person's feelings. Again, to be willing to enter the emotional world of the other with a caring attitude, it must be safe to do that.
- *A balance of power must exist.* This means, there must be equality of power between people to achieve intimacy. This equality is never a perfect balance, but the scales must not tip too far on either side.

Another important part of intimacy and closeness is the ability to distance, to return to ourselves and our lives after getting close. Intimacy and closeness are altered states of consciousness and energy. They are altered or softened states of boundaries. After we get close or intimate, we need to restore our boundaries and energy to normal, healthy, intact conditions. We need to close the gaps in our borders and restore ourselves to a state of completeness and individuality. People cannot sustain permanent states of intimacy and closeness. That's not desirable, and it would probably preclude getting anything else done. We need to get our balance and selves back.

The need to distance is instinctive and healthy after times of closeness.[8] The best ways to accomplish distancing aren't as instinctive. Many of us know all about distancing behaviors. They are the same behaviors we've used as substitutes for intimacy; they're the same behaviors that block and prevent intimacy. To distance we may resort to fight-picking, faultfinding, withdrawing, or any number of anti-intimacy behaviors.[9] If it pushes someone away, protects us, constructs a barricade, or somehow creates distance, it's a distancing behavior. For those of us who have a limited capacity for intimacy, it may not take much closeness or intimacy to propel us to use distancing behaviors.

An option to these behaviors is learning to accept our need to distance after closeness, and choose how we would like to do it. Often, a simple closure of our energy and return to our lives and normal activities is enough.

The more nurturing we are with ourselves, the easier it will be for us to handle both the merging and reemerging that are part of intimacy and closeness. Intimate, close relationships require a strong and nurtured self from both people involved.

Mutual respect and self-awareness are also necessary. We need to be able to say what hurts, what feels good, and what we need. So does the other person.

We deserve intimate, close relationships. Our capacity for intimacy and closeness will increase as we grow in recovery. We need to go slowly and gently as we learn the art of conditional surrender: surrendering for a while, surrendering with limits, surrendering with safe people, and surrendering with the knowledge that we'll come back a whole person. Once we learn to love ourselves, we can learn to love and be loved in exciting new ways in our relationships. Often, the greatest challenge isn't learning to love others. It's learning to let them love us.

Intimacy and closeness may be a struggle, but they're worth it. You've learned to accept powerlessness. You've found a Higher Power. You're learning to own your power. Now you can learn to share the power.[10]

ACTIVITY

1. What would you like intimacy and closeness to look like in your life and relationships?

2. What are your distancing patterns? Nagging, faultfinding, criticism, relationship termination, anger, controlling, getting busy with work? What other, more positive ways could you reestablish your boundaries after periods of intimacy?

17

NEGOTIATING CONFLICTS

"Do you want an argument or an explanation?"
the clerk finally asked the irate customer. The customer thought
for a moment. "I guess I want an argument," she said.

—Anonymous Al-Anon member

"Mommy, please don't fight with Daddy anymore! My friend Elizabeth told me when a mom and dad fight, they get divorced."

My daughter's words cut into my heart. It was sad she and Elizabeth thought conflict meant somebody went away. But they had reason to believe this. Elizabeth's mother and father argued, then divorced. My husband and I argued, then divorced. My mother and father argued, then divorced. It was sad I believed conflicts ended relationships.

Many of us have difficulty handling conflict and dealing with problems. Many reasons contribute to this. We may have lived in a family with a "no problem" rule. If it wasn't okay to have, identify, or talk about problems, we may still feel ashamed and anxious about having them. We may feel unequipped to solve them. If we lived with the "be perfect" and "be right" rules, we may be so intent on being perfect and right that we're ineffective.[1] Difficulty dealing with feelings, especially anger, can limit our negotiation skills. The issue may switch from "How can I solve this problem?" to "What can I do to punish you for making me angry?"

On the other hand, if we lived with too much trauma and anger, conflict may trigger our codependent reactions. The threat of conflict may send us into a tailspin of controlling, caretaking, anxiety, and denial.[2]

Growing Up With Poor Messages

"My mother said my dad tried to kill her with a butcher knife," recalls one woman. "She said I hid behind the couch, watching and screaming in terror. I don't remember this, but I still remember the fear. I feel it each time people get angry or raise their voice."

Whatever our circumstances, many of us grew up with poor role models and messages concerning problem solving and conflict resolution. We may have decided that we could resolve differences by ignoring, denying, avoiding, giving in, giving up, forcing, coercing, arbitrating, or walking away. These approaches don't solve problems or resolve differences. They create more conflict by teaching us and other people to ignore, deny, avoid, give in, give up, force, coerce, arbitrate, or walk away.

To complicate matters, many of us have spent much time trying to solve problems that we couldn't solve if we lived to be five hundred, because the problems weren't ours to solve. We may have spent years trying to negotiate with people who didn't play fair.[3] Diseases such as alcoholism don't negotiate. They win—until recovery begins.

Some of us became so enmeshed and overwhelmed with problems and pain we become martyrs. We learned to give all the power and energy to the problem, instead of the solution.

A lack of faith—in ourselves, the process of life, our Higher Power, and our problem-solving skills—can hinder our ability to deal with difficulties and differences. We may not believe in conflict resolution. Some of us may not believe in conflict.

Wasting Personal Energy

I used to maintain a naive attitude toward problems, differences, and difficulties. I didn't think there should be any. I was baffled when one problem after another kept cropping up. Why was God picking on me? What was I doing wrong? Why were other people doing this to me? I spent more time and energy reacting to the presence of problems than I did to solving them.

One day, while bemoaning a particular problem, someone threw the classic cliche at me: *Nobody ever said it was going to be easy.* Right! Nobody ever said it was going to be easy. But no one told me it was going to be this damn difficult, either.

It took me years to learn three concepts:

- I can have problems;
- I can solve some problems in ways that benefit me and my relationships;
- I can let go of problems I can't solve because my Higher Power is there to help me.

It took more years to learn my instinctive reactions to problems: denial, panic, avoidance, controlling, fatalism, and self-pity. These reactions often made things worse. I've since accepted several variations of Murphy's Law:

- Things that work, break.
- Some things that can go wrong, do.
- And frequently, things are harder to do than we think they'll be.

M. Scott Peck summed it up in three words in his opening line in *The Road Less Traveled.* "Life is difficult."

Once we see this great truth, we transcend it, Peck says. The sooner we accept that life is difficult, the easier life becomes.[4]

I've accepted another premise too. A. P. Herbert summed it up when he said: "The concept of two people living together for twenty-five years without a serious dispute suggests a lack of spirit only to be admired in sheep."[5]

Problem Stoppers

Problems are a fact of life and conflicts in relationships are too. But problem *solving* is also a fact of life. Learning to solve problems and negotiate differences will propel us forward on our recovery journey.[6] The rest of this chapter focuses on ideas for problem solving and conflict negotiation. We'll discuss the following suggestions:

- Identify and accept the problem.
- Look for solutions that are in the best interest of the relationship.
- Be open to various solutions.
- Learn to combine emotion with reason.
- Don't take problems and differences personally.
- Don't deny an adversary reaction if it's present, but don't assume one either.
- Learn to combine detachment with appropriate action steps.
- Practice deliberate, time-limited patience.
- Be clear about what you want and need.
- Consider the wants and needs of yourself and others as important.
- Separate issues from people.
- Communicate.
- Healthy boundaries are crucial to conflict negotiation.
- Consistently foregoing what you want and need isn't conflict negotiation.
- Avoid power plays.
- Learn to recognize when you're negotiating with yourself.
- Forego naïveté and cynicism.
- Save ultimatums for absolute nonnegotiables or late stage negotiation.
- Don't waste time negotiating nonnegotiables.

- Let each person keep his or her respect and dignity.
- Take full responsibility for your behavior.
- Look for the gift or the lesson.

Identify and Accept the Problem

- Reduce a problem to its simplest form.

Then, begin empowering and affirming the solution. Entering the problem and solution on a goal list under "problems to be solved" is one way to do this. Be specific about the problem. Be clear about what is and isn't your responsibility. If you don't know what's wrong, you can't fix it. If you don't accept the problem, you won't be in the necessary frame of mind to solve it.

Sometimes in my work, I know there's a problem with a certain piece of writing. If I get too anxious and attempt to fix the piece without clearly identifying the problem (structure, tone, content), I waste my time running in circles and ultimately get back to the starting gate: pinpointing the problem so I can pinpoint the solution. I've used the same hasty approach in relationships, and it hasn't worked any better.

Look for Solutions That Are in the Best Interest of the Relationship

- It means that we value the relationship, and the solution we seek will reflect that.

Yes, we're learning to take care of ourselves and act in our own best interests. But at some point, to preserve relationships—and some are worth preserving—we can learn to act in the best interest of the relationship. That doesn't mean we negate ourselves or our needs, or act in ways that aren't in our best interests.

Be Open to Various Solutions

- Good conflict negotiation means eliminating traditional black and white thinking; it means brainstorming. Sometimes obvious solutions are overlooked.

Grant and Sharon both worked full time. They had two children, and lived in a large home. Grant liked an immaculate house. Sharon's approach to housekeeping was relaxed. It became an ongoing source of irritation to them. Sharon believed if Grant wanted the house cleaner, he should do it. Grant thought he already did more than his share. The arguments took a nonconstructive tone. Then, they decided to stop arguing and solve the problem. Grant wanted a clean house. Sharon wanted to relax when she had time off. They both chipped in and hired a housekeeper.

Learn to Combine Emotion with Reason

- Exclusively using either an emotional or rational approach to solving problems and negotiating differences will reduce our effectiveness.

If we don't consider our own or other people's feelings—and don't consider them important—we'll run into trouble. Feelings often motivate behavior. If we ignore emotions and rely solely on reason while the other person is in the height of anger, pain, disappointment, or fear, our efforts may be futile, self-defeating, and misunderstood.

If we deal solely on the basis of emotions, we'll be ineffective too. Feelings need to be listened to and heard. But we don't allow them to control us or dictate our thinking.

Heavy emotions such as anger, hurt, or fear are best dealt with apart from problem-solving sessions. Anger helps us identify problems, but it usually doesn't help solve them.[7] Learn to call "time out" until heavy emotions subside.

"I had a problem that was driving me wild," says Jeff. "I bought a new car, and the hood popped every time I drove it. I took it in five times to be fixed. Each time, the hood popped open again before I got home. I was furious! One day, driving home from the dealership after the problem was supposedly fixed, the hood popped again. I was so mad! When I got out of the car, I slammed the hood down with my keys in my hand and put a five-inch gouge in the hood. That's when I knew it was time to deal with my anger apart from solving the problem. My anger was justified, but it wasn't solving the problem; it was creating more problems."

Don't Take Problems and Differences Personally

- This approach to problem solving wastes a lot of time and energy.

It's tempting to take problems personally. It also gives us an inaccurate perspective on probable solutions.

Don't Deny an Adversary Reaction if it's Present, but Don't Assume One, Either

- Approaching relationships and conflict negotiations with a "win-lose," "down with the enemy" approach creates a hostile atmosphere. Start by asking for what you want instead of demanding.

Sometimes we may create a negative situation that doesn't exist except in our own minds. On the other hand, we need to beware of a tendency to keep the peace at any price; in other words, don't throw away your integrity for the sake of making others happy.

Learn to Combine Detachment with Appropriate Action Steps

• Don't rely solely on detachment—Letting Go and Letting God—as a problem-solving tool. Don't rely solely on doing it yourself either.

Too much detachment may be denial and avoidance. Too many action steps may be controlling behavior. Strive for balance.

Practice Deliberate, Time-Limited Patience

• Sometimes, waiting helps accomplish challenges that seem impossible, despite our most ambitious efforts.

As with ourselves, the people around us sometimes also need time to figure out what they really want and need, and how to resolve feelings. We don't want to act too hastily, but we don't want to wait too long either. That invites denial. Select an appropriate time limit for each stage of negotiation.

"I impulsively committed myself to buying a product for much more than it was worth," Marv says. "The contract was possibly binding and borderline unethical. I wanted out before the ink dried on my signature. While I sat there regretting my decision, the salesman tap-danced in joy. He had just made a heck of a commission. When I informed him I was canceling, he got furious.

"We got into a go-nowhere confrontation," Marv recalls. "That's when I decided to back off. I excused myself from the negotiations, gave him back his product so he'd know I intended not to buy it, and left. I told him I would contact him in two days to get my money back. That gave us time to settle down. Two days later, I called and gave him and the sales manager an ultimatum: either give me my money back, or I pursue legal action. I also gave them another twenty-four hours to make their decision. The next day, they returned my money. I accomplished more by waiting three days than I could have by hollering for a week."

Sometimes, people need time to collect their thoughts, save face, resolve feelings, or figure out an appropriate solution.

Be Clear About What You Want and Need

• At the heart of most conflicts is a clash in needs.[8]

It's easy to let conflict exist for its own sake. We forget what we're arguing about; we forget about solving the problem. We begin arguing just to argue. Sometimes, arguing clears the air. But arguing isn't conflict negotiation; it's arguing.

Sometimes, we're not even arguing about the real problem. For many reasons—shame, fear, lack of trust or awareness—the real issue gets fogged, disguised, or lost. Certain issues can become "sacred cow" issues in relationships. We may not feel safe enough to state the problem, and how we feel about it. It may be an "off-limits" problem, too highly charged to discuss. We may feel ashamed to have certain problems or feelings, so we focus our anger and attention on a safer problem—a red herring, as some call it. Or we may be uncertain about the real problem. The problem may be an intangible one, such as "I feel you have more power in this relationship than I do."[9] It helps to ask ourselves and each other if what we're arguing about is what we're arguing about.

Until we understand negotiation goals, we aren't ready to negotiate. The more tangible and specific we can be about what we want from any particular negotiation, the greater our chance of achieving that.

Consider the Wants and Needs of Yourself and Others as Important

- This is a basic recovery concept.

When our sights seem to be getting lost in the heat of the moment, we can slow down and ask ourselves these questions:

- Why is the other person acting this way? What does he need?
- Why am I acting this way? What do I need?
- Is there some way we could solve the problem and meet both our needs?
- Is there an underlying common need?

The more emotionally charged the situation, the more we need to stay focused on our goals. We may want to write them down before negotiating so we don't get diverted.

Separate Issues from People

- Accept people and confront problems.

Doing otherwise invites shame, hostility, defensiveness, and rebuttal. These factors set us up for nonproductive negotiations. Our attitude toward people and relationships makes a difference when we're working through differences. Relationships don't have to be destroyed, abandoned, or abated because a conflict or problem emerges. Neither other people nor ourselves deserve to be discounted because of the presence of problems.

Communicate

- Talk and listen.

Sometimes discussion is the only way to get to the heart of the matter—what's the problem and what can we do to solve it? We may not know as much as we think about ourselves and other people. Understanding our own, and each other's, family of origin messages is helpful here.[10]

A friend told me a story that exemplifies this point. One day, after thirty years of marriage, the wife exploded, told her husband she wanted a divorce, but agreed to see a counselor first. During their first counseling session, the wife went on and on about how angry she was.

"And do you know what I really resent?" she said. "Each morning, when he made toast, he always gave me the crust. I hate the crust."

The husband then replied, "I did that because I love you. You see," he said, "I always thought the crust was the best part."

Healthy Boundaries are Crucial to Conflict Negotiation

- The ideal is having firm boundaries—neither too permeable, nor too rigid.

We need to know when we cannot yield, and when we can. We need to know what we want and need. And we need to know our bottom line. Our wants, needs, and bottom lines are important. What's negotiable? What's not?

Consistently Foregoing What You Want and Need Isn't Conflict Negotiation

- We need to constantly beware of the tendency to take care of other people while neglecting ourselves.

That old pattern of caretaking others' problems doesn't solve problems; it creates angry, deprived victims of ourselves. Caretaking doesn't resolve conflict; it creates more. And if we've learned to avoid conflict by forcing the other person to give in, we haven't resolved conflict—we've postponed it. The cost of peace at any price is inevitably high.

Avoid Power Plays

- Power plays don't work.[11] Power plays usually escalate conflict.

Mother to daughter: "I need you to baby-sit this weekend."

Daughter: "You're always making me baby-sit. I wanted to go out this weekend."

Mother: "I haven't been out in weeks. You're going to stay home this weekend and baby-sit."

Daughter: "If you go out, I'm not staying home and baby-sitting. I'll leave."

Mother: "If you leave, I'll ground you."

Daughter: "Go ahead. I'll run away."

Mother: "If you run away, I'll call the police."

The statement of conflicting need happened immediately in this conversation. Both the mother and daughter wanted to go out on the weekend. Instead of negotiating from that point, they used power plays—each in turn threatening something more severe. What follows is how they resolved the conflict:

Mother: "We're both getting angry and upset. We're saying things we don't mean. Why don't we call time-out? Let's talk about this later and see if we can solve the problem."

Daughter (an hour later): "How about if I go out on Friday night and baby-sit on Saturday?"

Mother: "That sounds fair to me."

Learn to Recognize When You're Negotiating with Yourself

- A good rule of thumb is: If you've asked someone three times for something and the person has refused you, lied to you, or promised to give something to you, then failed to deliver, you're probably negotiating with yourself. Remember, once isn't a pattern.[12]

Some people don't play fair. Their intention isn't to negotiate; they intend to sabotage, coerce, manipulate, or otherwise control events so they can go forward with their course of action. When you're dealing with someone's compulsive disease, you're negotiating with yourself.

When you find yourself negotiating with yourself it means it's time to set or enforce a boundary, or deliver an ultimatum. You need not make your own choice about what you need to do to take care of yourself based on the premise that the other person is not going to change his or her course of action.

Forego Naïveté and Cynicism

- Learn to trust yourself, and make good individual decisions about who you can trust.

Save Ultimatums for Absolute Nonnegotiables or Late Stage Negotiations

- Too often, we begin negotiating by delivering ultimatums.[13] This is ineffective.

Ultimatums need to be handled carefully. We need to avoid turning ultimatums into power plays. We deliver ultimatums as a way of taking care of ourselves, not controlling the other person. Ultimatums are either/or stands: either you do this, or I do this. Effective ultimatums require two ingredients:

- reasonable, fair, and appropriate time frame for the other person to deliver; and a commitment to following through with the "or."

Don't Waste Time Negotiating Nonnegotiables

- Sometimes, at the heart of our conflict lies two nonnegotiable, conflicting needs.

We've set a boundary we're not willing to negotiate—no matter what happens, what someone offers us, how long we talk, or how much we understand about the other person. Our goal here may not be to negotiate; it may be to terminate the relationship or change the dimensions of the relationship. Some conflicts can't be successfully negotiated. The people may either be unwilling to negotiate or unable to achieve a mutually satisfactory solution.

Let Each Person Keep His or Her Respect and Dignity

- Even if the relationship is ended, be kind to your adversaries, even—especially—when you "win." Avoid the use of humiliating tactics, and shake hands at the end of the game.[14]

We don't know when we shall encounter certain people again, and what the circumstances may be. We can strive to deal with people in such a way that whenever we encounter them, they will have reason to respect us for our conduct. This doesn't mean we resort to "people-pleasing" tactics. A certain person doesn't need to like us or the outcome of our negotiations. But we can give them reason to respect us for the way we've treated them: fairly and with dignity.

Take Full Responsibility for Your Behavior

• Our behavior isn't "conditional" on the other person's behavior. And it's preferable if our behavior isn't a reaction to the other person's behavior.

If we've been recovering from codependency for even a short time, we've learned we have no—and I mean *no*—control over other people and their behavior. But we do have some control over ourselves and our behavior.

We can be responsible for our behavior even if the other person isn't behaving responsibly. We try not to allow others to control our course of conduct. In recovery and in conflict negotiations, we're learning to behave rationally and responsibly because it's the course of conduct we choose, and because it's ultimately in our best interest to do that.

Look for the Gift or the Lesson[15]

• Some problems exist to be solved; some come with a particular territory; some bring a lesson or a gift we need. Be open.

Somewhere between asking for nothing and demanding everything is the middle ground of conflict negotiation. We reach that ground only when we relinquish our need to be perfect and right, and we pay attention to our true needs—including our need to participate in working relationships.

There may be times when we engage in nonproductive arguments. There may be times when the scope of a relationship changes. There will be times when walking away from a relationship is the thing to do. But recovery is about more than walking away. Sometimes it means learning to stay and deal. It's about building and maintaining relationships that work.

Some conflicts can be resolved in a mutually satisfactory way. Sometimes, we can both get what we really want—especially when we know what that is.

ACTIVITY

1. How do you usually react to conflict? Do you usually give in? Do others usually give in to you? Do you avoid conflict by denial or ending relationships?

2. Have you ever gotten involved with power plays—trying to force the other person into behaving the way you want? How has this worked for you? Are you involved with someone who tries to control you by power plays?

3. Think about one or two times you've successfully negotiated conflict. By successful, I mean times when both parties have entered into negotiations that resolve the conflict in a mutually acceptable way. How did you feel? What attitudes and behaviors were present in you?

18

DEALING WITH FEAR OF COMMITMENT

. . . let me never be afraid of endings or beginnings.
Teach me to embrace all of life with joy.

—Helen Lesman[1]

"I wasn't interested in Greg, but he pursued me arduously," Mary recalls. "I turned down his invitations for two months before he wore me down and I agreed to date him.

"The date turned out surprisingly great. We went to dinner, then back to his place," Mary remembers. "He talked about issues he had worked through. He asked questions about me, and listened when I answered. He didn't try to get me to go to bed with him. We sat up half the night talking about feelings. When he took me home, he gave me a quick kiss. What a nice man, I thought."

Greg continued to impress Mary. He brought flowers. He offered to help with household chores. He took her fishing. He called often, and Mary sensed that if she wanted to call Greg, that would be okay too.

"Somewhere, I passed the line from disinterest to interest," Mary says. "The kisses turned from nonsexual to sexual. Greg and I ended up in bed. I started to fall for this guy, and it looked like he really cared about me.

"Things were great after our sexual encounter," Mary explains. "Greg was romantic. I felt romantic. We spent the night together. He called from work the next day to tell me how much he enjoyed being with me. We made plans to spend the weekend together. He showed up for the weekend, but he wasn't the man I had grown to care for. We sat down to watch television, and I felt like I had an eagle strapped in my living room chair.

"The closeness and good feelings disappeared. I could feel something shift when I became interested in him. The moment I became emotionally involved, Greg stopped being involved. He was emotionally gone. I started to feel desperate, dependent, controlling, and scared. I didn't know what was wrong. When I tried to get him to talk about it, he mumbled something about feeling strange when he made plans, and how he needed to be spontaneous. It took less than a week for the 'relationship' to crumble. He wouldn't talk. He didn't call. I no longer felt comfortable calling him. What happened to the nice guy who shared feelings? What happened to the guy who was so interested in me? I spent a week trying to figure out what I was doing wrong. Then I realized that my mistake was getting interested in him. Greg wasn't pursuing me in spite of my disinterest. He was pursuing me because of my disinterest."

Kathryn's Story

Kathryn was ecstatic. She had finally saved enough money to buy the car she wanted. She had taken months to shop around and close the deal. Now, it was time to go to the lot and drive away in her gorgeous red Bonneville.

Kathryn sat in the sales manager's office, signing one form after another. As she put her signature on each successive form, her ecstasy turned to distress. She felt irritable, jumpy, and anxious. The salesman led her to the new car, opened the door, and handed her the keys. Kathryn slid into the seat. She barely heard the salesman's final instructions.

"I started perspiring. My hands trembled. The salesman was standing right next to me, but it sounded like he was in a tunnel. All I wanted was out," Kathryn said.

She drove the car around the block, then returned to the car lot, ran to the sales manager's office, and demanded that he cancel the sale. He refused. The salesman was confused. The sales manager was confused. They tried to calm her down. When they tried to placate her, Kathryn became more upset.

She walked to the nearest phone and called her attorney. After explaining what happened, as best she could, Kathryn asked how she could get out of the deal. The attorney told her to leave the new car at the lot if she definitely didn't want it. Kathryn hung up the phone.

"The minute I thought I could get out of the deal, I realized I didn't want to," Kathryn said. "What had I just done? I really wanted the car! I didn't want to leave it here. I got in my new car and drove away feeling embarrassed and confused."

Those Two Words: "Commitment" and "Relationship"

What happened to Greg and Kathryn happens to many people: fear of commitment. Some call it a sign of the times; some call it a symptom of the adult child syndrome. And for some, it's not fear; it's panic bordering on phobia.

When I ask men and women what they consider to be the biggest problem with members of the opposite sex, men tell me women seem to get bored and lose interest if a man acts interested and treats a woman well; women complain men won't commit.

"Fear of commitment?" says Allen, who's been recovering for several years. "I see a bunch of people doing it, calling it a lot of different things."

The problem of trying to deal with someone frightened of commitment, or trying to understand our own fear of commitment, perplexes many of us. I used to joke I could clear out a crowded nightclub by walking around to the tables and whispering two words in each man's ear: "commitment" and "relationship." I said it would scare everyone away, but the fact is those words scare me.

A commitment means pledging our time, interest, care, love, money, presence, energy, *ourselves,* or any combination of these, to a person, place, project, or thing for a specified time period. The commitments we fear may be as minor as finishing a project or as major as walking down the aisle and saying, "I do." People may fear committing to many situations: a rent lease, a major purchase; specific plans with lovers, friends, or relatives; joining a church or synagogue; a structured nine-to-five job; an extended volunteer position such as serving on a board of directors; or a relationship.[2]

We might not call our "fear of commitment" a "fear of commitment." We may call it "liking to be spontaneous," "not believing in a silly piece of paper," or "liking our space and freedom."[3] But the bottom line is this: our inability to commit, whether it's 'til death do us part or for three hours on Friday night, can spoil our chances for the good stuff.

Many of us have different degrees of fear about commitment, and we may each have particular commitments that set our hands and hearts to trembling. For some, the fear becomes an intense reaction caused by the thought of being caged, trapped, burdened, obligated, or forever and hopelessly *committed.*[4]

"When a person senses some type of threat or danger, the body has a very specific way of reacting," write Steven Carter and Julia Sokol in *Men Who Can't Love,* a good book about men who fear commitment and the women who love them.

An extreme fear of commitment can actually produce different degrees of one or more of the following symptoms, according to Carter and Sokol.

- Waves of anxiety
- A sense of dread
- Hyperventilating
- Labored breathing
- Suffocating sensations
- A skipping or racing heart

- Stomach distress
- Sweating or chills ("cold feet")

In many situations this response is entirely appropriate and expected. It is not surprising, for example, to experience these symptoms when confronted by a snarling Doberman or an armed assailant. But often these very same symptoms are triggered by a far more subtle threat, even a seemingly innocuous object or circumstance, such as an elevator, a bridge, a spider, or a relationship. When we have an inappropriate reaction such as this, when the body's fear response seems greatly exaggerated or totally irrational, we call it a phobic response.[5]

In *Men Who Can't Love,* the authors describe typical and predictable stages of relationship behavior for a person afraid to commit.

The Beginning: All he can think about is how much he wants you. The Middle: He knows he has you, and it scares him. The End: You want him, and he's running scared. The Bitter End: It's all over and you don't know why.[6]

The fear of commitment can set in at any stage in a relationship: after a good first date; after the first sexual encounter; when it's time to settle in, typically when two people decide to live together; or after they march down the aisle and pledge love for a lifetime.[7]

It can be confusing and painful to date, love, or be friends with a person afraid to commit. It can be confusing and painful to be a person who fears commitment.

Friends may wonder why Harry refused to make plans to go out with them.

Relatives may wonder why Jan refuses to commit to coming for Christmas dinner.

Lovers may wonder why the person who pursued them so arduously disappears, backs off, or gets cold feet.

The answer is that people truly do get "cold feet."

People afraid to commit aren't necessarily "unhealthy." They aren't necessarily uncaring "womanizers" or "man haters." They're people with a fear, sometimes a dreadful fear, of committing. Some of us who are afraid of committing may not know we harbor this fear. All we know is an uncomfortable feeling is present, and getting out of the commitment soothes the feeling.

Getting Cold Feet

The anxiety produced by making a particular commitment can be overwhelming, like the terror experienced by a claustrophobic who has been locked in a closet. Getting out of the commitment can be like the claustrophobic getting out of the closet. Creating distance, getting out, or getting away makes it feel better, since this is an instinctive reaction to feeling trapped. Once away and relaxed, we may feel safe enough to examine the feelings that led to the commitment in the first place. We may discover we really want who or what we've run from.[8]

"Marsha and I dated for months," Tom says. "It felt like we just couldn't be together enough. We made plans to move in together. I couldn't wait. But the day I was supposed to move in, something happened inside me. I panicked. I forced myself through the move, kind of. I brought my body to Marsha's house but I left my suitcases in my car. I couldn't bring myself to move one piece of furniture in with me.

"Each day, I got what I needed from the car. Slowly, I accumulated a few items in the house, but I never completely moved in. I woke up and left the house at 5:30 A.M. to work out. I'd get to the health club ten minutes before it opened! I'd get home late at night just in time to go to sleep.

"Marsha was patient for a while; then she started complaining. I accused her of being too demanding. She said she wasn't going to demand anything from me because I was history. I said fine, I wanted my space and freedom anyway. And I moved out.

"The minute I got my space and freedom, all I wanted was to be with Marsha. I was ready to commit. But Marsha wasn't. That was months ago and we're still not back together."

The perplexing and painful aspect about being in a relationship with a person who fears commitment is this: The fear of commitment emerges when a relationship is at its best, finest, or closest.[9] When the relationship isn't going well or the other person isn't interested, those of us who are afraid to commit feel safe enough to be interested. There's no threat. A person afraid to commit can only be "in" if the other person is "out." When the other person moves "in," the person afraid to commit moves back "out." Sometimes, the person afraid of committing chooses to be in a relationship with a person he knows he won't (or can't) commit to. Then when it's time to get "out," the excuse is ready.[10]

Other Factors Contributing to Fear of Commitment

Our fear of committing may be intertwined with fear of intimacy and closeness, unresolved shame issues, a previous commitment gone sour, not feeling safe, or not trusting ourselves to take care of ourselves. Fear of commitment may be caused by weak boundaries, fear of losing control, anxiety over whether we can live up to our promise, unresolved guilt over failed promises, fear of being hurt, or a fear of being trapped.

Many of the situations and people we've lived with could reasonably cause us to fear commitment. Some of us spent years overcommitting and overextending ourselves. We may react to this tendency in ourselves by refusing to commit to anything. Our tendency to remain committed to people who use our commitment and loyalty against us, can cause us to be leery of commitments.

"I was so committed to my marriage and my husband," says Darlene, "I used to joke that love was a ten-letter word spelled c-o-m-m-i-t-m-e-n-t. The problem was, my husband wasn't committed. He ran around on me and lied to me. He assumed I would always honor my commitment no matter what he did. He was almost right. It was hard for me to back out of my marriage vows. It's going to be a long time before I make that kind of commitment again."

Sometimes, our fear of commitment isn't our issue. It's an instinctive reaction to unresolved desperation and dependency issues in the other person.[11]

Not trusting ourselves and our choices can make us afraid to make long-term, or even short-term, commitments. Some of us were deprived of enough protection, permission, nurturing, and role modeling to learn that we could follow through on a promise and feel good about doing so.

Some of us have a thinking "disorder" about what constitutes a commitment. Some of us confuse accepting an invitation to dance with accepting an invitation to get married. Some of us are frightened by anything remotely resembling "forever," so one year, one month, or one evening can feel like an eternity, especially if we tend to "get lost" in other people.

Some of us can become as afraid of ending a relationship as we can to beginning it.[12] Some couples get stuck in the never-never land of distance dancing in relationships, afraid to commit either way.

"Karen was interested in having a relationship with me, until I decided I was interested in her. When I stopped balking, Karen started balking," Ralph explains. "We've gone back and forth this way for two years now. When one of us gets too close, the other one backs away. But the moment one of us backs too far away, the other one moves in closer. We can't seem to get in, and we can't seem to get out."

This is the good news: We'll each work through our fear of commitment at our own time and pace. We can each figure out what our fears are trying to tell us.

Sometimes, our instincts are telling us we don't want to commit. Not all relationships are meant to be forever. Some relationships are healing relationships, some are transitional, and some are "practice" relationships.[13] We can value the friendship and appreciate the learning experiences, but we don't have to marry everyone we date.[14]

Sometimes, our fear is signaling that we're not yet ready to commit to someone or something. I've seen couples distance dance for years, then decide, "That's it. It's time to settle down and stop this."

I've seen people refuse to commit to someone or something one month, then change their minds the next, make a commitment, and feel pleased they did.

I've seen people commit and regret it.

I've seen people despair one year because they loved someone who wouldn't commit to them, then rejoice the next year because they see the relationship would have been a disaster.

There's not one way to deal with fear of commitment. Each situation requires individual consideration. Sometimes our fear signals that a particular move is wrong for us. Sometimes it's just the fear of pledging ourselves to something new. Other times, it's an overreaction to making a decision that seems extremely long-term or perhaps mistaken.

When the Other Person Is Afraid to Commit

It can be "crazy-making" to love or care about someone who's afraid to commit. It can trigger all sorts of the codependent crazies in us—from desperation to wondering, "What's wrong with me?"

When we love someone who's afraid to commit, our worst possible reactions are usually our instinctive ones: taking things personally, trying to make him or her feel guilty, and becoming aggressive, needy, or demanding. If someone is feeling trapped, our tendency to get demanding, controlling, or desperate makes them feel more trapped. The best thing we can do is allow that person, without shame or guilt, to have his or her feelings. In other words, we detach; we allow the person to make a choice about what he or she wants to do. Then we concentrate on taking care of ourselves.[15] Nevertheless, there comes a time, as part of taking care of ourselves, when we do expect certain things from people, including a commitment to a re-lationship. When it's appropriate, we may need to set boundaries and deliver well-timed ultimatums.[16]

If the substance of a relationship is good and it's moving forward, we can be patient. If a person is acting committed, but is afraid to ver-balize that commitment, we may want to be patient.[17] It's normal for anyone to have some twinges of panic and a few second thoughts about committing. If the substance of a relationship isn't good, re-member that a commitment doesn't change the content of a relation-ship. Marriage or commitment is a continuation, not a cure.

If we're regularly attracted to people who refuse to commit, we may question whether we're being attracted to their unavailability. Some of us may also want to examine whether our desperation or de-pendency issues are causing people to run from us.

When We're Afraid to Commit

If we're afraid to commit, the first step toward dealing with our fear is to become aware of it. Strive to understand it. As with all feel-ings, we need to pay attention to the feeling, but we don't let it con-trol us. Sometimes, merely having information on this process can help us figure out how to deal with it. It helps to talk things out.

"I know I'm going to panic whenever I make a commitment," says one man. "I try to make careful decisions. I go slowly, so I know that what I'm doing is what I really want. Then, after I commit, I give myself a few days to feel nuts. I let myself go through the panic process, because I know I'll settle down."

The key is knowing and trusting what we want, don't want, and don't want to lose. To do that, we must know, trust, and listen to our-selves. There comes a time when to have what we want, we must commit to it. Each of us who fears commitment must understand that as we progress through life, we'll lose out on certain things if we're unwilling to commit.[18]

We'll lose certain jobs and opportunities. We'll miss out on closeness and fun times with friends and family if we're unwilling to commit to plans. We may lose our friends, because friendships require commitment. We'll miss out on owning certain items. We'll miss out on belonging if we can't commit to churches or other organizations. We'll miss out on the thrill of worthwhile accomplishments if we can't commit to projects. We'll miss out on recovery if we can't commit to that. We'll miss the confidence and self-esteem that comes from knowing we can make and follow through on a commitment. We may miss out on a love relationship that could be good and last a lifetime.

Let me paraphrase a comment of the Rev. Robert Schuller's that has stuck with me for years: In each undertaking, we'll be required to commit three times—in the beginning when it's new, in the middle when it's hard work, and at the end when we need that final burst of energy to break through to the finish line.[19]

Sometimes, you may find yourself making commitments that aren't in your best interest. Making a commitment doesn't require giving up your ultimate commitment—that of loving and caring for yourself. Talk to people. Trust your Higher Power. But don't forget to trust yourself too. Weigh what you want against what you're willing to give up. If you want it, there's a price to pay, and that price is committing yourself. I'm as afraid of committing as the next person. It's possible I'm more afraid than most. But I've learned one thing: in spite of my fears, trembling hands, hyperventilation, and anxieties, I'll commit and follow through when I'm ready, when the time is right, and when I want to.

So will you.

ACTIVITY

1. Do you know anyone who's afraid to commit? How has their inability to commit affected you?

2. How are you at making commitments? What's your history of commitments to relationships, organizations, purchases? Have

you ever lost something or someone because you couldn't or wouldn't commit? Have you ever had a panic attack after making a commitment? What commitments have you made and felt good about?

19

SHARING RECOVERY WITH OUR CHILDREN

Children are gifts, if we accept them.

—Kathleen Tierney Crilly[1]

"My spouse is finally recovering. I've been recovering for a while. Now, what can I do for my children? What do they need? If we're recovering, do the children need anything more?"

People often ask these questions. I've asked these questions. This book, and this section on relationships, wouldn't be complete without addressing this issue. It's become a growing concern for professionals in the recovery field. It's an issue facing many recovering people who have children. It's an important issue facing our children.

We've established that codependency and adult children issues are progressive. We know that one thing leads to another, and, without recovery, things get worse. We know that many people who recognize themselves as adult children and codependents develop problems with chemical dependency, develop stress-related medical problems, are prone to mental or emotional problems, and sometimes contemplate, attempt, and commit suicide. We know that adult children and codependents tend to have problems in their relationships and other areas of life. We've also acknowledged that codependency and adult children issues become self-defeating habits that "take on a life of their own." We know that many codependents and adult children have been abused verbally, physically, or sexually. We've recognized that each person affected by other people's problems, including alcoholism, needs to find his or her own program of recovery apart from anyone else's recovery program.[2]

Of course, the children need something more. It doesn't do us any good if someone else is recovering and we aren't. If our children have lived with parents with active alcoholism, food, or sex addictions, unresolved adult children issues, or with parents lacking the ability to deal with feelings and be nurturing, then our children may have these problems too. If our kids have lived with parents who have been in pain, then our children are probably in pain too.

They may not show it. They may not talk about it. The walking wounded often don't. They may not know it. We may not see it. We may not want to see it. *But we can know it.* We can know it as certainly as we know how much we've suffered from this problem called "codependency."

Not every child from a dysfunctional family will have troubles in his or her life, but many will. Some will adapt and people please until they bottom out in mid-life. Some won't know they're in trouble until they've had enough time struggling through life and relationships to understand they aren't doing well at either. Some will crash head-on at a young age into jails, mental institutions, and morgues.[3]

Our recovery movement has come into its own time. We've come into our own time. We know our problem was painfully real. We each know how much our problem affected our lives. One of these days, and maybe that day has already arrived, we're going to collectively slap ourselves on our foreheads and wonder why we're waiting for our children to grow up before we give them the hope of healing and recovery.

We're going to wonder why in heaven's name we're limiting our "prevention" efforts to classroom education on the effects of particular drugs. It's helpful to know that amphetamines and cocaine can increase our blood pressure. It's also helpful to know that living with an alcoholic or drug addict can increase our blood pressure. When I wanted to end my life, when I was certain there was something fundamentally wrong with me, when I suspected I was crazy, when I lost hope, I needed to learn about me, about codependency, about recovery, and self-love.

We don't have to wait until our children are addicted or in trouble to intervene. We don't have to wait until our children hate themselves before we begin to teach them how to love themselves.

The purpose of this chapter isn't to blame or shame. We can't afford either. My intent is to encourage us to examine what we're doing and change what's needed. Certainly, we can't prevent all children from becoming troubled adolescents or adults. But we can help some.

We've come a long way in responding to codependency and adult children issues. We've come even further in responding to alcohol and other drug addiction issues. But it's easy to forget we're still in the early stages of understanding and treating alcoholism and other drug addiction, and a host of other behavioral and emotional disorders.

We've taken our heads out of the sand. We've stopped denying many of our problems. We've gone a step further and are now actively, and in some instances aggressively, addressing these issues the best we know how. Our best is all we can do. That's good enough, for today. But doing our best means evaluating what we're doing and making changes when we gain new insight.

That's called growth.

As I travel across the country meeting people in recovery communities in small, medium, and big cities East, South, West, and North, I ask questions: What are you doing for the children? Do you have anything for them? How's it working? Are you going to do more? What? And when?

People are telling me about programs that are already operating or in the planning stages. Chemical dependency treatment program staff talk about being lucky enough to have someone in their agency committed to working with the children. I'm hearing about plans for summer camps, school programs that gently intervene in the lives of high-risk children from dysfunctional families, and treatment centers that offer groups for the children.

We have the National Association for Children of Alcoholics. We have agencies like Children are People, Inc., of St. Paul, and Rainbow Days, Inc., of Dallas. Such programs diligently carry the message of recovery to these children who really are people. I also hear something else, something unspoken: *We're on the cutting edge of making tremendous breakthroughs in reaching our children, but there is so much more to be done.*

What Children Need to Recover

What can we do in our families, schools, and communities to reach the children? What do they need? They need the same things we need on an age-appropriate level. The children need to lose their invisibility. They need to be recognized as people who need their own healing process. Did it help us when someone we loved changed, even if that change was for the better? It may have confused us if we weren't given our own help and hope. Often, children who weren't acting out when Mom and Dad were drinking or troubled, begin acting out when Mom and Dad begin recovering.[4]

Children need to know about the effects of alcohol and other drugs, but they also need to learn how to stop their pain. They need to learn how to love, nurture, and accept themselves. They need to know the family problems are not their fault. They need to understand they've been reacting, protecting themselves, and taking care of themselves in the best and most logical way they knew. They also need to know that some of their efforts to stop the pain don't work; some behaviors create more pain. They need to learn about options.

They need to be recognized, accepted, loved, and empowered. They need time to heal from feelings too painful to feel. They need new messages to motivate healthier behavior. They need to learn about controlling and caretaking, and they need to learn about alternatives.

We need to convince them they're lovable. We need to help them convince themselves they're lovable. They need to learn the difference between shame and guilt, and they need to know how to deal with both. They need to stop being shamed and start being given healthy limits and discipline.

They need to learn how to detach and walk away from craziness before they lose their minds. They need to learn how to deal with anger, but let go of resentments. They need to learn that too much food, sex, alcohol or other drugs doesn't stop the pain. And *we* need to know that if they're already indulging in these substances or behaviors they're trying to tell us they're already in pain. Thirteen-year-old promiscuous girls aren't bad; they've probably been sexually abused and they're trying to tell someone. We need families, churches, schools, and communities filled with healthy people so our children will have healthy role models and adults to interact with. They need to be surrounded by people who are enjoying life and doing their own recovery work, so they can see what the good life looks and feels like.

They need parents who role model intimacy, closeness, feelings, problem solving, fun, and self-love. They need to learn how to break any unhealthy rules they've learned and follow healthy rules. They need to know they're special. They need to begin affirming themselves and everything that is and could be special about them.

We can help them. First, we need to stop our pain. We need to start doing our recovery work and continue it. Then, we need to teach them how to love themselves. We can do that only by learning to love ourselves. Actually, we can learn a great deal about loving ourselves from how we deal with the children.

We wouldn't blame or shame children for their parents' problem. We wouldn't be harsh with the children. We'd do all we could to make them feel safe, loved, and good enough. We'd give them gentle, nurturing, unconditional love balanced with discipline. We'd teach them about not doing things that hurt themselves, not ever, because they're too special. We'd teach them to develop a positive connection to a Higher Power, other people, and themselves. We'd teach them how to listen to and trust themselves. If we taught our children these ideas, we could be confident they'd emerge as people who loved themselves and others, because the two ideas are absolutely and irrevocably connected.

Once we learn how to give the child in ourselves the care it needs, we'll know how to deal with the children.

"Is there really any hope for families and children?" a woman asked me. "Or are we all doomed to continue playing out and passing on our pathology?"

To that I say this: Yes, there is hope for our families, our children, and ourselves. I believe in recovery. I believe in changed lives. I believe in children. I even believe in childhood. My children and I are learning. It's been a struggle and a process, but it's been a worthwhile struggle and process. Together, we're getting better all the time.

We've been given so much. Let's share some with our kids.

ACTIVITY

1. What could you do to help your children increase their self-esteem?

Section V:

GOING FORWARD

No matter how it feels, we're moving forward.
No matter how good it gets, the best is yet to come.

20

WORKING ONE (OR MORE) PROGRAMS

*"Al-Anon is more than a Ladies Aid Society or a
women's auxiliary meeting," she said.
"It's where I go to keep on track."*

—Anonymous

"I can't figure out what's wrong," Jane said. "I feel disconnected from people and God. I'm worried and frightened. I'm having trouble sleeping. And I feel so helpless. What's going on?"

I told her it sounded like codependency, and asked if she was going to her Al-Anon meetings.

"No," she said. "Why should I? I'm not living with an alcoholic anymore."

"I'm not living with an alcoholic anymore either," I said. "But I'm still living with myself, so I still go to meetings."

No matter who we begin reacting to, codependency takes on a life of its own. I suspect our commitment to self-care and self-love may be a lifetime one. We may always need to pay attention to our attitudes, behaviors, and emotions. Regularly investing time and energy in our recovery programs is a good way to do that.

Does that mean we *have* to go to meetings or groups all our lives? No. I think it means we'll *want* to.

Although I'm prejudiced about Twelve Step groups being a good vehicle for recovery, other groups offer help and hope for people recovering from codependency and adult children issues too.

Whichever way we choose, this chapter is about our need to continue working at it.

There are two ideas central to working a recovery program: (1) going to meetings and being involved with other recovering people, and (2) working a program.

We need to go to groups or meetings, or find some way to be involved with other recovering people who have similar issues and goals. If we're trying to recover in isolation, what we're doing is probably not recovery. We need involvement with other recovering people. We need support, encouragement, fellowship, and bits and pieces of information. We may know something in our minds, but hearing this information from someone else helps us know it in our hearts. A benefit of our involvement with people and groups is we get to "belong."

"I grew up in a dysfunctional family. I never felt like I belonged anywhere. One thing I like about my support groups is I finally feel like part of something," says one woman.

"But I can't find any good groups!" some people object.

Some recovery groups are in the beginning stages and lack the focus, consistency, and strength found in groups with "old-timers." Some groups are floundering. Some consist of people going to a meeting and doing what they're there to learn how to stop doing: caretaking and controlling. But there are many good groups out there too. Look until you find one. If a group isn't right, you don't need to become stuck or stop recovering. You can voice opinions, suggest alternatives, or find another group.

Finding a Sponsor

As part of going to meetings and connecting with other recovering people, you'll also want to find a sponsor. A sponsor is someone you develop a special relationship with. This relationship entitles you to call on this person for support. If you've been recovering for a while, you probably need to be sponsoring somebody. Recovering people need to "give away" what they've been given. That's how it works.

How Many Groups Do You Need To Go To?

If we have a problem with chemical dependency and adult children or codependency issues, the addiction will always be a primary problem requiring its own recovery program. Our codependency issues probably will too.

When I first began recovering from chemical dependency, I heard much talk about how sobriety was more than staying straight or dry. It meant dealing with all the stuff underneath our disease, the issues that were there before we drank or used other drugs. I've now come to believe the stuff underneath my alcoholism is codependency.

Some people start the recovery journey by going to Al-Anon, then move into A.A. Some start by attending A.A., and later move into the Al-Anon room. Some of us need to go to both rooms. Ultimately, recovery is one big room called "lives and relationships that work." We do what we need to do to get and stay there.

Some people go to one or two meetings a week for chemical dependency and one a week for codependency issues. Some go to a weekly meeting for chemical problems and a biweekly meeting for codependency issues. Some people recovering only from codependency issues go to one meeting a week; some go to one a month. Whatever it takes to stay on track is what we do. This holds true for any combination of issues we face.

We each need to find our own kind of groups and the number of groups that work for us. It may be helpful in the beginning stages of recovery to go to more meetings. During stressful times, it's helpful to go to more meetings than usual. But the purpose of recovery isn't to spend our lives sitting in groups. The purpose is to go to enough groups to get and stay healthy enough to live our lives in ways that work.

The second idea important to ongoing recovery is "working a pro-

gram." We need to do more than sit at groups and talk to people. We need to do our own work. We need to do our part. This means applying the recovery themes, concepts, and the Twelve Steps to *ourselves.*

"We've got a Twelve Step group going for adult children of alcoholics," one woman told me. "Guess what? We've found the most phenomenal growth occurs when we work the Steps."

We try to do something each day toward recovery. That something can be brief: taking time for daily meditation, chanting an affirmation of "I love you" when we look in the mirror, or, asking our Higher Power to remove character defects such as shame or low self-esteem.

It requires hard work. We may do an inventory of our lives or our relationships. We might make a particularly tough amend. We might sit down and tackle our family of origin work, deciphering our destructive messages and creating new, healthy ones for ourselves.

But do something each day. Whether what you've done takes five minutes or five hours, try to feel good about it. Tell yourself it's really great that you're loving yourself that much and doing that for yourself. Tell yourself it's great you're moving forward, because you are. Tell yourself it's okay to be right where you are today—because it is.

Some days, we may do particularly well. We may assertively refuse someone's invitation to be codependent. We may deal well with a particular conflict or a feeling. We may have a few moments of intimacy or closeness. We may buy ourselves something special, then not wreck it by telling ourselves we don't deserve it.

Some days, we may have to look more closely to notice what we did. Maybe we took time out to rest when we were tired. We said The Serenity Prayer during a trying moment. Things got crazy and we detached when we noticed ourselves getting hooked in.

On our worst days, we still look for something we've done toward recovery. Sometimes the best we can do is feel good about what we did not do. We pat ourselves on the back because we didn't run to the nearest bar, drag home an alcoholic, and fall in love with him or her. For some of us, that's real progress and not to be overlooked on the gray days.

All the days count. Believe in recovery. Our lives and experiences can be different and better. The process of getting better is happening right now, this moment, in our lives.

Someone once asked me if I was still "in process." I think this person wanted to know if I was still doing my own recovery work, how much of it I had done, and how crazy my life was today, compared to yesterday.

I answered this way. "There was a time when life was mostly pain and problems, and occasionally something good happened. I used to joke about going through ten bad experiences before one good thing happened, and how small the one good thing seemed compared to the bad. But it wasn't a joke. I hurt most of the time. Somewhere, something changed. The record flipped over from Side B, negative, to Side A, positive. I still have bad days. I still feel hurt and afraid sometimes. But the constant pain I lived with for most of my life is gone. And the pain is so far gone that I can hardly remember it. It's like childbirth: it hurt so much I was afraid it wouldn't stop, but when it did, I could hardly remember it."

Am I still in process? Yes. I probably will be all my life, because that's what life and recovery is. The difference is, now life is mostly good, with some problems. Mostly sunny, with a little rain. And I don't know how much better it can get.

21

LETTING THE GOOD STUFF HAPPEN

*All I have seen teaches me to trust the Creator for
all I have not seen.*

—Ralph Waldo Emerson[1]

My friend and I were talking one day. She was feeling frustrated because something wasn't working out the way she hoped and planned it would.

"I work my program. I trust God. I do my part," she finally said. "But how much, *how much* do I have to let go of?"

I thought about her question. I thought about my life. "I'm not certain, but maybe we need to let go of everything," I said.

Let's concentrate for a moment on the spiritual part of the program. I use the word *spiritual* instead of *religious*. Although attending church is an important part of life and recovery for many of us, I'm not talking about going to church. What I'm talking about is finding a personal relationship with a Higher Power, *God as we understand Him*. I'm talking about finding the "church" inside us.

Our journey is many things, but it's primarily a spiritual one. We need people on that journey, and we need a Creator, and a Caretaker to guide and help us. We can't recover in isolation from other people and call it recovery; we can't recover in isolation from a Higher Power, or our spiritual selves, and call that recovery. Our spiritual selves are as much "us" as our bodies, minds, and emotions.

No matter which route we take to recover, the only way to walk

the path is unencumbered. Two of the most important recovery behaviors we can learn are surrendering and letting go. We don't do
those acts in isolation. We do them in collaboration with a Higher
Power. We need a *Power greater than ourselves* to surrender and let go
to. We need to know our Higher Power loves and cares for us, and
cares about the greatest and most minute details of our lives.

What's surrendering? What does it mean to "let go"? Surrendering is accepting; letting go is releasing. Surrendering is acknowledging the authority of a Higher Power; letting go is trusting His
authority.

What do we need to surrender to and let go of? Our past, present, and future. Our anger, resentments, fears, hopes, and dreams.
Our failures, successes, hate, love, and desires. We let go of *our* time
frame, our wants, sorrows, and joys. We release our old messages,
our new ones, our defects of character, and attributes. We let go of
people, things, and sometimes ourselves. We need to let go of
changes, changing, and the cyclical nature of love, recovery, and life
itself.

We release our guilt and shame over being not good enough, and
our desire to be better and healthier. We let go of things that work
out and things that don't, things we've done, and things we haven't
done. We let go of our unsuccessful relationships and our healthy relationships. We let go of the good, the bad, the painful, the fun, and
the exciting. We surrender to and let go of our needs. Often, a hidden need to be in pain and suffering is underneath our failed relationships, pain, and suffering. We can let go of that too.[2] All of it must
go.

Surrendering doesn't mean we stop desiring the good. It means
that after acknowledging our desires, we relinquish them and get
peaceful and grateful about circumstances, people, and our lives exactly as they are today.

*For those of us who have survived by controlling, surrendering and
letting go may not come easily.* But they work better. "Surrendering"
and "letting go" are intangible concepts that don't mean much until

we've practiced them. Then we realize that the concepts are real. Surrendering and letting go can be encouraged, but they can't be taught. They must be learned, and they must be learned anew each time we practice them.

When I began recovery from chemicals, I had to do an inordinate amount of surrendering. I lost a son, a family, my relationship with chemicals, my identity, and all my material possessions. I figured I'd done my share of surrendering, enough to last a lifetime. I was about to learn that I wasn't finished with this business of surrendering, I was only beginning to learn how.

I started believing I deserved good things: a husband, children, a home, and enough money. I tried to believe that my life, including my relationship, was going to work out well. Seven years later I was financially destitute, on the verge of divorce, and standing in my first Al-Anon meeting crying.

I was furious. I felt cheated. I believed God had let me down. I had surrendered and let go. It wasn't fair that I had to lose some more. It wasn't fair that I had another big issue to deal with in this lifetime—codependency. Why? I wondered. Why? Why? Why? Then I got my answer. Rather, I got another question. I had to come up with the answer.

"Are you still willing to surrender? Are you still willing to let go? Are you still willing to trust God, even when—especially when—it hurts?"

Surrendering and letting go are about willingness and trust. They're about having enough faith to want something so much that we can taste it; then deliberately letting go of our desires and trusting our Higher Power to do for us what He wants, when He wants. They're about believing in God and His love for us even when it hurts.

"I've learned that surrendering isn't a sign of weakness," says one man. "It's a sign of strength."

We don't have to surrender or let go perfectly. We only need do it as well as we can, today. I believe in empowerment, affirmations, and doing my part. But I've learned that I probably won't be empowered to do anything until I first surrender and let go. I surrender and let go on whatever level I can muster. This must happen first, and all along the way.

Someone once asked how much he needed to surrender before he'd become empowered. I asked him if he'd started attending meetings yet. He said he had been going to adult children groups for about three months. I told him if he had surrendered enough to go to meetings, he had surrendered enough for now.

Surrendering and letting go are frightening. They feel like dying, losing control, losing ourselves. They are losing control. But then we get back a new kind of power. That power includes, among other ideas, manageability of ourselves and our lives.

I hate losing control. I still try to hold on to things that are worthless on my recovery journey: resentments, anger, fear, and my desire to "make things happen." It's hard to trust. I've spent most of my life walking around convinced of my unlovability. Believing actual people in my life love me is difficult enough. Believing a God I can't physically see or touch loves me—especially when things hurt—requires a great leap of faith. But every time I leap, I land in His arms.

Sometimes, it feels like I have to work as hard at maintaining my relationship with God as I do with people. Sometimes, it feels like I have to work so hard at recovery. But I really do so little. It's called "the Grace of God."

"This is what I've learned about recovery and surrender," one man told me. "One day, my daughter got a sliver in her finger. It really hurt and I had to take it out. But taking it out hurt too. I held my daughter on my lap. I talked softly to her. I tried to be gentle. But she kicked, screamed, and fought all the way. I tried to tell her that if she relaxed and stopped fighting, it wouldn't hurt as much. I tried to tell her if she just trusted me, the pain would be gone before she knew it. But she was too scared to trust. When I got the sliver out, she was so mad she just cried and beat on my arms. It hurt that she didn't trust me. It hurt more that she had made her pain worse than it had to be."

Many of us surrender and let go the hard way, by struggling through frustration, intense desire, anger, hurt, and fear—to that cherished point of yielding, that moment when we loosen our grasp. When we do, something happens. When we stand unencumbered by the past or the future, with empty hands and open arms, we'll find a loving, caring Higher Power who fills us with what He chooses. And we can trust what He gives us, because it will be good.

When my children were young, they loved brightly colored helium balloons. But sometimes either accidentally or purposely, they'd let go of the string. There they'd stand, with tears in their eyes, watching their precious balloon fly high into the heavens until it disappeared from sight.

When that happened, I'd tell them a story.

"Don't cry," I'd say. "God's up there. And you know what? He catches every balloon you let go of. He's keeping all of them just for you. Someday, when you get to heaven, you'll get every one back."

My children are older now; so am I. But we still believe God's saving our balloons for us.

And I believe God catches all our balloons too—each one we let go of. Only we don't have to wait until we get to heaven to get them back. The best and most perfect of our balloons, the ones just right for us, He gives back as soon as we're ready to accept them. Sometimes, He gives back better ones than we let go of.

That's the secret to letting the good stuff happen.

It's connected to our deepest beliefs about what we deserve. It's connected to God's absolute, unconditional love for each of us. It's connected to our desire and His desire that we be and have the best possible. It's connected to our willingness to let go.

Wouldn't it be easier to skip this whole business? If we can't hang on to our desires, wouldn't it be simpler not to acknowledge them in the first place?

Probably. But it doesn't work that way. There's something magical and necessary about the process, the way it stands. The victory, joy, and growth aren't achieved by avoiding. The rewards come by overcoming. Each time we surrender, each time we let go, we'll be propelled forward on our journey. We'll be moved to a deeper level of play.

Discoveries along the Recovery Path

We've covered much ground in this book, but we'll cover a lot of territory in our recoveries too. We'll take detours. We'll take short-cuts that turn into "longcuts."[3] And sometimes we'll stop to rest.

We'll go to extremes. "I spent the first thirty years of my life taking care of everyone around me," says one woman. "Then, for a while, I refused to even sew a button on a shirt for someone!" We may have spent years hurling ourselves headlong into relationships with no forethought; then, for a while, we hold a microscope over everyone we meet. That's okay. That's how we grow. The goal of recovery is achieving balance, but most of us reach that middle ground only by exploring the peaks and valleys.

No matter how it feels, we're moving forward. And the further we travel, the more we rely on the concepts we learned at the beginning of our journey, the basics of self-care. The important idea is that we make ourselves available to the recovery process and participate in it as best we can, one day at a time. If we do, recovery will work for us. We'll see that all the parts and pieces of our lives weave together in a perfect design.

Some of our greatest mistakes may become crucially beneficial parts of our lives. Some of our codependent character traits may become the basis for some of our finest characteristics. We may find that our ability to be responsible will qualify us for positions of leadership. We may discover that our ability to put up with deprivation enables us to accomplish something extraordinary that couldn't be accomplished without the ability to delay gratification. We may find that healing from our pain helps others heal from theirs.

Let me close this chapter with a quote from Ellen Goodman, my favorite columnist. Goodman shared the following story with a college graduation class.

Eighty percent of life is showing up. Day by day, year by year we were presented with choices and made them. We showed up. And up. And up.

Some are paralyzed by choices. But there is much uncertainty about the decisions that start narrowing options, whether career options or love options.

The twenty-fifth class reunion reports are full of our 'mistakes.' Our lives are littered with mid-course corrections. A full half of us are divorced. Many of the women have had career paths that look like games of Chutes and Ladders. We have changed directions and priorities again and again. But our 'mistakes' became crucial parts, sometimes the best parts, of the lives we have made.

How do you make a life? Put one foot in front of the other. Make some choices. Take some chances.[4]

I know, I know. You don't want to make the same mistakes again. You don't want to lose yourself *that much* again. That's a healthy fear, but don't let it stop you from living and loving. You may have been burned from getting too close to the fire, but getting close to the fire is the only way to get warm.

Surrender to the pain. Then learn to surrender to the good. It's there and more is on the way. Love God. Love Family. Love what you do. Love people, and learn to let them love you. And always keep loving yourself.

No matter how good it gets, the best is yet to come.

EPILOGUE

And the greatest of these is love . . .

—1 Cor. 14:13 *The Living Bible*

Several reasons compelled me to write this book. It seemed a logical next step in my writing career. I have an interest in this field, and wanted to be part of the growing movement of help and hope for recovery from codependency and adult children issues. I thought I had a few things to say. And I wanted to. I had a dream, a vision, for this book. It was "today's work" for me.

But there was another reason too. On Valentine's Day, 1986, I submitted to my publisher the manuscript for what was to become *Codependent No More*. That date turned out to be appropriate. I've been writing since 1979. I've written many types of pieces to many different audiences. In all my writing, I've strived to write warmly and personally. But never in my writing career have I felt the overwhelming and heart-warming connection I've experienced with you, my readers.

I believe we've developed a relationship. I believe the connection I feel is love. I wrote this book to maintain our relationship. I wanted to spend some more time with you.

Thank you for letting me back into your lives. Thank you for the success you've given me.

May God bless you richly.

Melody

NOTES

Introduction

1. Ruth Peterman is a Minneapolis writer and writing teacher. She told this story during a class she taught.

2. Lawrence Block, "Messages for Your Most Important Reader," *Writer's Digest* (June 1988): 68.

Chapter 1

1. Charles Leerhsen, with Tessa Namuth, "Alcohol and the Family," *Newsweek* (18 January 1988).

Chapter 2

1. Lonny Owen, C.A.C. Facilitator, has been working in the codependency field for eight years as of the writing of this book. He and I facilitated a ten-week workshop/support group for codependents in Minneapolis in 1988.

2. This statement came from Bedford Combs, M.Ed., LMFT, at a workshop he presented entitled, "Moving Through Unfinished Business: The Recovery Journey from Codependency." The workshop took place on 25 March 1988, in Charlotte, North Carolina. Combs is founding president of the South Carolina Association for Children of Alcoholics, Director of CHAPS Family Care in South Carolina, and is a clinical member of AAMFT.

3. This thought has been around recovery circles for years, but I derived it specifically for content here from Combs' workshop (footnote 2).

4. Robert Subby, "Inside the Chemically Dependent Marriage: Denial & Manipulation," quoted in *Co-Dependency, An Emerging Issue* (Hollywood, Fla.: Health Communications, Inc., 1984), 26.

5. Robert Subby, and John Friel, "Co-Dependency—A Paradoxical Dependency," quoted in *Co-Dependency, An Emerging Issue* (Hollywood, Fla.: Health Communications, Inc., 1984), 31–44.

6. My writing on codependency and Post Traumatic Stress Disorder is based on writings by Timmen L. Cermak, M.D. Cermak is a founding board member, president, and chair of the National Association for Children of Alcoholics and co-director of Genesis, a San Francisco-based treatment and consultation program for the family aspects of chemical dependency.

7. Timmen L. Cermak, *Diagnosing and Treating Co-Dependence* (Minneapolis: Johnson Institute, 1986), 55.

8. Ibid.

9. Ibid.

10. Ibid., 56.

11. Ibid., 57.

12. Ibid., 57–58.

Chapter 3

1. Timmen L. Cermak, *Diagnosing and Treating Co-Dependence,* (Minneapolis, Johnson Institute, 1986), 68–93. The stages (names and information) are based on this book and Cermak's *A Time to Heal.* (Los Angeles: Jeremy P. Tarcher, Inc., 1988).

2. Robin Norwood, *Women Who Love Too Much,* (New York: Pocket Books, 1986), 140.

3. Scott Egleston. Mr. Egleston who is a private therapist and lives in the Twin Cities.

4. Cermak, *Diagnosing and Treating Co-Dependence,* 73.

5. Anne Morrow Lindbergh, *Gift from the Sea,* (New York: Pantheon Books, 1975), 24.

6. Marian Perkins, of Saint John, New Brunswick, has stated this concept in relation to codependency.

7. This exercise was adapted from material developed by Lonny Owen of Minneapolis.

Chapter 4

1. *The Living Bible* (Wheaton, Ill.: Tyndale House Publishers, 1971), 481.

Chapter 5

1. This is a diagram often used to represent recovery from chemical addiction, recovery from codependency, and recovery and growth.

2. Scott Egleston and others have used this to diagram codependency and recovery.

3. Lonny Owen used this to diagram recovery from codependency. He got the idea from someone else, who got the idea from another. . . .

4. Scott Egleston suggested this term.

5. *New World Dictionary of the American Language, Second College Edition* (New York, Simon & Schuster, Inc., 1984), 1198.

6. *New World Dictionary of the American Language, Second College Edition* (New York, Simon & Schuster, Inc., 1984), 1189.

Chapter 6

1. This is an edited quote from a letter I received from an anonymous woman in New South Wales, Australia.

2. Schaef made this comment when we both appeared on a radio show, via the telephone.

3. Timmen L. Cermak, M.D., *Diagnosing and Treating Co-Dependence* (Minneapolis: Johnson Institute, 1986), 55.

Chapter 7

1. These signs are based in part on "Co-Alcoholic Relapse: Family Factors and Warning Signs," Terence T. Gorski and Merlene Miller, from *Co-dependency, An Emerging Issue* (Pompano Beach, Fla.: Health Communications, Inc., 1984), 82.

2. Based in part on an interview with Donna Wallace, "Donna Wallace on Empowering ACoAs at Work," *Phoenix* 8, no. 5 (May 1988): 2.

3. This is wisdom from Scott Egleston.

4. I got this wisdom from a woman I met at an airport. I neglected to get her name, but she travels across the country teaching nurses about codependency, bases much of her teaching on *Codependent No More*, and shared this tidbit with me.

5. Based in part on information in *Here Comes the Sun*, Gayle Rosellini and Mark Worden (Center City, Minn.: Hazelden Educational Materials, 1987).

6. Lonny Owen is a C.A.C. facilitator with eight years experience counseling codependents and families.

7. This came from Lonny Owen.

8. Based in part on "Relapse Warning Signs for Co-Alcoholism," developed by Terence T. Gorski and Merlene Miller, from "Co-Alcoholic Relapse," in *Co-Dependency, An Emerging Issue,* 82.

Chapter 8

1. This is an indirect quote taken from Earnie Larsen's Adult Children seminar at Trinity Lutheran Church, Stillwater, Minn., spring, 1988.

2. The geneagram method is a popular one, used by many counselors and family programs across the nation. Most counselors develop their own method of using it. I developed this adaptation with Lonny Owen's help during the ten-week workshop and support group we co-facilitated.

3. Scott Egleston generated the core of these fantasy ideas in one of our conversations about family of origin work. He uses it in his family of origin work with teenagers.

4. Melody Beattie, *Denial* (Center City, Minn.: Hazelden Educational Materials, 1986).

5. Again, this thought emerged from the mind of Scott Egleston during a family of origin conversation.

6. Originally, Jessie Roberts taught me this during Transactional Analysis training in the mid-seventies. It's been around for years, and applies to adult children of alcoholics and dysfunctional families syndrome.

7. Earnie Larsen and other family systems counselors teach this.

8. Louise L. Hay, *You Can Heal Your Life* (Santa Monica, Calif.: Hay House, 1984), 78–79.

9. This is a paraphrase from Earnie Larsen's adult children lectures.

10. This idea was generated by Bedford Combs.

11. This idea was also generated by Combs. In his lecture he says that in his therapy program for codependency issues, he has a chorus of people actually "sing" the disease in the background, to help people recognize dysfunctional messages and patterns.

Chapter 9

1. The codependent rules I refer to throughout this book are based on Robert Subby and John Friel's work in "Co-Dependency—A Paradoxical Dependency," in *Co-Dependency, An Emerging Issue* (Pompano Beach, Fla.: Health Communications, Inc., 1984), 34–44.

2. Ibid.

3. Robert Subby, "Inside the Chemically Dependent Marriage: Denial & Manipulation," in *Co-Dependency, An Emerging Issue*, 26.

4. Ibid., 27.

Chapter 10

1. This phrase is borrowed from the pamphlet *Shame Faced: The Road to Recovery*, by Stephanie E. (Center City, Minn.: Hazelden Educational Materials, 1986).

2. Ibid., p. 1.

3. Merle A. Fossum and Marilyn J. Mason, *Facing Shame—Families in Recovery* (New York: W. W. Norton & Company, Inc., 1986), 44.

4. This idea, and many in this chapter, came to me from Scott Egleston.

5. This example came from Scott Egleston.

6. Stephanie E., *Shame Faced*, 1.

7. Fossum and Mason, *Facing Shame*, 29.

8. This idea came from Lonny Owen during the workshop we co-facilitated.

9. This definition is fairly common, but I got it from Scott Egleston.

10. Based on Step Six and Step Seven of the Al-Anon Twelve Step program.

11. From Lonny Owen.

Chapter 11

1. The details about this test, the sketches, and what each sketch resembled, are compiled from Jason's memory and may not be entirely accurate. The crux of the story is.

Chapter 12

1. This quote from Louise Hay appeared in an article by Carolyn Rebuen, "Healing Your Life with Louise Hay," *East West* (June 1988), 41.

2. *New World Dictionary of the American Language, Second College Edition* (New York: Simon & Schuster, Inc., 1984), 23.

3. Ibid., 459.

4. This idea grew from Nita Tucker's writing with Debra Feinstein on empowerment in *Beyond Cinderella: How to Find and Marry the Man You Want* (New York: St. Martin's Press, 1987), 155.

5. Louise L. Hay, *You Can Heal Your Life* (Santa Monica, Calif.: Hay House, 1984). Many of the ideas in this chapter were inspired by Hay's work.

6. Bernie S. Siegel, *Love, Medicine & Miracles* (New York: Perennial/Harper & Row, 1986).

7. This idea has been touted by different therapy modalities for years, including Transactional Analysis. Hay and Siegel are saying it again.

8. This idea has been touted for years too. I believe I heard it recently from Louise Hay and from my massage therapist.

9. This idea is from *New World Dictionary of the American Language*, 459, and Nita Tucker's book, *Beyond Cinderella*.

10. This idea based on Hay's writing in *You Can Heal Your Life*.

11. This is based on ideas by Louise Hay in *You Can Heal Your Life* and lectures on the use of affirmations by Earnie Larsen.

12. Based on a quote by Haim Ginott in "Quotable Quotes," *Reader's Digest* (June 1988), cover page.

13. The somatic, or body component, to emotional distress has been explored for a long time by many therapies.

14. This thought was generated years ago by the Rev. Phil Hansen, a pioneer in the chemical addiction recovery movement.

15. This idea based on a suggestion by Louise Hay in *You Can Heal Your Life*.

16. Hay, *You Can Heal Your Life*, 15.

17. Based on Ps 118:24.

18. These ideas inspired by Louise Hay.

19. Based on Phil 4:19.

Chapter 13

1. Martin Blinder, M.D., "Why Love Is Not Built to Last," *Cosmopolitan* (June 1988): 223.

2. This idea was inspired by my friend, Bob Utecht.

3. This gem originated with Earnie Larsen. It is his definition of recovery from codependency.

4. This thought originated with Earnie Larsen. It is my paraphrase of his idea that many relationships were doomed from the beginning because there is no way they possibly could have worked.

5. Earnie Larsen says, "Love is a living thing."

6. Blinder, "Why Love Is Not Built to Last," 221–22.

7. This idea came from Dan Caine, Executive Director of Eden House Rehabilitation Center in Minneapolis, Minnesota.

8. This idea was inspired by Martin Blinder, "Why Love Is Not Built to Last."

9. This idea came to me from Scott Egleston.

10. Blinder, "Why Love Is Not Built to Last."

11. This phrase is based on another writer's phrase: "achieving the exalted state of cliche-hood"—but I cannot remember where I read it. Probably in a writer's magazine.

12. Many people have expressed this idea. It is more recently and most loudly touted by Earnie Larsen.

13. This thought inspired by Nita Tucker with Debra Feinstein, *Beyond*

Cinderella: How to Find and Marry the Man You Want (New York: St. Martin's Press, 1987).

14. The quote, "Adult children deserve another chance in relationships" is said to have originated with Robert Subby, a recovery professional residing in Minnesota.

Chapter 14

1. Nita Tucker, with Debra Feinstein, *Beyond Cinderella: How to Find and Marry the Man You Want,* (New York: St. Martin's Press, 1987), 61.

2. Ibid.

3. Based on ideas from: Yehuda Nir, M.D., and Bonnie Maslin, *Loving Men for All the Right Reasons: Women's Patterns of Intimacy* (New York: Dell Publishing Co., Inc., 1983).

4. My thanks to Nita Tucker for something I've always known, but haven't been able to verbalize until I read her book.

5. Tucker, *Beyond Cinderella,* 58.

6. This idea is also from Tucker's *Beyond Cinderella.*

7. Ibid., 42–43.

8. For years, Earnie Larsen has been saying, "Who we're in a relationship with says as much about us as it does about them." Tucker also discusses our unavailability in *Beyond Cinderella,* 50–51.

9. Tucker, *Beyond Cinderella,* 41.

10. Paraphrase of Tucker's expression.

11. From Tucker's course: "Connecting."

12. Tucker, *Beyond Cinderella,* 75–76.

13. Ibid., 52.

14. Ibid., 60.

15. Louise Hay writes about the idea of dealing with panic separately in her book, *You Can Heal Your Life* (Santa Monica, Calif.: Hay House, 1984), 105.

16. Hay, *You Can Heal Your Life,* 124–129.

17. Scott Egleston is the first one that explained this "switch" to me.

18. Hay, *You Can Heal Your Life,* 105.

Chapter 15

1. *New World Dictionary of the American Language, Second College Edition* (New York: Simon & Schuster, Inc. 1984), 167.

2. Many professionals and recovering people have discussed this phenomenon. Merle A. Fossum and Marilyn J. Mason discuss it in *Facing Shame: Families in Recovery* (New York: W. W. Norton & Company, Inc., 1986), 76.

3. Anne Jefferies, "Rokelle Lerner: ACA's, Intimacy & Play," *The Phoenix* (October 1988): 1.

4. Some of my definition and explanation of boundaries is based on Fossum's and Mason's *Facing Shame*.

5. Jefferies, "Rokelle Lerner," 1.

6. Fossum and Mason, *Facing Shame*, 60–65.

7. Ibid., 73.

8. Jefferies, "Rokelle Lerner," 1.

9. This is Scott Egleston's approach to boundary setting.

10. Jefferies, "Rokelle Lerner," 1–2.

11. This idea emerged in part from Lonny Owen during the course of co-facilitating our workshop and support group.

12. This idea is from Fossum and Mason, *Facing Shame*.

13. These ideas are based in part on Rokelle Lerner's interview with *The Phoenix* (October 1988) and on M. Scott Peck's *The Road Less Traveled* (New York: Simon & Schuster, Inc., 1978), 97.

14. Janet Geringer Woititz, *Struggle for Intimacy* (Pompano Beach, Fla.: Health Communications, Inc., 1985), 46–48.

15. This tip came from a woman who travels across the country lecturing nurses about codependency. I met her in an airport and can't recall her name.

16. Woititz, *Struggle for Intimacy*, 48.

17. This idea originated with Scott Egleston.

18. The concept of being "robbed" is one that Fossum and Mason discuss in their book, *Facing Shame*.

19. This came from an Al-Anon member.

Chapter 16

1. John Powell, *Why Am I Afraid to Tell You Who I Am?* (Allen, Tex.: Argus Communications, 1969).

2. M. Scott Peck, *The Road Less Traveled* (New York: Simon and Schuster, 1978), 117.

3. This observation comes from Scott Egleston.

4. Eric Berne, M.D., *Games People Play* (New York: Ballantine Books, 1964), 18.

5. Earnie Larsen is the first person I've heard discuss the concept of surrendering to relationships. I heard it on his tape series, *Adult Children of Alcoholics.*

6. M. Scott Peck discusses this concept in *The Road Less Traveled.*

7. Stephanie Covington, and Liana Beckett, *Leaving the Enchanted Forest: The Path from Relationship Addiction to Intimacy* (San Francisco: Harper & Row, 1988), 24, 26.

8. Bedford Combs is the person who told me this.

9. Some of this came from Earnie Larsen. Some from observation and discussion with people. Much came from extensive personal experience in distancing behaviors.

10. The concept of sharing the power emerged during discussions with Scott Egleston.

Chapter 17

1. Again, I credit Robert Subby and John Friel (from *Co-Dependency: An Emerging Issue*) with the "rules," although other recovery professionals have discussed them.

2. Timmen Cermak discusses this in *Diagnosing and Treating Co-Dependence* (Minneapolis: Johnson Institute, 1986), 55.

3. I read about this concept—negotiating with people who don't play fair—in a magazine article at the doctor's office two years ago. I got the phrase from it, but I can't remember the author or article.

4. M. Scott Peck, *The Road Less Traveled* (New York: Simon & Schuster, Inc., 1978), 15.

5. A. P. Herbert, quoted by Gene Brown in *News Times* (Danbury, Conn.) from "Quotable Quotes," *Reader's Digest* (May 1988), 137.

6. This is the theme of M. Scott Peck's book, *The Road Less Traveled.*

7. Scott Egleston.

8. Scott Egleston.

9. Harriet Goldhor Lerner, *The Dance of Anger* (New York: Harper & Row, 1985), 37–40.

10. This is from Earnie Larsen.

11. I first learned about power plays in Claude M. Steiner's *Scripts People Live* (New York: Grove Press, 1974).

12. Michael Kelberer from *The Phoenix* came up with this tip.

13. Earnie Larsen.

14. Christopher Matthews, "Be Kind to Your Adversaries," *Reader's Digest* (May 1988), 135.

15. Richard Bach talks about the concept of problems being gifts in *Illusions, The Adventures of a Reluctant Messiah* (New York: Dell Publishing Co., 1977), 71.

Chapter 18

1. Helen Lesman, comp., *Heart Warmers,* (Minneapolis: Lighten Up Enterprises, Northwestern Products, 1985), October 10.

2. Steven Carter and Julia Sokol, *Men Who Can't Love: When a Man's Fear of Commitment Makes Him Run from the Women Who Love Him* (New York: M. Evans and Company, Inc., 1987), 56–61.

3. Ibid., 191–92.

4. Based on Carter and Sokol's *Men Who Can't Love,* 43, and Nita Tucker with Debra Feinstein, *Beyond Cinderella: How to Find and Marry the Man You Want,* (New York: St. Martin's Press, 1987), 136.

5. Carter and Sokol, *Men Who Can't Love,* 43–44.

6. Ibid., 29.

7. Ibid., 21–23.

8. Ibid., 32–34, 41.

9. Ibid., 52.

10. Ibid., 192.

11. Tucker, *Beyond Cinderella,* 136.

12. Carter and Sokol, *Men Who Can't Love,* 65.

13. Martin Blinder, M.D., "Why Love Is Not Built to Last," *Cosmopolitan* (June 1988): 220–23.

14. Tucker, *Beyond Cinderella,* 135.

15. Ibid., 136–37; Carter and Sokol, *Men Who Can't Love,* 157–228.

16. Earnie Larsen teaches this; it's also in Tucker, *Beyond Cinderella,* 139–41.

17. Tucker, *Beyond Cinderella,* 132–41.

18. Earnie Larsen teaches this.

19. I heard the Rev. Schuller say this in a television sermon around 1979.

Chapter 19

1. *Each Day a New Beginning* (Center City, Minn.: Hazelden Educational Materials), October 22.

2. This list is based in part on the Charter Statement of the National Association for Children of Alcoholics. The statements are under the category of "Established Facts about Children of Alcoholics." NACOA, 31706 Coast Highway, Suite 201, South Laguna, CA 92677. (714) 499-3889.

3. This fact based partly on the NACOA charter.

4. Bedford Combs talks about this idea.

Chapter 21

1. Ralph Waldo Emerson, "Quotable Quotes," *Reader's Digest* (March 1988).

2. Louise Hay discusses the concept of releasing, or letting go, of everything. She's the first person I heard mention the concept of letting go of our need to be in destructive relationships, and the more general concept of letting go of our underlying, destructive needs.

3. My friend Bob Utecht told me about "longcuts."

4. This is an excerpt from Ellen Goodman's column in the *St. Paul Pioneer Press Dispatch* (10 June 1988): 14A.

BIBLIOGRAPHY

Books

Al-Anon's Twelve Steps & Twelve Traditions. New York: Al-Anon Family Group Headquarters, Inc., 1981.

Beattie, Melody. *Codependent No More.* Center City, Minn.: Hazelden Educational Materials, 1987.

Berne, Eric, M.D. *What Do You Say After You Say Hello.* New York: Bantam Books, 1971.

————. *Games People Play.* New York: Ballantine Books, 1987.

Bissell, Le Claire, M.D., and James E. Royce. *Ethics For Addiction Professionals.* Center City, Minn.: Hazelden Educational Materials, 1987.

Brandon, Nathaniel. *How to Raise Your Self-Esteem.* New York: Bantam Books, 1987.

Carter, Steven, and Julia Sokol. *Men Who Can't Love: When a Man's Fear Makes Him Run from Commitment.* New York: M. Evans & Company, Inc., 1987.

Cermak, Timmen L., M.D. *Diagnosing and Treating Co-Dependence.* Minneapolis: Johnson Institute, 1986.

————. *A Time to Heal: The Road to Recovery for Adult Children of Alcoholics.* Los Angeles: J. P. Tarcher, Inc., 1988.

Covington, Stephanie, and Liana Beckett. *Leaving the Enchanted Forest.* San Francisco: Harper & Row, 1988.

Cowan, Connell, and Melvyn Kinder. *Smart Women—Foolish Choices.* New York: Signet Books, 1986.

Each Day a New Beginning. Center City, Minn.: Hazelden Educational Materials, 1982.

Fisher, Roger, and Scott Brown. *Getting Together.* Boston: Houghton Mifflin Co., 1988.

Forward, Susan, and Joan Torres. *Men Who Hate Women—The Women Who Love Them.* New York: Bantam Books, 1986.

Fossum, Merle A., and Marilyn J. Mason. *Facing Shame.* New York: W. W. Norton and Company, 1986.

Harris, Amy Bjork, and Thomas A. Harris. *Staying O.K.* New York: Harper & Row, 1985.

Hay, Louise L. *You Can Heal Yourself.* Santa Monica, Calif.: Hay House, 1984.

Larsen, Earnie. *Stage II Recovery—Life Beyond Addiction.* Minneapolis: Winston Press, 1985.

Lerner, Harriet Goldhor. *The Dance of Anger.* New York: Harper & Row, 1986.

Lesman, Helen. *Heart Warmers.* Minneapolis: Lighten Up Enterprises, 1985.

Lindberg, Anne Morrow. *Gift from the Sea.* New York: Pantheon Books, 1975.

Mornwell, Pierre, M.D. *Passive Men—Wild Women.* New York: Ballantine Books, 1980.

Nir, Yehuda, M.D., and Bonnie Maslin. *Loving Men for All the Right Reasons: Women's Patterns of Intimacy.* New York: Dell Publishing Company, Inc., 1983.

Norwood, Robin. *Women Who Love Too Much.* New York: Pocket Books, 1985.

Peck, M. Scott, M.D. *The Road Less Traveled.* New York: Simon & Schuster, 1978.

Powell, John. *Why Am I Afraid to Tell You Who I Am?* Allen, Tex.: Argus Communications, 1969.

Rosellini, Gayle, and Mark Worden. *Of Course You're Angry.* Center City, Minn.: Hazelden Educational Materials, 1985.

———. *Here Comes the Sun: Dealing with Depression.* Center City, Minn.: Hazelden Educational Materials, 1987.

Rubin, Theodore Isaac, M.D. *Compassion & Self Hate.* New York: Macmillan Publishing Company, 1986.

Russell, A. J. *God Calling*. Old Tappan, N.J.: Fleming H. Revell Company, 1984.

Schaef, Anne Wilson. *Co-Dependence: Misunderstood—Mistreated*. Minneapolis: Winston Press, 1986.

Schuller, Robert H. *Be Happy—You Are Loved*. Nashville: Thomas Nelson Inc., 1986.

Siegel, Bernie S., M.D. *Love, Medicine, and Miracles*, New York: Harper & Row/Perennial, 1986.

Smith, Marcell J. *When I Say No I Feel Guilty*. New York: Bantam Books, 1975.

Steiner, Claude M. *Scripts People Live*. New York: Grove Press, 1974.

The Living Bible. Wheaton, Ill.: Tyndale House Publications, 1971.

Trina, Paulus. *Hope For the Flowers*. New York: Paulest Press, 1972.

Tucker, Nita, and Debra Feinstein. *Beyond Cinderella—How to Find and Marry the Man You Want*. New York: St. Martin's Press, 1987.

Walker, Alice. *The Color Purple*. New York: Simon & Schuster, 1985.

Webster's New World Dictionary of the American Language. New York: Simon & Schuster, 1984.

Woititz, Janet Geringer. *Struggle for Intimacy*. Pompano Beach, Fla.: Health Communications, 1985.

Pamphlets

Beattie, Melody. *Denial*. Center City, Minn.: Hazelden Educational Materials, 1986.

Shame. Center City, Minn.: Hazelden Educational Materials, 1981.

Stephanie, E. *Shame Faced*. Center City, Minn.: Hazelden Educational Materials, 1986.

Articles

Blinder, Martin, M.D. "Why Love Is Not Built To Last." *Cosmopolitan* 204 (June 1988).

Block, Lawrence. "Messages For Your Most Important Reader." *Writer's Digest* (June 1988): 68.

Emerson, Ralph Waldo. "Quotation Quotes." *Reader's Digest* 132 (March 1988).

Ginott, Haim. "Quotable Quotes." *Reader's Digest* (June 1988).

Goodman, Ellen. "To Graduates—March On, Make Mistakes." *St. Paul Pioneer Press and Dispatch* (10 June 1988): 14A.

Herbert, A. P. "Quotable Quotes." *Reader's Digest* (May 1988): 137.

Jefferies, Anne. "Rokelle Lerner: ACA'S, Intimacy & Play." *The Phoenix* (October 1988): 1.

Leerhsen, Charles, with Tessa Namuth. "Alcohol and the Family." *Newsweek* (18 January 1988).

Matthews, Christopher. "Be Kind to Your Adversaries." *Reader's Digest* (May 1988): 135.

Subby, Robert. "Inside the Chemically Dependent Marriage: Denial & Manipulations." *Co-Dependency—An Emerging Issue.* Pompano Beach, Fla.: Health Communications, Inc., 1984.